THE STRANGE DEATH OF
LABOUR SCOTLAND

GERRY HASSAN AND ERIC SHAW

EDINBURGH
University Press

To Edwin Hassan (1933–93)
Communist, nationalist, Dundee United fan
GH

To the memory of my mother, Paulette
ES

© Gerry Hassan and Eric Shaw, 2012

Edinburgh University Press Ltd
22 George Square, Edinburgh EH8 9LF
www.euppublishing.com

Reprinted 2013

Typeset in 10.5/13 pt Goudy by
Servis Filmsetting Ltd, Stockport, Cheshire, and
printed and bound in Great Britain by
CPI Group (UK) Ltd, Croydon CR0 4YY

A CIP record for this book is available from the British Library

ISBN 978 0 7486 4001 0 (hardback)
ISBN 978 0 7486 4002 7 (paperback)
ISBN 978 0 7486 5555 7 (webready PDF)
ISBN 978 0 7486 5557 1 (epub)
ISBN 978 0 7486 5556 4 (Amazon ebook)

Contents

Tables

Acknowledgements

There are numerous people who have made this book possible. First and foremost, we would like to thank all the Labour MSPs, MPs and MEPs, current and former, who gave of their time and views, alongside councillors, officials and activists.

Second, our indebtedness is due to the support and encouragement of Edinburgh University Press from the outset, even as the project evolved into something more ambitious and wide-ranging as the Scottish political scene developed. In particular, we would like to show our gratitude to Nicola Ramsey who has been a pillar of editorial advice and wisdom.

It is worth acknowledging the genesis of this book and its two authors. One has written extensively on the character of the British Labour Party over the last twenty years (Shaw 1988, 1994, 1996, 2007); the other has analysed much of the Scottish political environment including the Scottish Labour Party, along with a companion volume on the SNP (Hassan 2004, 2009). We felt our mutual areas of expertise and knowledge would aid the researching, planning and writing of this book, which we thought needed to be written.

A word on our personal pasts. Both of us have at points been involved in the politics of Scottish Labour and in some of the debates and events discussed in the party's near-past. One was involved in the Labour Co-ordinating Committee, the soft left pressure group, in England, not Scotland, coming north of the border in 1990; the other in Scottish Labour Action, the party's home rule group. We would like to think, while not trying to claim objectivity, that this past involvement, along with our research and academic interests, has made this a richer, more human book.

We would like to acknowledge and thank for the support we have received for this project from the Carnegie Endowment Trust, the University of Stirling's Research and Enterprise Fund, the University of Stirling

Division of History and Politics, and the Barry Amiel and Norman Melburn Trust.

We interviewed a large number of people for this book, many of whom were very generous with their time. Some we interviewed twice and even three times (enumerated in the list below). Given the paucity of both secondary literature and archival material on Scottish Labour, information gathered from interviews was of vital importance to the book. Some interviews were conducted on the record, some off the record and some a combination of both. The interviews took place between 2003 and 2011, mainly between 2009 and 2011. To all who agreed to be interviewed we are extremely grateful.

The interviewees were James Adams, Wendy Alexander (two interviews), Jimmy Allison, Sarah Boyack, Rhona Brankin, Bill Butler, Malcolm Chisholm, Campbell Christie, Mike Connarty, Margaret Curran, Susan Dalgety, Susan Deacon (two interviews), Alex Falconer, George Foulkes, Sam Galbraith, Tom Harris, Sylvia Jackson, Michael Keating, Mark Lazarowicz, Richard Leonard (two interviews), Doug Maughan, Frank McAveety, Tom McCabe, Jack McConnell (three interviews), Katie McCulloch, Anne McGuire (two interviews), Ann McKechin, Rosemary McKenna (two interviews), John McLaren, Bob McLean, Henry McLeish (two interviews), John McTernan (two interviews), Sarah Miller, Bristow Muldoon, Derek Munn, John Parks, Peter Peacock, Danny Phillips, Simon Pia, Stephen Purcell, Lesley Quinn (two interviews), George Robertson, Godfrey Robson, John Rowan, Alex Rowley, Dave Scott, Tommy Sheppard, Jim Sillars, Richard Simpson (two interviews), David Smith, Grahame Smith, Matt Smith, Stewart Sutherland, Bob Thompson, Dave Watson, Mike Watson, David Whitton and Alf Young.

We circulated drafts of parts of this work to a number of people. We are extremely grateful to the following for reading and commenting on these drafts: James Adams, Malcolm Chisholm, Richard Leonard, Jack McConnell, James Mitchell, Peter Peacock, Danny Phillips and Lesley Quinn.

We would like to thank Valerie McNeice and Dot Kirkham who transcribed many of the interviews. We are also grateful to David Denver, Cailean Gallagher, Phil Hanlon, Michael Keating, Richard Leonard, Dave Scott, David Shaw, Nigel Smith, Colin Smyth and David Torrance who helped in a number of ways. A special big thanks and appreciation from both of us goes to Rosie Ilett who read the entire manuscript, checking arguments and prose with great attention. Douglas Robertson provided advice on housing statistics, Gregor Gall on trade union membership figures, and Sarah Mackie, senior officer of the Electoral Commission in Scotland, gave advice on numerous queries on voting figures.

We take full responsibility for the perspective put forward, and any errors and omissions are the responsibility of the authors. We hope that readers, whether supporters or opponents of Labour in Scotland, or members of the general public, enjoy the book and hope and recognise that while we may at points be critical, we have tried to be generous and fair to all concerned.

Gerry Hassan
Eric Shaw

The Strange Death of 'Labour Scotland'

Scottish Labour has until recently dominated Scottish politics and society. Despite its influence and reach, it has not, astonishingly, been the subject of a serious survey, although there are numerous studies of the history of Scottish Labour, of the rise and fall of the Independent Labour Party (ILP), of the realities and folklore of 'Red Clydeside', and assorted studies of some of its most famous figures of the distant past. The sole exception to this is the collection published by one of the authors of this book, *The Scottish Labour Party: History, Institutions and Ideas* (Hassan 2004).

This book seeks to fill the gap by providing the first in-depth study of a party that has played such a formative role in shaping Scotland's recent history. Our aim is to offer a detailed account of Scottish Labour's recent history over the three decades since the 1979 defeat of Labour and arrival of Thatcherism, and even more, since the establishment of the Scottish Parliament in 1999. This analysis scrutinises the multi-dimensional nature of Scottish Labour, a party operating at a Scottish and British level, and examines the politics and dynamics of the party in the arenas of the Scottish Parliament, Westminster and, to some degree, local government.

There are many paradoxes about Scottish Labour: that it had been Scotland's leading party for several decades, but never won a majority of the popular vote; that it sees itself as a radical party drawing on a rich set of traditions, but has often embodied conservative practice; and that it has emphasised its own distinctiveness and narrative of difference, while the very idea and practice of what 'Scottish Labour' is has always been more complicated and negotiated than first appears.

Our study attempts to grapple with these paradoxes. What kind of party is Scottish Labour, and what kind of politics has it articulated and expressed? In addressing this question we explore the following themes:

1

- Was there ever a 'Labour Scotland'? If so, in what way and why was Scotland peculiarly Labour? What were the characteristics of 'Labour Scotland', what were its underpinnings and what was the reach and potency of 'myth' associated with it? These questions are explored in Chapter 1.

- How did Scottish Labour's character evolve and change as it established and strengthened its position as Scotland's leading party until fairly recently? The party has been characterised in this period as 'Scotland's political establishment', which ran large swathes of Scottish public life, and in so doing changed its character and purpose. We explore whether this thesis is grounded in reality, assessing the pre-devolution years in chapters 2, 3 and 4, the post-devolution era in chapters 5, 6, 7 and 8, and some of the main cleavages and alignments of the era of Scottish Labour's dominance in chapter 12.

- What does Labour stand for? What, if any, are its distinctive doctrines and beliefs, its animating spirit? What is its culture, feel and sense of itself? Is there a Scottish variant or expression of social democracy or labourism that is different from the mainstream British variant? In chapters 2, 3 and 4 we address the evolution of Labour from the watershed year of the election of the Thatcher Government in 1979 to the arrival of Tony Blair in 1997.

- We question whether Scottish Labour, while in power, developed and pursued a distinctive policy agenda. We address the character, culture and mindsets of Labour in office from 1997 to 2010 at a UK level and 1999 to 2007 in the Scottish Parliament. We examine the different dynamics and tensions between Scottish Labour and New Labour, the evolution of devolution, the slow unravelling of the Scottish Labour constituency, and the demise of New Labour. These issues are considered in chapters 5, 6, 7 and 8.

- Scottish Labour may not have been renowned for its programmatic detail or radical ambitions, but it aided a politics of difference and divergence across a number of policy areas in the Scottish Parliament. We seek to investigate the relationship between the party's character and policy formulation, exploring these questions through a series of case studies of key areas within the remit of the Scottish Parliament, namely, education, health and free care for the elderly. These issues are covered in chapters 9, 10 and 11.

- Who rules Scottish Labour? How is power distributed within it? To what extent do its internal operations conform to democratic norms? How has it reconciled competing pressures for party unity and local autonomy? In probing these questions we appraise many aspects and levels of Scottish

Labour, from its membership to candidate selection, policy-making and formulation, relations with the trade unions, and its relationship to British Labour. These issues are explored in chapters 13, 14, 15, 16 and 17.

- How Scottish is Scottish Labour? Pre-devolution the party was seen as an effective bridge- building project and transmission belt between Scotland and Westminster, Scottish and British interests, advocating for Scotland at Westminster and the merits of Westminster in Scotland. This is the Scottish Labour of what can perhaps now be seen as its 'golden era' from Tom Johnston to Willie Ross. How has this approach adapted to the age of devolution and Scottish nationalism? What is Scottish Labour's relationship with British Labour and the British state? These challenges are addressed in chapters 5–8, 12 and 18.

- Finally, how has the party coped with the more recent demands and processes of devolution and the challenge of the Scottish National Party (SNP)? How has the party at different levels understood (or not understood) the politics of Scottish nationalism and the rise of the SNP? Is the party still defined after two election defeats at the hands of the SNP by a widespread anti-Scottish nationalism, or is there evidence of a more nuanced, strategic approach? What is the case for arguing that Scottish Labour's massive rejection in the polls at the 2011 Scottish Parliament elections does not matter, or should not be read as a fundamental watershed in Scottish politics given Labour's impressive showing in the 2010 UK election? These questions are examined in chapters 8, 12 and 18.

The book offers an in-depth analysis of the recent history of Scottish Labour, exploring the politics and events of Scotland from 1979 from the vantage point of Labour. As such, it offers an account of modern Scotland, politics and society over this period, of huge changes, challenges and transformation in many parts of life. In many respects we argue over this timeframe that Scotland has become a very different kind of place, with multiple consequences which are only beginning to be understood.

This is the thesis of our book *The Strange Death of Labour Scotland*, by which we argue that the rise of Scottish Labour gave birth to an entity we call 'Labour Scotland': the society and institutions that the party gave encouragement and support to so as to allow its dominance to be strengthened and reproduced. This political and social order, we argue, has now passed into history, leaving the Labour Party with a shortage of ideas and resources and little sense of what to do. It is possible that Scottish Labour will in the future find a new role and politics, but to do so it will need to understand that times have fundamentally changed, the old politics will not work anymore, and that it will have to embark on a new course. This book is a contribution to understanding what has happened, that journey, and what it means for Scottish Labour and others.

The book covers many events, past issues and controversies, and is also filled with people and personalities – Labour people in the widest sense, national politicians, local politicians, activists, trade unionists, and people in other parties and no parties. The recent history of Scottish Labour contained many big characters and players, from Gordon Brown to John Smith, Donald Dewar, Robin Cook, Jack McConnell, Henry McLeish and Wendy Alexander. We have at points written extensively about episodes in which they have been involved, but we have aspired to put these actions in a wider political and social context. This is not a political account which dwells on who said what to whom in the Andrew Rawnsley world of court politics (2000, 2010). That means by its nature we tell a story of politics which is more complex, nuanced and subtle, where for most of the time there are few heroes and villains, just a group of pressurised people trying their best.

This book has been a joint intellectual exercise. We have worked closely together in developing the original prospectus, engaging in the research and developing its conclusions. Each of us has contributed and commented on parts drawn up by the other, with Gerry Hassan principally responsible for chapters 1–8 and 12 and Eric Shaw for chapters 9–11 and 13–17. The introduction and offered Chapter 18 conclusion have been jointly authored, and the analysis and theses laid out in the book is a shared one.

We hope people from all political traditions, and none, will find something of interest in this book. It tells an important story in the life of modern Scotland. This is of relevance to Labour members and supporters, but also for those in other parties, and members of the general public interested in the wider public life of Scotland. We hope anyone who opens the pages of this book finds an accurate, interesting and original account of the events and cases examined, one which does justice to the passion, commitment and engagement of the people involved, whatever their political stance.

CHAPTER I

The 'Myth' of 'Labour Scotland'

INTRODUCTION

The idea of an all-powerful Scottish Labour Party pervades many accounts of how the party is described and perceived. Whether in popular politics or media discussion, even specialist literature, Scottish Labour is described as 'hegemonic', 'Scotland's leading party' and 'a political machine'. Such descriptions are widely used by supporters, opponents and observers of the party.

There is a central paradox in Scottish Labour; namely, how has a party which has never won a majority of the popular vote, which has a specific appeal to certain parts of Scotland and not to others, and which through most of its history has had few members and resources, seemed so powerful?

One of the main contributory factors in explaining how this seemingly 'weak' party has managed to extend and maintain its influence over much of society can be found in the concept of 'Labour Scotland'. This is something very different and distinct from Scottish Labour. It can be described as the 'myth' of 'Labour Scotland'. The term 'myth' is used in this context to denote 'an idea or set of ideas whose importance lies in being believed or accepted by a significant body of people sufficient to affect behaviour or attitudes whether grounded in fact or fiction' (Mitchell 1990: 4).

This 'myth' of 'Labour Scotland' was centred on the widespread belief both inside the party and among many of its opponents that Labour spoke for and represented most of Scotland. This was shaped by the party's increased dominance of Westminster representation, along with local government, pre-devolution, and this influenced and altered the normative values, attitudes and actions of many in the party. Scottish Labour politicians increasingly mistook the dynamics and distortions of the First Past the Post (FPTP) electoral system as a true indication of the scale and breadth of support that

5

Labour could claim to speak for. Thus, a minority popular support increasingly became a majority, all-encompassing Scotland. This affected how the party saw itself, its place in society, its relationship with other Scottish parties and with British Labour.

This 'myth' influenced Labour's collective memory and understanding of itself, its sense of time, history and, crucially, its past. Henry Drucker, in his penetrating analysis of British Labour, recognised the potency of the latter as critical:

> This sense of its past is so central to its ethos that it plays a crucial role in defining what the party is about to those in it. Labour's sense of her past is, of course, an expression of the past experience of the various parts of British working class. It is these pasts which dictate that Labour must be a party of the future and what kind of future policies it will tolerate. (Drucker 1979: 25)

Scottish Labour's sense of its past draws from several reference points that are part of the history, culture and politics of Scotland. There is the egalitarian 'myth' which has stressed that Scottish society is less hide-bound to class and hierarchy than England; the radical 'myth' of protest and socialist Scotland from 'Red Clydeside' to anti-Thatcherism; and the collective 'myth' of a society of shared values, difference and cohesion. All of these have contributed to making the 'myth' of 'Labour Scotland', its understanding of itself, its place and past, and where it has seen itself going.

What then is this 'Labour Scotland'? It is the society shaped by Labour's reach over aspects of political and public life, which has resulted from the party's use of power, influence, relationships and networks. This has allowed it to shape Scottish society and operate in alliance with much of institutional society (Labour's relationship with the Catholic Church being a good example), while at the same time preserving its own radical credentials.

Three institutional pillars strengthened Labour dominance of Scottish politics and society, namely, council housing, trade union membership and local government.[1] In the immediate post-war era of 1945 to 1965 these were associated with a powerful idea of 'Labour Scotland', connected to a feeling of optimism, hope and a shared collective vision of the future which gave Labour great strength and confidence, and influenced its opponents, while shaping society.

First, the role of council housing. This rose to a peak of 54.4% of all homes in 1977, before falling back; in 1988 owner-occupation surpassed council housing by 46.6% to 43.9%. When Labour were elected in 1997, council housing had fallen to 27.8% and by 2005 had reached 15.1% (Communities Scotland 2008). Between 1945 and 1965, 70.6% of all new homes built in Scotland were council housing, and 13.7% private sector (Murray 1973: 44).

These national figures disguise the huge concentrations of council housing which characterised parts of the country. Glasgow went from 38.0% council housing in 1961 to 63.5% in 1980 (Keating 1988: 117). In 1981, forty of Scotland's seventy-one constituencies had a majority of council housing; Glasgow Garscadden, Donald Dewar's seat, had the highest percentage of council housing, 96%, followed by Glasgow Provan with 90%. By 1991, significant change had occurred: only fourteen out of seventy-two con-stituencies had a majority of council housing, with Airdrie and Shotts and Motherwell and Wishaw joint highest with 62.5%. Ten years later, Scotland had undergone further dramatic change, with not one of the seventy-two FPTP constituencies having a majority of council housing, Motherwell and Wishaw having the highest percentage with 37.2% and Airdrie and Shotts next with 36.2% (Hassan and Fraser 2004).

Council housing transformed life across Scotland. It gave many working-class, along with middle-class, people decent homes with modern amenities. It also provided a system of patronage and control through letting policies which often used narrow and subjective criterion about 'good housing' and 'good tenants' that formed part of the Labour state which extended far into the lives of communities in a way unimaginable now (Robertson 2011). In return it gave people, until the advent of the Thatcher Government, security and freedom from the exploitation of private landlords via low council rents.

Second, the importance of trade union membership. This was 55% of the Scottish workforce in 1980, but it fell to 39.2% in 1991 and then 32.5% in 2001 and 32.2% in 2010 (Leopold 1989: 70; Paterson et al. 2004: 70; Achur 2011). STUC membership fell from a high of 1,093,056 in 1980 to 659,871 in 1997 and 640,000 in 2011 (Gall 2005: 104; STUC 2011). Scottish trade unions for a large part of the twentieth century drew from an economy with a significant manufacturing base, and as that declined, an expanded public sector. In 1951, manufacturing was 35.9% of employment, while even at this point service industries were larger at 44.7%; by 2000 manufacturing had fallen to 14.1% employment, while services accounted for 76.1% (Cameron 2010: 238). The long decline of manufacturing produced a less unionised industry, 42% unionised in 1991 compared to 29% in 2001 (Paterson et al. 2004: 55). In 1979, 50% of trade union members were working class, but this had fallen to 41% by 1992 (Brand et al. 1994: 217).

Scottish trade unionism for much of its history has had a reputation as being male, muscular and located in manufacturing. Contemporary Scottish trade unionism is more female and public sector, and concentrated across a number of sectors. The most highly unionised sectors in 2001 were education (67%), electricity, gas and water (63%), and public administration (62%); the least unionised sectors were hotel and catering (7%), fishing (10%), and mining and quarrying (11%), the last a reflection of the decline of deep mining (Paterson et al. 2004: 170).

Third, Labour post-1980 increased its dominance of Scottish local government in terms of the numbers of councillors elected and councils it controlled. In the first local government elections in 1980 after the election of the Thatcher Government, Labour won 45.4% of the vote and 494 councillors out of 1,182 seats (41.8%), winning control of twenty-four out of fifty-three district councils (45.3%) (*The Scotsman*, 3 May 1980). The 1995 unitary elections after the Conservative re-organisation of local government saw Labour win 43.6% of the vote, 614 out of 1,155 seats (53.2%) and twenty out of thirty-two councils (62.5%). This was Scottish Labour's high point in terms of local government reach and control.

Labour slowly declined from this point, aided by coming to office at Westminster in 1997 after the defeat of the Conservatives. In 1999, Labour won 36.6% of the vote, 545 seats out of 1,148 (47.5%) and fifteen councils out of thirty-two (46.9%). Four years later the party won 32.6% of the vote, 509 seats out of 1,222 (41.7%) and twelve councils (37.5%) (McConnell 2004: 139). Then came the political earthquake of the first council elections held using the single transferable vote (STV) method in 2007, which saw Labour win 28.1% of the vote, 348 seats out of 1,222 (28.5%) and a mere two councils (6.3%) – Glasgow and North Lanarkshire (Denver and Bochel 2007). The STV elections hurt Labour, but rather than being a one-shock blow to Labour (as widely perceived in the party) they came at a point of cumulative decline from the previous elections. These results shook many within the party's ranks, which measured its strength over the years in terms of seats and not votes.

Scottish Labour built up, through its years of dominance of local government, a powerful base of support, of local preferment and reach which amounted in its heartlands in the West of Scotland and urban Scotland to a networked local state. In some places such as Glasgow, Lanarkshire and Ayrshire, opposition councillors became at Labour's height an endangered species, developing a one-party politics where councillors and officials saw little conflict of interest, and the main debates went on behind closed doors inside the Labour Group or between senior councillors and officials. In the 1995 local elections in Glasgow, Labour, on 61.5% of the vote, won seventy-seven out of eighty-three seats (92.8%), with the Conservatives on three, and the SNP, Liberal Democrats and Scottish Militant Labour each on one (Clark and Beveridge 1998: 127).

These three entities can be seen as the primary pillars of the Labour state. All were mechanisms by which Labour could entrench itself in the political, economic and social life of Scotland, mobilising and reinforcing the Labour vote and a Labour way of life. All three crucially gave Labour majority constituencies of Scotland, with council tenants, trade union members and in local government. And each subsequently began to decline, the first two in the immediate aftermath of 1979 and the third from the end of the Tory era, from 1995 onwards.

Supporting the three pillars was the issue of religion. The Catholic vote was a powerful part of 'Labour Scotland', a cross-class constituency concentrated in the West of Scotland and Glasgow, which acted as a barrier to the challenge of first the Conservatives, then the SNP. Labour's relationship with the Catholic community went back to the 1918 Education (Scotland) Act, which brought Catholic schools into the state sector, with Labour seen as the main advocate of what was then in large part a poor immigrant community with little voice or influence. The Protestant working-class Conservative vote began to wither from the late 1950s, but Labour's Catholic constituency remained through the first challenges of the SNP in the 1960s and 1970s, before weakening in the 2011 Scottish Parliament elections.[2] This process of religious de-alignment altered one of the supposed certainties of Scottish politics: that there was a reliable Catholic majority vote for Labour.

The existence of 'Labour Scotland' had a number of far-reaching consequences. First, it gave the party an enormous influence and reach unlike in most other parts of the UK. The only other comparable Labour experience would be in Wales. Second, it changed the character and nature of Scottish Labour, making it a certain kind of party; one which was shaped by power and the exercise of it. Even more, it did so by a diffuse set of networks and relationships which gave the party huge reach. Third, this set of arrangements created a Labour politics and party where any prospect of a radical centre-left politics was restrained by a politics of patronage and administration, and which left at its core a rather small, under-resourced party. Fourth, all of this had a significant impact on Scottish society, aiding a more institutionally dominated and influenced society where elites, professional groups and expert interest groups had a much bigger role and influence than south of the border. There is a wider argument about the managed nature of Scottish society, of the negotiated autonomy in the union and managed character of society, with its powerful committees of the great and good during the nineteenth and most of the twentieth centuries, which can postulate that the Labour Party, rather than challenging this social order, made its accommodation with it (see Paterson 1994).

Another dimension to this was how Scottish Labour presented and advocated for Scottish interests pre-devolution. This is captured in R. H. S. Crossman's description of Willie Ross, Secretary of State for Scotland 1964–70 and 1974–6, prior to the start of the House of Commons debate on the Social Work (Scotland) Bill 1968:

9

Willie Ross and his friends accuse the Scot. Nats of separatism but what Willie Ross himself actually likes is to keep Scottish business entirely privy from English business. I am not sure that this system isn't one that gets the worst of both worlds which is why I'm in favour of a Scottish Parliament. (Crossman 1977: 48)

Crossman understood that the entire edifice of 'Labour Scotland' was aided by the party being able to maintain a balancing act of Scottish and British interests which saw Labour politicians north of the border see their dominance, influence and authority as being off-limits to scrutiny from others, including their party colleagues south of the border. And he thought that this state of affairs would be unsustainable with a Scottish Parliament.

HALFWAY TO PARADISE?

Scottish Labour's dominance is often explained by over-romanticising the party, public opinion and culture. Seldom is the disjuncture between Scottish Labour and 'Labour Scotland' explored. Instead, explanations have been offered which sentimentalise the radical character of Scottish socialism, with another perspective stressing the reach of Scots collective values and culture – from the power of the folklore and mythology of 'Clydesidism' – to the idea of 'the democratic intellect' (McCrone 1992). A further prevalent perspective has been to see Scottish Labour at its peak as an all-powerful, impregnable political force:

The system had come to rest on cliques of the orthodox. It inevitably fostered careerism, corruption and a positive aversion to anything smacking of public participation. Labour, long centralised and authoritarian enough, grew suspicious of all criticism and new ideas. This was especially true of the West, where the resemblance to a one-party state was closest . . . Labour commanded the centre of the stage, pontificating as the people's party on every Scottish issue. (Fry 1987: 228)

The explanation for Labour's dominance and entrenchment for a large part of the post-war era cannot be found by looking solely at the party. Henry Drucker, writing in the late 1970s, commented that 'The Labour Party in Scotland is based on the apparently unshakeable support of people who live in municipally owned housing, of the trade unions and of the Roman Catholic Church' (Drucker 1977: 8). Instead, we need to address the idea of 'Labour Scotland', a vision of a society whereby a generation of working people were liberated, their lives made infinitely better, poverty and hardship reduced, and more opportunity and choice created. This was a Scotland where the social democratic idea of citizenship, solidarity and positive freedom related to economic and social rights was expanded; central to the Scottish version of 'the good society' was the notion of 'good authority' (see

Paterson 2002). Planning, experts, government action and intervention were to be the primary tools in what was seen as a Scottish 'Brave New World'.

This can be seen in some of the accounts of the immediate post-war era: an age of full employment, the establishment of the National Health Service (NHS), mass slum clearance and the building of new homes and council estates. The old working-class communities of many of Scotland's cities, and Glasgow in particular, were seen as synonymous with dank, dark times, disease, filth and disorder. The new world was to be bright, shiny and tidy. Here is one account of a new council estate in Edinburgh in the 1950s:

> Here indeed was paradise. A shining new house, running hot and cold water and a bath – luxury indeed! A little strip of garden where my father grew roses and won prizes in the local garden competition. Great stretches of field in front of the house over which we ran daily to the little red brick school, built on the banks of Niddry Burn and named after the ancient mill which for centuries had graced its banks. (Crummy 1992: 25)

There is, however, a difference in some of the accounts between Glasgow and the West of Scotland and the rest of the nation, the latter having more pronounced and long-standing expressions of optimism and hope; many of the Glasgow perspectives start with a sense of positivity and then lose it, or have none or very little to begin with. In part this reflects the massive scale of the challenges housing-wise and socially in post-war Glasgow that the Corporation faced, leading to the mantra 'the maximum number of homes in the shortest possible time' (Checkland 1976, Damer 1980, Maver 2000, Craig 2010). This is a Glasgow resident reflecting on moving to a council estate in the 1960s:

> The scheme was considered a paradise when our family arrived in 1966. But like other social planning nightmares around Glasgow, it was only paradise on paper. It's a familiar tale. The adults missed stopping for a chat at Govan Cross. They missed going to the pictures, the dancing, the shops. In Pollok there was no centre of organisation. Nowhere to stop and chat. Nowhere to have a drink or a dance. Only churches, schools and a bit of windswept turf. (Sheridan and McAlpine 1994: 6)

The above two quotes are from first, Helen Crummy, a community activist in Craigmillar, the second, Tommy Sheridan, who later became a political activist, on arriving in Pollok.

People left the tenements filled with great hopes and optimism, as Castlemilk resident Iris MacDonald remembered: 'Everybody was very happy to come out of the old tenements into new houses with facilities they had never enjoyed before' (quoted in Dudgeon 2009: 297). In many cases this feeling did not last long. This is a 1983 reflection on the experience of moving to Pollok:

There was nothing in the scheme at all. The men missed the pubs the most. People used to go back to the old places all the time to see their friends and visit the old haunts. People who came from Govan took others who came from other areas back with them to the Govan shops. In any case, the shops in the older areas were cheaper than the shops in Pollok and the vans were expensive. (quoted in Kynaston 2007: 617)

This is a story of massive social change and dislocation and of people living through it and trying to cope and understand. The above Pollok voice reflected that, 'All the people settled down well together . . . but there was no community spirit' (ibid.). In the immediate post-war era there was widespread enthusiasm and elation at the possibilities of starting new lives, of liberation, cleanliness, and freedom from private landlords. The potency of reminiscing about the tenements, the community spirit, people knowing their neighbours and looking out for one another, came after the reality and disillusion kicked in with moving to the new estates found all across Scotland. Before this the stories associated with tenement life had been characterised by emphasising the grimness and widespread poverty. The universal sense of loss and grief people now sense for a world that passed away, came later, when the new utopia they were promised failed to live up to the billing.

The 'Labour Scotland' of the post-war era was, in the minds of those leading it, a modernist, rationalist, ordered world where the great challenges of the day were addressed, where people and their wants and needs were seen as pliable and changeable. There were huge public challenges to be faced – ill-health, poverty, poor housing and illiteracy – but Labour had a belief in the power of collective action and values which had been validated by 'the people's war'. Such a set of attitudes was given voice by Thomas Johnston, Secretary of State for Scotland from 1941 to 1945:

> It was this unity of purpose that saved us, took us from the brink of destruction and gave us the strength to achieve victory. It was this corporate all-in national effort, each for all, that enabled us to match the hour, and to withstand – at one period entirely alone in the world – the organised fury of the Fascist and Nazi powers of darkness. If we could only recapture part of that enthusiasm, elan and common purpose, recapture it for the much needed reconstruction and betterment of our world – if only we could lift great social crusades like better housing and health from the arena of partisan strife, what magnificent achievements might yet be ours. In unity lies strength: in concurrence, the possibility of great achievement in better housing, better health, better education, better use of leisure, greater security in income, and employment. In barking at each other's heels; in faction fighting and strife over non-essentials lie frustration and defeat for everybody. (Johnston 1952: 170)

A central plank in Labour's economic and social vision was the extension of public ownership. This was hoped to challenge the harshness, unpredictability and inefficiencies of the market, and no nationalisation was arguably more symbolic than that of the mining industries. Robert Smith, a Scottish miner, reflected on that momentous occasion:

> When Vesting Day [Nationalisation Day] came in 1947, all the pits passed into state hands. We had all been to meetings and listened to speakers telling us about the new utopia of nationalisation. We were told there would be a rosy future, wages increased, holidays with pay, improved sickness and injury payments – it all sounded good as we discussed it between ourselves. The more cynical asserted there would be no change. It would be the old team in new jerseys, they said, and they were right. (Duncan 2005: 248)

This was an age of ambition and believing in huge undertakings, of embracing a kind of brutalism in the call of a higher humanity, as David Gibson, Glasgow's Housing Convener in the 1960s, conveyed:

> In the next three years the skyline of Glasgow will become a more attractive one: to me because of the likely vision of multi-storey houses rising by the thousand ... The prospect will be thrilling, I am certain, to the many thousands who are still yearning for a home. It may appear on occasion that I would offend against all good planning principles, against open space and Green Belt principles – if I offend against these it is only in seeking to avoid the continuing and unpardonable offence that bad housing commits against human dignity. A decent home is the cradle of the infant, the seminar of the young, and the refuge of the aged. (Devine 1999: 561)

A whole industry of activity, personnel and general busy-ness was created to build the new post-war society, as one fictionalised account of 1950s activities showed:

> From the local towns each morning the bus loads of clerks, and in the little beaver-boarded cubbyholes, with their cups of tea and their doggy calendars ... would begin the long little jealous rows of bureaucracy. In the servants' bedrooms the major bureaucrats would sit with their feet upon a carpet and all their dreams would come true. And lastly there would come the men with the big machines. (Scott, 1954: 203)

Vince Cable, reflecting on his period as a Glasgow councillor from 1971 to 1974, commented, 'Leading councillors saw new motorways, like blocks of multi-storey council houses, as emblems of a modernistic, dynamic city' (Cable 2009: 125). Glasgow was a centre of activity, clearing whole neighbourhoods of the city, building whole new areas, and engaging in mass population decanting, both within and outwith the city. When problems began to arise, the first reaction of the council was one of denial: 'Initially, many councillors and housing officers refused to accept that there was a problem and developed a language for describing "choosy" and "difficult" people who lacked "gratitude" for what the council had done' (Cable 2009: 123).

THE END OF 'LABOUR SCOTLAND'

'Labour Scotland' is viewed by many critics as a method of all-pervasive authority and control, but it had a benign side to it. Planning, science, technology, experts all had a part to play in this: the rise of the New Towns, the creation of hydro-electric power, the belief in the triumph of man over nature, and the over-arching faith in 'planned freedom' (Cowling 1997, Miller 2007). All of this had a potent, emotional resonance, seen in the Glasgow Corporation Public Information Films made about the future of the city and the challenges city authorities faced, from slum clearance to poor health and raising children; the tone of these films was that such huge obstacles could be overcome and a better, cleaner, fairer city created (Lebas 2007). The last articulation of this positive spirit can be observed in Bill Forsyth's *Gregory's Girl* from 1981, set in Cumbernauld, a world still characterised by hope and humanity inherent in the idea of Scotland's New Towns (Yule 2010).

Post-1979 the idea of 'Labour Scotland' began to wilt as council house sales took off and new building ground to a halt, trade union membership began to decline, and the Thatcher Government began its long war of attrition on local government. However, as in other areas of the Conservatives' attack on the institutions and values of the post-war consensus, the decline and decay of 'Labour Scotland' had begun to manifest itself long before 1979.

The mammoth changes post-1945 produced a vast state and bureaucratic empire which reached into most aspects of Scottish public life. This changed fundamentally the character and nature of Scottish society, ameliorating hardship and poverty, and extending life chances and prosperity. However, at the same time it created new problems of uniformity, insensitivity, poor-quality housing estates and insensitive, unresponsive public services, with people wanting to be treated more as individuals and to have a greater say in their lives. These feelings of disenchantment with state provision and the post-war consensus were felt across the UK, and in England gave Thatcherism a receptive public mood to play to; in Scotland, such sentiment did not express itself in support for a populist right-wing agenda (see Hall 1979).

A few isolated perspectives at the time offered an understanding of the changing dynamics of Scottish society and the consequences for Scottish Labour, but were not paid heed to. Writing just after the peak of Scottish Labour's electoral fortunes in 1966, William Marwick painted a picture of an atrophied party with few members, little energy or political edge, engaging with a complex, managed society:

> The trend to the 'corporative' or 'managerial' society, characterised by large-scale centralisation and bureaucratic administration, both public and private, which is

common to all western countries, together with the achievement of the 'Age of Affluence' and the welfare state, have blunted the edge of the working-class movement. (Marwick 1967: 113–14)

Drucker, writing before the 1979 election, could discern that all was not well in Scottish Labour: 'There are signs of decay in the Labour Party. Many local constituency parties are controlled by tiny groups of elderly members. Too many local councillors are corrupt, as a series of scandals and court cases has shown' (Drucker 1977: 8–9).

The slow demise of 'Labour Scotland', of a vision of the future and its three main pillars, left the party exposed and vulnerable. Once there had been a specific Labour story of Scotland: one which came from Scottish traditions and values and responded to Scottish conditions, while playing its part and contributing to the Labour story of Britain. This latter account was one which at its heart and its best was a people's story of these isles, of the forward march of progress and fairness (Aughey 2001: Ch. 5).

This profound change began to become evident post-1979 but its existential roots lie earlier, and left Scottish Labour in a state of denial. In the period 1979 to 1997, as Scottish society changed from the more ordered, managed, deferential demeanour of the post-1945 order, and the idea of 'Labour Scotland' weakened, the Scottish Labour Party seemed unsure how to respond. At the same time, British Labour explored the challenges it faced in society, the economy and politics by having numerous, often painful, debates and exploring political options from the Bennite new left to Blairite New Labour.

Scottish Labour remained relatively impervious to such deliberations, instead displaying a quiet self-assurance to Scotland and the wider British Labour Party. This was a party which post-1979 continued winning elections, sending a significant bloc of MPs to Westminster, and saw these factors, along with its impressive local government base, as an accurate barometer of the state and strength of the Scottish party's appeal.

This contributed to a situation whereby Scottish Labour became increasingly unaware of the society it claimed to represent and understand, and the true nature of its own strength. Large swathes of the party chose, given that they continued to win elections by impressive margins in the 1980s and 1990s, to believe the comforting stories they told themselves, that Scottish Labour had an omnipotence, a special ability to win friends and influence people, and did not have to face the harsh truths that New Labour south of the border had.

This resulted, as each of the three pillars weakened, in the party finding it difficult to adapt, comprehend and change. Some elements in the party embraced a politics of defiant conservatism and traditionalism, of believing

15

that the party had a deep connection with Scottish voters aided by a more centre-left, collectivist culture. This led them to express their anger and wrath at what they saw as the perfidy and sell-out of New Labour. Another group positively celebrated rejecting anything which smacked of radical reform and 'modernisation'. A further smaller group, containing influential Westminster politicians, embraced with enthusiasm the language of change and renewal, key New Labour terms, but were met with widespread suspicion in the party.

This set of events has left Scottish Labour poorly equipped to deal with a society where it no longer has the majority constituencies it once had in council housing, trade union membership and local government. It has produced a party that lacks many of the most important skills and resources, as well as the understanding of its situation to fundamentally change and alter course. And at the same time, the wider cause of 'Labour Scotland', a pioneering vision of Scotland and its future and people, has exhausted itself and not been replaced. Henry McLeish articulated inadvertently the narrow parameters of 'Labour Scotland', or at least the Fife version of it, when he compared his experience to that of the West of Scotland, commenting that 'there were no Labour networks, clubs or universities to draw from in Fife' (interview), oblivious to St Andrews University.

There is a longer story and relevant account which we have to acknowledge; namely the demise of the Scottish radical tradition, a set of ideas which went far beyond the boundaries of Scottish Labour and wider labour movement, and which pre-date them into the era of the nineteenth-century Liberals and assorted radical currents. This is an argument put forward by the historian T. C. Smout in his celebrated *A Century of the Scottish People 1830–1950*. In the closing chapter, 'The Rise and Fall of Socialist Idealism', he writes:

> The coming of the collectivist state, and its determination to turn over decision-making to the experts once it had been agreed that a combination of economic growth and welfare was to be the main aim of government, bears much of the credit for the improved state of Scottish welfare since 1945. (Smout 1986: 275)

He then observes that in all this something valuable has been lost:

> It would be a blind observer of the Scottish scene who thought that Scotland today enjoys the vibrant popular political culture it enjoyed from the 1830s to the 1920s . . . The Friends of the People, the Chartists, the Liberal Working Man, Keir Hardie and the Clydesiders shared a common belief that, at the close of the twentieth century, we are in danger of losing: by the exercise of political will, the people hold their own future in their own hands . . . (ibid.)

Any historical understanding of Scottish Labour has to reflect this wider story. Our thesis is that the congruence of events we describe and analyse

16

in detail in this book has contributed hugely to the current state of Scottish Labour. At the same time, the rise and fall of 'Labour Scotland' and Scottish Labour did not happen in isolation, but as part of the decline of the radical imagination.

Our argument is not, we should be categorically clear, that the Scottish Labour Party is terminally and clinically dead, but that the wider story of 'Labour Scotland' which it brought into being, and which gave succour and support to the party, is now completely over. This is part of a bigger picture of fundamental change which has altered post-war Scottish society and resulted in a more secularised, less deferential, more disputatious, less predictable and controllable nation.

Very little is pre-determined in politics, but the long-term economic, social and cultural environment shape a significant part of political realities. Therefore, if Scottish Labour is to have a positive future and role in Scottish politics, it has to recognise that the terrain of politics has dramatically altered, its post-war social order is no more, and that it needs to understand what has changed, change itself and change the nature of its politics.

NOTES

1. Any analysis of Scottish figures on council tenants, trade union membership and local government has to put this in the context of how these compare with UK and English trends. English council housing rose to a peak of 29% of homes in 1975, before falling back to 18% in 1995. UK trade union membership peaked at 13,212,000 in 1979 (55.4% density) before falling back to 7,054,000 in 2009 (23.5%). In English local government, Labour elected 9,630 out of 20,380 councillors in its peak year post-1979 of 1996 (47.3%), falling back to 3,743 out of 18,216 in 2009 (20.5%); the party controlled 169 out of 386 councils in 1998 (43.8%) and 33 out of 351 in 2009 (9.4%) (Regional Trends 1996, *The Guardian*, 30 April 2010, Tetteh 2010).
2. Labour's support in the Catholic community in Scotland was 79.3% in February 1974, when the party won 36.6% of the national vote, 67% in 1979 and 53% in 1992 (Brand 1978: 152; Bennie et al. 1997: 114).

Part One
The Context of Scottish Labour:
The Opposition Years

CHAPTER 2

Fighting For What Really Matters:
The Politics of Scottish Labour 1979–87

INTRODUCTION

The 1970s were an uncomfortable decade for Labour and Scottish Labour. The party faced economic and social problems, the unravelling of many of the assumptions of post-war politics, a bitterly divided Labour Government which governed for much of the time with no overall parliamentary majority, and the rise of a challenging right-wing agenda which became known as Thatcherism.

At the same time, and connected to all of this, Labour's electoral and ideological base was slowly fragmenting and eroding, with the rise of a more fluid and multi-party politics, and the emergence of 'the forward march of labour halted' thesis (Hobsbawm et al. 1981).

Nowhere was more multi-party in its politics in the 1970s than Scotland. The October 1974 general election saw Labour win 36.3% of the vote – the party's lowest share of the vote since the debacle of 1931 – while the Scottish Nationalists' 30.4% to this day is their best showing in a Westminster election. All that preserved Labour's dominance in 1974 was the way in which the FPTP electoral system worked in Labour's favour, rewarding them with forty-one out of seventy-one seats to the Nationalists' eleven and Conservatives' sixteen. Behind these figures, though, thirty-five out of forty-one of Labour's seats had the Nationalists in second place: a position of strength they were to prove unable to build on from 1974 (Steed 1975).

THE POLITICS OF THE SCOTTISH DIMENSION:
DEVOLUTION AND OPPOSITION AFTER 1979

Scottish politics, and even to a large extent British politics, were shaped by the politics and dynamics of devolution in the October 1974–79 Parliament,

21

the consequences of which are explored elsewhere in this book. The long march to the 1979 referendum involved bitter Labour divisions and recriminations, a Labour 'Yes' campaign which refused to work with the Nationalists, and a Labour 'No' campaign which contained a significant number of party grandees, senior local government figures and a sizeable element of the party's grass roots.

The result of the 1 March 1979 Scottish referendum vote was both conclusive and inconclusive. Scottish voters were 51.6% to 48.4% in favour of a Scottish Assembly; this translated on a 63.6% turnout into 32.9% yes and 30.8% no. This meant that the 40% threshold, originally moved by George Cunningham, Labour MP for Islington South and Finsbury, scuppered the assembly proposals (Bochel et al. 1981).

Even at this point the Labour Government's proposals might have been saved, but such were the divisions in Labour on devolution, and antipathy towards the SNP and SNP parliamentary group and vice-versa, that the events post-referendum worked to shatter any chance of devolution for a generation, and in the process soured even more Labour–SNP relations. A vote of no confidence was put down, first by the Nationalists, then the Conservatives, and on that famous Commons night of 28 March 1979 Labour fell from office by 311 votes to 310. Labour legend has it this was the night that the SNP 'brought down the Labour Government', but the truth was more complicated, and instead gave validity and added passion to an existing array of prejudices on both sides.

Labour divisions on devolution were put on public display at the March 1979 party conference in Perth, despite the fact that the party knew an election had to be held that year. In a heated debate on devolution chaired by Janey Buchan, there were accusations that she significantly misused her position to call more anti-devolutionists. The debate had begun quietly, with Gordon Brown calling for 'no rancour, no recrimination, and no bloodletting', while Brian Wilson opposed the Executive policy statement on devolution, arguing that 'devolution should be out of the way, finished with!' (*The Scotsman*, 12 March 1979).

The party's statement was overwhelmingly carried, but tensions in the debate erupted towards the end of conference. Dennis Canavan stated his anger at the 'incredible spectacle of a Labour conference chaired by a person who had voted in the referendum against Labour Party policy', and accused Buchan of aiding at conference 'traitors who had collaborated with Tories' (ibid.).

The Scottish Trades Union Congress (STUC) at its Annual Congress held before the election had, like many in the party and wider labour movement, little awareness of the huge changes that were to come. Sam Gooding,

Scottish Labour chairman, told the Congress that they could 'look forward to an early implementation of the devolution measures when we return a Labour Government' (Aitken 1997: 261).

The Scottish dimension of the 1979 general election was almost quiet by comparison with the divisions in Labour recently shown. The key issues were the same as the rest of Britain, with a System Three poll rating the top issues as 47% the cost of living and 28% jobs and unemployment; devolution was mentioned by a mere 3%, behind trade union power on 4% (Hetherington 1979). Labour ran a professional campaign, concentrating on the party's achievements in office on the economy, protecting public spending and curbing inflation. It challenged the right-wing agenda of Margaret Thatcher, while having a field day against the SNP, for their many parliamentary votes against Labour and with the Tories over five years, and the devolution debacle. One commentator came to such a view after the election: 'Labour effectively managed to set the tone of the campaign from day one, to drive the Tories into a corner from which they found it difficult to escape' (Hetherington 1979: 95).

Labour had reason to feel confident in Scotland, as the party had begun to turn the Nationalist tide in the previous year, winning with relative ease three by-elections in Glasgow Garscadden, Hamilton, and Berwick and East Lothian. On 3 May 1979, across Scotland Labour saw its vote rise to 41.5%, while the Conservatives increased their support to 31.4%, as the Nationalist vote fell to 17.3%. This meant that Scotland swung by 1.5% from Labour to Conservative, the smallest national or regional swing in Britain, while across the UK the Conservatives achieved a 5.2% swing from Labour (Miller 1980).

Labour returned forty-four seats, a gain of three; the Conservatives twenty-two, a gain of six. Labour won back the previous Nationalist gains of Clackmannan and East Stirlingshire from George Reid and Dunbartonshire East from Margaret Bain; the party's most celebrated and noteworthy victory came in Glasgow Cathcart, where John Maxton defeated Margaret Thatcher's Scots favourite and potential Secretary of State for Scotland, Teddy Taylor (the only Tory seat to be lost across the UK in the election). If any result was indicative of the future pattern of Scottish politics over the next two decades it was Cathcart. This was an emblem of the slow decline of the Scots Tories in both Glasgow and the West of Scotland; in a matter of three years the city would be a Tory-free zone at the level of parliamentary representation, and the populist working-class Tory politics, which Taylor came from and gave voice to, a thing of the distant past. On election night Donald Dewar struck an unusually defiant note in his acceptance speech at Glasgow Garscadden, saying that the desire for self-government would get stronger under a right-wing Thatcher Government and declared, 'It may be that many who did vote No, or who abstained, may come to regret the indecisive result of the referendum as Mrs Thatcher's shock troops ride rough-shod . . . over Scotland' (Hetherington 1979: 100). George Foulkes defeated Jim Sillars, standing under the banner of the 'breakaway' Scottish Labour Party, in South Ayrshire by 1,521 votes, causing Sillars to reflect post-count, 'I pointed out to the victorious Labour supporters that we in Scotland still had not resolved the paradox of rejoicing in Labour winning in our country, while the English were voting in a Tory Government' (Sillars 1986: 74–5). One former Labour official of the time reflected that 'Labour organisation and commitment was motivated in elections to get the Nationalists' and that 'Labour members would literally be up for street by street in Garscadden, Hamilton and '79 taking back areas from the SNP. We saw them as interlopers and intruders in Labour areas' (interview).

The Thatcher Government came to office with an overall majority of forty-three, but was in a minority in seats and votes in Scotland, and moreover, its right-wing agenda was at odds with most of Scottish society, public opinion and institutional forces (Kemp 1993: 209–11). This was a profoundly unionist administration, and for all the signals given out in the devolution referendum from Lord Home and others that the Tories would be open-minded to better proposals, the Tories passed the Repeal of Order Act which repealed the Scotland Act 1978 within two months of winning office.

The Thatcher Government in its first term presided over a massive increase in unemployment which hit Scotland hard. A whole host of manufacturing jobs and industry were to be lost which were profoundly painful and deeply felt. From May 1979 a roll call of losses began: Singer, Clydebank; Monsanto chemicals, Ayrshire; Pye TMC electronics, Livingston; VF Corporation, Greenock; Massey Ferguson, Kilmarnock; along with Peugeot Talbot's Linwood plant, Invergordon aluminium smelter and Corpach pulp mill. This was a Scottish experience of the Thatcher Government's British monetarist policies, equally felt in the North of England, Yorkshire and Wales. In Scotland this was seen through a national dimension which was to weave itself in folklore, myths and even song. A future MP commented that 'Thatcherism felt like an onslaught on everything we believed. It turned our world upside down' (interview). Michael Gove, Conservative MP, identified the phenomenon of 'the "Letter from America ideology", where distant figures seek to impose an alien ideology' (Torrance 2009: 59).

One of the first areas in which the Thatcher Government and George Younger, Secretary of State for Scotland, pushed by Malcolm Rifkind, Minister for Home Affairs and the Environment at the Scottish Office, began to make an impact in Scotland, which challenged Labour's dominance, was council house sales. The Tenants' Rights etc. (Scotland) Act 1980 was to prove one of the most far-reaching pieces of post-war legislation seen north of the border. The act offered a generous package of discounts for council tenants buying their homes, and importantly, it forced councils to sell homes to those tenants who wanted to buy them.

This was a Scotland shaped by and defined by council housing, with 54% of households being council tenants. At first Labour councils attempted to resist the provisions of the bill and considered a policy of complete non-co-operation. This was not just a Labour stance; all across Scotland there was a prevailing opinion that the right to council housing, to access, maintenance of stock and different types of council housing in an area, was a social entitlement. But as with Labour opposition to the local government cuts by the Thatcher Government, resistance eventually collapsed. By September 1982, 28,535 sales had taken place, with a further 17,000 applications outstanding, representing just over 2% of the public stock (*The Scotsman*, 30 September 1982).

Despite the popularity of council house sales, the local elections of 1980 and 1982 saw Labour re-emerge from its unpopularity in the 1977 district and 1978 regional elections. The 1980 elections in particular saw Labour win 49.5% to the Conservatives' 26.5%; a huge swathe of young, leftist Labour councillors was elected, eager to take on the Tories, adopt radical stances, and distance themselves from the Labour establishment way of doing things. On council house sales, Labour continued to drag its feet as much as it could on this policy, with as late as January 1983 Allan Stewart, Scottish Office minister, writing to nineteen councils pointing out their failure 'to give sufficient priority to meeting the wishes of tenants to buy their council houses' (*The Scotsman*, 8 January 1983).

The Thatcher Government tried to control local government expenditure by establishing new ways of calculating and restricting Rate Support Grant (RSG) to councils which were deemed to be over-spending. In England, this agenda was promoted by Michael Heseltine, who was seen at the time as abrasive and challenging, whereas in Scotland it was the responsibility of the Scottish Office and George Younger; for all the difficulties politically, Younger's style here and elsewhere was to be the personification of genteel charm.

This agenda resulted in the Local Government (Miscellaneous Provisions) Scotland Act 1981, which gave the Scottish Office power to withdraw RSG from councils whose spending was judged to be 'excessive and unreasonable' (Heald et al. 1981: 40). This was precipitated by the case of Labour-controlled Lothian Regional Council, who in order to fund spending increases in 1980–1 put up rates by 41%. In the financial year 1981–2 a number of Labour authorities planned spending well above government guidelines. These included Lothian, Stirling and Dundee, all Labour councils and all associated with younger, more radical groups of Labour councillors; Lothian planned a rise of 24.7%, Stirling and Dundee of 122% and 150% respectively. This was the era of 'the loony left' and ratepayers' revolts, which was to lead in Labour's case to the hubris of Liverpool ultra-left posturing, and in the Conservatives the disaster of the poll tax.

In July 1981, Younger reduced RSG payments to Lothian, Dundee and Stirling councils by £47 million, £2 million and £1 million respectively. Lothian offered the most powerful resistance to Younger, claiming under its Labour leader John Mulvey that it had a popular mandate to protect jobs and services, and increase local expenditure to do so. At the end of 1981, Younger eventually decided to cut Lothian's budget by £30 million, and the council caved in to pressure.

Lothian was the nearest Scottish Labour got to embracing the politics of defiance and resistance, which eventually erupted in England in 1985–6 with the popular front of English Labour councils. The Lothian episode closed in the May 1982 regional elections with the defeat of Labour and election of a Tory administration led by Brian Meek supported by the Liberal-SDP Alliance, which reduced expenditure after Labour and the Tories finished neck and neck on twenty-two seats each. There was a much wider context at play which had a longer legacy. Younger was playing a subtle 'divide and rule' approach with his Labour local government opponents. He was happy to isolate and take on Lothian while at the same time accommodating the West of Scotland Labour establishment and, in particular, the much more powerful Strathclyde Regional Council. It was an approach which could be said to pay dividends for both Labour and Conservatives.

A PARTY DIVIDED: LABOUR, THE NEW LEFT AND MILITANT

Post-1979 the composition of Scottish Labour began to change and the party leadership faced internal challenge and pressure. Across the UK, the Bennite left organised in the Labour Co-ordinating Committee (LCC) and Campaign for Labour Party Democracy (CLPD) and challenged the party establishment and constitution, developing a list of left-wing policies and an agenda of intra-party democracy (Minkin 1980).

In Scotland, this Bennite 'new left' was associated with LCC (Scotland) who brought together a group of activists, councillors and feminists, many of whom became future MPs. It quickly identified a number of specific Scottish themes: the importance of a socialist agenda for local government, a feminist political sensibility which led to the formation of LCC (Scotland) Women's Committee, and, in particular, the Scottish dimension and home rule question (see LCC (Scotland) 1980).

People associated with this group were nearly all in their late twenties to thirties and forties, with little support from older or more senior colleagues, from parliamentary colleagues, even of a notional 'left' tradition. Prominent supporters included Mark Lazarowicz, later leader of Edinburgh Council and MP for Edinburgh North and Leith; George Galloway, Secretary/Organiser of Dundee Labour Party and later MP for Glasgow Hillhead; trade unionists Bill Speirs, later General Secretary of the STUC, Bill Gilby and Harry McLevy; along with Labour feminist activists such as Margaret Curran, Johann Lamont and Rosanna McCrae, the first two becoming MSPs and ministers in the Lab-Lib Dem Scottish Executive. Robin Cook and Dennis Canavan were that rare species: MPs who were prepared to associate with what was as much a generational movement as one of left versus right.

LCC was always more prominent than CLPD north of the border. It organised local groups in places like Dundee and Glasgow, held regular meetings, and produced a steady supply of publications including a bulletin, 'Scottish Labour Activist'. However, contrary to myth, it never won a secure majority on the Scottish Labour Executive on its own: in that the dynamics of Scottish Labour were more complex and nuanced than the British party where the Bennite left held a comfortable majority on the NEC from 1973 to 1981. In Scotland, the LCC worked with a wider, more fluid, difficult-to-define left, and also at significant points did not automatically set itself in opposition to the leadership, but sought to influence and work with it.

What is incontestable is that in the period post-1979 LCC and the wider left had a major impact on the party and national executive. LCC (Scotland), despite or because of the reality of facing an entrenched culture of conservative labourism in the upper echelons of the party, consistently chose to avoid the politics of frontal assault. Instead, LCC (Scotland) engaged in a politics of change by persuasion and omission which was to pay significant dividends, but eventually lead to incorporation into the leadership and then left fragmentation.

On 2 April 1981 the politics of Labour and the left entered a new phase after which everything would be different: Tony Benn announced his decision to challenge Denis Healey for the deputy leadership of the party. The aim of the campaign was to use and thus legitimise the newly created Electoral College of trade unions, constituency parties and MPs which had been agreed at the January 1981 Wembley conference (Kogan and Kogan 1981). In Scotland, the broad left around LCC (Scotland) swung behind Benn, but divisions and differences began to appear in what became known as 'the soft left' and its priorities versus what was called 'the hard left' or 'outside left' to its followers.

In July 1981, William McKelvey, MP for Kilmarnock, and Ernie Ross, MP for Dundee West, put forward a proposal that all Labour MPs should sign what was seen as 'a loyalty oath' to stand by conference decisions. McKelvey later reflected that 'the PLP thought we were nutters' (Morley 2007: 71). Several months of Labour infighting followed until on the opening day of the Labour conference on 27 September 1981, Denis Healey narrowly defeated Tony Benn by 50.4% to 49.6%; 81% of constituency parties voted for Benn, while in the second round after John Silkin was eliminated, thirty-seven 'soft left' MPs abstained, thus ensuring that Healey won; these included future Labour leader Neil Kinnock and MPs Joan Lestor and Jeff Rooker.

Tensions within the Labour Party and left boiled over at a meeting of the Scottish Labour Executive on 14 November 1981. This was a meeting Michael Foot attended as leader. Jimmy Allison, party organiser, called it 'an extremely unpleasant meeting', as George Galloway, in his position as chair of the Scottish party, denounced Foot for his exclusion of Benn from the Shadow Cabinet (Allison 1995: 94). This was a debate about power and who made policy: the Shadow Cabinet or Annual Conference. Donald Dewar commented to the press afterwards, 'I deeply regret that the Scottish Executive have been trapped into a counter-productive and totally unnecessary display of factional politics' (Morley 2007: 74).

Scottish Labour conference in March 1982 saw the party left push for a more powerful Scottish Assembly and the cause of internal party devolution, with the two becoming more intertwined in the eyes of supporters. The party chair, George Galloway, in an article in *New Socialist*, a party journal, leading up to conference gave an indication of the party mood on the left. There was an increasingly overblown rhetoric seeing Scotland transformed as 'Mrs Thatcher's holocaust further devastates Scottish society'. The national dimension was central: 'Scotland knows as a nation, that it did not vote for Mrs Thatcher; indeed it decisively rejected her'. This led him to argue:

> The Tory writ in Scotland is increasingly seen as that of an occupying power, with millionaire George Younger as governor-general. Tory diktat in Scotland is seen as essentially vindictive. (Galloway 1982)

Galloway even went down an unheard-of path in Labour circles: acknowledging and talking about the power and influence of 'British nationalism' in the party and the prospect that it could stop a distinctly Scottish autonomist approach.

At the 1982 British Labour conference the Bennite-inspired 'Labour's

Programme 1982' was passed by 6.42 million votes to 224,000 (*The Scotsman*, 30 September 1982). The 284-page document was the most comprehensive and radical post-war document ever presented to party conference: an Alternative Economic Strategy (AES) with extensive public ownership; withdrawal from the European Economic Community (EEC) and unilateral nuclear disarmament. This reflected the ferment of left-wing activity in the past few years. Yet on Scotland and devolution, in place of radicalism and sweeping ambition there was hesitancy and ambiguity.

The section 'Democracy and Human Rights' stated after rejecting Welsh devolution, respecting the wishes of the Welsh people in the 1979 referendum, 'we accept the decision of the people of Scotland who opted for an Assembly and we re-affirm our commitment to devolution for Scotland' (Labour's Programme 1982: 209). It went on to say:

> The party's 1982 Scottish conference has since re-affirmed its wish for a Scottish Assembly with significant industrial and limited fiscal powers. This will obviously have to be carefully examined in terms of its consequences for the machinery of government as a whole. (ibid.)

The careful wording was based on deep tensions and disagreements within Labour thinking, and within the left itself, between the power of the British state, Labour's centralism, and its need to nurture and promote a Scottish dimension and encourage its de-centralist traditions. Labour had tried to square this circle in 1974 when its limited devolution proposals were positioned within affirming the integrity of the British state, Scottish MPs and the Secretary of State for Scotland: the politics of 'the Dalintober Street devolutionists' (McLean 2004).

Nowhere were the fault-lines within Scottish Labour more clear than in Labour local government and the different agendas of the new radicals and party establishment. Whereas south of the border post-1979 an explosion of 'local socialism' and 'new left' initiatives took route, in Scotland these were much more limited. Apart from the brief episode of Lothian resistance, the only real 'new left' council experiments were seen in Stirling and Edinburgh. It was no accident that these were highly electorally competitive areas where Labour had to defeat local Conservatives to win control. Labour only won control of Edinburgh for the first time in its history in 1984. This was because intense electoral pressure gave younger Labour candidates, who won selection, election in winnable Labour seats, changing the composition of the city and Labour Group.

Another model was provided by the politics of Dundee, where Labour took control of the council in 1980 and a youthful George Galloway was Secretary/Organiser of the local party. Dundee District Council quickly earned a reputation for left-wing politics with its low council house rents, opposition to council house sales and Tory cuts, and most publicly, its decision in 1980 to fly the Palestinian flag in the City Chambers and twin with the West Bank town of Nablus.

This came at a point when the Palestinian cause had less profile and respect, was seen as synonymous with the Palestine Liberation Organisation (PLO) and viewed as controversial by Jewish groups in and beyond the city. It was even less of a cause célèbre on the British left, and in this Galloway and Dundee Labour were ahead of the game. Their stance was so contentious that ITV's *World in Action*, then itself prestigious and influential, devoted an entire programme to it.

What Dundee did not do was embrace a politics of 'the new left' or municipal socialism, addressing how council services were run, and in particular such issues as housing management and participation. Somehow such issues were seen as marginal to the politics of socialism; even in 1980 left politics were a mixture of 'bread and butter' issues for 'our people'; de-centralisation of council services was seen as 'trendy Hillhead politics', as one senior councillor put it at the time. One party member mentioned 'the prevalence of Stabianism, combining Stalinism and Fabianism, people who talk left and act right such as Ernie Ross' (interview).

The juxtaposition between rhetoric and reality has to be underlined. Dundee District Council liked to strike the militant pose in the early 1980s while engaging in the politics of symbolism. Yet at the same time Dundee was a relative hotbed of left activity in the district party, supported by Galloway, Harry McLevy, Chris and Mary Ward and others. The focal point for this was the LCC Dundee group, which began life as a group set up by Galloway entitled North East Debating Society, or NEDS as it became known.

With Dundee's long tradition of an active Communist Party which remained strong until the late 1980s, NEDS and then LCC Dundee brought together Labour and Communist members in what was in effect a broad left forum. In 1982, LCC Dundee decided to attempt to formalise this by asking the national office to give its permission to this local arrangement in its standing orders. It was refused by the LCC General Secretary Nigel Stanley; LCC Dundee responded to this by ignoring the decision and just carrying on.

Labour–Communist co-operation of course was not unusual in Scotland. In Fife, in Ayrshire, in various trades councils and in the STUC similar alliances occurred, but what made Dundee interesting was how late this continued at a local level. LCC Dundee held well-attended monthly meetings, had political education classes and guest speakers, but did not, despite all of this, develop an agenda of radical local council politics. It was far easier to talk about the politics of opposing the Tories on general issues or taking symbolic action on international issues. The Dundee example points to how strong and enduring the conservative ethos of Scottish Labour was even on the left under Thatcherism; and even when a local left politics came to fruition, rather than it embracing 'the new left' agenda it was in the context of a left municipal agenda of labourism, firmly based on the politics of the traditional Labour state.

The politics of Stirling, Edinburgh and, even more, Dundee attracted lots of attention and controversy at the time, but can now be seen in hindsight as atypical and as outliers from the dominant Scottish Labour model. Much more influential was the West of Scotland Labour approach to council politics, of which the most powerful was Strathclyde Regional Council, which because of its size, resources and make-up of its Labour Group developed a distinct political agenda. It was neither Greater London Council (GLC)-style self-professed 'new left', nor was it old-fashioned Labour municipalism; it allowed for different Labour leaders from the usual mould – Geoff Shaw in the 1970s, then the more traditional Dick Stewart, and following him the thoughtful Charlie Gray. In policies, it was pro-European, imaginative in economic development, regeneration and social strategy, while being big enough to prevent the Conservatives railroading it into submission (eventually contributing to its abolition).

The Scottish Labour left was not at this time just made up of LCC (Scotland). An alternative left perspective was provided by the Trotskyite Militant Tendency, who had been practising the politics of entryism into Labour since the 1960s (Crick 1984, Callaghan 1984). Militant's involvement in Scottish Labour saw them win their first representation on the Labour Party Young Socialists' Scottish Committee in 1972 and win control of the committee in 1973. In the 1979 general election Militant had only one Scottish Labour candidate, Alex Wood (who later went on to become a post-Militant Labour leader of Edinburgh Council from 1984 to 1986), who stood in the safe Tory seat of Dumfries held by Sir Hector Monro.

Post-1979 defeat, as the left's fortunes rose so did those of Militant. It was part of the broad left umbrella group the Rank and File Mobilising Committee (RFMC) which would subsequently play a major role in organising Tony Benn's campaign for the deputy leadership in 1981. The first sign of Militant's rising fortunes came in the selection for the Glasgow Central Labour nomination for the by-election caused by the death of Tom McMillan in April 1980. It took until the third ballot for Bob McTaggart to defeat the Militant candidate Ronnie Stevenson. Labour went on easily to win the by-election, with the SNP a distant second, in June.

The British party leadership began to act against Militant in 1982, expelling the tendency's national leadership for being 'a party within a party'. In the selection contests running up to the 1983 election, Militant put a considerable effort into two Glasgow seats: Pollok and Provan. In the former, Jimmy White, the sitting MP, held off Militant supporter David Dick by nine votes; in the latter, Hugh Brown, sitting MP, was challenged by Ronnie Stevenson, with Brown winning by five votes. Thus, Militant's first serious attempts to win Labour representation in Scotland ended in failure; it was not to be their last attempt.

The Labour centre-right were weakened in this period by the breakaway of Labour MPs, councillors and members to establish the Social Democratic Party (SDP) in March 1981. Scotland was less affected than the rest of the UK, with several prominent centre-right wingers who elsewhere would have been ideal candidates to defect remaining with Labour. These included George Robertson, John Smith, Donald Dewar and Helen Liddell. Two Scottish Labour MPs were part of a group of twelve Labour MPs who signed a declaration in September 1980 calling for comprehensive reform of the party; seven of the twelve joined the SDP the following year; the two Scottish MPs, George Robertson and Willie Hamilton, MP for Fife Central, did not (Crewe and King 1995: 48). There was something in Scottish Labour's belief system, its ethos and the 'myth' of 'Labour Scotland' which influenced many who might have joined the new party not to do so.

Two Scottish Labour MPs joined the Social Democrats: Robert Maclellan, MP for Caithness and Sutherland, and Dickson Mabon, MP for Greenock and Port Glasgow. Both were from a professional, elite, middle-class Labour tradition, which did not sit within the party's mainstream even on the right. This was to have wider consequences in the 1983 election, and further afield, in the influence Scottish Labour had on the British party.

The Liberal–SDP Alliance turned British politics upside down, creating a string of high- profile by-elections which began with Roy Jenkins nearly winning Warrington, followed by victories by Bill Pitt in Croydon North West and Shirley Williams in Crosby. Then came Glasgow Hillhead and Jenkins' victory in a tight, competitive contest in March 1982. Labour felt they were in with a chance in this seat, and threw significant resources behind David Wiseman's campaign, while the Conservative campaign with Gerry Malone encountered all sorts of difficulties. The end result had Jenkins win with a majority of 2,032 over the Conservatives, who finished 222 votes ahead of Labour. It was to be the last famous Liberal–SDP Alliance by-election victory, for within days of the result the Argentineans invaded the Falkland Islands and British politics were to be utterly changed. Closer to home, the result showed the changing nature of Glasgow politics. Hillhead was the last Conservative seat in Glasgow – a city they had once won nearly half the vote in and seven out of fifteen seats in 1955.

The 1983 general election was an uncomfortable one for Labour: a divided party, a resurgent Thatcher, the threat of the Liberal–SDP Alliance, and the prospect of Labour being pushed into third place in votes across the UK. In Scotland, the Scottish Labour Party campaign was more sure-footed and less accident-prone, with the party under less pressure. The Conservatives were becoming more unpopular, the Liberal–SDP Alliance were less of a challenge north of the border and particularly in Labour's Central Belt fortresses, while the SNP were still post-1979 in the doldrums after their bout of intra-party fratricide.

Bruce Millan, Shadow Secretary of State for Scotland and previously Secretary of State for Scotland from 1976 to 1979, laid out Labour's thinking before the election in an officially approved collection of essays edited by Gerald Kaufman and published to coincide with the run into the 1983 election. Millan summarised the four years of Tory Government as 'one of catastrophic industrial decline' in Scotland (Millan 1983: 139). He invoked the closures of the 'car plant at Linwood, the pulp mill at Fort William, the aluminium shelter at Invergordon', which produced a potent 'bitterness' aided by the destruction of the post-war hopes and dreams which had seen their establishment in the first place.

Millan then addressed Labour's failings in the 1970s on devolution: 'It is futile to pretend that Labour's plans for Scottish devolution, which resulted in the Scotland Act 1978, had nothing at all to do with the rise in the Nationalist vote' (ibid.). He emphasised, 'The case for devolution does not wax and wane with the rise and fall of the SNP' (ibid.). Instead, Labour had to give due emphasis to a counter-story which tapped deeply into the party's history and roots; Labour had to say about devolution that, 'We were, in fact, picking up a thread that has run through Labour's history, in Scotland for fifty years or more' (ibid.: 144). George Galloway predictably struck a much more radical stand, invoking the experience of Irish home rule and parliamentary disruption: 'Fifty or more Members of Parliament, with the will and imagination, can render Parliament inoperable as the struggle for the Irish Home Rule Bill almost 80 years ago showed' (Galloway 1983).

The more representative voice of party opinion came from John Smith in an interview he gave with *Radical Scotland* magazine in the months just before the 1983 election, where he hesitantly explored the options and terrain the party found itself in. A Scottish politics and devolution which 'expresses itself in such a way that it appears like disguised nationalism, then its not likely to succeed at Westminster'. He ruled out talk of wider re-alignment or co-operation between Labour and the SNP, stating, 'I think the Labour Party in Scotland will want to remain part of the Labour Party in the UK' (Smith 1983).

Yet at the same time the currents and dynamics of Scottish and British politics were pushing Scottish Labour in a more radical direction. This was something even the party establishment north of the border were at points open to conceding, with a former Scottish Labour Cabinet minister of the 1970s being quoted in 1982 as prophesying:

> We are certain to lose the next election in England. We will return even more MPs from Scotland, but we will be out of office down here for another ten years. We will have to play the nationalist card in Scotland. We will have to go for an Assembly with substantial economic power short of independence, but not much short. (*The Scotsman*, 28 July 1982)

The election saw Labour see its vote fall back significantly to 35.1%, the party's lowest share of the vote since 1931, while at the same time continuing its overwhelming parliamentary dominance in Scotland with forty-one seats thanks to FPTP and the fragmented four-party system. Labour lost Stirling to right-wing Tory Michael Forsyth, and failed to hold Renfrewshire West and Inverclyde after Norman Buchan retired, which the Tories gained (in both cases aided by significant boundary changes). The party retook Greenock and Port Glasgow after Dickson Mabon had joined the SDP, but could not succeed in regaining Caithness and Sutherland from Robert Maclellan.

Scottish Labour's health was very different from the threat to Labour's very existence south of the border across nearly every social demographic. Labour led in every age group; it won 54% of the semi-skilled working class and 42% of skilled manual working class along with 49.5% of trade unionists. In a country which had a majority of council housing, Labour won 53% of council tenants and 22% among owner occupiers versus 47% for the Conservatives. Bochel and Denver's analysis of the 1983 election showed the dangers of future prediction: 'What of the future? It would be unrealistic to expect Labour to do a great deal better in Scotland, certainly in its tally of seats, even if the fortunes took an upturn nationally' (Bochel and Denver 1983: 17).

There now began to appear in Scottish politics a new phenomenon – talk of the Conservative Government having 'no mandate' in Scotland. To begin with this would appear only on the margins of Labour in Scotland along with the SNP, but by its very articulation a kind of political stance was emerging which would in time, across the decade of the 1980s, reshape Scottish politics.

Something was stirring in parts of Scottish Labour in the aftermath of the 1983 election. George Foulkes, MP for Carrick, Cumnock and Doon Valley, drew up what became known as 'the Foulkes Memorandum', which suggested possible strategies for the party to resist Tory rule. It called on Labour to be bold, stating:

We must be clear that the action proposed will go beyond more vigorous resistance to new legislation on Scottish affairs . . . challenging the legitimacy of administrative directives and circulars which the majority of Scottish MPs have not endorsed . . . (Hepburn 1983)

This memorandum caused serious panic in the Scottish Labour leadership, who were content to pursue a strategy of relative inaction post-election. A discussion paper written by a group of Scottish Labour MPs entitled 'Defending Scotland Against Thatcher: An Action Plan for the Labour Movement' outlined a strategy for radical resistance and disobedience and attracted some interest, but was blocked by the leadership (*The Scotsman*, 17 September 1983). The official voice of the party emerged in a paper by Scottish Labour staff, where it laid out the case for not undertaking what it termed a 'little Scotland strategy'; it addressed the conflicting options and tensions the party faced between, first, protecting Scotland from the consequences of the Tory Government, and second, recognising 'our relatively preeminent potential to contribute towards the general recovery of the movement throughout Britain' (*The Scotsman*, 6 July 1983). This latter perspective was best summed up by John Maxton, MP for Glasgow Cathcart, at the 'Which way now for the Scottish left?' conference in July 1983, where he spoke of 'scotching the idea that there could be a realignment of the left in Scotland' (*Radical Scotland*, 1983)

Gordon Brown, newly elected MP for Dunfermline East, and Norman Godman, MP for Greenock and Port Glasgow, attempted as 'two new boys' in the Scottish Labour Group of MPs to bridge the divisions between the maxi-devolutionists and sceptics. The Brown–Godman proposals centred less on parliamentary disruption and focused on building a wider coalition for devolution and in particular convincing English Labour colleagues. They suggested ways of pressing the case in parliamentary terms which did not fall into oppositionalism; in the debate in the Labour Group, Bruce Millan showed he still had reservations about even committing to this cautious strategy; it took John Smith to throw his influence behind this to win the argument for the Brown–Godman position, a pro-devolution middle way between the radicals and sceptics.

Ernie Ross, left-wing Labour MP for Dundee West, saw the 1983 election result as offering a challenge and opportunity to the party:

The degree and dimensions of Labour's general election defeat in Britain makes Scotland perhaps the place where, with its representation substantially intact, Labour can provide a lead for the rest of Britain. (Ross 1983: 195)

Ross was confident that Labour could embrace, lead and shape the Scottish dimension:

> The Scottish nationalism of the Labour movement has recognised the differences in social class in the community, unlike the right-wing leadership of the SNP who tend to ignore this aspect. Part of the traditional message of the Scottish labour movement has always stipulated the need and the demand for Scottish self-government to attack social inequality in Scotland – together with the view that socialism would win the argument in Scotland before it did in England. (ibid.: 191)

This climate was ripe for a major re-appraisal and transformation of what Labour stood for across Britain, what its values, vision and ideals were, and how it did politics. This was led by the forces of Labour's 'soft left', organised around the formerly Bennite LCC who now spoke for the need for a 'popular socialism', which lay emphasis on connecting with voter concerns. This group was integral to Neil Kinnock's campaign to become Labour leader: a campaign which saw him easily see off the challenge of the centre-right Roy Hattersley by 71% to 19%, with the 'hard left' candidate Eric Heffer polling a derisory vote. Hattersley emphatically won the deputy leadership against the left's Michael Meacher by 67% to 28%, with a majority of constituency parties voting for Hattersley (Butler and Butler 2005).

In Scotland, this sense of urgency and desperate need for renewal was less acutely felt. Labour was after all the dominant party in Scotland and this was evident in the attitude of the left groups such as LCC post-1983 which were less eager to adopt the Kinnockite mission of modernisation.

Labour strengthened its position in local government in the 1984 district elections, winning Edinburgh for the first time, and in the 1986 regional elections, winning minority control of Tayside and winning back Lothian. Labour re-emphasised its commitment to a Scottish Assembly in 1984 in its Green Paper on devolution, which stated that 'the case for a devolved assembly is as compelling and as urgent as ever' (Scottish Labour Party 1984: 1). The language was beginning to change and evolve in a more radical, quasi-nationalist way, stating that measures 'opposed by the majority of Scotland's parliamentary representatives [have] nevertheless been forced through the House of Commons because of the Government's overall majority' (ibid.: 10).

POLITICS AS STRUGGLE: THE MINERS AND THE POLL TAX

Other factors were to dominate Scottish politics in the 1983–7 Parliament. The first was the miners' strike, while the second was the poll tax. The latter was to lead to a huge increase in the salience of the Scottish dimension, the home rule question, and constitutional reform.

36

The year-long miners' strike began on 5 March 1984 when the Yorkshire National Union of Mineworkers (NUM) announced strike action in response to the National Coal Board (NCB) decision to close Cortonwood colliery. On 6 March Ian MacGregor, NCB Chair, announced a national programme of job losses and the closure of twenty 'uneconomic' pits, with the Scottish NUM the same day calling for strike action. Three days later the NUM Executive and Arthur Scargill, NUM President, gave Yorkshire and Scotland action his approval, thereby avoiding the need for a national strike ballot which many thought would be lost. This turned out to be one of the pivotal issues and crucial controversies during the year-long strike. Mick McGahey, President of the Scottish NUM and Vice-President of the NUM, declared at the time, 'we shall not be constitutionalised out of a defence of our jobs' (Crick 1985: 100–1).

Scottish divisions in the strike were visible from the start, with Bilston Glen in Midlothian, Polkemmet in West Lothian, Comrie in Fife and Barony and Killoch in Ayrshire all voting against strike action. Within a matter of weeks of the strike beginning, all Scottish NUM members were out, such was the culture of discipline and solidarity. Ravenscraig steelworks in Lanarkshire proved to be one of the strike's central sites, with mass picketing, policing and, at points, violence. There was a related conflict at Hunterston deep-water terminal in Ayrshire which provided Ravenscraig with coal and iron ore. At one point Ravenscraig was left with just enough coal for one week. Despite everything it remained open throughout the strike to the fury of Scargill, pickets and the miners. Scottish Labour councils, in particular Strathclyde and Fife, provided free meals to miners' families' children, and prioritised benefit claims (*The Herald*, 22 March 1984). The STUC provided a co-ordinating role and called for negotiations with the government, and a Scottish Miners' Relief Fund was set up, raising £2 million in funds for assistance.

The strike began to crumble in the winter of 1984–5 as chances of a settlement proved elusive. By the end of February 1985 nearly half of Scottish miners – 46.7% – had returned to work, while Fife remained the most pro-strike area (*The Scotsman*, 28 February 1985). The return to work was a bitter and messy affair, with several Scottish mines damaged during the strike due to safety cover being withdrawn, and a much more hostile attitude by the NCB towards victimised miners. The National Coal Board was privatised in 1994, and when Longannet pit closed in 2002 the passing of a way of life into history was completed.

Scotland showed in the miners' strike a different kind of politics compared to the rest of the UK. This is not always reflected in commentaries on the strike, with John Campbell in his biography of Thatcher stating of Scargill and McGahey that they were 'militant left-wingers looking to break another Tory Government' (Campbell 2003: 356). This ignores the significant difference between the two. McGahey represented an older Communist Party (CPGB) class loyalty which stressed building alliances and choosing your battles. Scargill gave voice to a vanguardist oppositionalist Marxism while paradoxically being a prominent member of the Labour Party (although he had been in his youth a member of the Communist Party). The miners' strike turned out to be the demise of both of these traditions.

The depth of support and sympathy for the miners' cause in Scotland often spilled over into a public defence of the tactics of the NUM leadership, a situation which many surmised caused McGahey much consternation and grief while publicly he remained loyal. These dilemmas erupted into the public domain when the erstwhile hero of Upper Clyde Shipworkers, Jimmy Reid, publicly criticised Scargill and his tactics. He damned the silence of Labour politicians, Neil Kinnock excepted, on 'the refusal to hold a ballot, and the conduct of the strike'. He argued in a Channel 4 broadcast at the time that 'Arthur Scargill's leadership of the miners' strike has been a disgrace' and that he 'destroyed the NUM as an effective fighting force within British trade unionism for the next 20 years' (quoted in The Herald, 26 August 2010). These were comments many on the left never forgave him for, equating his actions with a kind of 'class betrayal', with McGahey himself calling Reid 'a broken Reid' (quoted in The Guardian, 10 August 2010). The deep divisions in the miners and the left which the strike created would for many never fully go away, lasting decades after the strike.

The defeat of the miners prefigured the continued transformation of the Scottish and British economies. The Thatcher Government felt it had to guarantee the future of the Ravenscraig steelworks for three years in part as payback for its continual working through the strike. It was decided that Gartcosh finishing mill in Lanarkshire would be closed, a decision which unleashed a high-profile national campaign led by the STUC ultimately to no effect. British Leyland's Bathgate truck assembly plant was also shut and added to the totemic list of closures of traditional jobs acutely felt in parts of Scotland.

The other seismic shift occurred in the most unlikely quarter: local government finance. It began with concern over the Scottish rates revaluation which galvanised Tory grass-roots concerns over rates which had been hypersensitive ever since the rates increases of 1980–1, and recent publications by Michael Forsyth and Douglas Mason making the case for a flat-rate poll tax.

The rates revaluation of February 1985 produced a huge shock in Scots Tory circles, and parts of middle-class Scotland. Average domestic rates went up by 8%, but this overall figure hid huge increases for some, including some commercial and industrial rates. In parts of Tory Scotland people were faced with massive increases of 40–50% and the Tory-voting single pensioner facing the full burden of rates was invoked. Torrance writes, 'These "little old ladies", be they in Troon, Bearsden or Morningside, were to become an important basis for . . . the poll tax' (Torrance 2009: 145).

The May 1985, Scottish Tory conference in Perth was a defining moment in change coming; Thatcher and George Younger pushed for radical change. As Thatcher reflected in her memoirs:

> On the strong advice of Scottish ministers, who reminded us continually and forcefully how much the Scottish people loathed the rates, we . . . accepted that we should legislate to bring the community charge in Scotland in advance of England and Wales. (Thatcher 1993: 651)

At this point, before a poll tax had been decided on, SNP MP Donald Stewart claimed the rates revaluation used Scots 'as guinea pigs for measures which would be unacceptable in the Tory shires of the Home Counties' (*The Scotsman*, 6 April 1985). *Radical Scotland* claimed Scotland was the 'guinea pig nation' (1985). This was nationalist rhetoric with the explicit use of Scotland as 'a guinea pig' predating the announcement of the poll tax; it was a harbinger of things to come.

On 6 January 1986 a Government Green Paper, 'Paying for Local Government', was discussed at Cabinet. It set out the case for a poll tax in Scotland, England and Wales, with transition periods, safety nets and proposals for a National Business Rate. It was imagined that the poll tax would be introduced in Scotland on 1 April 1989 with a three-year transition period, and in England and Wales in 1990 with a four-year phasing in. The Cabinet spent a mere fifteen minutes discussing this document, distracted by Michael Heseltine's resignation from the Cabinet over Westland helicopters. The Green Paper was published on 28 January when the height of the Westland affair was consuming Westminster.

The logic behind this was clear and simple. Scotland has an electorate of 3.9 million adults: 1.9 million were households liable to pay rates, with 1.1 million paying full rates, 400,000 receiving a partial rebate and 400,000 paying no rates (Fairley 1988: 53). The Conservative logic was that 'a large proportion of the electorate has little or no interest in restraining high spending local councils, or calling them to account' (The Conservative Campaign Guide 1987: 458). The Conservatives believed 'that three quarters of all households will either be better off, or lose less than £1 per week under the new system' (ibid.: 439).

The aim was to tackle the alleged socialist, high public spending culture of Scottish local government by massively expanding those who paid towards local services, including the unemployed and students. And behind all this was a Thatcherite zeal to address the Labour dominance of local government in Scotland. It was the same kind of partisan politics and blinkered dogma which in England saw the abolition of the GLC and six metropolitan authorities.

The Abolition of Domestic Rates Etc. (Scotland) Bill published on 26 November 1986 proposed that the poll tax, instead of being phased in over three years, would now be introduced in one go on 1 April 1989. The bill achieved its second reading in the Commons on 9 December 1986 and passed onto the statute book on 15 May 1987, weeks before the 1987 election. At the time public opinion was becoming increasingly opposed to the charge. A mere 26% of Scots were in favour of the poll tax in November 1986; in January 1987 an emphatic 80% were opposed to the introduction of the poll tax one year ahead of England and Wales.

The language about the poll tax began to change. Timothy Raison, Conservative MP for Aylesbury, commented that 'as an English MP I cannot help being relieved that Scotland is to be the legislative pacemaker or guinea pig' (The Guardian, 24 November 1987). Donald Dewar described the proposals as 'a combination of the ludicrous and the menacing', while the STUC came out in favour of a local income tax and the Convention of Scottish Local Authorities (COSLA) noted the 'massive redistribution' involved in the National Business Rate (Stewart 2009: 173–4). As the election of 1987 approached, the rhetoric of opposition to the poll tax became more pronounced and became connected to the Scottish dimension and issue of democracy. Radical Scotland coined the phrase 'Doomsday Scenario' to describe Scotland getting a Conservative Government it didn't elect being voted for by a minority of Scots (Radical Scotland, 1987).

To many in Scottish Labour this rhetoric was welcomed as a new tonic implying a willingness to take on the Thatcher Government and challenge its basic legitimacy. However, large parts of Scottish Labour including the leadership were sceptical of such an approach. Bob Middleton, party chair, took the view that the 'Doomsday Scenario' implied that 'if the Tories won another election Scotland was in great danger of getting into a situation similar to that which prevailed in Northern Ireland at the time' (Middleton 2001: 136). This was as over the top as some of the fantasies of Scotland as a land of 'restless natives', but indicated the different viewpoints which the leadership had to navigate.

The poll tax was going to have a huge impact on Scottish politics and indeed on British politics, but one small group it was to have a transformative effect on was Militant in Scotland. As Labour prepared for the 1987 general election, Militant pushed its resources into a number of constituencies in Glasgow and the West of Scotland. In the Glasgow Provan seat, the retirement of Hugh Brown left a vacancy which saw Jimmy Wray contest the selection against Militant's Jim Cameron, with Wray winning by one solitary vote. Jimmy Allison reflected after the event, 'If it had not been for Jimmy Wray, Militant would have won the selection with ease' (Allison 1995: 68).

In Glasgow Pollok, Jimmy White's retirement produced another knife-edge contest, with Militant's David Churchley seen as having a realistic chance of winning the nomination with matters made more complicated by the sizeable local presence of the International Marxist Group (IMG). There was no love lost between Militant and the IMG. After a first ballot in which Churchley led Bob Gillespie, a Society of Graphical and Allied Trades (SOGAT) official, and Jimmy Dunnachie, Dunnachie defeated Churchley by nine votes. This was in many respects the high point of Militant's influence in the party.

The 1987 election campaign pitted Neil Kinnock's new-look, semi-modernised Labour against Margaret Thatcher facing the prospect of a third consecutive term and at the time at the peak of her powers. The result was never really in question, given the scale of her 1983 victory and 146 seat overall majority she was defending; yet the campaign proved anything but predictable with a number of wobbles and scares thrown up for the Conservatives. By the end of the campaign, the Tories were returned to office with an overall majority of 102; Labour polled unimpressively and made a small number of gains in votes and seats nationally. A very different picture and politics emerged north of the border; whereas Kinnock's Labour made a mere 20 gains across Britain, nearly half of them – nine – were in Scotland.

Labour's impressive tally of gains in Scotland included a host of middle-class Tory seats, the sort of Scottish equivalents of Basildon, which the party at this point found incapable of winning in England, and the south of England especially. These included Aberdeen South, where Frank Doran defeated Gerry Malone, Edinburgh Central where Alistair Darling beat Alex Fletcher, Edinburgh South where Nigel Griffiths defeated Michael Ancram, along with Strathkelvin and Bearsden (Sam Galbraith), Cunninghame North (Brian Wilson) and Renfrewshire West and Inverclyde (Tommy Graham). At the same time, Labour won the previously SNP seats of Dundee East (John McAllion) and Western Isles (Calum MacDonald), finally managing to dislodge the Nationalist Gordon Wilson from Dundee, while in Glasgow Hillhead, Labour's George Galloway triumphed over Roy Jenkins, turning Glasgow into an all-Labour city at Westminster.

The Tories saw their parliamentary representation fall from twenty-one to a mere ten; the SNP won Moray, Banff and Buchan, and Angus East, all from the Conservatives, while the Liberal Democrats won North East Fife and Argyll and Bute from the Tories. This seemed like a vindication of a Scottish popular front of voters, and the validation of the dreams of the cross-party 'Tory-free Scotland' campaign. *Radical Scotland* believed that there was a Scottish dimension which meant 'there seems to be a simple egalitarianism emerging, wherein people won't just vote Tory because they themselves would be better off . . . they don't want to be better off if it's at the expense of someone else living in poverty' (*Radical Scotland*, 1987). Bochel and Denver, on the other hand, were unsure of the extent of anti-Conservative voting, stating 'that there was, in 1987, far less tactical voting than many had hoped for' (Bochel and Denver 1988: 33).

The shift in votes across Scotland which achieved these impressive changes in seats was much less stark. Labour increased their vote to 42.4%, a rise of 7.3%, while the Conservatives won 24.0%, a fall of 4.4%, the Lib Dems winning 19.4% and the SNP 14.0%. Labour's lead over the Conservatives at 18.4% was the largest the party had ever achieved; and given that England had decisively voted Tory with a 16.7% lead over Labour, the gap between the two nations was the largest ever on record (35.1%). This was a thesis which had been gaining ground post-1979: 'the end of British politics' which now seemed to many vindicated (Miller 1981). Labour's Scottish landslide was achieved on a minority of the vote winning over three-quarters of parliamentary representation, with one post-election analysis putting this in historic context: 'It should be remembered that Labour's 42.4% of the vote in 1987 was lower than they received in any election between 1945 and 1970' (Bochel and Denver 1988: 35).

Labour's fifty seats was then an all-time high, and as impressive and commented on was the quality of some of Labour's new intake: Alistair Darling, Sam Galbraith, Brian Wilson and Nigel Griffiths. Yet Labour's self-styled 'fighting fifty' also posed a huge problem for Labour. What were the 'fighting fifty' to fight for? And how exactly were they to fight? These questions were to come back quickly to haunt Labour. And the Nationalists were quick off the mark to label them the 'feeble fifty'.

In the immediate election aftermath such sentiments were left unexplored and unstated in public at least, as Scottish Labour sat back in the glow of its most impressive parliamentary results in its history, and the most emphatic Scottish parliamentary landslide for one party since the Liberals in 1910. Such a feeling and Scottish honeymoon was to prove to be a very short-term affair.

CHAPTER 3

'What Do You Do When Democracy Fails You?' – 'The Scottish Dimension' and Thatcherism

AFTER THE LANDSLIDE

The aftermath of the 1987 general election left all of Scotland's political parties with difficult questions. Labour, as the leading party of Scotland facing a UK Conservative Government, perhaps faced the most taxing. There was a mixture of elation in Scottish Labour post-1987 – which contributed to the strengthening of the 'myth' of 'Labour Scotland' – combined with anxiety and humility which Donald Dewar, Shadow Secretary of State, captured in an important post-election Fabian Society essay: 'In Scotland, Labour won the election. We took the seats. We carried the argument. Scotland voted not just against the Tories but emphatically for Labour' (Dewar 1987: 15).

But even at this moment of triumph, Dewar foresaw potential problems ahead:

> The Nationalists have been quick to accept the scale of Labour's Scottish victory and to lay down their challenge. Can Labour deliver? Can 50 MPs protect Scotland from Mrs Thatcher? Can the poll tax be stopped? Can Labour set up the Assembly?' (ibid.)

He went on, 'If the answers are in the negative the Nationalists will be there to draw some very uncomfortable conclusions.' Dewar saw the only feasible answer as parliamentary activity and in the short term forcing the Tories to address the 'essential sensitivity that has been disastrously absent' from their government (Dewar: 16–17). Ultimately the only solution was a Labour Government, but Dewar concluded his post-election analysis with a warning:

> Labour MPs are not a Scottish pressure group at Westminster; but in moral and electoral terms the real representatives of a real majority. If the government does not recognise that they will be set on a very dangerous course. (Dewar: 17)

Others had different views. Dennis Canavan believed that the Labour Party, despite having fifty Scottish Labour MPs, 'seemed devoid of ideas on how to pursue an effective campaign for home rule . . .' The leadership knew what it was against, such as disapproval of 'guerrilla tactics', but no clear strategy on how to advance the objectives it itself had set out post-election (Canavan 2009: 212).

Mark Lazarowicz, then Labour leader of Edinburgh Council, commented at the time:

> People on the left came together at the time of the Assembly campaign. Many of us saw it as an opportunity for radical policies, rather on the lines of those since carried out in some local authorities – Stirling, Edinburgh – following the example of the GLC. I mean at that stage the party had – still has – a very strong right-wing and we didn't want the Assembly to be a traditionalist kind of authority writ large. (quoted in Wainright 1987: 146)

'The Scottish Dimension' and Preparing for the Poll Tax

The issue of the campaign for a Scottish Assembly and a more radical, cam-paigning party came up against the cold reality of many local Labour parties, particularly in the West of Scotland. Wainright commented on the post-1987 environment that 'in most parts of Scotland the Labour Party has little campaigning, activist tradition' (Wainright 1987: 149).

In the immediate post-election environment the Scottish Tories faced some very practical problems, the most pressing of which was putting together a Scottish Office ministerial team from the small amount of talent they had on offer. Malcolm Rifkind, Secretary of State for Scotland, had no realistic option but to suspend the Scottish Select Committee when two Tory backbenchers, Bill Walker and Allan Stewart, 'the awkward squad', refused to serve (Macwhirter 1990: 23–4).

The Scottish Tories were unsure at this point on which way to go forward; the Scottish dimension could not be ignored, but how should it be embraced and challenged? A Conservative Party report, 'The Policies, Questions and Options: The Way Forward', came to the conclusion that the Tories were widely seen as an 'English party' (*The Scotsman*, 10 September 1987).

All of this did not directly help the situation Donald Dewar and Scottish Labour found themselves in. What was the best way to respond to Tory weakness and hesitancy? How should Labour build the widest popular front? And should it lead an anti-Tory alliance giving voice to the 76% of voters or pursue a Labour-only campaign?

The first signs of Labour wanting to pursue a cautious agenda were evident when Sam Galbraith easily defeated Dennis Canavan for the post of chair of the devolution sub-committee of the Labour Group. A subsequent group discussion rejected Canavan's call for parliamentary disruption in Scottish Question Time to challenge the way the Conservatives were ruling Scotland. Subsequent events exposed Labour's own deep divisions, as English Tory MPs intervened to make points in Scottish Question Time. Canavan responded by calling 'I Spy Strangers' and in the subsequent parliamentary vote fifteen Scottish Labour MPs and one Liberal MP supported Canavan's stand (Dowle 1988: 16–17).

This showcased publicly Labour's bitter divisions and differences; and yet the political environment and agenda of the Thatcher Government meant that these divisions were going to come increasingly to the fore. The party faced having to answer how it would respond to the introduction of the poll tax, on what grounds it would oppose it, and the issue of legitimacy and legality, alongside the wider dilemma of the Scottish democratic question. All of these were to become central questions in Scottish politics over the next few years, and defining issues for Scottish Labour.

On 21 October 1987 the party leadership launched 'Stop It: The Scottish Campaign against the Poll Tax', chaired by Brian Wilson, recently elected MP for Cunninghame North and previously arch-anti-devolutionist. The launch itself was high profile, bringing together celebrities and public figures from across Scottish life, including Billy McNeill, then manager of Celtic FC, and Elaine C. Smith, comedian and actor. Wilson claimed at the launch, 'we aim to stop the bills coming through the doors in the first place' (*The Scotsman*, 22 October 1987).

'Stop It' asked people to bring the registration system for the poll tax to a grinding halt or clog it up via sending in incomplete registration forms and asking various legal enquiries. The entire logic of the campaign was threadbare and transparently self-defeating, provoking widespread criticism and cynicism. This was seen as an exercise in the Labour leadership being seen to do something and going through the motions. Huw Lewis, of Edinburgh South CLP, said that the campaign 'seems to consist of little more than chanting "The Poll Tax is bad . . . Vote Labour"' (Lewis 1988).

With six months to go to the introduction of the poll tax, one estimate claimed that 95% of all registration forms had been returned; Tayside Regional Council's Registration Office commented that 10–15% of their forms had been returned with questions aimed at disrupting the process resulting in a 'significant increase in costs' (*The Glasgow Herald*, 13 September 1988). However, registration estimates did not take account of people coming off the electoral register because of the poll tax, and a Glasgow University study found that between October 1987 and October 1988 the voting public in Scotland's four main cities fell by 26,054 or 2.1%; and that two-thirds of this was due to young voters coming off the register (Enston 1990: 104).

Many different voices were raised in Scottish Labour at this point. Peter Russell, personal assistant to Glasgow Council leaders Pat Lally and Jean McFadden, wrote a memorandum on the subject in 1988 which stated that the 'Stop It' name and rationale was 'unrealistic' and that it was 'inevitable' the poll tax would be introduced in Scotland. He went further, challenging the whole basis of much of the anti-poll tax debate in the party, explicitly challenging the 'no mandate' argument increasingly used against the Conservatives. Instead, Russell proposed a political strategy which 'set the poll tax into the overall political and moral context: one which displays the Labour Party's virtues to the Tory Party's vices' (Stewart 2009: 177). This was the voice of mainstream, right-wing Labour down the ages: the mindset of pragmatic, power-orientated politics which had defined Scottish Labour for generations. Now it was increasingly struggling to be heard and hold the line in the post-1987 environment.

The tactic of poll tax non-payment was debated across the party, most prominently by Scottish Labour Action (SLA), of whom more later. Such were the times that consideration of non-payment, a strategy of illegality, could be found across the party, and not just on the margins of the left. A young Iain Gray, later to become leader of Scottish Labour in the Scottish Parliament, was forthright in his opposition and outlined a thoughtful strategy of non-payment. Gray argued, 'No one doubts that many will be unable to pay, but the debate is about whether we should organise non-payment as action against the tax' (Gray 1988). He proposed 'a "Committee of 100" Scots prepared to withhold payment of their poll tax and instead pay their current rates into an account, the interest of which would offset some campaign costs'. Labour should provide leadership in this: 'Scottish Labour MPs should provide the first fifty, and the others must be prominent Scots from all sectors of society including the Church, Trade Unions, universities, etc'. This stance 'could lead to rather than replace mass action' (ibid.).

This was a careful, considered and nuanced position, rather than oppositional positioning, and one representative of a large swathe of mainstream Labour which recognised that something radical had to be done which went beyond the caution and conservatism of the leadership position. Another position was also emerging which put pluralist politics above the national question. Huw Lewis articulated this when he accused Scottish Labour Action of adopting 'a vanguardist position on the poll tax' by seeing 'the party as the flag bearer of the Scottish people on this issue' (Lewis 1988). He argued, 'The party could never fulfil this role, even if it wanted to.' This was because of the simple fact, 'Labour does not have 50% of the Scottish vote. All Labour can say is that it can be part of a Scottish anti-poll tax majority' which would recognise 'the anti-Tory majority of 76% of Scottish opinion, rather than just the pro-Labour 42% . . .' (ibid.).

Such a principled and highly pluralist democratic politics was usually missing from most of the party debates and considerations, pointing to the problematic and flawed nature of these debates. Those who most criticised the Thatcher Government's over-reach and politics of 'no mandate' in Scotland, often pointed to its limited UK mandate on 42% of the votes; many of the same people often demanded that Scottish Labour act, lead and be the centre of opposition on a similar mandate of 42% of votes. Both British Conservatives and Scottish Labour were parliamentary majorities and popular minorities.

LABOUR AND CROSS-PARTY CO-OPERATION: THE ROAD TO THE CONVENTION

Scottish Labour's post-election sensitivities were heightened by the first popular event called to bring together the forces of the anti-Tory majority in Scotland. The STUC, now under Campbell Christie's leadership, called a 'Festival for Scottish Democracy' on 13 September 1987 on Glasgow Green. Instead of being a celebration and declaration of Scotland's unity against Conservative minority rule, it was 'marred by sectarian inter-party squabbles' (Deacon 1990: 64). The purpose had been to show the breadth of support for devolution, but participants had to endorse a statement which referred to devolution 'within the UK' which caused the SNP to withdraw, along with the Liberal-SDP Alliance, who felt they had only been invited as an after-thought (McLean 2005: 102).

Slowly things began to move from these inauspicious beginnings. The month before the Festival, LCC (Scotland) held a conference in Edinburgh. The agenda was comprehensive and ambitious; the day was well-attended and filled with excitement and radical talk. What could be done in Parliament? What were the practicalities and possibilities of cross-party co-operation? How could the Tories be best resisted – including on the poll tax? And how could a Scottish Assembly be achieved? The LCC (Scotland) pre-discussion paper argued that Scottish Labour was 'becoming the "national party" in Scottish politics' and that 'the campaign for an Assembly and the campaigns for industrial and economic regeneration, are not alternatives, but complementary objectives. The Assembly is a radical demand because it challenges the current power structure in Britain.' It stated, 'We want an economic policy determined by interests beyond those of the City of London.

And we don't want Labour's redefinition of itself to be simply aimed at Home Counties yuppies' (LCC (Scotland) 1987).

The conference saw a convergence of Labour traditions – Scottish, democratic socialist and nationalist. George Galloway said at the event, 'Fifty years ago, Robin [Cook] and I would have been standing on a platform not of devolution but home rule; it was the evacuation of that ground by the Labour Party post-1945 which left a political vacuum for the SNP to occupy.' He concluded that today 'as a nation, Scotland is entitled to as much self-determination as it wants'. Robin Cook apologised for 'getting it wrong' in the 1970s, and supported devolution in the wider context of its potential 'to knock a hole in Thatcher, and create an unstable situation in the rest of the centralised British state'. Bill Speirs showed how far the Labour left had gone and adopted the nationalist language of resistance, stating, 'We need a struggle for national liberation. We have the right to choose the form of self-determination', linking this to the more prosaic subject of Scottish Labour autonomy, observing that 'we can't even change the wallpaper without referring it to London' (*The Scotsman*, 31 August 1987).

The LCC (Scotland) conference was a backdrop to a special Scottish Labour conference in November 1987. Given the rich array of discussions which took place at the LCC event and LCC influence on the Scottish Executive, it was expected that the executive's statement to conference would reflect some of this and point the way forward. Instead, to many peoples' surprise, it did none of this, being in the eyes of some 'one of the most forgettable Labour movement gatherings in recent years'. The party executive statement boldly declared:

> The Labour Party in Scotland has the clear objective in the next four years of working for the return of a Labour Government for the whole of the United Kingdom at the next election. (Scottish Labour Party 1987)

There was little else on offer in the statement, which was in Bob McLean's words, 'a catalogue of missed opportunities' and a 'bland "business as usual" statement which fails to address the critical questions facing the party in Scotland' (Tribune, 20 November 1987). It instead offered no real suggestions for the party's future direction, 'No cross-party work, no Convention, no campaigning initiatives on the poll tax' (McLean 1990b: 42). The only direct result from the conference was the publication of Labour's new Scotland Bill, a tactic which had served the party well in 1984, but which was now totally out of kilter with the demands and expectations of the times; the party leadership had gone into the conference explicitly aiming to 'tone down the missionary zeal' evident in parts of Labour (Tribune, 20 November 1987).

The bill was in due course presented in Parliament and predictably voted down. This impotence had been predicted in the executive statement, which had openly called the bill 'a campaigning party for the whole party' and went on:

> We cannot expect it to be passed this time. Neither should the government – or the other parties – expect it to go away. It will remain as a standing reproach to the government for as long as they choose to ignore the wishes of the Scottish people. (Scottish Labour Party 1987)

It was this potent sense of disappointment and inadequacy to the challenges and context of the environment which led to the establishment of Scottish Labour Action (SLA), a pro-home rule, nationalist grouping that was impatient on the national question and poll tax while being dismissive of old-fashioned labourism and equally old-fashioned leftist grandstanding. They have since been called a whole host of names from 'the first modernisers in Scotland', a term loaded with baggage, to 'the Scottish Liberation Army' by their enemies (Hassan and Lynch 1999).

Many of SLA's membership came from LCC (Scotland) and caricatured the latter's politics as part of a complacent, new party establishment which they summed up in the phrase 'Labour Careerist Committee'. LCC (Scotland) had after its initial burst onto the scene post-1979 become more and more incorporated, less radical and less challenging to the party leadership; the post-1987 manoeuvrings which saw LCC (Scotland) unable to respond to the need for leadership and ambition was not an isolated incident, but part of a deeper shift. Hilary Wainright, examining Scottish Labour after the 1987 election, saw LCC (Scotland) as giving the appearance 'to have been marking time' after the fallout from the miners' strike, local government struggle and divisions on the Scottish dimension. She took the view that 'the majority of its founding members are either in leading positions on the party executive or on local councils, or they are parliamentary candidates' (Wainright 1987: 119).

Scottish Labour Action was formally launched at the March 1988 party conference. It drew a small smattering of support from pro-home rule Labour MPs such as Dennis Canavan, Dick Douglas, Robin Cook and, later, John McAllion and George Galloway. Its main support and stalwarts came from constituency activists such as Bob McLean, Ian Smart and Susan Deacon, later to be an MSP and minister. A host of future MSPs also gave their support: Jackie Baillie, Jack McConnell, Sarah Boyack, Pauline McNeill and many more. This grouping proved over the next decade to be a small group in number but one which had tenacity and the commitment to challenge some of the central tenets of Scottish Labour. Some of them they were to succeed in changing, others were to be less successful.

SLA's founding statement called on Scottish Labour to:

1. Assert Scotland's right to self-determination on such a basis as the people of Scotland themselves decide;
2. Adopt the argument that the Conservative Party has no mandate in Scotland and to campaign on that basis;
3. Support a policy of tactical non-co-operation with the Government in the conduct of Scottish business in the House of Commons;
4. Urge the party to place more emphasis on initiatives launched in Scotland, where the Tories are in an embarrassing minority, rather than at Westminster where they enjoy a massive majority;
5. Support mass civil disobedience in Scotland as a legitimate means of protest for the Scottish people;
6. Support, in particular, obstruction and civil disobedience in the implementation of the poll tax leading to a mass campaign of non-payment and to seek early and public declarations of intent not to pay from leading figures in the party and beyond;
7. Encourage the early establishment of an alternative democratic forum in Scotland.
   (Scottish Labour Action 1988a)

The party's divisions on the poll tax meant that a decision on non-payment had to be postponed to a special conference later in the year. Neil Kinnock's address to conference was seen as 'spectacularly uninspiring', not mentioning once devolution or the poll tax, nor addressing the issue of cross-party co-operation. In a TV interview later that evening, Kinnock was challenged about these omissions and answered with the dismissive remark that he had not mentioned many other issues including 'the environmental conditions of the Himalayas'. And he dismissed out of hand the possibility of a cross-party Constitutional Convention (*The Scotsman*, 14 March 1988).

'A Claim of Right for Scotland' was published on 13 July 1988, the product of a Constitutional Steering Committee set up by the Campaign for a Scottish Assembly and the work of Sir Robert Grieve as Chair and Jim Ross as Secretary. This was the work of serious, public-minded Scotland making a scathing and damning critique into the way Scotland was governed and offering a strategy for addressing it: a cross-party Scottish Constitutional Convention.

In powerful prose it declared 'the English Constitution – an illusion of democracy' and that 'there is currently a Prime Minister dedicated to preventing the creation of a Scottish Assembly and equipped within the terms of the English constitution, with overwhelming powers to frustrate opposition to her aims' (quoted in Dudley Edwards 1989: 18–19).

Labour's leadership had until this point had a long-standing uneasy relationship with the Campaign for a Scottish Assembly, rejecting calls for the party to affiliate. At the 1983 Scottish Labour conference the party leadership claimed that affiliation was not possible after receiving guidance from the British party. Instead, the party executive report declared that 'it was hoped that contact could be maintained' with the Campaign for a Scottish Assembly (Scottish Labour Party 1983: 10).

When the issue of a Constitutional Convention was first raised at Scottish Labour's Executive in June 1986, after the publication of Campaign for a Scottish Assembly, the party briskly dismissed them, stating:

> We have considered the CSA proposal for a Constitutional Convention. Since we believe that a Labour Government will be formed after the next election with a firm commitment to establish a Scottish Assembly, such a Convention is considered to be unnecessary . . . Only in the unlikely event of Labour not winning the next election, could the party then assess its reaction to the proposal. (Scottish Labour Party 1986)

Labour gave a cautious welcome to 'A Claim of Right for Scotland', acknowledging it as 'a major contribution to thinking on constitutional change in Scotland'. However, the party still felt the need to state that 'any major decision by the Scottish party on a matter of such importance would need to be taken by full conference in March next year' (quoted in Deacon 1990: 64).

Labour was both moving and playing for time. In August 1988, the party agreed to undertake an internal consultation on 'A Claim of Right', with submissions to be in by the November party executive meeting. The same meeting agreed an executive statement for the special conference on the poll tax in September, and only narrowly defeated by two votes poll tax non-payment.

It was a moment of significant change in Scottish Labour, as Jack McConnell reflected:

> We took the view that in the absence of an assembly, which she'd [Thatcher] promised in 1979 but not delivered, that the gap between the party's power and representation meant that they had no mandate to govern. The divide in the Labour Party was between those who looked at that from a Scottish perspective and those who felt the retention of the union was more important. (Torrance 2009: 189)

The momentum in Scottish Labour was now shifting decisively in favour of radical action. George Foulkes commented that the 'Claim of Right' document 'should be used as the spring board for eliminating the democratic deficit we now have' (Foulkes 1989: 69). He argued: 'There is a socialist case, a nationalist case, an efficiency argument and an historical claim but above all the case, the cause, the argument is for democracy' (ibid.: 68–9). There were still reservations, as David Martin MEP put it, about 'the authors' desire to locate the Claim of Right in Scotland [in] the nation state rather than with the Scottish people' (Martin 1989: 79). The Convention, he stated, in a prophetic remark of things to come, must be 'about increased democracy and not independence' (ibid.: 85).

At this point Donald Dewar provided a crucial lead in an important intervention in a lecture he gave at Stirling University on 21 October 1988. He stated: 'Any talks should be a genuine attempt to find that common ground and to evolve an agreed package that means that the process must be seen as a way of finding the right reform within the United Kingdom and not breaking away from it.' He went on, 'The people must decide if they are prepared to live a little dangerously in order to achieve what they want' (*The Scotsman*, 22 October 1988).

THE BATTLE OVER THE POLL TAX AND THE ROAD TO GOVAN

Scottish Labour's special conference on the poll tax had taken place the month previously, on 17 September 1988 in Govan Town Hall, Glasgow. The idea of having the conference in Govan, in the words of Jimmy Allison, had been to think ahead to the forthcoming parliamentary by-election, and 'to use it as a launching pad for our campaign. It was the wrong decision' (Allison 1995: 185). It was a bitter public debate, showcasing in public a party which contained deep divisions on one of the most fundamental issues of the day. Donald Dewar told the conference:

> This is a party which aspires to be in government. I don't believe such a party can afford selective amnesia when it comes to the law of the land. That would be to sacrifice its credibility to the vast majority of electors. (*Scotland on Sunday*, 18 September 1988)

The Transport and General Workers' Union (TGWU) was for non-payment, the GMB against non-payment, while constituency party delegates were fairly evenly divided with some observers thinking there was a slender majority for non-payment. As with British Labour a decade earlier, the tried and tested methods of party leadership and management at conference had broken down. Jimmy Allison recognised this:

> The divisions inside the hall would never have reached such a pitch if Hugh Wyper had still been around as the TGWU Secretary in Scotland. Hugh would have consulted with Jimmy Murrell, the GMB Secretary, and the two of them would have reached a compromise position in private. (Allison 1995: 185)

Susan Deacon reflected that 'the poll tax non-payment campaign was a fight that we could have won in Labour and Scotland' (interview). The eventual result, despite the hopes of SLA and the poll tax non-payment campaign, was never really in any doubt. Poll tax non-payment was defeated by a resounding 512,000 votes to 225,000 (*Scotland on Sunday*, 18 September 1988). One supporter of non-payment remembered it differently, stating that 'the vote was close and in doubt until the last minute. We really shook the leadership' (interview). The end of the conference was filled with a drama and high theatre in a charged atmosphere. Outside Govan Town Hall there were scenes of acrimony as anti-poll tax campaigners showed their displeasure to Labour delegates. Allison commented, 'Militant supporters demonstrated outside the hall and Donald Dewar was jostled and heckled by the crowd – all of which was covered by the media' (Allison 1995: 185).

This was all of immediate, as well as long-term, political impact. Labour had decided to nominate Bruce Millan, MP for Glasgow Govan, as one of Britain's two European Commissioners, creating a by-election in what was normally a safe Labour seat. The Govan by-election turned out to be another defining moment in Scottish politics. The SNP chose Jim Sillars, former Labour MP and now prominent Nationalist, while Labour selected SOGAT official Bob Gillespie. It turned out to be one of the most uncomfortable by-elections Scottish Labour had ever experienced, with all of the high drama covered by Scottish and UK media.

Labour's 19,509 majority melted away in an inept campaign of epic proportions. This was aided by two TV debates in which Labour's Bob Gillespie was shown as completely out of his depth. On 10 November 1988, Jim Sillars was returned with a 3,554 majority over Labour. The BBC Exit Poll showed that 32% of Govan voters thought representing Scotland's interests was the single most important issue, followed by 21% citing the poll tax and 19% unemployment; 55% rated the performance of Scotland's Labour MPs as either poor or very poor; a mere 7% rated them as very good in what had been a safe Labour seat (BBC Scotland, 10 November 1988). George Galloway said on election night in the immediate aftermath, 'The Labour Party has fallen short. It has not taken up the Scottish question' (*The Glasgow Herald*, 12 November 1988).

The result registered in the Westminster corridors of power in Labour and elsewhere. Tony Benn even managed a rare entry in his diaries on Scottish politics, reflecting on Labour's defeat and the SNP's triumph: 'There had been no socialist policies in our campaign – just the idea that if you keep your head you'll win.' He concluded that it had been 'an unnecessary by-election' which showed that 'if you don't offer people analysis they go for separatism, and it was also a reflection of our failure to discuss constitutional questions,

which are at the core of the devolution argument' (Benn 1992: 553). Jim
Sillars commented that 'his victory tapped into the desperation people felt
looking for opposition and leadership to take the fight to the Tories', and that
his triumph 'was not a rejection of socialist values, but of Labour compromise,
spinelessness and continual retreat' (interview).

Dennis Canavan believed that the Nationalist victory was down to the
poll tax and Labour's failings: 'Sillars would be telling the voters: "Don't pay!"
Whereas Labour would be telling the voters: "Stump up!"' (Canavan 2009:
214). Nigel Griffiths, looking at post-Govan possibilities, argued that the
defeat 'gave focus to those people within the Labour Party whose patience
with Labour as a credible force for change had been exhausted. They viewed
the Govan campaign, reiterating as it did a Labour commitment to opposition within the law (especially on the poll tax) as the last straw' (Griffiths
1989: 57).

Two days after the Govan debacle, Scottish Labour's Executive met to
discuss its approach towards the Constitutional Convention. Party responses
were massively in favour of the party co-operating with the establishment of
a Convention: twenty-five for and a mere two against. Labour's Executive
voted by thirty-two votes to two for Labour to participate in the Convention
(*Scotland on Sunday*, 13 November 1988).

SLA issued within days of the Govan defeat a statement entitled 'Gubbed
in Govan' which stated, 'Questionable organisation, local issues and the
merits of candidates all contributed in some minor way to Labour's rout at
Govan. It would be folly, however, to explain away the Southside slaugh-
ter on those grounds alone. Govan was a vote of no confidence in Labour's
Scottish leadership and their inability to come to terms with the Scottish
dimension.' It argued, 'Labour's defeat in Govan was not inevitable. The
people of Govan, in common with people all over Scotland, share Labour's
values', and concluded, 'People didn't question democratic socialist policies
in Govan, they questioned Labour's ability to deliver for Scotland' (Scottish
Labour Action 1988b).

LABOUR, THE NATIONALISTS AND
THE CONVENTION

Events were now moving fast. The Scottish Constitutional Convention held
its first cross-party talks on 27 January 1989, with Donald Dewar, Jim Sillars of
the SNP and Malcolm Bruce of the Lib Dems leading their respective delega-
tions. The SNP had three major concerns: the number of Convention seats
more accurately reflecting the popular support of parties, the issue of sovereignty, and a referendum on the final proposals. There was an air of goodwill

and possibility in the meeting, but in the aftermath the SNP leadership quickly turned volte face, leading Jim Sillars to declare the SNP would not take part in 'Labour's rigged Convention' (The Glasgow Herald, 29 January 1989).

Labour's proposals for its annual conference saw Donald Dewar unveil the party's new thinking. This was entitled 'independence in the UK', the response to the SNP's 'independence in Europe' policy which had proved enormously popular. Labour thinking was shifting away from the 1970s usage of the term 'devolution' and towards the older, more radical phrase 'home rule'; people still talked of a 'Scottish Assembly' rather than a 'Scottish Parliament', but distinctly the thinking about what this body would do, its place in society, its politics, powers and ambitions was evolving and moving slowly in the direction of the latter.

This was evident in the publication of a new SLA pamphlet, 'Proposals for Scottish Democracy', which shaped much of the agenda and discussions at the March 1989 party conference. It called for a Scottish Assembly being a catalyst to widen and renew democracy and participation across Scotland, a proportionately representative Assembly, attacking gender inequality, recall elections for voters, and an Assembly which was constitutionally guaranteed and protected. Jack McConnell, writing in the introduction, saw this as 'the full development of Scottish democracy'. He went on to stress that such policies would not be met 'by creating a replica of the House of Commons or Strathclyde Regional Council' (Scottish Labour Action 1989: 2). This was powerful code for rejecting not just the discredited Westminster system, but also the Labour Party one-party rule across much of the West of Scotland.

The most controversial debates at party conference were on two other SLA-related matters: 'the dual mandate' and party autonomy. 'The dual mandate' position argued that Scottish Labour MPs should seek a specific Scottish mandate and then use it as a platform for action irrespective of the British result. Ian Smart of SLA set out pre-conference what such a position entailed:

> . . . a majority Labour Government at Westminster was the ideal which we aimed at, then there could be no contradiction in pledging that – in the event of falling short of that goal – achieving a majority of Labour MPs in Scotland (or of pro-Assembly votes, or both) would be regarded as a mandate to negotiate with any Westminster Government for an Assembly . . . (Smart 1988)

Opponents would, Smart conceded, label such an approach as defeatist, but he argued, 'Other people in the Labour Party remain more devoted to the British constitution than to the interests of the Scottish people.' The dual mandate position would 'carry the huge majority of the constituency delegates. But what of the unions, unionists in more sense than one?' (ibid.).

In a heated conference debate, the dual mandate position was heading for defeat after being subject to concentrated criticism from Brian Wilson, MP and others. At the last minute it was remitted back to the party executive for further consideration. The party autonomy debate proved no less animated, touching a set of perennial concerns in parts of Scottish Labour about lack of autonomy and distinctiveness. However, this debate came alive and some-what bitter when it got stuck in the practicalities of accountability and the issue of who would control Scottish Labour Party staff, and no progress was made (*Scotland on Sunday*, 12 March 1989).

At the same time the rhetoric of Labour home rulers was becoming both more radical and oppositional. Jim Ross, one of the key figures in 'A Claim of Right for Scotland', penned a seminal *Radical Scotland* article entitled 'A Fond Farewell to Devolution' (1988). In the same issue, in a sign of the changing political weather, Robin Cook gave an extensive interview on the Scottish dimension, devolution and Thatcherism. His language was dramatic and powerful for a senior frontbencher: 'To all intents and purposes Scotland is an occupied country in which the ruling power depends for its support on a powerbase which is outside the country' (Cook 1988). This didn't exactly endear Cook to many of his senior colleagues, Donald Dewar in particular.

The first meeting of the Scottish Constitutional Convention took place on the Mound, Edinburgh on 30 March 1989. There were no Conservatives or SNP present. The Scottish Labour Group of MPs (minus Tam Dalyell), Liberal Democrats, Scottish Greens, Communists and representatives of Scottish public life gathered in a historic setting. The Labour MPs present and others signed 'A Claim of Right' – a declaration of the sovereignty of the Scottish people.

Two days later, on 1 April 1989, the poll tax was introduced in Scotland, one year ahead of England and Wales. The 'Stop It' campaign by this time had become seen as both impotent and overtaken by events. The SNP had taken up a position of non-payment and aspired to lead an army of 100,000 non-payers who failed to materialise. All over Scotland there were cam-paigns, resistance and non-payment. There was the cross-party 'Committee of 100' involving a range of prominent Scots in public life and Labour MPs such as John McAllion and Maria Fyfe (*The Glasgow Herald*, 22 November 1988). Then there was the Anti-Poll Tax Union, which included Strathclyde Anti-Poll Tax Federation, whose secretary was Tommy Sheridan and where the Militant Tendency played a significant role (Sheridan and McAlpine 1994: 64).

Attempting to provide a co-ordinating role was the STUC Anti-Poll Tax Steering Committee, which brought together a wide array of political and civic opinion. It engaged in campaigning, support and local activities, but was handicapped by political difficulties. Previewing Convention disagreements, the SNP 'suspended their involvement' in the committee in April 1988 (*The Glasgow Herald*, 15 April 1988) and rejoined it a year later in May 1989 (*The Glasgow Herald*, 18 May 1989).

The reality of poll tax non-payment began to take shape, define local government and its finances, and damage the Scottish Tories. Poll tax non-payment was estimated at 16.8% of bills in September 1989, but collection costs were spiralling compared to the rates (Butler et al. 1994: 135). Non-payment was also higher in some areas than others, with one estimate suggesting 20% of Strathclyde Region's poll tax was unpaid. Scotland at points seemed like a nation in convulsion over the poll tax and its lack of legitimacy.

LABOUR'S EVOLUTION OF DEVOLUTION

In June 1989 another difficult by-election posed itself for Labour in similar territory to Glasgow Govan – the neighbouring Glasgow Central. This time Labour learnt the lessons and chose the much more capable Mike Watson, while the SNP had Alex Neil, a competent, populist candidate, but not in the league of Jim Sillars. The SNP was hamstrung in its attempts to develop a by-election bandwagon by the Euro elections being on the same day – but more important was the political environment post-Convention pull-out.

Labour's campaign in Central was all Govan was not: sure-footed, well-resourced and professional. Jimmy Allison reflected that Labour 'never had a shortage of workers', unlike Govan, while the SNP hit difficulties when Tayside Regional Council, which they ran with the Tories, announced they were sacking local cleaners (Allison 1995: 192). Labour were not without their embarrassments, most famously when Gerald Kaufman in a press conference showed he had no idea what 'independence in the UK' was, when it was official Scottish Labour policy. He replied, 'It's not worthy of the name "idea". If someone knows what it means I wish they'd tell me.' Murray Elder, Scottish Secretary of Labour, had to tell him in full public glare that was Labour Party policy in Scotland (Macwhirter 1990: 21).

Labour saw a 17,253 majority reduced to 6,462, with Mike Watson polling 54.6% of the vote. The SNP by-election bandwagon had well and truly stalled. On the same day the Euro elections gave a picture of the state of Scotland. Labour won 41.9% to the SNP's 25.6% and the Conservatives' 20.9%. These were the first national elections since October 1974 where the SNP finished in second place and ahead of the Conservatives, but given the scale of post-Govan expectations, these results were seen as disappointing for the Nationalists and good for Labour. Significantly in terms of future omens, Scotland became for the first time at any elected level 'a Tory-free zone', electing seven Labour MEPs, a gain of two from the Tories, and one SNP MEP.

As the Convention got down to its detailed work, Labour began to debate the issue of electoral reform for any future potential Scottish national body. Labour's 1970s plans enshrined in the Scotland Act 1978 had proposed a 144-seat Assembly, which would give on current voting preferences a massive in-built Labour majority and which would have had a West of Scotland dominance. It also had the potential on a low share of the vote for the Nationalists to deliver them an overall majority and trigger a constitutional crisis.

Scottish Labour undertook an internal party consultation on the issues related to the Convention at the end of 1989. The response rate was low, but overwhelmingly in favour of a radical Labour home rule agenda: 'a constitutional guarantee, sovereignty, wide-ranging economic powers, a reverse block grant, a meaningful role in Europe, etc.'. In January 1990 the Scottish Labour Executive deferred the issues of economic powers, financial powers, Europe and the electoral system to party conference in March; it agreed a constitutional guarantee for the Scottish Parliament, 'but rejected its establishment through returning sovereignty to the Scottish people, then handing back powers to Westminster' (McLean 1990c). In its place, the party chose to support a Scottish Parliament with defined powers from Westminster, and the possibility of revisiting the sovereignty issue in the context of UK-wide regionalism.

Pivotal to this different kind of politics and Parliament evolving and Labour making a success out of the Convention was electoral reform; without it there was the risk that the Lib Dems might withdraw, leaving the Convention looking even more like a Labour talking shop. The March 1990 Scottish Labour conference saw the party debate the issue of electoral reform for a future Scottish Parliament; the influence of the debates in and around the Convention were already shaping Labour thinking and language: slowly disappearing was any reference to an 'Assembly' and in its place was the idea of a 'Parliament'. The reformers were a wide coalition including SLA, the TGWU and a minority of Labour MPs and CLPs; a narrow majority of CLPs were anti-reform and a substantial majority of MPs. George Foulkes, arch anti-electoral reformer, accused Malcolm Bruce, leader of the Scottish Lib Dems, of putting a gun to Labour's head. Labour was to many 'running scared of the Liberal Democrats, who were determining much of the work of the Convention, and Labour should call Bruce's bluff' (Bruce 1990). Dennis Canavan, reflecting on this wider debate, commented, 'The weaknesses of the first past the post system are obvious when we consider that, at the last general election, the Conservatives won 58% of the UK parliamentary seats with only 42% of the vote. In Scotland, the Labour Party won a similar share of the vote, but captured 69% of the seats' (Canavan 1989: 75).

This was still anathema to a large swathe of Scottish Labour and had been historically, but such people now found themselves on the back foot: having to defend FPTP and Labour's massive parliamentary representation on minority votes. Bob Middleton, chair of the party, looking back on the debate still thought it inexplicable that Labour would champion an electoral system which would give the Tories representation, producing 'an electoral system giving them a power base once again', and saw it as an example of 'the lack of political intelligence' in Labour's leadership (Middleton 2001: 137). Many would have argued the exact opposite: that it was a sign of mature political intelligence.

Conference voted 372,000 votes to 285,000 for electoral reform and the notion of a Scottish Parliament elected by the Additional Member System (AMS): a watershed moment for Scottish Labour and the campaign for a Scottish Parliament, and a victory for the Convention and home rule radicals. Malcolm Bruce, Lib Dem MP, welcomed the result, calling it with a slight degree of hyperbole, 'a political earthquake comparable in Scottish terms to the opening of the Berlin Wall' (Bruce 1990).

Labour then announced its policy to replace the poll tax in the run-up to the 1990 regional elections: what became known as 'the roof tax' which was to lead the party into all sorts of bother. Labour's tax was a property-based one, taxing actual house prices or capital values. The Conservatives had a field day, calling 'the roof tax' a tax on aspirations, home improvements and everything they could think of. The regional election results showed Labour comfortably ahead with 42.7% of the vote to the SNP's 21.8% and the Conservatives' 19.6%. Any Labour embarrassment and difficulty on 'the roof tax' was more than cancelled by Tory weaknesses and problems with the poll tax (Bochel and Denver 1991).

In early 1990 senior Labour figures attempted to address the ideas deficit in Scottish Labour and followed the example of British Labour, which had in 1988 encouraged the establishment of the centre-left think tank the Institute of Public Policy Research (IPPR). This led to the setting up of the John Wheatley Centre at the initiative of a host of Labour figures such as George Foulkes and Anne McGuire; the aspiration was that this would come up with a range of detailed policy proposals for Labour and the wider progressive cause in a future devolved Scotland. It was a noble intent, but the organisation was hamstrung from the outset from a lack of funds, the perception it was a 'Labour body', and Labour's culture of conservatism and lack of engagement with ideas. It did, in the pre-devolution times and around the time of the establishment of the Parliament, have some notable success and influence, particularly with the publication of Bernard Crick and David Miller's draft standing orders for a new Parliament.

As 1990 ground on, the Conservatives' and Mrs Thatcher's problems escalated, with Neil Kinnock's Labour establishing at a UK level huge leads in the polls. When Geoffrey Howe resigned from the Cabinet, Michael Heseltine stood against Thatcher for the Conservative leadership, and inflicted a fatal wound on her premiership, forcing her to resign on 22 November 1990, resulting in the more consensual John Major becoming Prime Minister. A few years later, Mrs Thatcher, looking back on her period in office and its impact on Scotland, said, 'The balance sheet of Thatcherism is a lopsided one: economically positive but politically negative' (Thatcher 1993: 623). This wasn't a very popular view at the time, but with hindsight it has become a perspective more people are willing to concede might have some truth in it.

Two by-elections were caught in this momentous change: both in Paisley and both voting two days into John Major's new premiership. Labour's Irene Adams and Gordon McMaster were returned with comfortable but massively reduced majorities. Even more significantly, one day after the Paisley votes the Scottish Constitutional Convention produced its report, 'Towards a Scottish Parliament' (Scottish Constitutional Convention 1990).

The document proposed a Parliament elected by a proportional system with wide powers, but many questions were left unaddressed such as the detail of the electoral system, relations with Westminster, the number of Scottish MPs and the role of the Secretary of State for Scotland. The launch itself at the newly opened Royal Concert Hall in Glasgow saw a procession of most of Scotland's council leaders, while the launch itself was introduced by Harry Ewing and David Steel, Joint Chairs of the Convention. John Smith, speaking for Labour, said the proposals were 'both more extensive in scope and stronger in substance than anything it had been possible to achieve in the Scotland Act which failed in 1979'. In a memorable phrase he spoke of the desire for a Scottish Parliament as being 'the settled will of the Scottish people' (Wright 1997: 142–3).

As the pomp and grandeur faded, many in the Convention came to realise that these proposals were merely a first draft of proposals and that substantially more work would be needed. Bernard Ponsonby, then working for the Lib Dems, commented hopefully that '1970s-style devolution has been consigned to the constitutional scrap heap'. He went on to ask the huge question at the back of everyone's minds: 'And what if Labour loses? Present Scottish strategy assumes this is unthinkable, but it is their lack of forward planning which is their real weakness' (Ponsonby 1990). This was touching on the terrain of the multi-option referendum, something which was to emerge after the 1992 election as a critical issue, but which for now Murray Elder, General Secretary of Scottish Labour, was prepared to rule out, declaring that he could 'see no purpose' in it (The Scotsman, 21 July 1990).

In the months before Scottish Labour's 1991 conference the anti-proportional representation supporters fought back. This involved politicians such as George Foulkes and Pat Lally, then leader of Glasgow District Council, who set up the Labour Campaign for Electoral Success, which included a significant swathe of senior Labour councillors. They wanted to make the case for FPTP, and for Labour not giving away its built-in advantage under the current system. They opposed electoral reform for the Scottish Parliament, seeing it as a thin wedge which could lead on to further reform, in local government and ultimately Westminster, thus eroding Labour's power base in Scotland. They were defeated at party conference, but they did succeed in articulating party reservations.

In the latter part of the year, a by-election was called in Tory-held Kincardine and Deeside after the death of Alick Buchanan-Smith. The seat, a Tory–Lib Dem marginal, was won by Lib Dem Nicol Stephen with a 7,824 majority. The result pushed the Tories into third place in Scottish parliamentary representation behind the Lib Dems. All seemed set for a 'Doomsday II' election. In early 1992, the Conservative Government finally announced the closure of Ravenscraig after years of trade union and civil Scotland campaigning. John Major looked back on a transformed Scotland in his autobiography:

> Margaret Thatcher's economic medicine served Scotland well, and I carried it forward in the 1990s. Such changes are always painful. There were job losses in the shipyards on the Clyde, in the coalfields and most symbolic of all, in the decline and closure of the steel plant at Ravenscraig. All were hurtful. And each one of them was presented as the result of an 'uncaring' English Government. (Major 1999: 476)

The 1992 general election was fought against the backdrop of popular expectations that for the anti-Tory parties it would offer the prospect of the continuation of 1987, and that the Tories would face further embarrassing and painful losses. It didn't turn out that way.

John Major decided mid-campaign to put the defence of the union centre stage. In an election rally he announced, 'If I could summon up all the authority of this office, would put it into a single warning: the United Kingdom is in danger. Wake up, my fellow countrymen. Wake up now before it is too late' (Major: 424). Whatever its effect, it was one of the defining moments of the campaign, and became part of the mythology of 1992 along with Major's 'soapbox' and Neil Kinnock's disastrous Sheffield rally (Seldon 1997: 261–3).

Labour polled 39.0%, a loss of 3.4%, the Conservatives 25.7%, up 1.7%, while the SNP's vote rose to 21.5%, up 7.5%. Compared to popular expectations this was presented as a great Tory recovery aided by Major's rhetoric. Labour lost Aberdeen South to the Tories while the Tories won back Kincardine and Deeside from the Lib Dems. Famously Labour retook

Glasgow Govan from the SNP's Jim Sillars, with Ian Davidson returning the seat to the Labour fold with a comfortable 4,125 majority. One analysis of the SNP's performance commented that 'the party is left with not a single seat where it is less than 10% behind a Labour incumbent' (Curtice and Steed 1992: 342).

Scotland had swung 2.5% from Labour to Conservatives, while England and the UK swung to Labour and reduced Major's majority to 21 seats, which was in due course to suffer attrition and elimination by by-election defeat and intra-party conflict. The immediate post-election environment in Scotland was one of shock and a sense of numbness in Labour, the opposition parties and home rule campaigners. This was soon to change. The next Parliament was to prove even more eventful and challenging to Scottish Labour than the last one, but for different and unforeseen circumstances.

CHAPTER 4

Northern Discomfort: Scottish Labour, New Labour and the Coming of Blair

INTRODUCTION

The aftermath of the 1992 election was one of confusion: filled with disappointment, shock and for some a sense that something had to be done. On election night, Charles Gray, leader of Strathclyde Regional Council and Labour's most senior figure in local government, floated the possibility of civil disobedience to resist the Conservatives (*The Herald*, 11 April 1992). He was quickly slapped down by colleagues. Pat Lally called Gray 'a little intemperate' and believed his 'brusqueness of manner' was counter-productive (Lally 2000: 104).

The weeks after the election saw agitation and deflation in equal measure. Jim Sillars dismissed the Scots with the phrase 'there are too many ninety minute patriots in this country' (*The Scotsman*, 24 April 1992). William McIlvanney commented on the agony he felt after the result: 'That day was like one terrible hangover, a national version' (*Scotland on Sunday*, 19 April 1992). Some of this feeling boiled over into blaming the Scottish populus, as Muriel Gray did: 'we are all going down with the ship and I have no fear in repeating that it is the people's fault and nobody else' (*Scotland on Sunday*, 12 April 1992).

Protest found voice in the creation of 'Scotland United', a coalition of home rule supporters from Labour and civic Scotland, including MPs such as George Galloway and John McAllion, the latter of whom wrote that 'no party on its own could deliver to the Scottish people. I will not wait for another five years' (*Scotland on Sunday*, 12 April 1992). After several rallies in Glasgow's George Square, 'Scotland United's main demand crystallised into pushing the idea of a multi-option referendum. Scottish Labour quickly agreed to support an official multi-option referendum which the government rejected; this then resulted in Labour doing next to nothing to advance a referendum, while 'Scotland United' argued for an unofficial referendum.

The local government elections one month after the general election painted a picture of a confused, deflated nation. Labour's vote at 34.1% was the party's lowest share of the vote in district elections since its poor showing in 1977; the SNP's 24.3% was its best ever, and the Conservatives 23.2% their best since 1980. Labour lost control of six councils, including Edinburgh, West Lothian and Falkirk, while gaining Cumbernauld and Kilsyth. One interesting development was the emergence in Glasgow of Scottish Militant Labour as an independent electoral force, with Tommy Sheridan becoming a councillor while in Saughton Prison for attempting to stop a warrant sale (Gall 2012).

The Labour defeat produced the resignation of Neil Kinnock as party leader, and the emphatic victory of John Smith over Bryan Gould in the leadership contest. Behind the scenes, in a discussion which was to have unforeseen consequences, Tony Blair attempted to persuade Gordon Brown to stand against Smith for the leadership to push the 'modernisers'' agenda, and challenge the 'safety first' approach of Smith. Brown refused, feeling duty-bound by loyalty not to stand against Smith.

The post-election Shadow Cabinet saw Tom Clarke become Shadow Scottish Secretary as Donald Dewar became Shadow Social Security Minister after nine years as Scottish spokesperson. This move was initially welcomed by Labour home rulers. Donald Dewar had been seen by some, despite his pro-devolution credentials, as too cautious and 'responsible', and perceived as 'failing to prosecute Scotland's case in Parliament with any vigour'. Clarke was viewed at first as a 'healer', someone who could bring together Labour's different factions, and give a different kind of voice and sense of urgency to the Scottish question (Macwhirter 1992: 5). This would all turn out to be seen as nothing but idle speculation, as Labour's post-election posturing ending up as doing as little as possible other than neutralising the Scottish dimension.

As some in Labour adopted more radical positions, others moved to embrace the party establishment. The Scottish Labour Action agenda of the late 1980s had not converted the entire party or leadership, but had been enormously influential in Labour and beyond in preaching a more pluralist politics and powerful Parliament. Post-1992, SLA felt a sense of exhaustion and fragmentation as its small cadre re-appraised what they had done and could realistically achieve with their numbers and resources.

One such person seriously re-appraising the situation was Jack McConnell, and when the post of General Secretary of the Scottish Labour Party became available he decided to apply. Pre-devolution, along with the post of

Secretary or Shadow Secretary of State for Scotland, this was the key Labour position, and held by such luminaries as Helen Liddell and Murray Elder. Jack McConnell, Anne McGuire and Johann Lamont were interviewed for the post by the British NEC. There was an expectation at the time that the party needed a woman in charge, to give Labour's poor track record with women's representation and the gender agenda of the home rule issue a major push. McConnell got the post because he 'had distanced himself from the hardliners within the home rule movement, the leadership knew they had found their man – a devolution enthusiast who was also a realist' (Davidson 2005: 74–5). The Scottish Labour establishment had again acted adeptly on how it managed party opinion.

Tom Clarke and his deputy John McFall were having trouble in the stormy sea of Scottish politics. They were seen as being against all the then current ideas such as a homegrown referendum or a shadow Parliament, and only seemed to be offering one solution: a future Labour Government.

The Major Government's re-election and any prospect of a Tory honeymoon and revival quickly fell apart as they became engulfed in problems, the most significant of which was 'Black Wednesday' on 16 September 1992 when the pound was forced out of the Exchange Rate Mechanism (ERM), leaving government economic policy discredited. There were huge Tory divisions over Europe and the Maastricht Treaty; and Michael Heseltine was forced into a humiliating U-turn when he attempted a nationwide programme of closing up to thirty-one of the remaining fifty pits with the loss of 31,000 jobs (*The Scotsman*, 14 October 1992). In Scotland, there was still anger and hurt in the aftermath of the decision to shut Ravenscraig.

The European Union summit on 12 December 1992 proved a catalytic public moment. Held in Edinburgh with John Major and numerous heads of state, a sizeable and impressive home rule march made a major national and even international statement. Organised by the cross-party Campaign for Scottish Democracy, it issued a 'Democracy Declaration' which stated that 'Scotland demands democracy' (*The Scotsman*, 10 December 1992).

A whole host of prominent figures addressed the protestors gathered at the Meadows in Edinburgh, with William McIlvanney and Alex Salmond, SNP leader, both capturing the mood of people to rise above differences and speak for a wider Scottish interest. In the weeks immediately after the rally, a national debate began about what was the best way for the home rule forces to advance, and the question of whether the political parties would maintain the spirit of co-operation so much of Scotland seemed to yearn for. George Robertson, who within months was to replace Tom Clarke as Shadow Scottish Secretary, led those pouring scorn on the possibilities of something happening, commenting that it was important not to get 'carried away' by the size of the rally. McIlvanney responded that Robertson was deliberately undermining the importance of what happened and that he believed 'any form of political life outside London is a joke' (Mitchell 1996: 298). In this climate, any search for cross-party co-operation was doomed at the outset. The SNP Westminster Group made matters even more difficult and supplied the ideal ammunition to their enemies, voting with the Conservative Government on the Europe of the Regions part of the Maastricht Bill; this was enough to begin a new Labour–SNP war of words with claims of 'tartan Tories' and worse.

Post-1992 all of the opposition parties had fears that the Tory Government would attempt to privatise Scottish water, which was still in public ownership, unlike in England and Wales where it had been privatised in 1989. This led Strathclyde Regional Council to organise an unofficial postal referendum on water privatisation which resulted in a 72% turnout, with 1.2 million people voting, and 97% of them against water privatisation (*The Scotsman*, 8 March 1993). Such an initiative seemed to show the possibilities of popular plebiscites in opposing Tory minority rule and offered lessons for the home rule cause.

The Problems of Lanarkshire Labour and the Monklands By-election

One of the dominant stories post-1992 in Scottish politics turned out to be about local government corruption in Monklands Council, which was given wider British resonance because John Smith, party leader, represented Monklands West which covered a large part of the council. Allegations centred on Catholic Coatbridge getting a disproportionate amount of council capital spending, and of discrimination in jobs, and nepotism in employment practice. Coatbridge received £21 million in capital projects; Airdrie, which was predominantly Protestant, got £2.5 million; all seventeen Labour councillors were Catholic, the three SNP councillors Protestant.

Scottish Labour's initial response was to do nothing. John Smith and Tom Clarke, the local MPs, believed it was a matter for the local council. Clarke in particular as a former Provost of Monklands went further and supported the council. Then David Shaw, Tory MP for Dover, decided to make political capital out of it to embarrass Smith and Labour. There were, after some delays, a Labour Party investigation, a council inquiry and an independent review with a limit remit, all of which found no wrong-doing, but something was rotten at the very heart of Lanarkshire Labour. And the party, including Smith and Jack McConnell, were slow to realise this. No one claimed that John Smith was involved or gaining anything from any potential malpractice, but it did allow people, including as it dragged on some in Labour, to question his political judgement. The BBC's *Newsnight* and the intrepid Michael Crick even ventured north into the relatively unknown territory for them of Scottish politics. This allowed Crick to ask Smith, 'Do you think Monklands is a model for how a Labour Government would operate?' (Stuart 2005: 361).

When Smith tragically died on 12 May 1994 Labour was faced with a huge challenge: a difficult by-election in about the most problematic circumstances you could realistically imagine. Helen Liddell was chosen as Labour candidate: high profile, previously General Secretary of the party, former advisor to Robert Maxwell and head of public affairs in his media empire, Catholic and well renowned as a formidable political operator. In the middle of the campaign Liddell stated of the differences between Coatbridge and Airdrie, 'This is unacceptable to local people and unacceptable to me' (*The Herald*, 22 June 1994). Labour's bitter and fraught fault-lines were suddenly thrust into public view in the middle of the by-election. Tom Clarke responded by accusing critics of the council of 'McCarthyite smears' (Stuart 2005: 391). He was backed by Jimmy Wray, Chair of the Scottish Labour Group of MPs, and as 'old Labour' as anyone could possibly imagine. Wray had to be lent on by the party hierarchy, and by McConnell specifically, to retreat from this position publicly and to back Liddell.

Labour's campaign was seen in the party and by Liddell as one of the most shambolic and unprofessional in years, and one which invited defeat. The party had at points lost control of its own campaign. The final result was a poor one for Labour and a missed opportunity for the SNP. Labour's majority was slashed from 15,712 to a mere 1,640. The losers were the people in the constituency, the reputations of most involved and Labour and the SNP, both of whom saw their activists raise the spectre of sectarianism. Helen Liddell emerged with her reputation as a street-fighting politician enhanced, and as someone who would take on and defeat both SNP and Labour opponents.

An opinion poll two days before voting showed more than half the local voters thought that the council did practice religious discrimination. It also found that 80% of Catholics supported Labour and 65% of Protestants the SNP (*The Scotsman*, 28 June 1994). And yet despite all this there were still significant and senior Labour voices of denial. Jimmy Allison, even after the event, wrote, 'By posing the question why does Roman Catholic Coatbridge get more done for it than non-Catholic Airdrie and the surrounding villages, the Tories and SNP played the sectarian card. They pointed discreetly to the fact that the Labour Party councillors were all Catholic' (Allison 1995: 144).

This was the powerful, certain voice of anger, indignation and denial, angry about being held to account and the effrontery of people asking questions and demanding accountability for public monies. And seeing this as somehow 'playing the sectarian card' rather than putting the responsibility where it belonged: with Labour.

Fortunately for the party there were prominent voices who were prepared to have courage and admit there was a major problem. Helen Liddell conceded that Monklands was 'tribalism at its worst', while George Robertson looking back on it commented that 'many of the local councillors did not believe they were doing anything wrong, partly because they had been in power for such a long time' (Stuart 2005: 351). As the Monklands by-election was fought, revealing a side of Scotland that shocked and dismayed many, Scottish and British politics were about to experience change and transformation on a scale which no one could have expected. For the death of John Smith meant that there had to be a Labour leadership contest.

THE ARRIVAL OF NEW LABOUR

The Labour Party after the death of John Smith was profoundly shocked and stunned. At the same time senior politicians in the party were also making cold calculations about who would stand for and win the leadership, and succeed Smith. The two most obvious candidates were Tony Blair and Gordon Brown, who had both grown in stature and reputation in recent years, and become increasingly impatient with John Smith's cautious conservatism and 'one more heave' mindset as they caricatured it.

While people positioned themselves, John Smith's funeral and the European elections were impending, with the party quickly agreeing that there would be no formal leadership campaigning until after the Euro elections. Smith's funeral was on 19 May 1994 at Cluny Church, Edinburgh. Donald Dewar, speaking at the funeral, said, 'The people have lost a friend – someone who was on their side and they know it.' He stated, 'John was not interested in the trappings of power. He wanted power not for what it did for him, but for what it might allow him to do for others' (Dewar 1994: 19–20). Gordon Brown, reflecting on Smith later, wrote, 'Public service was for John, the purpose of politics' (Brown 1994: 61).

Just one week later the contours of the party environment were shaken when *The Scotsman* published a survey of Scottish Labour MP opinions. They contacted forty-two of the then forty-eight Scots Labour MPs; fifteen said they would support Brown, six Blair, and a further six said they felt a 'personal obligation' to support Brown, but hoped he would not stand and instead back Blair (*The Scotsman*, 27 May 1994). The effect of this poll was to emphasise that even in his own supposed 'heartland' Brown could not be confident of winning majority support among MPs, and that even many who did or were prepared to support him were only doing so out of a sense of duty and obligation.

Two days later Brown gave a powerful, emotive speech in Swansea addressing the mission and purpose of Labour after Smith and his legacy. He stated, 'The flame still burns, the work continues, the passion for justice endures and the vision will never fade: the vision of Labour in power' (Routledge 1998: 203). This was the missionary man and genuine credo of Gordon Brown.

Brown then announced on 1 June 1994, the day after the now infamous Granita restaurant meeting between Blair and Brown, that he was not standing for the leadership, and would be backing Tony Blair. A few days later, on 9 June, the Euro elections took place and showed Labour significantly ahead of the Tories across the UK. In Scotland, Labour polled 42.5% to the SNP's 32.6% and the Tories 14.5%. This was Scottish Labour's best-ever Euro performance, while it was also the highest-ever national SNP support, with the Tories, the party in government, reduced to also-rans.

Tony Blair, John Prescott and Margaret Beckett contested the leadership. On 21 July 1994 Tony Blair was elected leader and John Prescott won the deputy leadership. Blair won 57.0% of the Electoral College to 24.1% for Prescott and 18.9% for Beckett, who had been acting leader in the period following Smith's death (*The Guardian*, 22 July 1994). The conduct of the leadership contest was widely seen as a huge positive for Labour and over a million people voted in the tripartite Electoral College. Many felt that the party had finally moved light years away from the internecine warfare of the 1981 Benn–Healey deputy leadership, but fear of that and anxieties about letting go were still to haunt the party for years to come. One activist commented about the mood in the party at the time, 'It was a very strange period, from the disillusion of '92 and the Tories getting back in, to picking ourselves up unlike '79 and not giving up. Then along came Blair and everything was different' (interview).

In October 1994, at Blair's first conference as leader, New Labour was born, the strategy of 'New Labour, New Britain' unveiled, and the abolition of Clause Four announced, or more accurately obliquely hinted at, then briefed, in a manner which showed the politics of the future. Almost immediately the Labour leadership found themselves facing significant opposition. Two days after Blair's speech, conference voted to retain Clause Four, Jim Mearns, Glasgow Maryhill CLP delegate, creating a flurry of excitement with his call to traditional socialism with his 'tough on capitalism, tough on the causes of capitalism' intervention deliberately invoking Blair's most famous soundbite at that point, 'tough on crime, tough on the causes of crime' (Routledge 1998: 221). A *Tribune* survey found that fifty-eight out of sixty CLP general committees were opposed to the dropping of Clause Four (*Tribune*, 3 March 1995).

Blair decided to take the high-risk approach and undertake a national tour speaking to 30,000 party members. At the March 1995 Scottish Labour conference the effort paid off as the party voted to abandon the old Clause Four. Kenny Macintyre reporting for BBC Scotland summed up the conference debate as 'a wee stushie', reflecting the raw nerves on both sides (Campbell 2010: 165). A week later Blair and Prescott announced the new Clause Four; it was a 344-word mission statement of forgettable blandness replacing the previous fifty-six words which had endured for seventy-seven years in the party constitution.

Then on 29 April 1995, at a special conference, the party approved the new clause by 65.2% to 34.8%, with a significant majority of constituency parties voting for change. Even more emphatically, of the 500-plus local parties who balloted their memberships only three voted to retain the traditional clause.

Out of the pro-Clause Four campaign in Scotland and traditional anxieties about the direction of New Labour, the Campaign for Socialism was born. It included at the outset Alex Smith and Alex Falconer, both MEPs, and Cathy Jamieson, later to be a MSP and Scottish Parliament minister; its support was always small scale in the party, but it could draw on a well of wider sympathy and, in particular, unease and distrust about New Labour. Jimmy Allison tapped into this when he wrote of Clause Four, 'It is not good enough for a political party such as Labour to increase membership numbers, it must continue to attract activists.' He believed that it would not 'increase the number of votes in favour of Labour on the ballot papers. It may, however, discourage traditional Labour voters' (Allison 1995: 234). Such opinions were not unusual, but they did not get much of a hearing at this time.

Scottish Labour may have had its internal tensions but it had few problems in the opinion polls at this point, with soaring ratings over 50% and an unpopular Conservative Government seen as out of touch in Scotland and facing huge internal divisions and problems at UK level. The Conservatives, desperate to undermine Labour's dominance of Scottish politics, came up with the idea of abolishing the regional tier of local government. They were increasingly furious at the growing influence of councils such as Strathclyde Region who with more and more frequency by-passed the Scottish Office and had developed a European profile and influence.

A new single tier of thirty-two local authorities was proposed to replace the old tier, with a widespread assumption that the motivation was Tory-style GLC gerrymandering and trying to create 'Tory safe havens' in Scotland. If that was the case it backfired, with the first elections in April 1995 proving the high point of Labour in local government. The party won outright control of twenty out of the twenty-nine councils up for election and 43.8% of the vote; the Tories won not one council and a mere 11.3%; the SNP took three councils and 26.2%; and the Lib Dems 9.7%. The results were seen as a 'catastrophe for the Conservatives' (Denver and Bochel 1995). The Tory wipeout could be seen in hindsight as an ominous sign in Scotland for the forthcoming UK election.

In May 1995 the Perth and Kinross by-election, caused by the death of Tory MP Nicholas Fairbairn, gave New Labour a chance to test some of its assumptions in a Scottish context. Douglas Alexander, Brownite ally and protégé, was chosen as Labour candidate and proceeded in a seat, where the party started off in third place behind the SNP, to run a campaign which created waves and made headlines. It was combative, unionist, anti-Scottish nationalist and, in particular, floated the idea of 'middle Scotland', which sank as soon as it was raised. Roseanna Cunningham, the SNP candidate, attacked New Labour for turning its back on 'traditional Scottish values of common decency' (*The Independent*, 17 May 1995). On 25 May Cunningham took the seat from the Tories, turning Fairbairn's 2,094 majority into a SNP majority of 7,311 over Douglas Alexander, who pipped the Tories for second place. Alexander was seen as a rising star, while the tone of Labour's by-election campaign was to be the shape of things to come (with the bitter Littleborough and Saddleworth by-election between the Lib Dems and Labour's Phil Woolas being only two months away).

The Westminster Boundary Commission review posed a potential headache for Labour as the leading party of Scotland, but in most cases the party managed the process smoothly. One seat was to prove an exception, and provide party officials with many sleepless nights and bad publicity: Glasgow Govan. The party selection pitted Mike Watson, victor in the Glasgow Central by-election, whose seat was being abolished, against Mohammed Sarwar, local councillor and Asian businessman, and Margaret Curran. It was a messy, nasty contest with accusation and counter-accusation, and at first Watson seemed to hold Sarwar off, winning 237 to 236 with fifty-two invalid votes (*The Herald*, 15 December 1995). The party, under threat of legal action from both Sarwar and Watson, ordered a rerun ballot, which Sarwar convincingly won, 279 to 197, a majority of eighty-two votes (*The Herald*, 25 June 1996). Sarwar's candidature continued to attract both publicity and controversy over his business practices, but there was a suspicion that the Scottish party and New Labour were prepared to put up with this for gaining such a well-known Asian businessman and multi-millionaire along with hopes to better court the Asian vote.

CONVENTION BLUES AND NEW LABOUR

The work of the Scottish Constitutional Convention continued post-1992 election with the setting up of the Scottish Constitutional Commission in

1993 to revisit the 1990 Convention proposals and in particular to look in detail at the electoral system and gender balance for a future Scottish Parliament, along with consequences for local government and the wider UK. This reported in October 1994, proposing a 112-seat Parliament elected by the Additional Member System (AMS), with 40% women's representation by the second term, while retaining seventy-two Scottish MPs and the Secretary of State for Scotland at least for the time being.

Labour and Lib Dem negotiations leading up to the final Convention document showed the tensions between the two parties; Labour's George Robertson argued for a Parliament of 112 members, while Jim Wallace of the Lib Dems made the case for 145. The eventual compromise which emerged was a Parliament of 129 members made up of 73 FPTP and 56 AMS; the overall number was the minimum the Lib Dems would agree to, below which they believed proportionality would be damaged. Both party leaderships suffered internal criticism over this compromise.

Labour felt uncomfortable about some of the changes and the need to explain them internally. Jack McConnell, in a note to George Robertson on 17 September 1995, laid out his thoughts about the proposals. He noted that the tax powers had been 'put in much more restrained and acceptable language' with 'other taxation specifically ruled out'; some of the far-reaching ideas on economic policy had been dropped, as had 'all extravagant references to transfer of sovereignty deleted', proposals for a gender-balanced Parliament replaced by voluntary agreement and deletion of any reference to a 'Scottish Civil Service'. Brian Taylor commented, 'It is plain from this memo . . . that Labour's aim was to contain its devolution scheme within what the leadership would regard as workable boundaries.' Part of this entailed recognising the need 'to build a balance between Scottish Home Rule and the UK dimension' (Taylor 1999: 68); part was also the arrival of Tony Blair and New Labour.

On St Andrew's Day, 30 November 1995, the Convention launched with much fanfare at The Mound, Edinburgh, 'Scotland's Parliament, Scotland's Right'. This was a more coherent and impressive set of proposals, not just in comparison to 1978, but to the first Convention package of 1990. The document proposed a Parliament elected by proportional representation of 129 members with economic powers, tax-raising powers and competence over large parts of Scottish public life (Lynch 1995). George Robertson commented at the launch that, 'we present with dignity and integrity a detailed plan worked out with pain and argument, time and travail, often mind-bending attention to detail, and built solidly and effectively on consensus and common sense' (*The Scotsman*, 1 December 1995).

The Blair leadership were uncomfortable with the commitment to a tax-raising Parliament, and when Tory right-winger and populist Michael Forsyth became Secretary of State for Scotland in June 1995 he decided to mix things up with a campaign against 'Labour's tartan tax', which was to prove hugely effective and have unforeseen consequences.

Rumours began to circulate that the Labour leadership were considering a referendum: anathema to the Scottish party, the Convention and home rule class. There was a wider critical unease about the shortcomings of the Convention's proposed package in places (McCormick and Alexander 1996). George Robertson, Shadow Secretary of State for Scotland, commented before the party's U-turn, 'There is no question of the Labour Party supporting calls for a referendum on a Scottish Parliament. The will of the people is behind the scheme and they will vote in that way in the election' (*Scottish Daily Mail*, 12 February 1996).

Then came the Labour Party announcement of a two-fold referendum. According to Blair, 'the strategy was clear: to devolve after a hundred years of waiting. The tactic was obvious: get the people to say yes, then the Lords could not say no' (Blair 2010: 252). It was seen by many as a 'mini-version of Clause Four' (Campbell 2010: 480). This was particularly so in the Blair leadership who saw it as a popular initiative, putting the leadership out in front showing courage, taking risks and being macho, challenging the party and conventional wisdom in a manner we were to grow increasingly accustomed too.

George Robertson, now defending a two-vote referendum, stated, 'the people of Scotland will be asked to endorse the [devolution] proposals in an early referendum to pave the way for legislation. There is now overwhelming support for a referendum. Politicians should trust the people' (*Scottish Daily Mail*, 27 June 1996). On 28 June, Blair met the Scottish Labour Executive and, according to Alastair Campbell, 'There was lots of talk of betrayal. One of them said they had been lied to' (Campbell 2010: 484). After Blair left, Campbell writes, 'Pat [McFadden] called to say we had won 20–4 on the new policy, and 16–12 on defeating the old one' (ibid.).

This wasn't the end of things. First, John McAllion resigned as Labour's Spokesperson on Constitutional Affairs, as did Harry Ewing, Joint Chair of the Convention. There was widespread frustration and opposition in parts of Labour, trade unions and the home rule movement. More crucially for Labour, significant opposition coalesced in the Scottish party executive and this came to a head at its crucial 31 August meeting. Its first vote was by the narrow margin of twenty-one to eighteen, defeating the notion of a one-vote referendum. However, to get this defeated a majority ended up backing Mohammed Sarwar's, later to be Labour MP for Glasgow Govan at the forthcoming election, compromise proposal. This entailed having three votes, comprised of the original two-vote question, and now a separate vote on activating the tax powers, which was passed by twenty-three to sixteen.

This briefly became Labour policy. Robertson announced the third Labour policy in less than three months: 'I think the people of Scotland want to be asked. They should be asked twice' (*Scotland on Sunday*, 1 September 1996). Within a week Labour changed again, abandoning the new policy and reverting to the two-question vote. Robertson now sold this, arguing, 'I am saying today to the party and the Constitutional Convention that a second referendum is not necessary and would not be pursued by the Labour Party' (BBC Radio 4, 6 September 1996). Campbell reflected on the fallout: 'Devolution, which had led the news all day yesterday, was a dreadful mess.' George Robertson 'was taking a real hammering', a set of events which Campbell did not lay the responsibility for on Tony Blair and the Labour hierarchy, but instead on 'the behaviour of the Scottish Executive' (Campbell 2010: 520).

Blair, looking back after a decade of New Labour in office, showed a similar lack of self-reflection. The whole episode, he believed, produced 'the most contorted cries of outrage from assorted nationalists and hacks . . .' (Blair 2010: 252). He went on to explore the motivations and reasoning, as he understood it, of opposition to his policy:

> I would be asked: Isn't having a referendum vote just a way of denying Scotland its due and proper Parliament? I would say: Er, but the Scots are the ones voting. Ah, they would say, but suppose they vote no? Well, I would say, in that case I assume they don't want one. And so on. Amazing. (Blair 2010: 252–3)

Thus began a phase of the relationship between the Blair leadership, sizeable parts of Scottish Labour and even parts of the home rule movement that can only be characterised as one of mutual antagonism, distrust and dislike. Things could only get worse, to paraphrase the song. Bob Thompson, a senior trade unionist, commented that, 'even at the time it was obvious something fundamental was happening. That the New Labour era wasn't just business as usual, but the start of something new and to those from a left political perspective, reactionary and playing the Tory tune' (interview).

At the end of 2006, Scottish Labour Party focus group findings about voter perceptions of Blair and New Labour were leaked to the press. Both publicly and in the party leadership, suspicion fell on Tommy Sheppard, Deputy General Secretary of the party, who was forced to leave as a result. The findings summarised detailed research into Scottish uncommitted voters in October 1996, stating, 'Tony Blair is perceived to be English, and his identity or image is associated with that of a Southerner.' It went on, 'There has been serious damage to the trust that voters have in New Labour's promises with regard to Scotland.' The paper concluded, 'Tony's easy smile arouses suspicion in the dour Scots. At worst this tends to be described as "smarmy". The Blairs are perceived to be emulating the Clintons' (System Three 1996: 6–8).

A Lanarkshire lady commented, 'I don't think Tony Blair is popular or genuine. I wouldn't trust him as far as I can throw him.' An Inverness man said, 'he seems to promise anything just to get support' (ibid.: 7, 15). The System Three findings found four main concerns among voters about Blair and New Labour. First, little difference was seen between New Labour and the Tories. Second, Blair was seen as focused on and from the middle class, and shifting Labour remorselessly rightwards with the loss of John Smith still acutely felt. Third, George Robertson was perceived as having little real power and as acting on London orders. Fourth, the disadvantaged were seen as having lost Labour as a voice and champion.

These were Scottish Labour's own research findings, and what was even more embarrassing and potentially damning was that these opinions chimed with a section of Scottish and even British voters. They became part of the pre-election story north and south of the border, with the Tories anxious to use such material to stop or hinder the New Labour bandwagon. It in effect showcased Scottish Labour's 'Northern Discomfort', the anxiety people felt at the direction and motivation of New Labour; it was the mirror image of Labour's previous 'Southern Discomfort' research by Giles Radice, which had shown a party out of touch with Southern aspirations (Radice 1992, Radice and Pollard 1993).

Sheppard reflects that the whole episode, and his sacking as a result of it, illustrated the deep tensions and divisions at the top of the party. He believes that 'I'm pretty sure it was George Robertson who really wanted me out, and given that Jack [McConnell] had his ear, he could have reassured Robertson that I was not the problem he thought I was' (Sheppard, quoted in Davidson 2005: 87). Then there was the amateurish and counter-productive attempt by McConnell and Sheppard to claim the SNP had obtained the documents by illegal methods, by breaking into Sheppard's car. He looks back on the episode, 'We never said outright that the SNP condoned breaking into their opponents' cars but it was an example of the political black arts that were practised then – and perhaps more so now – by the highest echelons of New Labour. It is not an episode of which I am proud' (ibid.: 86).

THE ROAD TO POWER

Scottish Labour approached its March 1997 conference in Edinburgh and the forthcoming election with a mixture of optimism and hope combined with disenchantment bordering in parts on cynicism. A prevailing feeling in the party was that the New Labour agenda was an entirely English election focused on 'middle England' and not needed north of the border. John McAllion articulated this post-election when he said, 'Old Labour was never unelectable in Scotland. Even at the high tide of Thatcherism in 1983, Michael Foot's Labour won a majority of seats in Scotland. In 1987, Scottish Labour recorded its best ever result' (*The Observer*, 22 March 1998). Another MP took a different line, feeling that 'New Labour should have more emphatically challenged the collectivist fantasies which had built up during the Thatcher years' (interview).

The Scottish conference saw the blowback from the events of the previous year and the U-turn on the referendum. A new centre-right group had emerged called the Network which briefly morphed into the Scottish Labour Forum (*The Scotsman*, 29 January 1997). Pro-Blairite, pro-leadership, it was associated with Rosemary McKenna and Jim Murphy, both of whom were standing as Labour candidates in winnable seats. Its aim was the politics of organisation rather than ideas: focused on targeting a group of non-loyalist members on the Scottish Labour Executive. Thus the party conference saw the defeat of five of the leading home rule rebels who all happened at the same time to be left-wingers from the executive and their replacement by loyalists. This was seen as payback time and an insurance policy against future trouble and troublemakers (*The Herald*, 8 March 1997).

The party was not yet completely out of trouble. This time it occurred in the middle of the 1997 election campaign – and the sole culprit was one Tony Blair. In an interview with *The Scotsman*, he compared the Scottish Parliament's tax-raising powers with those of 'the smallest English parish council', and declared that 'sovereignty rests with me as an English MP and that's the way it will stay' (*The Scotsman*, 5 April 1997). Opponents made as much mischief as possible over these remarks, with Alex Salmond claiming that Labour was a single-issue party focused on 'the pursuit of power by Tony Blair in Middle England' (*The Herald*, 30 April 1997).

Campbell, reflecting on Blair's comments, lost his once sensitive political antenna over the furore which ensued: 'It was totally dishonest – he had been making a pro-Parliament point, saying that if a parish council could levy taxes, why was it such a big deal if the Scottish Parliament could' (Campbell 2010: 695). It was no wonder Campbell saw the Scottish media as 'unreconstructed wankers' and regularly viewed Scotland as 'a disaster'; here was a political terrain the usually reliable Campbell and the whole Blair leadership saw as alien and just could not comprehend and understand.

Campbell, in his diaries at the time, in the middle of the 1997 campaign, caught perfectly the contradictions and different logics pushing Labour policy. Thus he could write, 'We were saying we believed in devolution, yet effectively deciding what a devolved Parliament would do' (ibid.). It was a set of tensions which was only to escalate once Labour won the UK election and the Parliament was set up; indeed, such a duality could be said to be one of the characteristics and contradictions of New Labour in office.

On 1 May 1997 Tony Blair was returned to office with an emphatic and historic 179-seat overall majority in the Commons. In Scotland, Labour increased its vote from 39.0% to 45.6%, while the SNP established themselves in second place in votes for the first time in a Westminster election since October 1974, with their vote inching forward by the smallest of margins to 22.1%. The Conservative vote fell from 25.7% to a paltry and new all-time low of 17.5%.

The story of the night in Scotland and Wales was the elimination of Tory parliamentary representation, something which had never previously happened in Scotland. All the opposition parties gained from Tory discomfort, with some element of an informal anti-Tory popular front of voters, but it was Labour who were the biggest beneficiaries by far.

While the Scottish Nationalists went from three seats last time to six seats, defeating Ian Lang in Galloway and Upper Nithsdale and Bill Walker in Tayside North, Roseanna Cunningham held on to the Perth seat which she had won in the by-election; the Lib Dems won Edinburgh West, defeating James Douglas-Hamilton, and Aberdeenshire West and Kincardine while losing Inverness East, Nairn and Lochaber to Labour. Scottish Labour took an impressive six Tory seats. Anne McGuire defeated Michael Forsyth, Secretary of State for Scotland, Lynda Clark took Edinburgh Pentlands from Malcolm Rifkind, Defence Minister, and in Aberdeen South Anne Begg pushed Raymond Robertson into third place. The party also won previous redoubtable Tory seats such as Ayr, Dumfries and Eastwood, the latter being the last Tory seat on the night to fall and make Scotland 'a Tory-free zone' in Westminster representation.

The results were devastating for the Tories, but there was some disappointment in the Scottish Nationalists that they had not been able to capitalise more on 'northern discomfort' with 'New Labour' and 'Middle England'. In particular, given the amount of negative publicity Labour had faced in the Mohammed Sarwar versus Mike Watson selection battle, many were surprised at how Sarwar held off the high-profile challenge from the SNP's Nicola Sturgeon in Glasgow Govan; while the SNP had targeted the seat, Labour had treated it like a marginal. Sarwar was to cover himself in controversy within weeks of the election, but the Labour and SNP contest would continue both in Govan, the West of Scotland and in preparations for the Scottish Parliament.

Scottish politics were set to begin a new era. As David Denver concluded, 'There is no doubt that the results of the general election in Scotland were dramatic – especially in terms of seats won. It seems likely, however, that they will bring about even more dramatic changes in Scottish politics' (Denver 1997: 32). The immediate future was to be shaped by a British Labour Government which had the potential to dominate and reshape British politics, the impending referendum on a Scottish Parliament and the politics of devolution, and a weakened and humiliated Conservative Party. It was clear that things would never be the same again.

Part Two
The Context of Scottish Labour:
Devolution Days

CHAPTER 5

The High Tide of New Labour, New Scotland

POST-ELECTION HONEYMOON: SCOTLAND MARCHES TOWARDS A PARLIAMENT

The election of the first Labour Government since October 1974 saw, as many had surmised pre-election, Donald Dewar rather than George Robertson become Secretary of State for Scotland. Dewar was the eighth Labour Secretary of State for Scotland, following the long-forgotten William Adamson in the 1920s, Tom Johnston in Churchill's wartime coalition, Attlee's three Secretaries, Joseph Westwood, Arthur Woodburn and Hector McNeil, and Willie Ross and Bruce Millan in the Wilson–Callaghan era. Dewar was to be a Secretary of State with a difference, legislating quickly for a Scottish Parliament, changing the nature of the post and of Scottish politics.

The Blair Government was characterised by a number of prominent Scots: Gordon Brown as Chancellor, Alistair Darling as Chief Secretary to the Treasury, Robin Cook as Foreign Secretary, George Robertson as Defence Secretary and Gavin Strang as Transport Secretary. Over the course of New Labour's thirteen years in office, only three ministers served in Cabinet from beginning to end: Gordon Brown, Alistair Darling and Jack Straw.

Dewar's Scottish Office ministerial team contained Ministers of State, Henry McLeish covering home affairs and devolution and Brian Wilson with responsibility for education and industry. Parliamentary Under-Secretaries were Sam Galbraith, Malcolm Chisholm and Lord Sewel.

Symbolically the Referendums (Scotland and Wales) Bill introduced on 15 May was the first piece of legislation announced to Parliament by the new Labour Government. Everything in action and design was meant to give the signal to supporters and opponents that this was to be the opposite of the experience of legislating for devolution in 1974–9. The legislation was a mere five clauses long, laying out the wording of the two questions to be put in a pre-legislative referendum. It passed through Parliament quickly and smoothly, and achieved Royal Assent on 31 July, after Lib Dem efforts to reduce the question to one vote and the SNP's to have a multi-option vote with independence on the ballot both failed (*The Scotsman*, 1 August 1997).

The White Paper, *Scotland's Parliament*, was published on 24 July. Dewar stressed in the foreword that 'Scotland will remain firmly part of the United Kingdom', while the paper underlined that 'The UK Parliament is and will remain sovereign' (*Scotland's Parliament* 1997: vii). Addressing the UK Cabinet that day, Dewar said, as recorded in Alastair Campbell's diaries, 'He said we're putting the whole package firmly within the context of the UK and the sovereignty of the UK Parliament.' In terms of Scottish Westminster representation, 'He and GR [George Robertson] spoke of the "untenable" seventy-two MPs situation and said it would be reduced' (Campbell 2011a: 100).

The entire document was a careful balancing act between the expectations of home rulers in Scottish Labour and the wider Labour Party. There would be a 129-member Scottish Parliament, a Scottish Executive and a First Minister, 'which will be similar to the relationship between the UK Government and the UK Parliament' (ibid.: 7). The Parliament would cover domestic affairs ranging from health to education, local government, transport, economic development and agriculture, fisheries and forestry.

The devolved issues were not to be identified one by one as they were in the Scotland Act 1978 and Convention proposals. Instead, the powers which were to be retained by Westminster – reserved powers – were identified, including macro-economic policy, defence, foreign policy, social security and the constitution of the UK. The financial arrangements emphasised the continuity and careful balancing: provision for tax-raising powers for the Parliament, alongside maintenance for the time being of the block grant from Westminster and the Barnett Formula. The paper proposed that the requirement for Scotland to have a minimum of seventy-one Westminster MPs should be abolished, an important development in Labour's devolution proposals compared to the 1970s.

There had been concerns in parts of the UK Government that earlier versions of the White Paper had been 'too Braveheart', reflecting Scottish considerations which might be seen as contentious to English voters or politicians. Scots Tory MP Michael Ancram, now representing the English constituency of Devizes, tried to make political capital of this in the Commons debate on the White Paper. He attempted to pull up Donald Dewar for using the term 'we' when he was talking about the Scots. Dewar effortlessly put down this argument with the retort, 'I am sorry I made the cardinal error of assuming I was a Scot for the moment' (House of Commons, 24 July 1997).

PROBLEMS WITH WEST OF SCOTLAND LABOUR

The referendum date was set for 11 September, but before the campaign began Labour got involved in a series of bitter, divisive controversies. Within weeks of Labour's election, Mohammed Sarwar, newly elected Labour MP for Glasgow Govan, was involved in a major scandal when *The News of the World* alleged he had bribed an election opponent with a £5,000 'bung'. Other allegations then emerged about electoral registration inaccuracies and irregularities, along with election expense allegations which resulted in Sarwar being suspended from the Parliamentary Labour Party for 'action grossly detrimental to the party' and 'unbecoming and totally inappropriate for a Labour MP' (*The Scotsman*, 17 June 1997).

Campbell wrote at the time of the widespread Labour fear 'that we were just the same as the Tories' and that 'we had a potential big problem on this because the sense was we were no different and he was seeming to get away with it' (Campbell 2011a: 18, 27). Sarwar was charged, tried and found not guilty.

Gordon McMaster, Labour MP for Paisley South, committed suicide three months after the election. He had been elected in a simultaneous by-election in November 1990 with Irene Adams, MP for Paisley North. The two had created significant local enemies in the party, including Tommy Graham, MP for neighbouring Renfrewshire West (*The Sunday Times*, 3 August 1997; *The Scotsman*, 9 August 1997).

It had been alleged that Graham engaged in a campaign of rumour and discrediting of McMaster and this included malicious gossip about his sexuality (Deer 1997). Graham was suspended by the party with significant public and media attention focused on Renfrewshire Council, with allegations made of intimidation, adversarial culture and corruption within it, from which neither Labour nor the SNP came out with any credit.

Another scandal involved Glasgow City Council, with Bob Gould, council leader, claiming of a culture of 'junkets for votes' among Labour councillors. The party announced an internal inquiry in an attempt to dilute it before the election. This reported in September 1997, as a result of which nine Labour councillors were suspended, including Gould and Lord Provost Pat Lally, for actions ranging from factionalism to corruption and inappropriate behaviour. As a result of this, Frank McAveety became leader of the council at the then young age, by Glasgow standards, of thirty-five (*The Scotsman*, 23 September 1997).

Lally and other accused colleagues took the party to court and six months later the party abandoned plans to expel them (*The Scotsman*, 25 March 1998). The whole episode reflected badly on the party in every way, from not dealing with various accusations of malpractice to what looked like incompetence, along with a widespread councillor sense of entitlement and reward. Donald Dewar and the Scottish party headed by Jack McConnell had been under enormous pressure to act both from London and public opinion, but they failed to follow due process. Lally, who had an enormous capacity for self-promotion and was seen by many as a popular champion of Glasgow, later reflected that he was 'hugely relieved and delighted' at the outcome, and 'angry that the Labour Party had ignored and abused its own procedures' (Lally 2000: 252).

THE SECOND TIME AROUND

None of this was exactly ideal preparation for Labour in the up-and-coming devolution referendum on 11 September. As David Denver and his colleagues wrote about the referendum campaign, 'Labour sleaze was becoming an issue to the embarrassment of the party leadership' (Denver et al. 2000: 65). The anti-devolution 'Think Twice' campaign ran adverts with the question, 'Can you really face a Scottish Parliament?' with the answer 'NO NO' and in the Os photographs of Tommy Graham and Mohammed Sarwar. This was the face of West of Scotland Labour – one of the formidable fears of other parts of Scotland, both geographically and politically.

The campaign saw, via the creation of the cross-party 'Scotland Forward', Labour and the SNP campaign together, and even Donald Dewar and Alex Salmond on occasion appear together with Jim Wallace, the leader of the Scottish Lib Dems: a very different kind of politics and mood compared to 1979.

The death of Diana, Princess of Wales had a dramatic effect on the campaign, shutting down political activities for a week. The last week saw Peter Mandelson strike a deeply unhelpful and partisan note, urging SNP supporters not to vote for a Scottish Parliament. He claimed that doing so would be voting for a 'Scotland that is an integral part of the United Kingdom' (*Scottish Daily Mail*, 10 September 1997). Fortunately, this created few political ripples at the time, but did illustrate a wider New Labour lack of understanding about Scottish politics.

The next day Scotland voted emphatically for a Parliament: 74.3% for a Parliament and 63.5% for tax-raising powers (*The Scotsman*, 13 September 1997). Tony Blair reflected the day after that it was, '"Quite a result", he said, "but we must get the message out loud and clear that there must be no pandering to nationalism, and we must stress that it's good for the UK, not just for Scotland"' (Campbell 2011a: 148). Blair was even at this stage, 'worried about English nationalism' and asked Campbell, 'Do you think a Scot can be

Prime Minister now there is a Scottish Parliament?', to which he replied 'Yes' (ibid.: 148–9).

On the Saturday after the vote, Blair asked, 'What will the English make of this Parliament?' and worried about the future direction of Scottish politics: 'He said DD [Donald Dewar] should be First Minister and also that we should have a series of measures to deal with sleaze and the quality of candidates' (ibid.: 149). Already, a profound disjuncture was beginning to emerge at this early hour between supporting the abstract and general principle of Scottish devolution, and a complete lack of ease about its consequences, giving away power, and the politics of devolution. This was to become a major defining feature of New Labour, not just in Scotland but elsewhere.

The post-referendum study underlined the extent the campaign showed at every level – voters, members, organisationally – that Labour was united, committed and enthused by the idea of a Scottish Parliament. In 1979, Tam Dalyell spoke for a significant section of the party with his arch-scepticism and hostility to devolution; in 1997 he was a lone, irrelevant voice, tolerated by the Scottish party. In 1979, a System Three survey before polling day found 66% of Labour supporters intending to vote Yes. The figures for 1997 showed 85% of Labour supporters along with 90% of SNP supporters planning to vote 'Yes, Yes' (Denver et al. 2000: 158–9).

At party level the change was even more emphatic. In 1979 one-third of Scottish Constituency Labour Parties had decided not to campaign, but in 1997 every one decided to campaign for a 'Yes, Yes' vote. In 1979 only 21% of CLPs reported their decision as unanimous; in 1997 this was true of all but one CLP. The proportion of Labour members reporting some of their members campaigning on the No side fell from 44% in 1979 to 8% in 1997. And Labour members became much more enthusiastic: in 1979 a mere 35% were enthusiastic compared to 73% in 1997 (ibid.: 106, 111).

Labour held the Paisley South by-election in November 1997 following Gordon McMaster's suicide, with Douglas Alexander winning with a 2,731 lead over the SNP on an 11.2% swing from Labour to the SNP. On 18 December the Scotland Bill was introduced into Parliament. Donald Dewar heralded the moment by quoting Clause One Part One of the bill: 'There shall be a Scottish Parliament'. He repeated it: 'There shall be a Scottish Parliament. I like that' (The Herald, 19 December 1997). The Scotland Bill was to pass through the Commons and, despite some Labour fears, the Lords, unscathed and received Royal Assent on 19 November 1998 (BBC News, 19 November 1998). It had proven a very different experience from the 1970s, with anti-devolution forces in the party and Parliament marginalised and politically impotent. The political attention and dynamic as the bill made its way through an uneventful Parliament slowly began to drift elsewhere, to the future and the impending electoral contest for the Scottish Parliament.

Preparing for the Parliament

All political parties had with the coming of the Parliament to identify, select and prepare candidates for standing, both for constituencies and regional lists. This posed the most serious of challenges to Scottish Labour, considering it was the party with the most constituency seats. Rosemary McKenna, MP for Cumbernauld and Kilsyth since the May 1997 election and leading Blairite in the Network group, was appointed chair of the Labour selection panel. Ernie Ross, MP for Dundee West, became her deputy. Ross was previously known as 'Afghan Ernie' for his support of the Soviet invasion of Afghanistan and rather rigid Marxism, but was now known as 'the fixer' because of his willingness to do the leadership's bidding when a difficult issue arose.

McKenna commented about the process, 'The Scottish Parliament has to be different. There's a wealth of new talent coming forward and we are going to choose the best, no matter whose nose maybe out of joint' (*Daily Record*, 15 May 1998).

Labour's selection panels comprised five representatives of the Scottish Labour Executive, five from the National Executive Committee, five 'experienced party members' and five independent advisors, including academic Alice Brown and Nigel Smith, former chair of the cross-party 'Scotland Forward'. They split into sub-groups of four each for interviewing candidates.

Labour followed conventional recruitment processes for its selections, asking people to apply by submitting a 500-word essay on what they wanted to achieve in the Scottish Parliament. It was a significant set of processes involving a sizeable swathe of the party: 1,100 requests were made for applications, 534 applications were then submitted, 326 selected for interview and 166 made the final list – a success rate from interviewees of just 51% – of which sixty-nine were women; a number of people rejected appealed against their exclusion, with only one being successful, Susan Deacon. One Labour insider who was party to the panel deliberations viewed that the process 'was neither conspiracy nor cock-up. Instead, there was an attempt to bring narrow management selection processes into a political set of decisions' (interview). One Labour MP went much further and claimed that 'the whole thing had a bad odour and bad faith, and the hands of Donald Dewar were all over it as a hatchet job, settling scores and keeping out people' (interview).

It was a bumpy experience, part deliberately played out in the full glare of the media. Blair said at the 1998 Scottish Labour conference at the start of the process:

This isn't about stopping any particular person – it is about ensuring high-quality candidates. No one has an automatic right to selection. Scotland deserves the best from Labour at local and national level. That is what it will get. (*Daily Record*, 7 March 1998)

Alastair Campbell recounts doubts at even this point, which can only be described as New Labour's and Blair's long honeymoon, as they were preparing Blair's speech: 'Donald came up and wanted to take out the word entrepreneurship, feeling it would go down badly in the party'. Blair reflected on this [writes Campbell], 'He said he was worried what might happen in the Scottish party once the Parliament was up and running. "There is a real rabbit in headlights feeling"' (Campbell 2011a: 315).

There was widespread suspicion that New Labour would use their methods of party management and control mixed with media briefings and manipulation. One of the main ways the media was beginning to define and categorise New Labour was as masters of 'spin' and control. The Scottish Parliament Labour selection process was to become seen within this context and therefore to strengthen further this perception.

In mid-May, the MPs Michael Connarty, Dennis Canavan and Ian Davidson (who had indicated they wished to stand for the Scottish Parliament) were profiled on the front page of *The Herald* as if facing criminal charges (*The Herald*, 13 May 1998). Connarty pulled out of the selection process. Davidson continued and was excluded, a process which turned him from a party loyalist into an inveterate rebel as he commented:

One peculiar feeling I have is a sense of liberation, because I now feel free to speak and act any way I wish. Despite never having voted against the Labour whip in six years, I have not made the panel, therefore I need feel no inhibitions now. (*The Herald*, 15 June 1998)

Dennis Canavan was similarly excluded but took a different path, standing as an independent in Falkirk West, which he won in May 1999 with the biggest constituency majority in Scotland. There had long been personal bad feelings between Dewar and Canavan since the latter beat the former for the Labour nomination of West Stirlingshire in the October 1974 election.

Canavan was interviewed to be a Labour candidate by Ernie Ross and Maggie Jones of Unison (later to lose the once safe Labour seat of Blaenau Gwent as a parliamentary candidate herself). Questions included:

Have you ever voted against the Government?
Have you ever asked an awkward question?
Have you ever said George Robertson should resign? (Canavan 2009: 232–3)

Reflecting on this and Davidson's exclusion, Canavan commented:

Davidson had allegedly treated the interviewing board with insufficient respect because he was not wearing a tie! As for me, I had been deemed 'too aggressive'. In truth, I had bent over backwards to be as courteous as possible, when faced with the most provocative interrogation and hostile body language I had ever experienced during any interview. (ibid.: 233)

The list of excluded members was a fascinating one: Murray Elder, special advisor to Donald Dewar; Tommy Sheppard, former deputy general secretary; Esther Roberton, who had worked for the Constitutional Convention and Labour quangocrat; Isobel Lindsay, who had left the SNP over the Convention; Jeanne Freeman, later Jack McConnell's head of policy; and Mark Lazarowicz, previously Labour leader of Edinburgh Council and later to be MP for Edinburgh North and Leith.

Labour's constituency selection process also posed difficulties and created controversy. The party adopted constituency twinning to advance gender equality and this resulted in a number of leading Labour men being excluded. East Lothian's twinning with Midlothian meant that John Home Robertson was favourite in the former, leaving home rule campaigner Bob McLean without a local seat. In Cumbernauld and Kilsyth's twinning with Strathkelvin and Bearsden, Ian Smart would have been favourite in the former, but for Sam Galbraith, sitting MP for the latter, going for the nomination in the Scottish Parliament. Many thought the exclusion of the two leading lights of Scottish Labour Action was a product of party fixing, but others thought it accidental. McLean and Smart had even wound up SLA at the end of 1997 to play the loyalist card, holding a swansong conference looking positively ahead to the future agenda of the Scottish Parliament. Sarah Boyack, a prominent SLA figure and future MSP, reflected, 'we were now in a position to actually influence policy. We no longer needed to organise a campaign' (interview).

SLA also published a pro-autonomy pamphlet, 'A New Scottish Labour Party' by Tommy Sheppard, which concluded with the following prophetic comments:

If the party does not devolve and is seen as having its Scottish policy run from London, it will put itself at a considerable disadvantage compared to its competitors. In time, the Scottish people will want their parties home grown, and Labour will have to change or leave the political stage to others. (Sheppard 2007: 24)

Labour's most creative pressure group of the previous decade, the nearest the Labour left had come north of the border to a sustained, pluralist Scottish new left, attempting to steer a course between incorporation and oppositionalism, wound up at the point where it was most needed. In a final sour note, its main protagonists and most committed radical voices found themselves without a platform.

The most bitter contest, Motherwell and Wishaw, saw Jack McConnell narrowly defeat AEEU trade union official Bill Tynan by 270 to 268 votes, with five spoiled ballot papers and twenty out of 180 postal ballots ruled out, with some thinking these were disproportionately pro-Tynan. Danny Carrigan, AEEU Scottish Secretary, said after the contest, 'We're forever having to fight major battles to get trade union people elected' (*The Scotsman*, 23 November 1998). It had at points been a particularly nasty selection contest: 'Tynan's camp claimed McConnell's supporters played the sectarian card. They said Tynan's Catholic religion was used against him on the doorsteps. McConnell's supporters claimed Jack's Protestant background was used against him' (Davidson 2005: 102). For the second time in a few years, the ugly, unacceptable side of Lanarkshire Labour politics went national, revealing the divisions and fraught nature of the sectarian issue.

The party also experienced problems in the regional list, with the Scottish Labour Executive announcing that it would have the sole say in how candidates would be ranked (*The Herald*, 26 January 1999). Peter Peacock was placed top of the Highlands and Islands Labour list, despite only just joining the party after being an independent councillor. Donald Dewar topped the Glasgow list, but was only notionally in first place as he was expected to win his Glasgow Anniesland seat. Publicly little-known Brian Fitzpatrick, Dewar and Brown ally, was placed in second position, and therefore in real first position, causing seven of Glasgow's ten CLPs formally to complain to party headquarters.

A study of people who made it onto Labour's long list – both those successful and unsuccessful in becoming candidates – showed deep disquiet across the party: 23% said the system for selecting panel and constituency candidates was undemocratic; 34% that constituency candidate selection was unfair; 83% that regional list candidate selection was undemocratic and 76% unfair (Bradbury et al. 2000: 159); 27% thought there was too much leadership influence in candidate selection, 74% in relation to regional lists. These figures showed deep dissatisfaction about a number of the processes, but at the same time, the depth and residual nature of party loyalism: a characteristic which was to be tried and tested to breaking point over the next few years. There is further exploration of these issues in Chapter 16.

TROUBLE AT THE TOP

Scottish Labour needed to elect a leader for the forthcoming election campaign and in September 1998 called a special one-day conference at the Scottish Exhibition and Conference Centre at Glasgow to elect as leader Donald Dewar. He was the sole candidate nominated and was elected on the day in a slightly surreal atmosphere with a nearly unanimous 99.8% of the vote; Falkirk West's CLP delegate, unhappy at the treatment of Dennis Canavan, pointedly abstained (Scotland on Sunday, 20 September 1998). One future MSP said 'that to disguise its North Korean tendencies the party leadership must have paid Falkirk West to stop the embarrassment of a 100% endorsement of Donald' (interview).

The focus on Labour's public difficulties on candidate selection contributed to a sense of visible difficulty, drift and lack of positive direction. Over the summer of 1998, the SNP moved ahead of Labour in voting intentions for the forthcoming Scottish Parliament elections. In May 1998, System Three showed the SNP led Labour by 41% to 36% and in June by 44% to 35%, leads of 5% and 9%, which caught many in Labour out. The first System Three poll to show constituency and regional voting intentions in July had the SNP 45% to 37% ahead in the first and 43% to 32% in the second (Hassan and Lynch 2001: 387). This contributed to an increasingly anxious, nervous British Labour leadership worried about losing Scotland, and which more and more implored Scottish Labour and Donald Dewar to become more pro-active, develop a professional political strategy and, in particular, embrace an aggressive anti-Nationalist approach.

While Labour's poll ratings looked distinctly unhealthy, so did Donald Dewar's. In September 1998 NOP for *The Sunday Times* looked at the appeal of the two main leaders, Donald Dewar and Alex Salmond, SNP leader. Asked to choose in a two-way contest the best First Minister, 44% chose Salmond and 40% Dewar. When asked who they would most like to meet, Salmond was ahead by 51% to 34%; when asked who they would most like as a next-door neighbour, Salmond led by 41% to 34%; when asked about trustworthiness, Salmond and Dewar tied on 33% each (*The Sunday Times*, 27 September 1998).

A Euro by-election in North East Scotland in November 1998 caused Labour even more problems. The Labour candidate, Kathleen Walker Shaw's nationality became an issue in the campaign after it emerged she had been born in England and not Scotland as she previously suggested. She attempted to explain the mix-up by stating, 'It is all a misunderstanding, I was born in Stafford, but I was conceived in Aberdeen' (*BBC News*, 27 November 1998). Not surprisingly, the SNP's Ian Hudghton was emphatically elected with 48.0% to the Conservative Struan Stevenson's 19.9%, with Labour on 18.5% in a seat it held until 1994. The result and campaign were widely seen in the party as disastrous, and Walker Shaw withdrew as a Labour candidate from the forthcoming Euro elections.

Senior members of Labour's hierarchy were being driven into apoplexy by this series of events. Labour were sleepwalking into a historic and embarrassing defeat. Campbell reflected on some of this criticism of Dewar: 'The same people savaging him now would suddenly elevate him to the status of Great Scot done in by trendy London Labour' (Campbell 2011a: 436). Lorraine Davidson, an under-pressure Scottish Labour Head of Communications in the 1998–9 run-in, commented that Dewar 'didn't really like going for the SNP hard' (ibid.: 457–8). The contradictions, tensions and powerplays within Scottish Labour were becoming more acute and critical, as Campbell illustrated:

> The message we were getting from the Scottish party was we needed to be more traditional and play to the Jock agenda etc. But Philip G [Gould] said the groups he did showed the opposite – they liked TB [Tony Blair] and wanted to be more New Labour not less. He said the SNP were worried about TB as a weapon up there. (ibid.: 458)

The Scottish Labour campaign saw a host of people become involved, and for a crucial period it was unclear who was really responsible and running things. Alex Rowley had become General Secretary of the party following Jack McConnell's departure. Rowley was widely seen as Gordon Brown's choice and candidate for the job versus the Blairite choice, Andy Kerr. This perception undoubtedly contributed to hurting Rowley as the Labour leadership north and south panicked that the election was running away from them, and amplified the scale of backbiting and internal positioning which went on during his brief period as General Secretary.

Rowley was to resign as General Secretary within weeks of the May 1999 elections, but in reality he had become sidelined before the end of 1998. Similarly, Lorraine Davidson, the party's Head of Communications, was seen as unable to get Dewar to develop a more professional media strategy and go for the SNP.

Dewar was nominally head of Labour's campaign, but the real drivers and shapers were Gordon Brown, aided by Douglas Alexander, who were assisted by John Rafferty, who took time out of his full-time job running the National Charities Board in Scotland. Other work was done by some of the key figures and architects in New Labour nationally, including Matthew Taylor, then working at Millbank, and Philip Gould, Tony Blair's pollster. It was as if the formal party structures and personnel had been displaced by a de facto team put in place with the intention of saving what was seen by some as an election being lost.

Having created this set of formal and informal campaign structures, the party had to attempt to get its organisational make-up, resources and personnel focused, devise a set of coherent messages and then communicate and disseminate them. And as crucially, it had to get its leadership to single-mindedly implement and articulate this. In this the party was to encounter numerous problems.

The Scottish Labour Party had never actually in its history had a proper leader. The Secretary of State for Scotland or Shadow Secretary had often in the past played this role, while the role of the party's General Secretary at points could also be seen to undertake this. Now the party faced the prospect of a Labour Group of MSPs who had not been selected and did not owe their position to Donald Dewar. This made the authority of the leadership conditional. Combining this with Dewar's known diffidence and dislike of New Labour methods created a leadership vacuum.

Dewar himself did little to rectify matters by creating a collective leadership team around him, either drawing from Scottish Office ministers or a mixture of special advisors and newly selected Labour candidates. Henry McLeish was thought by some not close to Dewar or trusted enough by him. Wendy Alexander was taken up with her candidature in Paisley North; Murray Elder had been rejected by the party panel; Jack McConnell had been sent to the party equivalent of Siberia, post-General Secretary, after attempting to serialise his memoirs in *Scotland on Sunday*, and was going to have to earn back his spurs.

There was a wider context to this. Scottish Labour had previously advanced a rather narrow notion of leadership, of the councillor class and nomenklatura of the networked state. There were always exceptions to this – Willie Ross, Bruce Millan, Donald Dewar, for example – but none of these attempted to change the nature and character of Labour in Scotland. Even ambitious politicians such as Jack McConnell or Wendy Alexander always saw the party as a platform for advancing 'modernisation', rather than something that needed reform itself. In all the febrile activities and anxieties in the run-up to 1999, Scottish Labour's preparations on how it might develop leadership, think about how to run things and how to act strategically in government were next to non-existent. Several future MSPs commented on this; that they felt they were, in the words of one, 'left in the dark, hanging on a thread, and it wasn't surprising that we didn't hit the ground running when the Parliament was set up' (interview).

This vulnerable position was increasingly filled by the towering figure of Gordon Brown, who had a proprietorial interest in what happened in his own backyard, Scottish Labour and Scottish politics. His reach and influence north of the border had always been more complex than portrayed by some of the simplistic conspiracy theories of politics, as the survey of Scottish Labour MPs had shown in the run-up to the 1994 leadership contest. Scottish Labour was not a straightforward Brownite heartland, no matter how he and some of his acolytes saw it, but his skills, acumen and intellect were to prove at this point vital to Scottish Labour's election campaign.

Brown and Douglas Alexander penned a Smith Institute pamphlet, 'New Scotland, New Britain', in March 1999 which laid out the New Labour message north of the border: one which even more than it drew from New Labour sensibilities, was proudly and unapologetically unionist and went in hard on the Nationalist 'separatist' message:

> So the real battle in Scotland in May 1999 will now be between those who put the politics of social justice first, and those who practice the politics of national identity above and before anything else. There is and always has been more to Scottish politics than identity politics. Solidarity – and working together – offers Scotland more than separation – and splitting ourselves apart. That is why a politics based on the expansive vision of social justice will defeat the narrow divisiveness of Nationalism. (Brown and Alexander 1999: 47)

At the same time, in the run-up to the Scottish Labour conference in March 1999, the party unveiled its new election message in February at a one-day event at the Royal Scottish Academy of Music and Drama in Glasgow. This was the unveiling of 'Divorce is an Expensive Business', which carried the strapline, 'It won't be a trial separation with the SNP'. The strategy and words had been inspired by Douglas Alexander, but the wider strategy was signed up to across the party.

Tony Blair, launching this approach, said, 'The decision the Scottish people will make is whether this election will be remembered as Devolution Day or Divorce Day.' He went on, 'In Scotland, step by step we are confirming that New Labour's values are Scotland's values . . .' (*The Herald*, 6 February 1999). For those who had grown up with Scottish Labour's championing of the Scottish dimension in the 1980s, this new bold strategy at the time came as a bit of a shock: a hard, abrasive, populist anti-Scottish Nationalist message. One Labour former insider commented that 'the strategy was a complete surprise to many of us. For ages the leadership had assured people it wouldn't go negative. And then it did big time with Douglas Alexander's strategy' (interview). And in many respects it was to prove effective, equally surprising and wrong-footing the SNP. The Scottish Labour conference in the Glasgow Royal Concert Hall had the feel more of a set of pre-election rallies than the conference of old. Campbell judged, 'The mood at the conference was good, and they were up for a proper message' (Campbell 2011a: 676). He records Tony Blair commenting, 'He said Donald was clever and smart and popular but at the moment he was like blancmange' (ibid.: 676).

Further into the campaign, both Tony Blair and Gordon Brown were losing their patience with Dewar and the lack of focus, professionalism or strategy. Campbell put it, 'GB [Gordon Brown] said it was exasperating and hopeless, especially as the strategy was clear – 1. hurt the SNP with business,

2. beat them on fairness, 3. make clear there was a process and this was the first instalment' (Campbell 2011a: 690).

Labour's nervousness and anxiety was in spite of the reality of the opinion polls. The election had increasingly been turning Labour's way from late 1998. In January 1999, System Three had the SNP ahead on 40% to Labour's 39% in the constituency vote and 39% to 36% in the regional vote; by March Labour were ahead 39% to 38% in the first and 40% to 36% in the second; by 2 April and the beginning of the official campaign, Labour had pulled ahead emphatically, leading 45% to the SNP's 32% on the first vote and 40% to 32% on the second (Hassan and Lynch 2001: 387).

All of the big events were now shifting things Labour's way: the 'Divorce is an Expensive Business' theme; Labour's tax-cutting budget taking one penny off the standard rate of income tax; the SNP's ill-judged, snap decision to respond with 'A Penny for Scotland'; the big business endorsements for Labour and high-profile advertising campaign; and Alex Salmond's broadcast during which he called the British-backed military action in Kosovo 'an unpardonable folly', words which were to prove hugely controversial and seen by many as ill-chosen.

Despite all of this aiding Labour into building a sizeable lead which had been emerging for months, and with the election now seen to be moving away from the SNP, Scottish Labour did not relax and revel in its new-found success and moment in the sun; instead, the top levels of the party were filled with rancour and division. Bob Thompson remembered that 'the campaign was dispiriting and there was little politics in it beyond Labour bashing the Nats' (interview).

Polling day on 6 May 1999 saw Scottish Labour poll 38.8% of the constituency vote, with the SNP on 28.7%, while Labour won 33.6% of the regional vote to the SNP's 27.3%. Labour won fifty-six seats to the SNP's thirty-five, Conservatives' eighteen and Lib Dems' seventeen, with three others in the 129-member Parliament (Denver and MacAllister 1999).

Labour held fifty-three out of seventy-three FPTP seats, all of which it had held in the 1997 Westminster election. It lost three seats it had held two years previously: Falkirk West to independent Dennis Canavan, Aberdeen South to the Lib Dems, and Inverness East, Nairn and Lochaber to the Nationalists. Labour supplemented this with winning three regional list seats in the Highlands and Islands, but otherwise the geographies and patterns of Scottish Labour support were as expected, with the party drawing heavily from the West of Scotland, and winning more votes than anyone in six of the eight Scottish Parliament regional constituencies, the exceptions being North East Scotland and Highlands and Islands.

The post-election environment with a newly established Scottish

Parliament would demand many things from Labour, but it also left a party which was in an unsure, uneasy, brittle state. Within weeks, Alex Rowley was gone as General Secretary, to be replaced by Lesley Quinn, while British Labour voices made sure their criticisms were heard.

Matthew Taylor, who had worked for the party in the pre-election period, in a key post-election piece criticised Scottish Labour critics of New Labour. He wrote that the debate was not, as some claimed, between Scottish Labour autonomy and London control freakery, but about consistency of message in Labour:

> It is between two equally legitimate positions: the expectation that governmental devolution implies some party devolution, and the principle that a party's integrity depends upon embodying a single set of values, principles and core policies regardless of where it operates. Devolution gives the people of Scotland and Wales the right to elect their own government, not to redesign the political platform of each party. (Taylor 1999)

He went on forthrightly making his case:

> The British Labour Party has every reason to have a stake in the policies and practices of Scottish and Welsh Labour. It is a question of branding. The emergence of a Scottish Labour brand very different from that of Wales and England would undermine the credibility and coherence of British Labour as a whole. (ibid.)

Conceding that the next few years would see 'four public policy laboratories' across the UK, he argued:

> But to suggest that devolution to the Scottish Parliament means that Scottish Labour politicians have free rein to redesign the party's values and core principles is to deny the very definition of a political party. (ibid.)

This was perhaps put starkly and was brutally honest, but this was increasingly over the next few years to be the dominant British Labour response to much of devolution, and Scottish devolution in particular. Taylor's view was unusual in its explicitness and lack of qualification, but in its principled, unapologetic Labour centralism and complete lack of understanding of the dynamics and dimensions of Scottish politics, it was very revealing. A hugely influential part of New Labour were shown to believe in and be happy to promote a politics of centralisation and standardisation *the like of which had rarely been seen in recent British politics*. The New Labour leadership over the next few years were going to have to slowly and painfully learn that such an approach was unsustainable and unpractical. However, the tensions and conflicts inside Labour in the meantime would cause severe problems and restrict the potential of Scottish Labour to adapt, evolve and thrive in the emerging Scottish political environment.

CHAPTER 6

Scottish Labour and 'the Early Days of a Better Nation'

THE NEW POLITICS?
A LABOUR–LIB DEM COALITION

The first Scottish Parliament had been elected with a great deal of excitement, enthusiasm and hope for the future. As had been nearly universally expected, the election produced no party having an overall majority. On the Sunday after the polls (9 May 1999) the Labour Group of MSPs met for the first time and then negotiations began between the Labour and Lib Dem teams. There was no assumption by any major players in any of the parties of any other outcome, such as a minority Labour administration, or more radically, the non-Labour parties coming together and excluding Labour from office.

The Labour team was led by Donald Dewar and included Henry McLeish, Sam Galbraith, Tom McCabe and the only woman in either team, newly elected Sarah Boyack, MSP for Edinburgh Central. The Lib Dem team was led by Jim Wallace and included Nicol Stephen, Ross Finnie, Iain Smith, Iain Yuill and, from the party executive, Andy Myles and Denis Robertson Sullivan.

Henry McLeish commented at the time, 'The fact that we have no overall majority focussed our discussions. However, over 70% voted for parties pledged to make the Parliament work' (McLeish 1999: 57). The starting point in discussions quickly became the issue of tuition fees, which the Lib Dems were against. Agreement was eventually reached on tuition fees for an independent review, allowing Donald Dewar and Jim Wallace to sign a joint statement in the Museum of Scotland, Edinburgh, committing them to a 'Partnership for Scotland'. This historic document itemised a 'Programme for Government' and the policies and principles for the Labour–Lib Dem Executive (*BBC News*, 14 May 1999).

96

'Was a coalition inevitable?', asked Mike Watson, Labour MSP for Glasgow Cathcart and former MP. 'Could Labour, having secured less than 40 percent of first votes, have used that as a step ladder from which to reach out and grab 100 percent of the power in Scotland's new democracy?' (Watson 2001: 3). Watson's phraseology belies his doubts about the proposition, and in the first Labour Group meeting after the coalition agreement, John McAllion, MSP for Dundee East, and others robustly put the case for a minority Labour administration, but this was very much a minority opinion, attracting at best no more than half a dozen colleagues.

It was not just Scottish Labour who were concerned about a coalition; British Labour were also anxious about the nature of the deal, as were the Lib Dems at both a British and Scottish level. The British Labour concerns were fixated during the coalition negotiations on the subject of tuition fees, and the consequences of their abolition as a principle and financially. Paddy Ashdown records Gordon Brown as claiming, 'There is no question of providing Scotland with more money from the Treasury coffers', with Ashdown responding, 'Will you people *never* listen to what we say?' and Brown commenting, 'the principle is the money' (Ashdown 2001: 447).

Both Blair and Brown were roadblocks on the path to coalition and equally ill at ease with the evolving politics of pluralism and policy divergence across the UK. This is an exchange recorded between Ashdown and Blair at the same time, talking about tuition fees:

> TB: You can't have Scotland doing something different from the rest of the UK.
> PA: Then you shouldn't have given the Scots devolution, including specifically, the power to be different on this issue . . .
> TB: Yes, that is a problem. I am beginning to see the defects in all this devolution.
> PA: Well, is this a matter of principle for you or a matter of practicalities? If it is a matter of principle, then we might as well call a halt right now. The principle we hold to is that the Scottish Parliament should be allowed to exercise the powers you bestowed on it. If you say that's impossible, then we do not want to be your partners. If on the other hand, it is a matter of costings, then I'm sure we can find a practical way through. (Ashdown 2001: 446)

With all these difficulties, the Labour–Lib Dem coalition happened because the central negotiating parties wanted to make it happen, wanted to work together and had an assumption that this would happen. All of this meant, whatever Blair, Brown or other major figures said, it did happen.

Before that the Scottish Parliament opened on 12 May 1999, with Winnie Ewing as the oldest member in the chamber declaring, 'The Scottish Parliament which adjourned on 25 March in the year 1707 is hereby reconvened.' David Steel was elected Presiding Officer later on the same day, and

Donald Dewar elected First Minister on 13 May with seventy-one votes, the combined Labour and Lib Dem groups minus Lib Dem maverick Keith Raffan. McLeish's comments at the time captured the sense of occasion and emotion:

> A man of deep integrity and conviction, a man who has fought for the Parliament all his life, now leads it. The Scottish Parliament breaks with Westminster tradition and rises to its feet to give Donald a standing ovation. (McLeish 2004: 60)

Campbell reflected at the end of the week, 'DD [Donald Dewar] was looking the part though I was still hearing there was zero news management up there' (Campbell 2011b: 23) On 17 May the first Scottish Executive was announced, with Jim Wallace as Deputy First Minister and Justice Minister. Henry McLeish became Enterprise and Lifelong Learning; Tom McCabe was Parliament Business Minister; Jack McConnell was at Finance; Sam Galbraith, Education; Wendy Alexander, Social Inclusion, Local Government and Housing; Sarah Boyack, Transport and Environment; Susan Deacon, Health; while Ross Finnie took Rural Affairs.

The Euro elections on 10 June 1999 saw Scotland's previous eight constituencies become one nationwide contest elected by PR. Labour's vote fell to 28.7%, narrowly ahead of the SNP's 27.2%. Labour's number of MEPs fell from six to three because of PR, with the SNP unchanged at two, the Conservatives gaining two and the Lib Dems one. The big Labour story had been the virtual de-selection of MEPs Hugh McMahon and Alex Smith by placing them so low down the party list as to make election impossible. This had been the fate of many anti-Blair rebels and Smith withdrew as a candidate as a result (*The Independent*, 23 September 1998).

LABOUR PAINS AND THE CHALLENGES OF OFFICE

The mixture of Westminster experience and newly elected relatively young ministers at the time caused a ripple of excitement and optimism. The new Parliament had been established, the Executive formed and the First Minister elected. There was enormous goodwill across institutional Scotland: a full legislative programme would shortly emerge, but already some problems were evident. This was about more than the lack of strategy and focus at the top and the corrosive effect of negative press coverage of the early days of the Scottish Parliament.

Scottish Labour's dominance of Scottish politics for so long had disguised the fact that outside of local government the party had limited experience in running anything. Scottish Labour now found itself in the dominant position in the Parliament, in coalition with the Lib Dems, with political and popular expectations but no collective experience or memory of developing and sustaining leadership. The previous two years of preparing for devolution had seen no substantive preparation in this arena, and this was increasingly to become self-evident and a problem.

The problem went beyond leadership. The Labour Group of MSPs were not before 6 May 1999 a collective group and it would take them time to develop and bond. There was also a sense of the low level of some of the political discussion in the Labour Group, vindicated by the raw nerves sometimes hit in the early days by *Scotland on Sunday*'s diary of Mungo MacKay, a fictitious Labour MSP. One early column had a Labour Group discussion dominated by people talking about the reliability and quality of local bus services; the satire on the Labour 'cooncillor' nature of the group was raised in the Labour Group as an issue. Mike Watson looking back believed that 'the Scottish Parliament did not create a political community. There were no real discussions in the Labour Group. Instead, we huddled together and kept our heads down' (interview).

The vacuum of leadership went beyond whatever failings Donald Dewar had as a politician, or all the complaints New Labourites made about the lack of strategy and media management. It affected core issues about style, values and cultures within the party, and permissible forms of leadership, and was to come back to hurt Scottish Labour in the coming years.

The first months of the Scottish Parliament were ones characterised by negative press coverage over a host of issues, mostly small but others cumulatively damaging, such as the rising cost of the Holyrood building project for the new Scottish Parliament. In a parliamentary debate on 17 June, the Holyrood project was only approved by sixty-six to fifty-seven MSPs. At the time the parliamentary costs for the new building had more than doubled to £105 million, but over the next five years they would escalate by a factor of four.

The day before, Dewar had announced the first legislative programme, including a range of bills (education standards, tackling traffic congestion, land reform, abolishing feudal tenure), and introduced the programme by claiming that it 'will touch on the lives of every man, woman and child in the land. This is fundamental, radical change' (*The Scotsman*, 17 June 1999). Peter Jones commented that the programme 'lacked a populist edge' and went on, 'The virtue of dullness, however, lay in providing a programme on which the new Parliament could cut their teeth without getting into too much party political controversy' (Jones 2000: 61).

Weeks later, 1 July saw the official opening of the Scottish Parliament attended by the Queen, and with Donald Dewar's poignant address capturing a moving sense of hope and expectation. His speech was a mixture of looking to the past, while trying to weave a narrative of a changing Scotland over the generations which reflected on that journey. He talked of a 'moment anchored in history' and the emergence of a new voice which connected to that past:

> ... the shout of the welder in the din of the great Clyde shipyards; the speak of the Mearns, with its soul in the land; the discourse of the Enlightenment when Edinburgh and Glasgow were a light held to the intellectual life of Europe; the wild cry of the great pipes, and back to the distant cries of the battles of Bruce and Wallace. (*The Herald*, 2 July 1999)

Dewar evoked a language which could be from a SNP member, particularly a sentimental and romantic one. 'For me, for any Scot, today is a proud moment: a new stage on a journey begun long ago and which has no end.' He noted, 'A Scottish Parliament – not an end, a means to greater ends' (ibid.). The following day, 2 July, the Parliament addressed a matter of significant political controversy: agreeing to an independent commission on tuition fees.

On 23 September, Labour's Bill Tynan held the Hamilton South seat in a Westminster by-election, with Labour's majority cut from 15,878 to a slender 556, a 22.6% swing from Labour to the SNP. Then days later another media firestorm began with what became known as 'Lobbygate'. *The Observer* ran a story about Beattie Media, a PR and lobbying company. Kevin Reid, John Reid's son, worked for them, as had Jack McConnell before becoming an MSP. The allegations centred on Kevin Reid's boasts of being able to get access to McConnell, along with Reid's boss, Alex Barr, who claimed access to other ministers.

McConnell was left with questions against his character and judgement, commenting, 'It was then like a steamroller that I didn't see coming and I couldn't stop it' (Watson 2001: 48). It led to a public spat between Donald Dewar and John Reid, who had become, after Dewar, Secretary of State for Scotland, at the British Labour conference. Lorraine Davidson put it in context: 'The Lobbygate row ignited because the accusations went to the heart of what Scotland's new democracy was meant to stand for – openness and transparency' (Davidson 2005: 108). Perhaps even more than that, it 'dramatically exposed some private aspects of "public life" in Scotland and the issue of "cronyism" in public life' (Schlesinger et al. 2001: 244). These were to become defining features about public life and the Labour Party in Scotland.

At the end of October, Wendy Alexander announced her intention to abolish Section 28/Clause 2A, preventing the 'promotion' of homosexuality in Scottish schools. This led to a divisive controversy which had all the characteristics of a 'cultural war', with a 'Keep the Clause' campaign funded by businessman Brian Souter, who called and organised an unofficial national referendum which on a 34.5% turnout produced an 86.8% vote against repeal.

There were numerous high-profile interventions, including Cardinal Winning, head of the Catholic Church in Scotland, other religious leaders, and the Labour-supporting *Daily Record*, in which Tom Brown asked, 'When did Scotland vote for pink politics?' (*Daily Record*, 16 December 1999). Catherine Macleod, writing of the role of the *Daily Record* in this, reflected, 'Scottish Labour has been stunned, like rabbits in the headlights, as the "Record" has in turned poured ridicule, contempt and condemnation on the party's performance' (*The Herald*, 14 March 2000).

All of this contributed to Labour anxieties about its relations with the Catholic Church, the concerns of Catholic Labour voters, and the social conservatism of many older Labour voters. This crystallised into the concerns of the three 'Big Macs': Tom McCabe, Jack McConnell and Henry McLeish. They indicated that they had concerns about the worries of Labour voters, particularly in parts of the West of Scotland and Lanarkshire, and they felt these should be listened to. There were allegations of briefings against the repeal of the clause in the press, and angry exchanges in the Labour Group of MSPs.

This was not Scotland's, or Scottish Labour's, finest hour, but eventually the clause was abolished. In the middle of the campaign, the Scottish Parliament's first by-election occurred in March 2000 in Ayr. John Scott for the Tories defeated Labour, turning a Labour majority of twenty-five into a Conservative majority of 3,344 over the SNP, with Labour reduced to third place.

On 17 July 1999, in a surprise announcement, Alex Salmond decided to stand down as SNP leader after a decade in charge. The SNP and Salmond had found it difficult to adjust to the politics of devolution. The transition to becoming a professional political party and the politics of effective, constructive opposition, mixing tactical and strategic intelligence, had proven a major strain. Salmond's style as well had not helped matters, and in September, John Swinney defeated Alex Neil in what was to prove an interregnum.

Donald Dewar had been seriously ill earlier in the year and in May 2000 had open heart surgery, taking time off afterwards to recoup while Jim Wallace deputised for him as First Minister and Henry McLeish took over Labour Party responsibilities. Wallace proved able in the role, but McLeish was visibly put out, as he later commented: 'I admit it was sometimes frustrating to be minding the Labour shop and looking after the party's interests in the coalition government without recognition.' As he added and was later to

101

rectify, 'there was no official position as Deputy Leader of the Scottish Labour Party' (McLeish 2004: 121).

Dewar returned to work but on 10 October he fell outside Bute House, Edinburgh, and suffered a brain haemorrhage. He died the following day at Edinburgh's Western General Hospital. It was a massive moment for Scottish politics, the Parliament, Labour, but even more for Scotland. It was a loss which palpably put Dewar's contribution to public life in proper context, for all his faults and quirks. Campbell reflected, 'He could be maddening at times with his old-fashioned ways, but he was a truly solid citizen and he had been a great help to me so many times' (Campbell 2011b: 410).

Labour quickly decided that the timescale of the Parliament electing a First Minister made it impossible to hold a full election with the widest franchise. Instead of holding an electoral college of MPs, MSPs and MEPs, trade unions and affiliated members, and individual party members, the party chose to hold an election based on a mini-electoral college made up of fifty-four Labour MSPs and twenty-seven members of the party executive. One MSP remembered that 'none of us knew what was going on. The leadership just made it up as it went along' (interview). A former Labour advisor believed 'that the party was under enormous pressure to speed things along and get a new leader which no one seemed to question' (interview). This was to prove a controversial and telling decision: on the one hand, the nearest Scottish Labour was to get in the first decade of the Parliament to a democratic contest, and on the other, by restricting it to the party selectorate, aiding any candidate backed by the party leadership and discriminating against any other challenger.

Dewar's funeral took place on 18 October 2000 at Glasgow Cathedral. It was a moving, almost state, occasion and featured an emotional peroration from Gordon Brown which Campbell thought 'very powerful, very socialist, more of the Old Labour than the New' (Campbell 2011b: 433). Brown stated:

> Donald's achievement is much more than a Parliament. Much more than the sum of his social reforms. It is that he ennobled the very idea of service and by his pursuit of a just society, he gave moral purpose to our public life. (Brown 2000: 41)

There were numerous other moving tributes, some with humour and reflections on Dewar's eccentricities, all deeply sad and filled with individual and collective loss. Dewar's death left his legacy naturally incomplete; he had been First Minister for less than a year and a half, but in that time a whole host of changes had happened which changed Scotland fundamentally. Peter Jones commented that there were 'three facets' to Dewar's thinking: 'social justice, radical reform, modernisation'. He quotes Dewar on the latter: 'Modernisation matters now. There is no time. But there are those who would waste it' (Jones 2005: 165). This seems an overstatement: Dewar was not a moderniser in the sense Jones means the term, but a traditional Labour centre-right politician, someone who operated within the political framework of 'Gaitskellism', the moderate social democracy which took its name from Hugh Gaitskell, Labour leader, that he and John Smith embraced in their student days at Glasgow University (McSmith 1994: 18–21).

Wendy Alexander, who worked with Dewar as a special advisor and minister, asked why Scotland suffered what she called a 'devolution hangover' under his leadership answered:

> The explanation lies in Scotland's collective ill-preparedness and the absence of a shared vision for the post-Parliament world as well as misplaced and contradictory expectations. (Alexander 2005: 213)

Alexander then listed fifteen measures Dewar advanced in his three years as Secretary of State for Scotland and First Minister. It is an impressive list: a new social justice strategy, land reform, housing reform, abolition of tuition fees, action on anti-social behaviour, Freedom of Information and much more. She called it 'a remarkable record for such a short tenure' and asked 'what difference has devolution made?' and answered 'a reforming legacy' (ibid.: 218). She commented that Dewar's 'creed of social justice and economic efficiency altered little throughout his long political career . . .' (ibid.). This is a more accurate analysis than trying to label Dewar, in the terms of today's political discourse, a 'moderniser'. But what this apposite analysis does not touch on is the role of Scottish Labour and Scottish social democracy in the post-Parliament environment.

The Accidental Leader: Henry McLeish

After Donald Dewar's funeral on 18 October, later that same day Henry McLeish was told by Angus MacKay, MSP for Edinburgh South and one of his supporters, of information from the McConnell camp that McConnell would not be standing for the leadership. This was a deliberate campaign of disinformation to wrong-foot McLeish. The next day by 9.00am McConnell had personally emailed every single Labour MSP announcing that he was standing.

McLeish and McConnell only had between 19 and 21 October to fight a mini-contest with a mini-electorate. McLeish reflected:

> The leadership contest after Dewar's death was something no one had expected or wanted, and I was very ill-prepared, both mentally and politically. Curiously, because of my lack of confidence earlier in life and because of my attitude of always doing things on my own I may have been a bit naïve. (McLeish 2004: 125)

In a clear swipe at McConnell, he referred to his own lack of engagement in plotting and positioning during Dewar's short period as First Minister:

> Unlike others, I was not fired up by the minutiae and intrigue and was not into the cronyism which is a major factor in Scottish Labour politics. I was not from Lanarkshire or the West of Scotland and had not been involved in continually wooing MSPs. (McLeish 2004: 125)

This was the perception many of Jack McConnell's colleagues had of him. Lorraine Davidson, writing in McConnell's biography, commented on the previous year, 'Most of the time, Dewar did not mind the jockeying for position within his team because he felt secure in his post' (Davidson 2005: 118). This is putting a gloss on what had really happened; the jockeying did hurt and undermine Dewar; he did mind it and it did hurt the reputation of Labour, the Scottish Executive and Parliament.

There was of course little substantial difference between McLeish and McConnell. The latter was keener to invoke the image of 'modernisation', the former put himself forward as the continuity candidate. Gordon Brown commented, speaking to Alastair Campbell, 'He said McLeish was not perfect but with Wendy Alexander as Number 2 he would be fine. He was worried about McConnell and said Reid would wind him up.' There was also the fear that 'Jack would flirt with neo-nationalism' (Campbell 2011b: 430).

The short contest had its moments of drama. Frank McAveety, a junior minister, came out for McConnell then recanted, thus damaging himself and McConnell. It became clear that all Scottish Labour Executive ministers would support McLeish and no one endorse McConnell, and given the small size of the electorate this would be a significant factor in the outcome. The final result was forty-four for McLeish and thirty-six for McConnell, showing that while McLeish had taken and secured 'the payroll vote', McConnell had polled impressively among Labour backbenchers and the party (*The Scotsman*, 22 October 2000). It was a result which showed, for all the absence of burning political issues dividing the party, that Labour was deeply divided on personality and style. The result was not going to make easy Henry McLeish's period as First Minister.

McLeish was elected First Minister by the Parliament on 26 October and then three days later began a mini-ministerial reshuffle. The main changes were that Jack McConnell went to Education, Wendy Alexander to Enterprise and Lifelong Learning, and Sam Galbraith to Environment, Sport and Culture, while two of McLeish's supporters were rewarded with Cabinet posts: Angus MacKay with Finance and Jackie Baillie with Social Justice (*The Scotsman*, 30 October 2000). In a significant party move, drawing from McLeish's experience with Dewar, the post of Scottish Labour Deputy Leader was created, which Cathy Jamieson won without an election. An erstwhile left-winger and Campaign for Socialism member, she was thought to offer a political shield for McLeish from the left.

A number of by-elections occurred towards the end of the year. In November, Glasgow Anniesland held simultaneous Scottish Parliament and Westminster contests following Dewar's death. Bill Butler won the Scottish Parliament seat with a 5,376 majority over the SNP, while John Robertson retained the Westminster seat with a 6,337 majority over the Nationalists (*The Scotsman*, 25 November 2000). These were both comfortable majorities, but the party had more trouble in the Falkirk West Westminster by-election following Dennis Canavan's resignation from the Commons. Canavan had, after Dewar's death, discussions with Gordon Brown and Henry McLeish on rejoining Labour, but had decided to remain as an independent in the Scottish Parliament (Canavan 2009: 277). Labour's Eric Joyce, a high-profile and controversial local choice, ex-military and an ultra-moderniser, saw Labour's majority slashed from 13,783 to a slender 705 (*The Scotsman*, 23 December 2000). The SNP's failure to win the seat, given Labour's many difficulties, was seen as a major missed opportunity.

Henry McLeish wanted to advance an ambitious agenda for Scotland and make his mark. His vision was of 'a confident, competitive and compassionate Scotland', addressing some of its key challenges such as its declining workforce and aging population (McLeish 2004: Ch. 12). One of the ways he thought of addressing the latter was through free care for the elderly.

McLeish found himself in a position where, as he puts it himself, 'The development of the policy within the Scottish Executive was certainly not a textbook example of government at work.' Instead, it was 'messy' and 'bedevilled by leaks'; called by many 'Making Policy on the Hoof', McLeish reflects, 'I am not sure it was even that sophisticated' (McLeish 2004: 141). The Sutherland Royal Commission on Care had been dismissed by the UK Government, yet there had been no real Scottish debate. Dewar had been opposed, as was Susan Deacon, the Health Minister, the Scottish Labour Group of MSPs along with Labour MPs, while the Scottish Lib Dems were in favour. McLeish put it, 'All the political parties in Scotland, with the exception of Labour, supported the Sutherland Report and so did overwhelming public opinion. So who was out of step?' (McLeish 2004: 145). The policy adoption raised numerous questions about the evidence base of policy and its sustainability, along with important distributional questions. As crucial was the politics: it had revealed a deeply divided Labour Party on a number of levels, one between MSPs and MPs, with some of the latter scathing in their contempt and disdain for the former. For a more detailed discussion of the political and policy dimensions, see Chapter 11.

Labour divisions were not completely straightforward. The public language was of 'Team McLeish', but the reality was very different. Weekly Cabinet meetings showed the fault-lines and fractures, with Jack McConnell judged by some of his colleagues as not a 'team player', McConnell feeling isolated, and Henry McLeish not trusting him or feeling he could sack him. Labour colleagues felt McConnell was the source of press briefings about them and their discussions, while McConnell felt some of his colleagues, Angus MacKay and Jackie Baillie in particular, had been given 'special permission' to undermine him.

Another political storm broke when Tom McCabe, Parliament Business Manager, floated the idea of calling the McLeish administration 'the Scottish Government'. This brought forward the following comment from an unidentified Scottish Labour MP: 'They can call themselves the White Heather Club if they want but they will never be the Scottish Government.' An unnamed UK minister said, 'Henry has made a fool of himself. The problem with Henry is that he is thick, and not a proper thinking politician.' McLeish not surprisingly backtracked, leading Tom Brown to observe, 'McLeish is accused of trying to undo the late Donald Dewar's more cautious approach to devolution' (*New Statesman*, 22 January 2001).

Then on 6 June 2001 Labour won for the first time its second UK consecutive term with an overall working majority of 167, only slightly reduced from 179 in 1997. The Scottish result showed little change from four years previously, Labour's vote falling a little from 45.6% to 43.2%; the party's number of seats showed no real change, falling from fifty-six to fifty-five, as Michael Martin went from Labour to being counted as 'The Speaker'. The only real change in Scotland's seventy-two constituencies was the SNP's loss of Dumfries and Galloway by seventy-four votes to the Conservatives. The SNP fell back to 20.1%, the Lib Dems rose to 16.4%, while the Tories, although winning a seat, fell back in votes to 15.6% (Mitchell and Bradbury 2002).

Sam Galbraith stood down as a Scottish minister, MP and MSP; Brian Fitzpatrick held Strathkelvin and Bearsden in a by-election held on the same day as the UK general election, with Labour's majority reduced from 12,121 to 7,829, with independent Jean Turner in second place. Fitzpatrick had narrowly beaten the NUM's Nicky Wilson by two votes for the Labour candidature, with David Martin, an MEP for seventeen years, vetoed by Labour's London NEC (*The Herald*, 28 March 2001). A Banff and Buchan Scottish Parliament by-election was held as well following Alex Salmond's resignation as SNP leader, seeing Stewart Stevenson elected with an 8,567 majority over the Conservatives.

In the aftermath of the election, Henry McLeish and Helen Liddell, the latter of whom had been appointed Secretary of State for Scotland in January, were caught on mic talking about their colleagues. Liddell called John Reid 'a patronising bastard', with McLeish saying 'He really is'. McLeish commented of Brian Wilson that he was 'a great communicator', but that he 'spends most of his time in bloody Dublin' (*The Scotsman*, 9 June 2001).

Blair's second term was to be dominated by the development of his 'choice' agenda and marketisation of public services, and, even more starkly, the 9/11 attacks on New York by al-Qaeda and the resulting 'war on terror'.

In October 2001, Henry McLeish became embroiled in a scandal which became known as 'Officegate' about rental arrangements in his constituency office in Glenrothes, Fife. What hurt McLeish more than the substance of the allegations was his inability to establish a definitive version even to his staff, let alone publicly, explain it and close it down as an issue. It was, in his own words, 'a muddle, not a fiddle' (*BBC News*, 13 November 2001).

The substance of the issue was McLeish subletting his constituency office to a range of bodies: Digby Brown solicitors, the local council and a local charity. What finally brought McLeish down was a combination of a number of events, the first of which was a disastrous BBC *Question Time* performance during which he admitted to the chair, David Dimbleby, 'I don't know how much money was involved' (*The Scotsman*, 2 November 2001). Previously the same day he had paid back £9,000 and claimed that this had been agreed with the House of Commons Fee Office. The following week, on 6 November, McLeish presented to the media what he claimed was a full account of all his sublets. He called it an 'honest mistake' and offered to pay back a further £27,000 to the House of Commons, bringing the total amount of subletting since 1987 to £36,122 (*BBC News*, 6 November 2001). He subsequently found another sublet that he and his staff had missed, to a small local charity (*The Scotsman*, 7 November 2001).

McLeish was faced with no option but to resign as First Minister. Even at the last minute Jackie Baillie, one of his key supporters, tried to persuade him to change his mind, a position Baillie would later find herself in with another Scottish Labour leader. On 8 November, McLeish's resignation was announced to the Scottish Parliament with a letter from him to Presiding Officer David Steel, followed by a personal statement later the same day by McLeish (*BBC News*, 8 November 2001). McLeish later reflected, 'My feeling of frustration was increased by the knowledge that I had not knowingly done anything wrong' (McLeish 2004: 8). This was accurate, yet had an element of denial and naïvety. One Labour former minister believed that 'McLeish could have survived if he had organised things better, but then the entire McLeish period was shaped by an accident-prone leadership' (interview).

The whole episode exposed the underbelly of the shady manner of networks and arrangements which characterised the local Labour state, one of the party, local government, trade unions and sympathetic businesses and third-sector bodies, with blurred boundaries and little recognition of conflicts of interests. The Scottish Parliament was just two and a half years old, but found itself having to find its third First Minister and Scottish Labour leader. It was in this context that the Scottish party looked to find a sense of re-assurance. What many Scottish Labour politicians yearned for was a period of calm and stability where there was less disruption and constant change. Some wished for a quieter life with a less difficult media and public responsibilities, while others in Westminster wanted to see the Scottish Parliament cut down to size, regarding the whole project as either a diversion or a mistake. Any future leader would have to tread a difficult path balancing all of these and more competing forces in Scottish Labour.

Chapter 7

The Politics of Stability and the Slow Demise of New Labour

The Third Man: The Coming of Jack McConnell

Henry McLeish's resignation left the door open for McConnell to become Scottish Labour leader in the Scottish Parliament and First Minister. There was the issue of whether McConnell would face a challenge from any of his colleagues. Wendy Alexander was the obvious person to stand against McConnell. She was widely seen as 'Brown's candidate', had an agenda – modernising, challenging, pro-enterprise – and she and McConnell had a history of antagonism; she also had a reputation for a formidable intellect but poor political instinct.

Alexander was weighing up whether to stand while many of her supporters had already gone public. She then decided she did not want to, citing as one of her reasons that she thought she 'would win', in the process leaving her supporters exposed and vulnerable. A second candidate emerged in Malcolm Chisholm, who could not get enough nominations. McConnell's camp debated whether to give Chisholm enough support to produce a contest. This did not happen. The challenger of the previous year had become the candidate of the establishment and party machine; last year democracy was vital, now it was seen as an irrelevance and troublesome.

The only other obstacle that McConnell faced was his decision to hold a press conference and admit that he had in the past had an affair, the reasoning being to take the disclosure out of the hands of the media and it blowing up out of control, sinking his candidature. This was a 'high risk strategy' (Davidson 2005: 142). Bridget McConnell, Jack's wife, announced her support at a high-profile press conference, chaired by Andy Kerr, MSP for East Kilbride. It was a success, but the press the next day chose to put their emphasis on her comment that her husband, Jack, had 'betrayed her trust' (*The Scotsman*, 14 November 2001).

On 17 November, McConnell became Scottish Labour leader and on 22 November First Minister. He then began engaging in a reshuffle which became known as 'the morning of the long knives'. Elements of 'Team McLeish', along with prominent Wendy Alexander supporters, were sacked, while several of Jack McConnell's supporters were promoted into the Cabinet. Five ministers went: Jackie Baillie, Angus MacKay, Tom McCabe and Sarah Boyack were all sacked; Susan Deacon was offered Social Justice, refused and resigned. In came Cathy Jamieson at Education, Andy Kerr at Finance, Mike Watson at Tourism, Culture and Sport, and Patricia Ferguson as Parliament Business Manager, while Malcolm Chisholm went to Health, Iain Gray was rewarded with Social Justice, and Wendy Alexander had her portfolio expanded to Enterprise, Transport and Lifelong Learning, causing a public spat with McConnell. Sources close to the First Minister called Alexander 'an extremely stupid woman', while she responded that there 'would be hell to pay' (*The Scotsman*, 18 November 2001). Sam Galbraith commented on McConnell, 'He is a typical town council fixer – he can't help himself' (Davidson 2005: 232). Another former minister commented that 'the day of Jack's election as First Minister was the moment the party rebels became the new establishment and we found out they weren't young turks anymore' (interview).

On the day of his election as First Minister, McConnell talked of his ambition and the scale of change he wanted to see. He talked of a Scotland where young people still leave school without qualifications and self-confidence: 'This is what makes me angry. And it needs to change. Lewis Grassic Gibbon said that anger is at the root of all change – but anger must be balanced. Too much anger and you're incapable of change, not enough and you don't really want it' (Scottish Parliament, 22 November 2001).

McConnell attempted to reflect on the lessons and mistakes of the Dewar and McLeish periods, commenting, 'We've spent too much time on politics and not enough on government, although the civil service machine has found it difficult to move away from government to politics and there's sometimes been a clash' (*Sunday Herald*, 25 November 2001). He began to articulate his philosophy of 'doing less better' and prioritising the myriad activities of the Scottish Executive, laying out five themes in January 2002: health, education, transport, crime and jobs. It was a conspicuous attempt to move away from the themes and buzz words associated with New Labour to a more 'bread and butter' agenda.

McConnell had previously established a reputation as dynamic and ambitious, and in the first year of the Parliament penned an essay, 'Modernising the Modernisers', in which he laid out some of his thinking, writing, 'Even the word "modernising" may spark fear and suggest treachery to many' and that, 'We have to move to the next stage of modernisation, what has been called "modernising the modernisation", reappraising the left's message . . .' (McConnell 1999: 69). He articulated a politics impatient at the inadequacies of contemporary Scotland:

> The truth about life in Scotland today is that existing public services fail too many working class communities for reasons of quality as well as quantity. Our education system fails children from poorer backgrounds, our health service is skewed in favour of the more prosperous households, and the environment is best where those who have most live. (ibid.: 68–9)

This voice of urgency and believing the existing state of affairs was not good enough, was one which McConnell held dear, but which was mostly missing from the public pronouncements and actions of his administration. One significant area where McConnell was to make a dramatic impact was electoral reform in local government. McConnell wanted to address this not just because the Lib Dems were in favour of it, but to set out a different kind of Labour agenda, and to challenge the old Labour fiefdoms and one-party councils across Scotland. The Local Government (Scotland) Bill was published before the 2003 elections, and after the elections a commitment to legislation was contained in the Labour–Lib Dem Partnership Agreement. Eventually the bill became law, despite significant opposition from Labour councillors and Labour COSLA colleagues. This was, putting it in context, a braver, bolder move than it now looks, put forward at a time when Charlie Gordon, Labour leader of Glasgow City Council, had unilaterally left COSLA and was fighting a two-front conflict with them and the Scottish Executive.

In May 2002, Wendy Alexander resigned as a minister feeling she had become over-burdened in her responsibilities, having become in the process known as 'the Minister for Everything'. Her departure from government saw Iain Gray succeed her and the Cabinet become more united than it had been previously. Alexander felt that serving for five years in government, working as a Special Advisor, and then under three First Ministers had taken its toil (*The Herald*, 4 May 2002). Others were more critical. *The Herald* stated, 'Her plans did not take others into account. Which business leader or senior executive in any other field could have behaved in such a way without incurring justifiable criticism?' (*The Herald*, 8 May 2002). Later it reflected, 'Lest there be any doubt, Wendy Alexander's departure from the Scottish Cabinet is a serious loss, certainly of more lasting damage than Henry McLeish's resignation last year' (*The Herald*, 11 May 2002). Iain Gray took the Enterprise, Transport and Lifelong Learning post, while Margaret Curran entered Cabinet for the first time leading Social Justice.

In a leaked letter to Jim Sillars, former SNP Deputy Leader, Alexander criticised the lack of ideas and vision in Scottish Labour, claiming that ministers were more interested in keeping their 'ministerial Mondeos' than anything else. She charged that the Scottish party was in crisis and had contributed little positive for years:

> I think the most relevant analogy for Scotland is that perhaps one of the last times the Labour movement in Scotland made a real intellectual contribution to the UK Labour Party was around the rapid growth of the Independent Labour Party following the establishment of 'Forward' newspaper in 1906. (*The Herald*, 1 October 2002)

She went on to make the general charge that:

> We have often spent so long obsessing about our constitutional choices that we have spent too little time reflecting on the sort of nation we wish to create. We are only a short way into the parliament and there is still much to achieve. (ibid.)

It was a damning indictment, leaked on the eve of the national Labour conference gathering and a keynote speech from Jack McConnell about the historic and contemporary contributions of 'Great Scots' to the wider Labour movement. Alexander's dismissal of the contribution of Scottish Labour for a century allowed most in the party to pour scorn on it, but within what had been a private letter there were a number of serious points about what Scottish Labour had actually positively contributed in ideas in a long time, and what was the party's vision for devolution and Scotland.

THE INEXORABLE MARCH TO WAR

The next year of British and international politics were dominated by the march to war with Saddam Hussein's Iraq and the Blair–Bush military axis. This had huge consequences for Scottish politics and was as divisive an issue in Scottish Labour as the rest of the party. On 16 January 2003, the first Scottish Parliament debate was held on Iraq, called because of an SNP anti-war motion. Tom McCabe invoked 'the sovereignty of the Westminster Parliament' to underline where power lay and said, 'Local authorities are free to debate the issues, as we are free to debate them, but we should never mislead the people of Scotland about our power to influence. The issue is reserved to the Westminster Parliament' (Scottish Parliament, 16 January 2003).

A Tavish Scott amendment was lost 67–51, with Labour anti-war rebels John McAllion, Pauline McNeill and Elaine Smith abstaining, while Gordon Jackson voted for the amendment; on Tommy Sheridan's motion only John McAllion voted for it from Labour; while the main SNP anti-war motion was defeated 67–51 with three abstentions, Gordon Jackson, Pauline McNeill and Elaine Smith, and one rebel, John McAllion.

A month later, on 15 February, as anti-war demonstrators the world over marched, more than 75,000 protested in Glasgow. The demonstration concluded at the Scottish Exhibition and Conference Centre where the Labour Party was holding a national conference. Tony Blair had to move the time of his speech for it not to coincide with the arrival of the marchers (*Sunday Herald*, 16 February 2003).

The second Scottish Parliament debate on Iraq took place on 13 March 2003, with a 62–57 vote against an anti-war motion with three abstentions. John McAllion's amendment to the motion saw six Labour MSPs support the anti-war position: Bill Butler, Susan Deacon, Cathy Peattie, McAllion, Pauline McNeill and Elaine Smith, with three abstentions: Gordon Jackson, Marilyn Livingston and Kate Maclean. McAllion stated in the Parliament, 'It matters to me that democracy should matter to the Scottish people', while George Reid, SNP MSP, invoked the call of the STUC for 'all silent MSPs to say where they stand'. Brian Fitzpatrick, Labour MSP, challenged what he saw as the distortions of the debate:

> People can cartoonise Tony Blair if they must, but he is no one's poodle. Regardless of their views, any honest person sees in Tony Blair a man who believes that he is doing what is right and necessary. (Scottish Parliament, 13 March 2003)

McConnell, in First Minister's Question Time the same day, treading a careful balancing act, declared that just as 'simplistic views are wrong in Washington and in Paris, they are wrong in this Chamber' (ibid.). Two days later, Malcolm Chisholm, having voted for the Labour loyalist and what some saw as the 'pro-war camp', did an about turn: 'I think, on reflecting on it, what happened was that I put loyalty to my colleagues before what I knew to be right' (*BBC News*, 15 March 2003). McConnell chose not to sack him, recognising the anti-war feeling in the party.

Robin Cook, former Foreign Secretary, resigned as Leader of the House of Commons on 18 March, saying in his resignation speech, 'I intend to join those tomorrow night who will vote against military action now. It is for that reason, and for that reason alone, and with a heavy heart, that I resign from the Government' (House of Commons, 18 March 2003). He questioned the existence of Iraq's Weapons of Mass Destruction and the scale and threat Saddam Hussein posed.

The following day the main anti-war motion was defeated in the Commons 396–217 with 139 Labour anti-war rebels, the largest backbench revolt in the age of modern party politics, with Blair's march to war underwritten by Conservative Party support. There were seventeen Scottish Labour rebels: Michael Connarty, Robin Cook, Ian Davidson, Frank Doran, George Galloway, David Hamilton, Jimmy Hood, Mark Lazarowicz, Iain Luke, John Lyons, Ann McKechin, John Robertson, Mohammed Sarwar, Malcolm Savidge, Gavin Strang, Bill Tynan and Tony Worthington; thirty Scots Labour MPs voted against the anti-war motion. John Reid, party chairman, said afterwards, 'It is now clear that Parliament has voted clearly to support the Government in its efforts to disarm Saddam Hussein' (BBC News, 19 March 2003).

Scottish Labour conference found itself happening at a time of huge political sensitivity and Labour Party opposition to the war. Labour at first tried to prevent any debate on Iraq but, when that failed, instead had a private debate with no vote taken. Jack McConnell said, 'We live in a free society and I would encourage the maximum possible debate on all of these issues. But I also want to make sure the conference this weekend does have a real debate about issues like health and education and business' (BBC News, 18 March 2003).

John Reid, party chairman, told the conference, 'We could have done nothing, we didn't do that and people are entitled to ask us to face the moral consequences of our actions, but please don't pretend there are no moral consequences of refusing to act' (BBC News, 22 March 2003). He tried to unify and focus the party on the impending Scottish Parliament elections: 'Make sure that it is another step in a unified effort in shaping a modern programme for progress based on [a] set of evolving values' (ibid.).

Labour anti-war supporters felt they had achieved something in forcing a debate, with John McAllion reflecting, 'It felt like being in the Labour Party again for the first time in years – to see the trade unions and constituency parties working together to try to get a grass roots view across and to say that the leadership can't tell them what to do or dragoon them into the sort of positions they don't want to be dragooned into' (ibid.).

A New Mandate

It was not exactly the ideal backdrop on which to open and fight an election campaign, but then Scottish Labour had little choice. The 2003 Scottish Parliament elections were to see both Labour and SNP fall back in popular support and parliamentary seats, while turnout fell below 50%, and the Scottish Greens and Scottish Socialists both made major breakthroughs.

Scottish Labour saw its constituency vote fall from 38.8% to 34.6%, a decline of 4.2%, while the SNP's fell from 28.7% to 23.9%, a decline of 4.8%; in the regional vote Scottish Labour's fell from 33.6% to 29.3%, down 4.3%, while the SNP went from 27.3% to 20.9%, down 6.4%. Labour's number of seats fell from fifty-six in 1999 to fifty, while the SNP's declined from thirty-five to twenty-seven, with the Scottish Greens winning seven seats, a rise of six, and the Scottish Socialists taking six, up five (Denver 2003). The surge of both radical parties was to give the Parliament its name as 'the rainbow Parliament'.

Labour's fifty seats were made up of forty-six constituency seats, where it had seven losses compared to 1999 (and six taking into account the Ayr by-election defeat in the 1999–2003 Parliament), and four regional list seats, a gain of one. These were made up of the following constituency losses: Edinburgh Pentlands where David McLetchie defeated Iain Gray; Edinburgh South, which the Lib Dems gained from Angus MacKay; Aberdeen North, an SNP gain from Elaine Thomson; Dundee East, an SNP gain from John McAllion; Strathkelvin and Bearsden, where Brian Fitzpatrick was defeated by independent Jean Turner by 438 votes; and Ochil, where George Reid defeated Richard Simpson.

Worryingly for Labour, its constituency losses and popular vote decline was across the political spectrum: Labour lost seats to the Conservatives, SNP, Lib Dems and an independent, while losing regional votes to the Greens and Scottish Socialists. The main factor which had prevented Labour's result looking worse or even losing was the decline in the SNP vote.

A post-election reshuffle saw Jim Wallace go to Enterprise and Lifelong Learning, and Cathy Jamieson take Justice, while Frank McAveety and Nicol Stephen took Cabinet seats on junior ministerial salaries at Tourism, Culture and Sport, and Transport respectively. Mike Watson was sacked, the only senior minister in the entire reshuffle. A month later, Alistair Darling became Secretary of State for Scotland, job-sharing with Transport, a sign of the post's diminished importance. One MSP commented 'that this was the point I began to have major doubts about Jack. What was he First Minister for?' (interview). A former advisor put it that there was 'a lack of Labour political intelligence, of how to govern politically', a charge they thought all the Labour–Lib Dem administrations were guilty of (interview).

The second Jack McConnell administration was characterised by a number of high-profile initiatives. One was the Anti-Social Behaviour etc. (Scotland) Act 2004, which was a populist and, to some, punitive set of measures. This shifted responsibilities for dealing with children in trouble from children's hearings to the courts. It faced major criticism from children's rights organisations and those working with young people (Cleland 2006). It was also a measure filled with paradoxes.

This legislation and other initiatives were championed and steered through Parliament by Cathy Jamieson, who had been head of a voluntary sector organisation (Who Cares? Scotland) which spoke out for young people in care. This agenda was popular with Labour's core vote, was repeatedly tested in focus groups, and went down well with West of Scotland working-class, older voters; where it did not go down well was with middle-class, liberal-minded voters. Leading advocates for this kind of politics alongside Jamieson were Margaret Curran and Johann Lamont; this seemed to symbolise the retreat of what was once a left politics and also what had become of Labour feminist politics, which had morphed into an espousal of moral authoritarianism.

A different tone was set by the Fresh Talent Initiative, launched in February 2004 as a deliberate attempt to address Scotland's different demographic challenges. The initiative allowed overseas students who had studied in Scotland to stay here after they had graduated for up to two years. Immigration is a UK reserved issue and agreement had to be reached with the Home Office before the scheme could go ahead. McConnell stated when launching it:

> . . . tackling our declining population is a priority for the Scottish Government which is why I want Scotland to be the most welcoming country in the world. Scots are renowned for being friendly, welcoming people. Scotland has a great quality of life, a fantastic environment, a first class education system. (McConnell 2004)

It had been quite an achievement in the age of New Labour's concerns on asylum and immigration to be able to launch such a policy. English universities were not happy, thinking that it could give Scottish universities a competitive advantage. In its first year 1,500 students from approximately seventy-five countries successfully applied (*The Scotsman*, 7 March 2006); in 2008 it was wound up with the arrival of a points-based immigration system.

McConnell was trying to find different issues to denote a different politics, support change and aid others pushing in the same direction. There was his St Andrew's Day speech of 2003 on the culture of Scotland which was seen as an important, thoughtful contribution. Other attempts were less successful; there was the launch of the Cultural Commission and with it a debate on 'cultural rights' and 'cultural entitlements'; the rebranding of Scotland as 'the best small nation in the world' attracted much scorn. On the other hand, McConnell's attempts to develop a Scottish international aid programme created a Scotland–Malawi Partnership focusing on development and tackling poverty that attracted many plaudits and created links between the two countries which are still flourishing (*BBC News*, 3 November 2005).

McConnell also wanted to address the long-running sore in Scottish society of the issue of sectarianism, what he called 'the nation's secret shame'.

McConnell, despite being a Lanarkshire MSP, was originally from Arran and had cut his political teeth in Stirling; part of what was taken as normal politics in the West of Scotland shocked him, and the collusion of elements of Labour with it. In February 2005, McConnell hosted a Scottish Government summit on sectarianism and the need to act in education, sports and marches and parades. Later in the year a review of marches and parades was published undertaken by John Orr. McConnell later reflected that he wished he had done more on the issue of sectarianism:

> I wished I had passed a Bill on Government action on sectarianism – we passed individual pieces of legislation to tackle sectarianism but we did not pull it all together and put duties on ministers to keep that work going . . . (*The Herald*, 15 May 2009)

The Euro elections of 2004 saw Labour win 26.4%, its lowest Euro vote ever, while the SNP won 19.7%, their lowest vote since 1999. Labour, SNP and Conservatives all won two seats each and the Lib Dems one, but the elections were seen as indicative that something had to happen in the SNP and John Swinney resigned as leader within weeks of the poll. In a three-way contest for the leadership Alex Salmond won 75.8% to Roseanna Cunningham's 14.6% and Mike Russell's 9.7%; Nicola Sturgeon won the deputy leadership with 53.9%. This was to change the fortunes of the SNP dramatically and wider Scottish politics, but for the meantime until the Scottish Parliament elections, Salmond as leader remained in Westminster and Sturgeon led the SNP in the Scottish Parliament (*BBC News*, 3 September 2004).

Jack McConnell reshuffled his ministerial team in October 2004, sacking Frank McAveety after he had turned up late for a Parliamentary Question Time. He moved one of his key allies, Andy Kerr, to Health, Patricia Ferguson to Tourism, Culture and Sport, and Malcolm Chisholm was presented as being 'demoted' in moving from Health to Communities (*The Scotsman*, 4 October 2004).

Two appointments stood out. Tom McCabe became Finance Minister; McCabe had been sacked in 2001, but had been allowed back as a junior minister for Health and Community Care, and now his competence and loyalty were rewarded. Margaret Curran, who had been seen as a significant success at Communities, was moved to Parliament Business Manager for very different reasons. In her period as a senior minister Curran had been the most high-profile minister apart from the First Minister, and was being widely talked about as a future leader. One view was that she was moved because she was increasingly seen as a threat to McConnell, another that her presentation skills would better suit the administration in her new post where she was dubbed 'Minister for *Newsnight*'. Recognition of Curran's impact in her previous job came the following month when she was awarded *The Herald*'s 'Politician of the Year' award (*The Herald*, 12 November 2004).

The UK general election of 2005 saw Labour returned with a much-reduced but workable majority of sixty-six seats. This was attained on a much lower 35.2% of the vote on a 61.5% turnout – a mere 21.6% of the electorate. Labour's problems post-Iraq, the growing unpopularity of Tony Blair and the increasing weariness of the public with the style and content of New Labour were all increasingly evident. Despite this, Labour had little prospect of losing, aided by the continued narrow appeal of the Tories and strength of the economy.

The Scottish campaign was fought against the backdrop of the reduction of Scottish Westminster representation from seventy-two to fifty-nine seats. Scottish Labour won 38.9% of the vote and forty seats, its vote falling 4.4% across Scotland compared to the previous Westminster contest and slightly less than the UK fall of 5.5%. While it had won fifty-five seats in the previous election, on the new boundaries this represented a fall of five seats.

The Lib Dems won 22.6% of the vote and eleven seats, the SNP 17.7% and six seats, and the Conservatives 15.8% and one seat. The Lib Dems gained East Dunbartonshire and Inverness, Nairn, Badenoch and Strathspey from Labour, the SNP Western Isles and Dundee East, and the Conservatives Dumfriesshire, Clydesdale and Tweeddale.

This was Jack McConnell's first UK election as First Minister, and Scottish Labour encountered difficulties around its different policies in Scotland and England. McConnell had to admit during the election that hospital waiting lists in Scotland could be twice as long as in England. This was widely seen as a 'gaffe' during the election (*The Scotsman*, 15 April 2005). It was also Alex Salmond's first election as leader of the SNP since his return, and the SNP, while seeing their vote fall, fought a focused campaign based on targeting key marginal seats, which paid dividends with their two gains – Western Isles and Dundee East (Denver 2005, Mitchell 2005).

It was also an election which witnessed the retiring of some of Labour's older generation of Westminster veterans. Tam Dalyell, George Foulkes, Brian Wilson and Helen Liddell were just a few of the thirteen Labour MPs standing down. Three Labour MPs, Jimmy Wray, Malcolm Savidge and Irene Adams, tried and failed to win selection in winnable seats. And then there was the special case of George Galloway, MP for Glasgow Hillhead, then Kelvin, from 1987 to 2005, who had been expelled from the Labour Party in 2003 over remarks on the Iraq war. Galloway now departed from Scottish politics and stood in the Bethnal Green and Bow London constituency against Labour's Oona King, where he was to prove successful.

Post-election there was some evidence of tension between Labour and the Lib Dems in Scotland. In the immediate aftermath, Jim Wallace announced that after thirteen years as Scottish Lib Dem leader and six as Deputy First Minister, he was standing down. The contest pitted Nicol Stephen against Mike Rumbles, with the former winning by an emphatic 77% to 23% (*BBC News*, 23 June 2005).

British politics were dramatically altered by the election of David Cameron as Conservative leader in December 2005, which coincided with Labour becoming increasingly unpopular. In February 2006 evidence of this was provided by the Dunfermline and West Fife by-election after the death of Rachel Squire. Labour was not aided by allegations of attempts to get the candidate the leadership wanted with 'evidence of a high-level "fix" to select [the Labour] candidate'. This had transpired because 'party bosses sent out a leaflet on behalf of Catherine Stihler's campaign hours before she was selected to fight the seat' (*Sunday Herald*, 29 January 2005). Stihler was subsequently chosen, but Labour's majority of 11,562 evaporated and was turned into a 1,800 majority for the Lib Dems' Willie Rennie.

The tragic death of Robin Cook in August 2005 forced a by-election in the Livingston seat. Labour defended a 13,097 majority and this was reduced to a 2,680 majority which saw Jim Devine returned to the Commons. On the same day, Glasgow Cathcart held a Scottish Parliament by-election following Mike Watson being charged and later found guilty of fire-raising. Labour yet again encountered problems with candidate selection when Jack McConnell let it be known that he would like to see Charan Gill, a local entrepreneur, become the party's candidate. However, he had only joined the Labour Party days before the deadline for applying to be considered a candidate, and was ruled ineligible by the Scottish Labour Executive (*The Herald*, 7 September 2005). Labour's Charlie Gordon, former leader of Glasgow City Council, won the seat, with the party's majority cut from 5,112 to 2,405.

In March 2006, one of the most significant public health measures in recent years came into force in Scotland: the smoking ban in public places. This had begun life as a SNP backbench motion tabled by Stewart Maxwell in July 2003 (building on work done by Kenny Gibson, SNP MSP, in the first Parliament), stating that he would bring forward a parliamentary bill in early 2004. The initial response of Labour was to oppose this measure, worried about practicalities and the effect on public houses. However, when the scale of public and expert opinion became evident, the Labour–Lib Dem Executive decided to back the idea and the legislation was passed on 30 June 2005. McConnell indicated his support and that of the Scottish Government:

It is clear that Scotland must not be held back by poor public health – the single biggest contribution devolved government can make is to reduce the toll of preventable death caused by smoking. (*BBC News*, 10 November 2004)

The Moray by-election in April 2006, following the death of SNP Margaret Ewing, was not in natural Labour territory, but the SNP won convincingly, and Labour fell from third to fourth, losing half their vote. At the same time, a YouGov poll commissioned by the SNP found that 56% of people agreed with the statement, 'The Labour Party has been in power too long in Scotland: it is time for a change' (*The Scotsman*, 18 April 2006).

Douglas Alexander became Secretary of State in May 2006, along with Transport Secretary. In a speech within days of being appointed he laid out his thinking. Speaking to a Press Club charity event in Glasgow, he said:

> The essential difference between myself and the Nationalists is this. They believe that what scars Scotland is the border with England. I believe that what scars Scotland is poverty, inequality and injustice. (*The Scotsman*, 20 May 2006)

This was an apt summary of Alexander's vision of the principle fault-lines in Scottish politics; whereas opponents would say that the Scotland scarred by 'poverty, inequality and injustice' was, more than anyone else's, Labour's Scotland.

McConnell gave the Annual John P. Mackintosh lecture in October in Haddington, East Lothian, arguing that the Scottish Parliament's current powers were sufficient: 'It can't be other than sensible for us to make the fullest use of those powers before demanding lots more.' To do so would invite 'a collective and wholly self-imposed inertia'; at the same time, McConnell invoked the idea of a 'union dividend' to explain how Scotland benefited from the union (*BBC News*, 24 October 2006).

With the Scottish elections approaching, several Labour politicians reached for apocryphal language in relation to the threat of the SNP at the Scottish Labour autumn conference in Oban. John Reid claimed that the SNP was not 'fit for purpose' (*BBC News*, 26 November 2006); Blair warned that an SNP victory would produce a 'constitutional nightmare' (*BBC News*, 24 November 2006).

Ministerial changes were forced on McConnell towards the end of 2006 with Peter Peacock resigning for health reasons and being replaced by Hugh Henry at Education (*BBC News*, 14 November 2006). More difficult politically, Malcolm Chisholm chose to voice his opposition to the UK Government's decision to replace Trident, and in a Scottish Parliament debate supported an SNP motion opposing a replacement to Trident, forcing his resignation as Communities minister (*BBC News*, 23 December 2006); he was subsequently replaced in the new year by Rhona Brankin, who had served in a number of capacities as a junior minister (*BBC News*, 7 January 2007).

A Scottish Watershed?

During the latter half of 2006 the SNP began to establish a lead over the Labour Party in both constituency and regional votes for the Scottish Parliament. This they maintained and reinforced in the first months of 2007, prior to the campaign proper. A TNS System 3 poll in March 2007 had the SNP on 39% to Labour's 34% on the constituency vote, and 36% to 25% on the regional vote; YouGov at the same time put the SNP on 36% to Labour's 27% on the constituency vote and 33% to 26% on the regional vote.

Labour faced numerous difficulties as the campaign approached: Tony Blair's unpopularity, Alex Salmond's relative popularity versus Jack McConnell, and Labour divisions at both a Scottish and British level. The party would face significant challenges with its traditional trade union supporters, business, and how it dealt with the media and its main opponents, the SNP.

In the middle of the election campaign, the STUC General Council passed a motion endorsing Labour which was to be presented to the Annual Congress by one vote, 14–13. The motion stated that Labour in office in Scotland was 'in the best interest of Scottish workers'. The TGWU and Amicus supported it, but several unions including Unison and the PCS, along with the Fire Brigades Union, UCU university lecturers and RMT opposed it; significant factors in the unprecedented scale of opposition were Labour's promotion of PFI/PPP and privatisation (*The Scotsman*, 17 April 2007).

McConnell told the STUC the following day, in what was widely seen and reported as a lacklustre speech which enticed a 'lukewarm response' from delegates:

> Last week Alex Salmond had the opportunity to debate with me and spell out his priorities. He was given the choice between education, the economy and independence. He chose independence. (*The Herald*, 18 April 2007)

The party was facing problems in the other direction support-wise: attempting to utilise in New Labour style the business community in support of its cause. This was worse on two fronts; business endorsements for Labour were few and far between and meagre compared to the rich pickings of 1997 and 1999. Michelle Mone, Glasgow entrepreneur, was one of the few to go public, threatening to leave Scotland if the SNP won. Even more seriously, Labour now had to compete on this terrain with the SNP, who published a list of their own business supporters including such prominent public figures as Sir George Mathewson, former chairman of the Royal Bank of Scotland.

Labour also encountered problems with the media, with several newspapers endorsing Alex Salmond and the SNP. Only the *Daily Record* could be completely relied on to propagate the party message without apology. It adopted in what were desperate times a number of key messages: Gordon Brown would soon replace Tony Blair as Prime Minister; emphasising the qualities of Gordon Brown versus Alex Salmond, which was an implicit criticism of McConnell; and stressing the importance of the union and the dangers of separatism.

Labour's campaign was characterised for the third Scottish election in a row by an abrasive anti-Nationalist message. Gordon Brown and Douglas Alexander, as in 1999, published a pamphlet on the progressive case for the union and challenging the appeal and logic of Scottish nationalism (Hassan 2009b). They confidently asserted, 'The union in 2007 is founded on social justice' (Brown and Alexander 2007: 25).

This election found Scottish Labour caught between the tensions of Blair and Brown, as Jack McConnell observed afterwards:

> The Labour Party in Scotland was actually in better shape than it had been for a while. But that battle plagued the Scottish campaign for months. We started to feel as if we were swimming against a tide, we were on the back foot. (Torrance 2010: 239)

The SNP's positive campaigning tone and message, involving a change in what Alex Salmond himself described as 'his mindset', the party's campaigning strategy and that of its candidates, not only caught the public mood, but wrong-footed Labour, playing to its old messages of Nationalist caricatures. McConnell reflected on this:

> During the campaign itself they [the SNP] picked up on the fact that Scots wanted to hear positive stuff so they ran with a very positive campaign and we ended up on the other side of that, sounding negative. (ibid.)

Voters noticed these differences. When asked in the post-election Scottish Election Survey to assess the campaign tones of the different parties, Labour came out as the most negative and the SNP as the most positive. Only 20% of voters thought Labour ran a positive campaign, whereas 59% thought it negative; the Conservatives and Lib Dems were in the middle ground with 36% and 35% respectively positive ratings; the SNP were seen as positive by 51% and negative by 29% (Johns et al. 2010: 128).

Then there was how the leaders were seen. In 1999 Labour had Donald Dewar, in 2003 Jack McConnell faced John Swinney, but now he faced Alex Salmond. In March 2007, when YouGov asked the public who would make the best First Minister out of all the party leaders, Salmond was on 31% to McConnell's 18% (*The Daily Telegraph*, 30 March 2007). Later in the campaign, YouGov found ratings of Salmond on 35% to McConnell's 23% (*The Sunday Times*, 22 April 2007). An earlier poll at the end of 2006, when voters were forced to choose between the two leaders, found Salmond beating McConnell by 54% to 27% (*The Herald*, 23 November 2006). One Labour MSP commented that 'McConnell's ratings given he had been First Minister for six years were a big problem' (interview).

The April 2007 YouGov poll found Salmond ahead on every positive. He led on who stands up for Scotland (55% to 24%), intelligent (33% to 22%); while McConnell led on negatives: out of touch (29% to 12%), not leadership material (31% to 15%) and dull (28% to 14%) (*The Sunday Times*, 22 April 2007). Voters were becoming less Labour. The British Election Survey from 1974 had painted a consistent picture of Labour identification at or about 40% and Conservative long-term decline. But things were becoming less clear-cut at Holyrood in 2007, with Labour on 40% to the SNP's 30% on party identification, which narrowed to 27% to 21% when leaners were added (Johns et al.: 42). Labour voters were also becoming more pro-union and anti-independence; the number of Labour voters who supported independence fell from 16% in 2003 to an all-time low of 6% in 2007; while those supporting independence who voted Labour fell from 31% in 1992 to a new low of 6% (Johns et al.: 87).

The result when it emerged was close: the SNP won 32.9% to Labour's 32.2% of the constituency vote, the former a rise of 9.0%, the latter down 2.4%; the SNP won 31.0% to Labour's 29.2% in the regional vote, the former up 10.1% and the latter down 0.1%. The SNP won forty-seven seats to Labour's forty-six seats in the 129-member Parliament, the Highlands and Islands regional list giving the SNP their narrow parliamentary victory (Denver 2007).

The SNP gained twenty seats, including twelve constituency seats, mostly from Labour. The Nationalists won Kilmarnock and Loudoun, Glasgow Govan, Western Isles, Edinburgh East and Musselburgh, Livingston, Fife Central, Stirling, Dundee West and Cunninghame North, all from Labour, along with Argyll and Bute and Gordon from the Lib Dems and Falkirk West from 'independent'. Labour lost nine FPTP seats overall, the nine above and Dunfermline West to the Lib Dems, while retaking Strathkelvin and Bearsden from independent Jean Turner.

There was controversy over the 141,891 rejected votes: 85,644 constituency votes and 56,247 regional votes (*BBC News*, 9 May 2007). In Cunninghame North, Labour's Allan Wilson lost by forty-eight votes to the SNP's Kenneth Gibson, with 1,015 rejected ballots. Wilson threatened to take legal action, but none was forthcoming.

On the same day as the Scottish Parliament elections, the first elections under the STV system of proportional representation were held. Labour narrowly finished ahead of the SNP in votes by 28.1% to 27.9%, but the big change was in seats and control of councils. Labour went from 509 seats in 2003 to 348 in 2007, a loss of 161, while the SNP went from 181 to 363, an increase of 182. In the last FPTP elections of 2003, Labour won thirteen out of Scotland's twenty-nine mainland councils with overall majorities. Under STV this fell to two: Glasgow and North Lanarkshire (*The Herald*, 5 May 2007, Denver and Bochel 2007). The political map of Scottish local government had been changed overnight, and a swathe of Labour councillors removed at one stroke.

Some voices in the New Labour establishment attempted to argue that the Scottish election had been a great triumph for the party; of Labour nearly pulling off victory and the last Gordon and Tony show. This was the argument of Philip Gould, Blair's pollster, in *The New Statesman*, where he described the odds that had been stacked against Labour: 'From the start the polls were against us. One had us 12 per cent behind the SNP with only weeks to go; another had us lagging by 10 points.' Despite this, 'In the last few days our campaign pounded a double message of SNP risk and "come home to Labour". As we strengthened the SNP melted, and we were sure that we would win or come close' (Gould 2007).

Gould painted a picture of epic proportions, the Labour team with their backs to the wall fighting one last fight:

> This was a campaign that showed Labour at its best: Tony Blair magnificent, leading from the front, finding exactly the right words, always able to change the political weather. Gordon Brown like a tank, indomitable, raging against the possibility of defeat, generating ideas and implementing them with an energy that was breathtaking. (ibid.)

Douglas Alexander was 'pathologically determined to win', and finally there was:

> ... Jack McConnell, so often criticised, but who never showed the slightest loss of nerve, in the end finding a street-fighting demeanour that made Salmond's helicopter tours look arrogant and presumptuous. (ibid.)

Gould, for so long the sage reader of the public mood, had written a piece that seemed almost completely disconnected from political realities, and whose only point had seemed to be to serve the New Labour pantheon and idea of its own mythology. As far as analysis went, it would not take Scottish Labour far.

Tony Blair proved a much more reliable reader of the Scottish political mood, reflecting:

> I knew once Alex Salmond got his feet under the table he could play off the Westminster government and embed himself. It would be far harder to remove him than to stop him in the first place. (Blair 2010: 651)

The Scottish Parliament elections were a seismic result: a huge moment in the advance of the SNP, their first-ever national triumph. And it was equally a massive moment for Scottish Labour, the dominant force of Scottish politics for decades. Stephen Purcell, former leader of Glasgow City Council, reflected that 'the election was a huge wake-up call for the party which it hasn't fully heeded' (interview). How Labour and the SNP reacted would shape politics for many years to come. Was the SNP victory an aberration? Their best result had occurred when Labour were at their weakest, at the fag end of the Blair Government waiting for the handing on of the baton to the more astute (on Scottish matters), so the argument went, Gordon Brown. If this was the best the SNP could do when so many factors were in their favour, Labour had little to fear. Some even dared privately to think of the 2007 election as a 'blip', after which normal service would be resumed.

All of this would depend on how all the parties reacted to the result, how successful or not the SNP were in office, and the wider picture of British and even global politics.

CHAPTER 8

A Different Political Landscape: Scottish Labour in a Cold Climate

Two Labour Leaders, No Election Contests

The 3 May 2007 Scottish Parliament elections produced a cliffhanger of a result. The SNP seized the initiative with the final results declared on Friday at 5.32pm and Alex Salmond declaring victory at Prestonfield House, Edinburgh. Crucially, he did not actually declare victory, but gave the appearance of victory and of declaring victory. With their one-seat margin confirmed, Salmond and the Nationalists went on later that night to a victory rally at The Hub.

McConnell seems to have admitted to himself and others from the earliest possible moment that the party had lost and something major had happened. Not everyone had the same views. Some in the party wanted to cling to power; the election result after all had been inconclusive. Discussions between Gordon Brown and Menzies Campbell on whether a Labour–Lib Dem coalition could be put together and McConnell be persuaded to stay in office got little traction (Campbell 2008: 280). A consistent Labour line in public over the first few weeks was to call the election 'a draw', a line taken by Wendy Alexander and David Whitton, and a phrase which seemed to suggest some delay in acknowledging reality (BBC Newsnight Scotland, 10 May 2007).

After discussions with the Lib Dems and Greens failed to produce any basis for coalition, the SNP became Scotland's first-ever minority government. On 16 May 2007 Alex Salmond was elected First Minister by forty-nine votes to Jack McConnell's forty-six, winning the support of the two Green MSPs. Alex Salmond then announced his administration, now named 'the Scottish Government', with a slimmed-down Cabinet with Nicola Sturgeon as Deputy First Minister and Health Secretary and John Swinney as Finance Secretary.

Tony Blair had declared on 1 May in the dying days of the Scottish election campaign that he would announce his resignation as Labour leader the

126

following week (*BBC News*, 1 May 2007). The following week, on 10 May, Blair told Sedgefield Labour Party that he would stand down on 27 June (*BBC News*, 10 May 2007). Labour then agreed a timetable, with nominations opening on 15 May and closing on 17 May.

Gordon Brown became Labour leader and Prime Minister without a proper election, receiving 313 nominations; John McDonnell had twenty-four nominations and Michael Meacher twenty-one, both left-wingers and both short of the forty-five needed to stand; Meacher then withdrew and McDonnell ended up with a final tally of twenty-nine, still short. This resulted in Brown becoming Labour leader unchallenged, something his campaign deliberately intended. The only debate which had taken place in the non-contest had been a Fabian Society event where one view was that Brown 'had agreed to participate in order to be seen taking on the left, or as a counter to those who argued that he was left wing' (Richards 2010: 253); other Brownites thought any criticism of Brown was disrespectful and likely to damage the standing of New Labour – a continuation of the paranoia which had characterised much of the Blair–Brown era about the nature of the party.

When Brown became Prime Minister he embraced change: 'I have heard the need for change. Change in our NHS, change in our schools, change with affordable housing, change to build trust in government, change to protect and extend the British way of life. That change cannot be met by the old priorities (*BBC News*, 27 June 2010).

Gordon Brown's new Government saw Alistair Darling become Chancellor, Douglas Alexander move to International Development, and Des Browne become Secretary of State for Scotland along with Defence.

Alex Salmond's speech at the opening of Holyrood in the presence of the Queen was to many appropriate for the occasion, with him declaring, 'Your Majesty, it will not have escaped your notice that I am the first SNP First Minister that this Parliament has elected. I believe in the restoration of an independent Scotland. Others in this chamber take a different view.' Andy Kerr attacked Salmond's words as 'outrageous and appalling', whereas Tory leader Annabel Goldie called the speech 'statesmanlike' (*The Daily Telegraph*, 2 July 2007).

Jack McConnell resigned as Scottish Labour leader in the Scottish Parliament on 15 August and Wendy Alexander formally announced her leadership bid on 17 August. At a campaign launch, Alexander acknowledged that Scottish Labour had 'lost' and stated:

> In May the people of Scotland told us loud and clear they wanted change. They didn't whisper – they shouted it. So change we must. Change how we behave, change how we engage and change how we respond to the people we represent. (*BBC News*, 17 August 2007)

127

Labour had to – Alexander argued – heed the lessons of defeat:

> Iraq and cash for honours allegations played their part, but we would be fooling ourselves if we didn't recognise that we, in Scottish Labour, were also at fault in that defeat . . . (ibid.)

And she addressed why the party's opponents had won:

> The SNP didn't just win with slick presentational tricks. Nor did they win thanks to their manifesto. They won because they seized Labour's agenda of hope and aspiration. Well I'm here to tell you that we're going to seize it back. (ibid.)

By the time nominations closed, Alexander had support from forty-one out of forty-six MSPs, whereas any alternative candidate needed six nominations. The Alexander camp had deliberately gone out of its way to stop a contest, while the Campaign for Socialism could only find four supporters; the left-wing group had five MSPs as supporters, but could not persuade Patricia Ferguson to support an alternative candidate. Elaine Smith, MSP for Coatbridge and Chryston, argued that the party wanted a contest not a 'coronation' (*The Herald*, 22 August 2007).

Alexander, in a speech on the day nominations closed, attempted to find a language for Labour embracing the need for change:

> Sometimes the very hardest thing to do is admit you have to change. Labour in Scotland have done this. We have accepted we lost in May and that didn't happen by accident. (*BBC News*, 21 August 2007)

On 14 September, Wendy Alexander became Labour leader in the Scottish Parliament unopposed, and in her victory speech said, 'Under my leadership Scottish Labour will be a party of vision. A party of compassion. A party for all Scotland' (*BBC News*, 14 September 2007).

Already Alexander was ready to take the fight to the SNP: 'Under my leadership we will hold the SNP's minority administration to account for every broken promise and every pledge they fail to keep' (ibid.).

From this early point in the political cycle this was the Labour strategy towards the SNP Government: the constant incantation of 'broken promises'. Labour tabled a motion in the Scottish Parliament on the SNP in office in its first 100 days, with Iain Gray opening the debate and finding the new Government characterised by 'a string of broken promises and lame excuses'. Gray said of the SNP in office:

> They say that, if one is going to tell a lie, it might as well be a big one. In exactly the same way, if one is going to break a promise, it might as well be a big promise. (The Scottish Parliament, 4 October 2007)

Andy Kerr concluded the debate, stating of the Nationalist Government in its infancy, 'That is a record of lack of delivery and of misleading the Scottish public. It is the big lie at the heart of the SNP Government.' Wendy Alexander was missing from her first big parliamentary debate, while others noted the rather shrill tone of Labour, with Patrick Harvie, Green MSP, accusing Labour of 'bitterness, sniping and negativity' (ibid.).

The early days of the Brown Government enjoyed what was called 'a Brown Bounce', with Labour and Brown's personal ratings buoyed by the post-Blair era and Brown's initial success in articulating a different agenda. Labour's poll ratings contributed to talk of an early election, which the party did nothing to dispel. This built into a crescendo pre-Labour conference, with Douglas Alexander, election co-ordinator, and Ed Balls escalating election speculation. Instead, the Labour conference and the first days of the Conservative conference became 'the death knell for Brown's leadership' (Richards 2010: 293). George Osborne seized the political agenda with his proposals on inheritance tax reform, and Brown had to announce there would not be an election so he could develop 'his vision for the country' (*The Guardian*, 7 October 2007). Gordon Brown's premiership would never be viewed the same again.

ANOTHER LEADER IN CRISIS

Wendy Alexander, in a St Andrew's Day speech, made what was planned as a significant contribution to the constitutional debate. She stated that there was 'unfinished business' from the Scotland Act 1998 and that it was up to the pro-union parties to 'fix it', and went on:

> My objective is for Labour, in partnership with other major pro-union party leaders at Westminster and Holyrood, to establish an expert-led independent Scottish constitutional commission to review devolution in Scotland in ten years and develop a more balanced home rule package. (*BBC News*, 30 November 2007)

This would, Alexander argued, have a mandate from the Scottish Parliament, unlike the SNP Government's 'national conversation'. A key issue would be strengthening the 'financial accountability' of the Scottish Parliament:

> In short, the financing of the Parliament almost wholly through grant funding does not provide the proper incentives to make the right decisions. (ibid.)

This speech's impact had been lessened by the emergence of a story about the financing of Wendy Alexander's leadership campaign. At the same time, Gavin Yates, Scottish Labour's new head of communications, had described in a blog Wendy Alexander as 'abrasive', Andy Kerr 'simply uninspiring' and

Jack McConnell as First Minister as a 'lame duck leader' (*Sunday Herald*, 25 November 2007).

The week before, the *Sunday Herald* had raised the first allegations about Alexander's leadership campaign, claiming that every one of her campaign donations was under £1,000, allowing them not to have to be publicly declared (*Sunday Herald*, 18 November 2007). The following week, Alexander refused to say whether she had returned a leadership campaign donation of under £1,000 from a non-UK citizen living in the Channel Islands, a donation from a non-UK citizen and non-UK taxpayer being illegal (*Sunday Herald*, 25 November 2007).

The Labour Party checked the donation with Paul Green who had made the contribution, who lived in the Channel Islands and who was now publicly identified. Charlie Gordon, MSP for Glasgow Cathcart, resigned as Shadow Minister for Transport after it was revealed he had solicited the £950 donation to Alexander's campaign (*BBC News*, 29 November 2007). Tom McCabe stated, 'at the moment, there's been a breach of the law, as it stands'. He said of Alexander, 'She's clearly very upset that having secured the leadership and having done so successfully, this kind of distraction, I think, casts a shadow over this entire campaign' (*BBC News*, 29 November 2007). On St Andrew's Day, Alexander's speech was overshadowed by this gathering crisis, with Paul Green commenting that 'I am very angry after innocently becoming embroiled in a national controversy' (*BBC News*, 30 November 2007).

The story was to run for the next few months, dominating and destabilising Alexander's leadership. Tom McCabe, who had been Alexander's campaign manager, stated that only Charlie Gordon knew about the illegal contribution (*Sunday Herald*, 2 December 2007). Geoff Hoon, Labour Chief Whip at the House of Commons, said, 'she [Wendy Alexander] has to explain how this came about and what she knew at the time' (*Scotland on Sunday*, 2 December 2007).

Two Labour peers, Baroness Adams and Lord Maxton, both former MPs, complained to the police about having their identities and actions revealed after donating less than £1,000 (*Sunday Herald*, 2 December 2007).

The Electoral Commission then received what it called a 'huge amount' of documents and materials from Wendy Alexander's office (*BBC News*, 5 December 2007). Charlie Gordon, who had been under pressure to consider his position as an MSP, stated that he had made 'serious errors' in relation to political donations, but that he would 'stay on as Cathcart's MSP' (*BBC News*, 7 December 2007). The Scottish Parliament Standards Committee announced it would undertake an inquiry into Wendy Alexander's actions and, in particular, allegations that she broke Holyrood rules on MSPs using parliamentary facilities for party fundraising. The same day, Willie Haughey,

Glasgow businessman and a major donor to the Labour Party, declared that he would not be doing so 'if there is not complete transparency in political giving in the future' (BBC News, 9 December 2007).

Another facet of the crisis emerged in the new year when the Scottish Parliament Standards Commissioner Jim Dyer stated that any gifts in excess of £520 needed to be declared. Previously Alexander stated Parliament officials had said that donations to the leadership campaign did not have to be recorded in the MSP register of interests (BBC News, 1 February 2008). Alexander commented that, 'In every other leadership election campaign, they've not been construed as gifts' (BBC News, 3 February 2008).

In February 2008, the Electoral Commission declared that there was not sufficient evidence to be able to prosecute Wendy Alexander. The increasingly beleaguered leader stated at a press conference, 'I welcome the commission's decision that there is no basis for any finding of intentional wrongdoing on the part of me or my campaign team.' She went on, 'Personally this has been both a salutary and bruising experience. Some of the coverage has hurt me and caused distress to many entirely innocent friends, family and donors' (BBC News, 7 February 2008).

Yet another strand of allegations arose when it became public that Alexander channelled £12,000 from the Labour-supporting Scottish Industry Forum to fund her constituency office in 2002 and 2003. Alexander responded, 'I'm getting used to the mud slinging from events from six years ago' and said that, 'The Scottish Industry Forum made clear that they were the main Labour business organisation for more than a decade. They were part of the prawn cocktail offensive' (The Sunday Times, 10 February 2008).

In the following month the Crown Office stated that Alexander would not be prosecuted over failing to record donations. Margaret Curran, Shadow Health Minister and long-time Alexander supporter, was reported as calling her leadership 'shocking and appalling' (Sunday Herald, 9 March 2008).

The Scottish Labour conference in March saw Alexander attempt to develop a new agenda, setting out clear, defining lines between Labour and the SNP and challenging the latter's belief that they owned 'Scotland':

> Scotland is a country I love to the core of my being. However, 'Scotland' is not a political philosophy. 'Scotland' can just as easily be Adam Smith as it can be John Smith. The world over, politics comes down to a choice: right versus left, conservatives versus progressives, nationalists versus internationalists. (Alexander 2008)

Alexander attempted to invoke traditional Labour themes against the SNP: 'Cutting poverty against cutting taxes. Rewarding hard work versus unearned wealth. Socialist versus Nationalist' (ibid.). The speech became known as 'Red Wendy'. Given the pressures Alexander was under, it was not surprising that even she felt the compulsion to return to the party's comfort zones; political strategy and the future it was not.

After a quiet three months the controversy came centre-stage again in June 2008 when the Scottish Parliament Standards Committee voted by five to two that Alexander had broken parliamentary rules by failing to register donations. The following day the Standards Committee voted by four to three to ban Alexander from Parliament for one day. David Whitton, Labour MSP for Strathkelvin and Bearsden and parliamentary aide to Alexander, stated, 'They wanted her hung, drawn and quartered. The result of this ballot didn't actually mean anything – whether it's one day, a week, a year – it doesn't really matter' (BBC News, 26 June 2008). There was now in the Alexander camp a visible anger and sheer exhaustion in dealing with these issues; to the end Jackie Baillie, as with the Henry McLeish 'Officegate' scandal, tried to persuade Alexander to tough it out, and had been prepared to put her own reputation on the line in the media; none of it would prove to be enough.

Two days later, on 28 June 2008, Alexander announced after more than seven months of the story running 'with deep regret' her resignation as Scottish Labour leader. She called the Standards Committee decision 'partisan' and went on, 'My pursuers have sought the prize of political victory with little thought to the standing of the Parliament' (BBC News, 28 June 2008). Acknowledging that mistakes had been made, she said there had been a series of 'politically motivated complaints' against her, and reflected that those 'vexatious complaints' would continue as long as she remained Labour leader, saying, 'I cannot ask Labour supporters in Scotland for further forbearance' (Sunday Herald, 29 June 2008). Cathy Jamieson, Deputy Leader, stated, 'Ever since this process began, anyone who knows Wendy Alexander has not for one minute questioned her integrity' (BBC News, 28 June 2008).

In the aftermath most commentary acknowledged that Alexander and her campaign team had brought this on themselves. Academic John Curtice stated, 'the lesson of this story is that Wendy Alexander actually mismanaged dealing with the problem of her leadership finance campaign once the story emerged' (BBC News, 28 June 2008). What had this affair been about in the end? Had it been a micro-drama blown out of proportion by a Scottish media whose own take on politics was part of the problem? Others pointed to the murky world of Scottish Labour finances, which the McLeish affair had raised as well, and the lack of boundaries, conflicts of interest and a culture of patronage, deals and getting things done. It was also ironic that Alexander's campaign had been undermined by raising £17,000 when they were also doing all they could to prevent an open leadership contest. Thus, one of the defining features in this episode was the dominant culture within Scottish

Labour of fixing, manipulating and lack of democracy, and those in leadership positions colluding in rather than challenging this.

It did seem a very Scottish kind of scandal, and a very Scottish Labour one. Wendy Alexander, one of the party's brightest talents, had been cut down and diminished in a party that was hardly awash with talent. Kenny Farquharson went further: 'Her term as leader was flawed, but her vision for Scotland was sound . . . Wendy Alexander was right to resign. But her demise is a terrible setback for Scotland' (*Scotland on Sunday*, 29 June 2008). Iain Macwhirter suggested the party faced huge issues post-Wendy: 'To meet the Nationalist challenge, Labour has to detach itself from Westminster and become more of a Scottish party' (*Sunday Herald*, 29 June 2008). One MSP commented, 'Wendy had much of the right analysis, but she just ruffled too many feathers and challenged too many vested interests. And did so with a style and touch which led to her having to resign' (interview).

'Bringing It On': The Independence Question

While the Wendy Alexander mini-scandal obsessed a small coterie of the Scottish media, normal politics were continuing as usual. Alexander herself had taken the first steps in the establishment of what became the Calman Commission. Not content to rest there, she then proceeded to launch a bombshell on Scottish politics, announcing her support for an independence referendum, a U-turn on all previous statements she had made. With the famous words 'Bring it on', live on the BBC's *Politics Show*, Alexander hoped to recapture the initiative and disorientate the Nationalists, but instead destabilised her own side.

There then followed an intense period of confusion, with it becoming clear that Alexander had not agreed with Brown on the way forward; Scottish Labour MPs were incensed, calling it 'a freelance operation' (*The Daily Telegraph*, 5 May 2008). Gordon Brown at Prime Minister's Question Time refused to support Alexander's call, and even denied she had called for an independence referendum. Afterwards Brown and Alexander spoke to attempt to establish a common line; Alexander critics labelled her 'bendy Wendy' over the affair, while Brown was seen as 'losing touch with reality' (*The Independent*, 8 May 2008). At First Minister's Questions, Alexander announced, 'I'm not the problem' (*BBC News*, 8 May 2008), leading *The Scotsman* to wonder whether Brown was 'losing his grip on Scotland' (*The Scotsman*, 9 May 2008).

Alexander's policy change ostensibly had the support post-announcement of the Scottish Labour Group of MSPs, but it could not be said to be enthusiastic, and it had raised the wrath of many Scottish Labour MPs, particularly those who detested the Scottish Parliament. With numerous twists, turns and re-interpretations over a short period of time, Scottish Labour on one count had six different policies on an independence referendum in as many weeks. Post-Alexander's leadership, the party reverted to its traditional anti-independence referendum stand. One former Labour advisor viewed that 'Wendy got it absolutely right on independence on the substance, but the tactics were a disaster' (interview).

Alexander had been typically right on the substance of the issue, but displayed a poor grasp of strategy and tactics. She had mixed up a desperate attempt to save her leadership and regain the political initiative with the biggest issue in Scottish politics. The brief pro-independence ballot stance of Scottish Labour had ruffled the feathers of many in Scottish politics. Scottish Labour MPs hated it and played a part in seeing it undermined and ridiculed. Gordon Brown detested it, but came out of the whole episode even more diminished, and after losing the trust of one Alexander (Douglas) over the election that never was in 2007, now lost the support of another (Wendy) on the independence question.

The group who had been most alarmed about Alexander's position ultimately were the SNP. Opinion polls consistently showed that Scottish people wanted in principle the right to have a referendum, while being unconvinced by independence. The call for an immediate referendum was one that the SNP Government found embarrassing, this being the last thing they wanted. And yet such were the fissures and disagreements in Scottish Labour that this fundamental political truth was not brought centre-stage.

Alexander's short and ill-fated leadership left one important legacy. Her St Andrew's Day speech in 2007 had led to the establishment of the Calman Commission on Scottish devolution, which was approved by seventy-six votes to forty-six in the Scottish Parliament on 6 December 2007. The commission then announced its membership, drawing from a range of expert and establishment voices from the three unionist parties to business, trade unions, media and churches, and held its first meeting in April 2008.

The commission's work entailed a range of task groups and an independent expert group on financial accountability. Its first report, published in December 2008, ruled out full fiscal autonomy. A final report, 'Serving Scotland Better: Scotland and the United Kingdom in the 21st Century', was published in June 2009 and proposed a significant extension of the powers and competence of the Scottish Parliament with new financial powers and a range of other measures (BBC News, 15 June 2009). This report was endorsed by Labour, the Lib Dems and Conservatives, while the SNP tried to dismiss it as 'devolution lite' and counter-posed the possibilities of 'devolution max' and full fiscal autonomy. Many of the measures of the Calman Commission were adopted by the newly elected Conservative–Lib Dem UK Government in 2010 and their Scotland Bill.

At the end of Alexander's leadership, Labour were forced into a difficult by-election in Glasgow East, following David Marshall's resignation from the House of Commons. Labour went through the painful embarrassment of finding it difficult to get a candidate. Its first, George Ryan, pulled out, failing to come to the selection meeting for approving his candidature. Stephen Purcell, leader of Glasgow City Council, Lesley Quinn, party General Secretary, and Frank McAveety, MSP for neighbouring Glasgow Shettleston, were all sounded out and refused. This left Labour with its fifth-choice candidate, Margaret Curran, MSP for Glasgow Baillieston, part of her seat covering the same area, to come forth for the party in their hour of need (*The Scotsman*, 7 July 2008).

A challenging contest ensued for Labour in its third-safest seat in Scotland at a time of major unpopularity for Gordon Brown as Prime Minister and immediately following Wendy Alexander's resignation. The campaign was an energetic one with significant UK media interest, and on polling day, 24 July 2008, the SNP's John Mason overturned a Labour majority of 13,507 into a narrow Nationalist gain of 365 votes on a 22.5% swing (*BBC News*, 25 July 2008). Labour had been outmanoeuvred and outgunned in their own heartlands, with polling day reports showing a motivated, professional SNP operation which knew how to run a campaign and get out the vote, and a lacklustre, unfocused Labour campaign which did not from the outset know where its vote was and ran an appalling polling day 'get out the vote' campaign.

A Labour Revival?

Post-Wendy Alexander and the Glasgow East by-election, Labour put its timetable into effect for a leadership contest. This would be for Scottish Labour's fifth leader in the Scottish Parliament in less than a decade, yet it would also be the first full contest, debate and election for a leader ever held in Scottish Labour's history. Up until this point, no leader had been endorsed by the party's grass roots, from individual members to trade unionists and affiliated members. Nominations closed for the leadership and deputy leadership on 1 August 2008 and this produced for the leadership Iain Gray with thirteen nominations, Cathy Jamieson with twelve and Andy Kerr with ten, and for the deputy leadership, Johann Lamont with eighteen to Bill Butler's seven.

An important contribution to the leadership debate was provided by Tom McCabe in an article in the *Sunday Herald*. McCabe argued that Scottish

Labour was caught in a major predicament: 'For too long, there have been Scottish Labour politicians at local government level and at Westminster who have been resentful, and even contemptuous, of the Scottish Parliament' (*Sunday Herald*, 3 August 2008). Henry McLeish commented that since the establishment of the Scottish Parliament, 'MPs and councillors have been uncomfortable with devolution. Labour must establish its Scottish credentials' (ibid.).

Various Labour MSPs described Iain Gray as 'the embodiment of mediocrity', 'London's man' and 'boring'. An unnamed Labour MP said of Cathy Jamieson, 'Can you imagine her as leader?'; a Labour MSP called her a 'left-wing hypocrite', while another MSP said, 'This is the minister who backed privatisation at every step. Now she is left wing after all.' One Labour politician described Andy Kerr as 'Jack McConnell without brains', while a Labour MP viewed him as 'the triumph of ambition over talent' (*Sunday Herald*, 3 August 2008).

Three weeks later, the *Sunday Herald*'s Paul Hutcheon reflected on the non-debate evident in the contest for the leadership, writing that 'the three-way battle between Iain Gray, Cathy Jamieson and Andy Kerr is perhaps the most anti-democratic farce you can witness in the UK this year' (*Sunday Herald*, 21 August 2008).

On 13 September 2008, Iain Gray was elected leader and Johann Lamont deputy. The results were as follows:

Significantly, the party did not provide a detailed breakdown of the figures

Table 1: Scottish Labour Leadership Contest 2008 (as a percentage)

	MSPs, MPs & MEPs	Individual Members	Trade Unions & Affiliates	Total
Leadership First Ballot				
Iain Gray	17.89	15.06	13.05	46.00
Cathy Jamieson	8.94	10.27	14.09	33.30
Andy Kerr	6.50	8.00	6.19	20.69
Leadership Second Ballot				
Iain Gray	22.52	19.10	16.17	57.79
Cathy Jamieson	10.81	14.23	17.17	42.21
Deputy Leadership				
Johann Lamont	24.68	18.31	17.19	60.18
Bill Butler	8.66	15.02	16.14	39.82

Source: *BBC News*, 13 September 2008.

beyond these overall percentages to show turnout or how many individual or trade union members had voted. For example, when Tony Blair was elected leader in 1994 the party provided a full account of voting, boasting that one million people took part in the exercise.

Gray, on his election, launched a major attack on Alex Salmond, comparing his career unfavourably to his own:

> While Alex Salmond was studying the dismal science – economics – in the academic birthplace of Thatcherism, I was studying natural science in the academic home of the enlightenment. When Alex Salmond was an official in the Scottish Office I was learning to be a teacher in a tough school and a community activist in the biggest council housing scheme in Edinburgh. While he moved to the Royal Bank of Scotland I moved to Mozambique where I taught for two years in a country literally fighting for its life. While he spent the eighties and nineties developing the tricks of politics in Westminster, I spent them developing my values working for Oxfam. (BBC News, 13 September 2008)

Gray stated that, 'It is time to close the manifesto in which we fought the 2007 election, and begin to write our programme for 2011 and beyond.' He ruled out support for an independence referendum: 'Wendy Alexander was right to challenge Alex Salmond to put the question to the public and get it out of the way', but Labour would not support a 'rigged referendum', offering Labour an escape clause (ibid.). He also revealed the extent of Labour sensitivities, talking of his wider 'mandate', provoking Des Browne to reply that Gray should 'respect the structure of this party' (BBC News, 15 September 2008).

At the same time, the economic and political climate began to change dramatically with the collapse of the US financial firm Lehman Brothers. Gordon Brown sprang into action within weeks, advocating and leading British and global co-ordinated intervention, attempting to prevent depression. This was Brown's 'save the world' moment, as he later mis-spoke.

A UK Government reshuffle on 3 October saw the surprise return of Peter Mandelson to office as Business Secretary. Jim Murphy was given the post of Secretary of State for Scotland; unlike his three immediate predecessors, he would not share his post with any other ministerial responsibilities. Murphy was to prove a formidable adversary of Alex Salmond over the coming months. He would work with him where appropriate at a governmental level, while taking him on in the realm of politics. This combination of skills was to help balance and focus Scottish Labour in the run-up to the UK election.

An immediate challenge came with the Glenrothes by-election which, following soon after the Glasgow East contest, did not look anything other than ominous for Labour. The party's prospects were widely written off. 'Brown is heading for an epic defeat in the Glenrothes by-election', wrote Iain Macwhirter, echoing many others (Sunday Herald, 7 September

2008). The campaign proved very different from how everyone imagined. A rejuvenated Labour Party found the verve and appetite to behave like an opposition and go after the SNP. They challenged in adversarial style the actions of the SNP-led Scottish Government and, in particular, the SNP-run Fife Council, aided by the SNP candidate Peter Grant being leader of the council. Power came with responsibility and accountability, the SNP found, and Labour were prepared to be opportunistic and populist in challenging them.

Labour turned out comfortable winners, Lindsay Roy winning with a 6,737 majority over the SNP on 6 November 2008. Labour's majority only fell slightly from 10,664 in 2005, and while the SNP managed a small 4.7% swing from Labour, Roy also saw his vote rise in percentage terms by 3.7%. The Labour victory was widely interpreted as a significant point, possibly even a turning point, not just for Scottish politics but for Gordon Brown's premiership.

In May 2009 the Westminster parliamentary expenses scandal became public, with *The Daily Telegraph* revealing a long-standing and widespread culture of entitlement and self-aggrandisement paid for by the public (*The Daily Telegraph*, 8 May, 9 May 2009). The tales of moat-cleaning and duck houses and other excesses became iconic, but more serious was the tax avoidance of many MPs and their 'flipping' of their first and second homes, a practice twice undertaken by the Chancellor Alistair Darling. Four MPs including Scottish Labour's Jim Devine would eventually be charged and imprisoned, but the wider stock of politicians as a class fell even further.

It was partly because Labour were in office that this came as more of a blow to them than the Conservatives, and opposition leader David Cameron was seen as more fleet-footed on the issue than Gordon Brown in taking a principled stand; several Tory MPs were pressurised not to stand at the next election. Brown apologised 'on behalf of all politicians' for their actions (*BBC News*, 11 May 2009).

In a related political controversy, former Labour MP and Speaker of the House Michael Martin was criticised for his handling of the parliamentary expenses issue and subsequent debate, where he named and attacked two MPs. After an unprecedented parliamentary motion of no confidence was tabled against Martin (supported by twenty-three MPs), he announced he would stand down as Speaker and MP, resulting in a by-election in Glasgow North East.

The Scottish results in the Euro elections demonstrated the weakness of Scottish Labour, while the UK results embarrassingly pushed Labour into third place in votes and seats behind the Conservatives and Eurosceptic UKIP. In Scotland, the SNP won 29.1% to Labour's 20.8% – only the second time the SNP has finished ahead of Labour in a national poll. The division of Scotland's six seats saw no change in Labour and the SNP's two each or the Lib Dems' one, with the Tories reduced from two to one.

On 20 August 2009 an announcement came that would become a defining moment of the first SNP administration and which sent ongoing shock waves round the world. Justice Secretary Kenny MacAskill announced the release on 'compassionate grounds' of Abdelbaset Ali al-Megrahi, diagnosed with terminal cancer, the only man found guilty of the bombing of Pan Am Flight 103 over Lockerbie in December 1988 which killed 270 people.

The SNP Government faced immediate criticism from the Obama administration, among others, while a more complicated and murky backstory emerged of the Blair Government's dealings with Gaddafi's Libya. There had been the signing of the Prisoner Transfer Agreement in 2007 between the two countries, and Britain's mixing of diplomacy and pursuing lucrative trade deals on oil. None of this stopped Scottish Labour politicians articulating their shock and anger at MacAskill's decision. Richard Baker, Shadow Justice Minister, said the deal was 'an act of unpardonable folly', echoing Salmond's comments on Kosovo a decade previously (*The Observer*, 23 August 2009). The Scottish Parliament was recalled on 24 August, with MacAskill stating, 'It was my decision and my decision alone', while the only politician on any side to break party lines was Labour's Malcolm Chisholm, who 'commended the Justice Secretary for a courageous decision' (*BBC News*, 24 August 2009). A subsequent debate saw a parliamentary motion criticising the SNP passed seventy-three votes to fifty (*BBC News*, 3 September 2009).

The Glasgow North East by-election was eventually called for 12 November 2009. It was a very different context compared to Glasgow East less than a year and a half before. Despite Labour's local embarrassments, the party had a bullish approach to contesting the seat, with Willie Bain, Labour candidate, commenting during the campaign, 'The SNP has been in power in Scotland for two years and I think people are thinking they have not delivered their promises' (*BBC News*, 15 October 2009).

Labour fought an even more motivated campaign than in Glenrothes, targeting the 'anti-Glasgow' bias of the SNP, particularly in relation to the Scottish Government's cancellation of the Glasgow Airport Rail Link (GARL). Labour won comfortably, with Bain achieving a 8,111 majority over the SNP's David Kerr. Labour managed to increase their vote in percentage terms by 6.1% compared to Michael Martin's last showing, while the SNP only put their vote up by 2.3% on a 33.2% turnout. It was the worst showing by the SNP in a Labour–SNP contest in over thirty years. Iain Macwhirter, reflecting on the result, stated, 'By rights, Labour should never have won this by-election', concluding that 'The SNP has no excuses here' (*The Herald*, 16 November 2009).

On 2 March 2010, Stephen Purcell, until this point viewed as one of the brightest stars and hopes for the future in Labour, unexpectedly announced his resignation as leader of Glasgow City Council and, two days later, as a councillor. Purcell who had embraced a forward-looking progressive agenda while leading Glasgow, advocating a Glasgow Living Wage, winning the Commonwealth Games for the city for 2014, and being prepared to acknowledge some of the weaknesses of Scottish Labour, had the potential, many thought, of becoming an even more significant national figure in the Scottish Parliament or even Westminster.

The scandal revealed an unattractive aspect of part of Glasgow and West of Scotland Labour, tapping into a set of stories about Strathclyde Passenger Transport (SPT), jobs for the boys and excessive global junketing. This led to the resignation from the public body of Labour insider Ron Culley, who had been its head, Bob Wylie, its head of communications, and Labour councillor Alistair Watson, the body's chair (*The Sunday Times*, 21 February 2010). Purcell had been viewed as close to Culley, who was seen by some as mentoring and influencing him. His abrupt resignation from the council and public life came with admissions of drug use, and that the police had previously advised him that this might make him a victim of blackmail (*Scottish Daily Mail*, 8 March 2010). He was quickly replaced by Gordon Matheson as leader of the council, but the murky side of Labour patronage was partly lifted because of this.

This developed into a much bigger story about the strange character of West of Scotland Labour. There was the mushrooming of arm's-length external organisations (ALEOS) in Glasgow City Council, where thirteen such bodies had been set up providing former council services, ranging from Glasgow Life, providing culture and sport services, to City Building and Cordia. *The Herald* analysed this and revealed that '"Labour backwoodsmen" . . . were given positions on outside bodies and commanded five-figure sums', while Labour councillors talked of 'a secretive web of political patronage' with consequences for accountability and financial responsibility (*The Herald*, 1 April 2010). Another strand emerged concerning what Jason Allardyce and Stuart MacDonald called the 'close proximity between political donations and municipal decision making' in Glasgow and Lanarkshire. This entailed a network of relationships involving property owners, developers and Labour councillors, of dubious land deals and money being made from the public purse (*The Sunday Times*, 11 April 2010). This was not a side of Scottish Labour that often became public, nor was it one most party members wanted to spend time thinking about.

This was the immediate backdrop for Scottish Labour as it prepared for the 2010 UK general election. It was not a contest in which Labour had to look far to find problems, as Gordon Brown's premiership had proven a major disappointment for any still harbouring hopes of a 'Red Brown' agenda or breaking free of the constraints of New Labour.

Nine Scottish Labour MPs announced they were standing down, including John Reid, Des Browne, Nigel Griffiths, John McFall, Rosemary McKenna and Mohammed Sarwar. Two were not allowed to stand: Jim Devine was facing criminal charges and Anne Moffat had been de-selected. A whole swathe of new younger Labour MPs were elected. Pamela Nash replaced Reid in Airdrie and Shotts; Gregg McClymont replaced McKenna in Cumbernauld, Kilsyth and Kirkintilloch East; Gemma Doyle in West Dunbartonshire replaced John McFall; and Anas Sarwar took over from his father in Glasgow Central. There was a real sense of generational passing and a commensurate hollowing out and dilution of talent.

The highlight of the election, leaving aside Gordon Brown calling Labour voter Mrs Duffy in Rochdale 'a sort of bigoted woman', was the innovation of the first TV debates between the UK party leaders. These were dubbed 'the Prime Ministerial Debates' between Gordon Brown, David Cameron and Nick Clegg on ITV, Sky and BBC. Mitchell and van der Zwet view that the effect of the debates contributed to 'marginalising any distinctive Scottish dimension' (Mitchell and van der Zwet 2010: 128).

Despite the existence of an SNP administration in Holyrood, some felt that the nature of the contest was the most British-focused since 1979. The Lib Dems benefited from the TV debates and exposure given, with 'Cleggmania' briefly bursting out across the UK, and the SNP suffered from being somewhat ignored. The effect of the TV debates led the SNP to go to the Court of Session after the ITV and Sky debates and claim that the BBC had breached its rules on impartiality by excluding the SNP, and asking for Alex Salmond to be included or the debate not to be shown in Scotland; their case was rejected (*The Scotsman*, 29 April 2010).

The Scottish election results told a story of both continuity and continued change: of Labour's powerful dominance of Scottish politics at Westminster, while the role of that institution in Scottish public life profoundly changed. The Scottish party held all the seats it was defending, won back Glasgow East and Dunfermline and West Fife with ease from by-election defeats, and held Glasgow North East (which had been a 'notional gain' from the Speaker), giving it forty-one seats, up one from 2005 (Denver 2010).

The most British of campaigns north of the border produced a result which paradoxically underlined Scottish politics' very different dynamics. While Labour's vote fell in England by 7.4%, in Scotland it rose by 3.1% to 42.0%.

141

The Conservatives on the other hand saw their vote rise by 3.9% in England and a more humble 0.9% in Scotland. The Tories gained ninety-two seats in England, but not one in Scotland. This account of Scottish difference was reinforced by the Welsh results, where Labour polled badly (down 6.5% in the vote) and the Tories did relatively well (4.7% rise in vote and five gains in seats) (Kavanagh and Cowley 2010: 353).

Despite Labour's problems at a UK level, Cameron's Conservatives fell well short of an overall majority, and there then followed what has been called *Five Days That Changed Britain*, the title of the BBC's Nick Robinson programme on the post-election negotiations which produced the Conservative–Lib Dem coalition government (BBC *Two*, 29 July 2010). The coalition government dramatically changed many of the assumptions and dynamics of British politics. It changed Scottish politics in that it addressed the issue of Conservative weakness and diluted the 'no mandate' argument, augmenting the sole Conservative representative with eleven Scottish Lib Dems. David Cameron from the outset talked of a 'respect agenda' between the UK and Scottish governments, aided by having a Lib Dem Secretary of State, briefly, Danny Alexander, and then Michael Moore.

Many felt that the return of the Tories with all that evoked in the Scottish collective psyche could offer the prospect of a kind of 'Back to the Future' mindset, rekindling memories of Thatcherism, job losses and public spending cuts. There was an element of this, along with the perception of seeing the Tories as anti-Scottish and a threat to Scottish interests, which contributed to post-May 2010 Labour moving into a commanding lead in Scottish Parliament voting intentions. The party's rating shot up dramatically after the May election, establishing a double-digit lead over the SNP which it was to retain until February 2011.

Many felt Scottish Labour's victory in 2010 had been a story of 'Labour coming home'. This was the kind of language that Iain Gray offered to the five candidates standing for the Labour leadership after Gordon Brown's resignation. At a hustings meeting held in Glasgow, Gray talked of 'one million Scots saying yes to Labour' and that 'we fought back and we won', showing that Scottish Labour 'was on the way back' (*The Scotsman*, 14 June 2010). Scottish Labour was being explicitly presented as a party that had learnt the lessons of defeat, suffered its trials and tribulations, renewed and reconnected with voters, and thus offered a road map for British Labour.

The Labour leadership contest saw the triumph of Ed Miliband over his brother David, winning in the final ballot by 50.65% to 49.35%, aided by the votes of trade unionists while losing in the parliamentary party and individual members (BBC *News*, 25 September 2010). Tory and right-wing press fantasies of labelling him 'Red Ed' and the prisoner of trade union barons were given a brief fillip by this.

An interesting secondary story emerged from the Labour leadership when it came to light that the national party had issued 13,135 individual party members in Scotland, whereas the party 'claimed' 20,133 members. Where were the missing 7,000 Labour members, asked Hamish Macdonell, to elicit the answer from the Labour Party that the 'missing' 7,000 were Labour Party members not entitled to vote in leadership elections. This was because they were members of the party through Labour Social Clubs in Ayrshire and Fife, a situation which led some to surmise they were not really fully paid-up, constituted Labour members. As Macdonell pointed out, this situation torpedoed Scottish Labour's long-standing claim to be the largest party in members, with the Nationalists' 15,945 members at the time clearly outnumbering them (*Caledonian Mercury*, 29 September 2010).

A Very Scottish Revolution

Scottish Labour maintained and built on its post-May 2010 lead in the polls for the Scottish Parliament. There came to be a view that Scottish Labour was going to win the next Scottish elections, and that the SNP Government had lost a sense of momentum and forward agenda. In January 2011 this state of affairs seemed to be underlined by a TNS-BMRB opinion poll which put Labour on 49% on the constituency vote and 47% on the regional vote, versus the SNP's 33% in both, producing Labour leads of 16% and 14% respectively (*The Herald*, 17 January 2011).

Numerous voices assumed the election was over. One of the most interesting perspectives came from Nick Pearce of IPPR, who commented that, 'Labour will now go into the Scottish election as the party claiming it is best placed to protect Scotland from a Conservative-led Government in Westminster', going on to say, 'the SNP will suffer from incumbency and a sense of drift over the last two years by comparison with their energetic start after winning in 2007'. A Labour–Lib Dem coalition, wrote Pearce, 'would give substance to Ed Miliband's claim that Labour can practice a more liberal and pluralist politics' (Pearce 2011).

A few days later, on 16 February, the first signs emerged that it was all going to be very different. An Ipsos-Mori poll saw Labour's lead built up over the last eight months evaporate overnight; the SNP were in the lead over Labour by 37% to 36% in the constituency vote and 35% to 33% in the regional vote (*The Times*, 16 February 2011). The Scottish election campaign was never going to be the same again.

Labour's campaign run by John Smith House had started from the basis of a high degree of over-confidence. The party had a lead, and all it had to do was sit on it and not lose it. There was an understanding that the race would necessarily tighten closer to polling day, but it was widely felt that the contest was Labour's to lose. One Labour MSP described the mood in the party's campaign: 'It's like we're walking across a highly polished ballroom floor carrying a priceless Ming Dynasty vase' (Torrance 2011: 8). Taking this analogy further, Labour slipped badly and smashed the vase into thousands of pieces. Stephen Purcell commented before the election that he felt 'the party didn't get the damage it did to itself by its lack of practising and championing of democracy' (interview).

Scottish Labour's manifesto, 'Fighting for what really matters', opened with the words, 'Now that the Tories are back, we need a Government in Scotland that focuses on what really matters' (Scottish Labour 2011a). The 96-page document, strewn with typos and mistakes, did not once mention anywhere the SNP. The focus was entirely on the Conservatives and the threat they posed. Labour's strategy was to marginalise the SNP and make them irrelevant in the big UK battle of Labour versus Conservatives. This implied some element of risk in a Scottish contest with an incumbent SNP Government (*The Scotsman*, 7 April 2011). A week later, the SNP launched their glossy, professional, focused manifesto, 'Re-elect A Scottish Government Working for Scotland', which was forward-looking, aspirational and optimistic in tone (SNP 2011).

Labour's campaign was handicapped by setbacks including the fire alarm going off during the election manifesto launch and Iain Gray being surrounded by protestors in Glasgow Central station and having to seek sanctuary in a nearby eatery. These images contrasted with Alex Salmond and the SNP. Salmond appeared on the BBC's *Question Time* in the middle of the campaign in Liverpool and dominated the show with his charm. Labour's problems masked much deeper difficulties. The party's strategy was wrong, ill-focused and unable to adapt in what from February to March had become a competitive contest.

The logistics of a campaign had been put in place, but organisationally and politically it was inept and unprepared for unforeseen eventualities. The party did not engage in private polling to the extent of the Nationalists, or have 'smart' resources like Activate (the SNP's software system), nor was it able to conduct a similar number of focus groups. The party's social media presence compared to the SNP was pitiful. While the party could claim that it could not match the SNP in money and resources, what was missing even more was political intelligence, and a sense of motivation and drive for the wider cause.

For years, a small core of Scottish Labour had been able to draw on trade unions and local government councillors and personnel, but these had become fewer in number and marginalised in the party. Scottish Labour's campaign started off without the advantages of previous party campaigns, facing a potent SNP, and handicapped by a lack of understanding of the changed environment of Scottish politics and the need for a different kind of Labour politics.

These mistakes were not the product of a disastrous Labour campaign, but of four years of denial and opportunistic opposition to the SNP. These four years cannot be seen in isolation, and need to be located in the broader context of Labour's continued inability to understand and come to terms with the SNP. Iain Gray and Labour's head of the campaign, John Park, had to take some of the responsibility for not counteracting this, but a whole pantheon of more senior Labour figures from Gordon Brown down had contributed to this.

The media campaign showcased and exaggerated Labour's problems, with *The Sun* coming out for Alex Salmond with 'Play it Again Salm' (*The Sun*, 19 April 2011). This was not only an endorsement for the SNP, but an explicit rebuttal of Labour and 'Labour Scotland'. In its inside pages, *The Sun* declared, 'Warning: Voting Labour is Bad for Your Health', with a detailed analysis of poverty and inequality drawing on the work of academic Danny Dorling. This was far removed from *The Sun*'s 'Braveheart' nationalism of 1992.

The Sun's endorsement of the SNP was damning of Labour, stating, 'Labour want this election to be a referendum on the coalition at Westminster. That is plain insulting. This election is NOT about Westminster, it's about who runs Scotland . . .' (*The Sun*, 19 April 2011). Moreover, the business and public endorsements of the SNP, ranging from David Murray, at the time of the election the owner of Rangers FC, to Annie Lennox, Irvine Welsh and Brian Cox, humbled any Labour efforts.

The election night and results was a watershed for Scotland. The last polls had predicted an SNP landslide and there were late signs of Labour's vote melting away. The final results were seismic. The SNP won 45.4% to Labour's 31.7% in the constituency vote, a rise of 12.5% for the Nationalists and fall of 0.5% for Labour; in the regional vote the SNP won 44.0% to Labour's 26.3%, a rise of 13.0% and fall of 2.9% (Denver 2011a). This was the highest-ever vote in the SNP's history, its biggest-ever lead over Labour, and Labour's worst showing in the popular vote (excluding Euro elections) since 1918 (Hassan 2011).

In parliamentary seats the SNP victory was even more striking: sixty-nine SNP seats to Labour's thirty-seven – an SNP overall majority in a Parliament which was not meant to allow this to happen and indeed meant to 'kill nationalism stone dead'. The SNP won fifty-three FPTP constituencies to Labour's fifteen, a gain of thirty-two for the SNP and a loss of twenty for Labour. The only feature of the election which made it slightly less one-sided for Labour was the Scottish Parliament's electoral system giving Labour twenty-two regional list seats, an increase of thirteen.[1]

Fifteen Labour incumbent MSPs lost their seats: Andy Kerr in East Kilbride; Frank McAveety in Glasgow Shettleston; Tom McCabe in Hamilton, Larkhall and Stonehouse; David Whitton in Strathkelvin and Bearsden; while nine Labour MSPs had already stood down. The latter group included two former leaders, Wendy Alexander and Jack McConnell, Peter Peacock and Rhona Brankin, and two MSPs already elected as MPs, Cathy Jamieson and Margaret Curran. Iain Gray just held his East Lothian seat by a narrow 151 votes over the SNP.

This left a Scottish Labour Group of MSPs bereft of the familiar faces of the previous decade, with only fourteen Labour MSPs who had served continuously since 1999 (less than the SNP's sixteen). Some in the party and wider Scotland had previously worried about the detrimental effect of Labour 'bedblockers', MSPs nursing seats for life. Now the party faced the opposite problem, bereft of experience and skills, and with a whole host of politicians unexpectedly elected on the regional list.

Scottish Labour's defeat was both national and in every area of Scotland. Whereas in the SNP's 2007 victory Labour still managed to finish ahead in four of the eight regional constituencies, now the SNP landslide carried all before it, with the Nationalists ahead in every one of the eight regional constituencies. Labour's traditional West of Scotland heartlands which had proven mostly resolute in 2007, now crumbled. For the first time since the 1930s Glasgow was no longer Labour, with the SNP finishing with 39.8% to Labour's 35.0% on the regional vote, while winning five FPTP seats to Labour's four.

Why had the SNP won so big and inflicted so heavy a defeat on Labour? The SNP's record in office was viewed across a range of issues as ambiguous: in nine policy areas from health to education, transport and environment, on not one did the SNP's record warrant majority support or that of a sizeable plurality (*Scotland on Sunday*, 17 April 2011).

The leadership question mattered. One Labour candidate said during the election:

We have simply not got to grips with the Salmond factor in this election. Some people in our campaign believe that if they hate Alex Salmond, everyone else should hate him . . . too many people in the party are at the stage of 2007. They have never got over losing to the SNP four years ago. (*The Times*, 19 April 2011)

When asked who should be First Minister in the midst of the campaign, respondents answered Alex Salmond 42%, Iain Gray 14%, Annabel Goldie 9%, Tavish Scott 3%. Asked to choose between Salmond and Gray, voters split 52% to 27% for Salmond; when asked to choose between an SNP and Labour Government they split 47% to 29% for the SNP, suggesting that Gray was a significant drag on Labour's fortunes. In the battle of perceptions between Salmond and Gray, Salmond led Gray on standing up for Scotland by 60% to 15%, on being intelligent by 40% to 18%, while only on being conceited did Gray find an advantage with Salmond leading by 32% to 10% (*Scotland on Sunday*, 17 April 2011).

The Scottish Election Survey showed the extent of the SNP's victory and Labour's defeat (Carman et al. 2011). The AB and C1 social groups both voted 41% SNP to 25% Labour and the C2DE group 47% SNP to 28% Labour; Church of Scotland voters 44% SNP to 26% Labour and, importantly, Catholic voters 43% SNP to 36% Labour. Parts of the electorate which had previously been less SNP – women, working-class and Catholic voters – swung significantly to the SNP.

The flow of the vote from 2007 to 2011 saw Labour retain 69% of its 2007 vote, with 21% shifting to the SNP; while the SNP retained 89%, Conservatives 75% and Lib Dems 35%. Then there was the perception of which party was thought effective at managing the impact of Westminster cuts; the Conservatives and Lib Dems were not seen as highly rated with 31% and 22% respectively saying they would be very or fairly effective; Labour had a 48% rating and the SNP 64% (ibid.).

The Labour election inquest began even before the polls opened, with one Labour activist calling the campaign 'uninspiring, ill-conceived and unsuccessful', and starting up a dedicated website for the post-election inquest. He wrote in explicit terms:

> ... the SNP has, of course, continuously positioned itself as the defender of Scotland, proclaiming that they will oppose or mitigate the Westminster imposed cuts. The SNP's slogan is 'A Scottish Government Working for Scotland', and this appeal to nationalism is arguably more effective than Labour's politically partisan approach. (Wright 2011)

A very different view came from John McTernan, who began his call for action with a week to go to the polls and Labour's need to attack the idea of independence, noting that, 'It is a fundamental law of political campaigning that you should always be talking about whatever it is your opponent doesn't want to mention' and went on:

> Everything in politics comes back to money, and the most important money for voters is their own. For all that the chatterati flirt with the notion that Scotland

is in some way more left wing, more social democratic than the rest of Britain, no-one has used the tax powers of the Parliament to raise taxes. (*The Scotsman*, 27 April 2011)

Post-election, McTernan expanded on his analysis. 'Labour did not build on their strengths' in the campaign, he wrote, particularly on their knife crime policies or going after the SNP's liberal policies on prisons. More crucially, Labour had to begin a debate about what went wrong and what it was for:

> The fish, the Russians used to say, rots from the head. Political parties start to decay when they stop thinking. Time to jump-start debate about progressive futures. (*The Scotsman*, 7 May 2011)

One Labour MP complained that the media and others somehow restrained Labour from scrutinising the Nationalists: 'They say when we challenge them that we are being negative. We are pulled up for calling their plans unrealistic and unaffordable, and told you can't do that, you are being too negative' (interview). From a very different Labour perspective, Ian Smart, one of the main protagonists in Scottish Labour Action, put forward a scathing critique of Scottish Labour, not just in this election but more widely. He pointed out that with the SNP in office, 'The country has not seen anarchy for the last four years', which had major implications for Labour:

> In 1999 and 2003 Labour ran its anti-nationalist campaign premised on the election of an SNP Government leading to a flight of capital, the collapse of the Scottish economy, schools and hospitals closing their doors out of a sheer sense of hopelessness and ultimately plagues of locusts ravishing the land. (Smart 2011)

He concluded that this perspective 'always did however have one major flaw': what happened if the SNP came to office, did not correspond to Labour caricature, and instead were competent. Even more fundamentally, he made the salient and heretical point, 'There is no such thing as the Scottish Labour Party', and then proceeded:

> What position will Iain Gray's successor actually hold? Under the Party's current constitutional arrangements it will not be leader of the Scottish Labour Party for that post is actually held, somewhat bizarrely, by one Ed Miliband. We need major change within the Party in Scotland: a rooting out of the deadwood at the top; a Party structure based on the ability to fight Scottish elections becoming an equal priority to fighting Westminster ones; a more inclusive candidate selection process; above all a means of involving our natural supporters fit for 2016 rather than 1916. All of that can only be achieved by a leader in Scotland with the power to set the terms of the debate and force through the changes required without constantly having to seek permission from London. (ibid.)

These were some of the first thoughts post-election of a party in a state of shock. There was the issue of the leadership as Iain Gray indicated his wish to resign as Scottish leader. Ed Miliband announced a party review into Scottish Labour, which at first was headed up by Jim Murphy with Ann McKechin and Anne McGuire, all of whom were MPs. Sarah Boyack, MSP, was later added to the review and made joint head of it with Murphy (*The Scotsman*, 10 May, 11 May 2011). The review's terms set out to identify 'Labour's vision for the future' and address such issues as 'Building capacity', 'the next generation' and 'campaigning strategy' (Scottish Labour 2011b).

Some sought to blame the party's predicament on Gordon Brown and his long shadow over Scottish Labour, arguing that he prevented the party from flourishing and growing in new ways, but this does not efficiently explain the last near-twenty years – from the death of John Smith in 1994 to Gordon Brown's election defeat in 2010. Contrary to myth, Gordon Brown's reach did not extend into every aspect of Scottish Labour; the problems the party had and has are much more complicated, deep-rooted and difficult to solve than the over-reach of one man. One former Labour minister reflected that blaming Brown was 'a deception' and 'a diversion' and 'unfair'. They went on to say that 'the deeper malaise was the Westminster class of Labour MPs, and the Scottish Group in particular, who as a class do not understand devolution, and in the most extreme examples detest with an over-the-top vengeance the Scottish Parliament' (interview). A former MP commented that 'the Scottish Labour Group of MSPs hardly helped matters with a lack of leadership, political courage or ideas' (interview).

The Scottish party looked forward, if those were the right words, to the new Scottish parliamentary term and an uncertain future. Kenny Farquharson caught this when he described the party as 'a cornered animal tearing at its own wounded flesh'. A new sweeping revisionism was finding voice in sections of the party:

> Devolution was a mistake, say some. Proportional representation was a bigger mistake say others, both for Holyrood and council elections. There is a rueful nostalgia for the days when Labour ruled unchecked and unbalanced, its power and patronage the fruit of a ridiculously unfair and untenable electoral system. (*Scotland on Sunday*, 21 August 2011)

Scottish Labour found itself in 2011 entering uncharted waters, some clinging to the wreckage and fond memories of past glories, the path back to popularity and power uncertain and unclear.

NOTE

1. All changes in terms of gains and losses at the 2011 Scottish Parliament elections compared to 2007 are notional due to boundary changes. The actual result of 2007: SNP 47, Labour 46, Conservative 17, Lib Dems 16, Others 3, has been calculated on new boundaries: SNP 46 (-1), Labour 44 (-2), Conservative 20 (+3), Lib Dems 17 (+1), Others 2 (-1) (Denver, *The New Scottish Parliament Constituencies 2011*, Lancaster University 2011).

Part Three
Scottish Labour in Power

CHAPTER 9

How Distinctive is Scottish Labour?
The Cases of Education and Health

LABOUR, SOCIAL DEMOCRACY AND THE REFORM OF PUBLIC SERVICES

What does Scottish Labour stand for? To what extent, while in office, did it pursue a programmatic trajectory distinctive from New Labour in London? There is no consensus on these questions. Keating and Freeman argue that, compared to the national party, Scottish Labour adopted a more collectivist, traditionally social democratic stance on key policy issues (Keating 2003: 435; Freeman 2007: 92). Mooney and Williams, in contrast, claim that 'the Scottish Executive has increasingly adopted the language, rhetoric and increasingly the policy and practice of New Labour in England in relation to public sector reforms' (Mooney and Williams 2006: 619), while Hopkin and Bradbury conclude that all Labour First Ministers 'were comfortable with the Blairite New Labour agenda' (Hopkin and Bradbury 2006: 144). Scottish Labour politicians, to the contrary, believed in the idea and 'myth' of 'Labour Scotland', of a more radical, collectivist political culture and community than south of the border, which they spoke for and represented.

In formulating its response, this chapter uses three case studies – education (focusing on secondary schooling), health and long-term care for the elderly – which were chosen for three main reasons. Firstly, they represent key areas for which the Scottish Parliament became fully responsible in the new devolved settlement. Secondly, in terms of funding requirements, centrality in people's lives and political salience, they are among the most vital areas of policy for any government. Thirdly, they cover some of the main areas of policy divergence between Labour north and south of the border during the years of the Labour–Lib Dem coalition. This chapter traces Scottish Labour policy on secondary education and healthcare, Chapter 10 seeks to explain why these policies diverged from those pursued in London, while Chapter 11 explores the quite distinctive case of free personal care for the elderly.

The character of the New Labour project in Westminster became increasingly defined by its programme of public service reform, notably in the fields of education and health. This programme proved to be intensely controversial within the Labour Party – causing major rifts and large-scale parliamentary revolts – because it involved a sharp break with the party's traditional collectivist approach. Underpinning this older approach were two central domain assumptions: that public services should be provided by monopoly public producers; and that public sector professionals could be trusted to deliver them in an effective, equitable, fair and efficient manner. New Labour rejected both assumptions. Monopoly public provision was seen as a core weakness of the traditional collectivist model. Without the spur of competition and consumer pressure, it was argued, public organisations tended to succumb to a wasteful use of resources, rent-seeking behaviour, weak and bureaucratic management and institutional inertia (Strategy Unit 2006: 50). Faith in professionalism was equally misguided. A system characterised by what Blair called 'professional domination of service provision' had too often led to a poor standard of service which left service-users 'disempowered and demoralised' (Blair 2004). Haltingly at first, but then with mounting urgency, New Labour unveiled its programme for 'public service modernisation'. This combined the party's traditional commitment to well-funded public services supplied free on the basis of need with an insistence on the need to reform the delivery of these services by promoting user choice, competition and diversity of provision. The modernisation programme only truly got under way by around 2000, by which time the two key sectors to which it was applied, education and health, were under the jurisdiction of the new devolved authorities. It soon became plain that New Labour-style modernisation would not cross the border into Scotland.

SCOTTISH LABOUR AND SCHOOL EDUCATION

Labour returned to power in 1997 committed to an expanded educational system, to higher standards for all, and greater equality of opportunity and social justice. The question was how to realise these goals. The party inherited a system of secondary education which had undergone wide-ranging changes during the Conservative government, designed to establish what came to be called an 'internal' or 'quasi' market. These changes included delegated budgets, the right to opt-out of Local Education Authority control, a funding system based on school rolls, greater diversity of school provision and league tables. Labour's response was two-fold. On the one hand (after 2000) it announced a major increase in the education budget, an ambitious school-building programme and negotiated significant improvements in the pay and conditions of teachers. On the other hand (to the indignation of many within the party and the education profession) it accepted and extended the basic thrust of the Tories' internal market reforms.

Its reasoning ran as follows. Giving parents the right to chose between a diverse range of increasingly differentiated and autonomous schools would create a competitive system which would incentivise schools to drive up standards, respond more sensitively to the needs of pupils and tackle with greater urgency the problem of widespread educational under-achievement among working-class children (Ranson 2003: 465; Taylor, Fitz and Gorard 2005: 54). League tables compiled largely from examination results, coupled with stricter audits of performance, would provide quantifiable performance indicators that would enable parents to make informed choices (Ranson 2008: 202). They would also identify failing schools, which would be 'named and shamed' and placed under tough remedial 'special measure' regimes. Mistrust of professional power also prompted a heavy emphasis on tight performance management, with providers regularly and rigorously monitored, inspected and scrutinised.

This market-oriented strategy was not only rejected in Scotland: it was never even seriously considered. Scottish education has always been autonomous, with its organisation, curriculum, structure and forms of assessment being quite distinct from its southern neighbour. The move towards an internal market under the Tories in England was only haltingly introduced in Scotland, so institutional realities were quite different. Hardly any schools in Scotland (in contrast to England) opted out of local authority control, there was less emphasis on competition and the testing regime was less intrusive (Arnott and Menter 2007: 254; Paterson 2003: 168). The concept of the universal comprehensive system, in short, remained intact.

The new devolved administration made it clear that it would remain so. Education Minister Jack McConnell declared unequivocally in 2001 that there would be no 'privatisation, selection or streaming' in Scottish education, no fragmentation of the schooling system, no standardised national testing in primary and early secondary schooling, and the existing league tables would be scrapped. The status of the comprehensive as the neighbourhood community school would be preserved (Paterson 2003: 177). In contrast to England, the Scottish Government was committed to, in McConnell's words, 're-invigorating the comprehensive ideal' (interview). The comprehensive system in Scotland, Labour contended, had suffered from decades of serious under-funding, poor pay and low teacher morale, and very troubled industrial relations. But over the years it had proved its resilience.

155

There was less debate or anxiety over failing schools compared with England and overall there was a belief that the calibre of the educational experience was higher. There seemed little case for massively destabilising changes.

Scottish Labour adduced practical considerations for denying the relevance of the New Labour strategy. Public services in Scotland were seen to be operating on too small a canvas for choice and competition mechanisms to work effectively with the population (outside Glasgow), and too dispersed to allow meaningful choice. Provider choice was 'simply impractical, or would require wasteful surplus provision' (Scottish Executive 2006: 10). Couching objections to the New Labour agenda on practical rather than principled grounds had political advantages, since it minimised the potential for conflict with Westminster. In reality, Scottish Labour's disapproval of market reform ran much deeper. The key to sustained improvement in the quality of schooling, Scottish Labour policy-makers averred, was not the importation of market mechanisms but a re-invigoration of what may be called the professional model of public service organisation. This holds that the key to bringing out the best of employees in public organisations is not competitive pressures or incentivisation but a sense of professional pride and public duty coupled with shared norms and co-operative working habits. As the Scottish Executive explained: 'Within a framework of clear national standards and local authority support, teachers and other professionals in schools must have the freedom to exercise their professional judgement to deliver excellent learning and teaching. We will act to give them that freedom' (Scottish Executive 2004: 5). Hence the policies of the Scottish Executive sought to foster trust and collaborative working relationships between teachers, local authorities, the Scottish Executive and parents.

Scottish Labour did not rely exclusively on the professional model, holding that a large measure of central direction, regulation and inspection was required to ensure that schools were under pressure to lift standards. Hence there were numerous policy initiatives, such as requirements to deliver an externally prescribed curriculum and the use of various performance indicators and quality controls to monitor and assess performance. But this stopped well short of what has been called 'the culture of performativity' in England (Arnott and Menter 2007: 20). The Scottish Government abandoned the school league tables and to a large extent scrapped the testing and oversight regime inherited from the Conservatives. It was interventionist in that it introduced a raft of changes to improve the quality of teacher training and leadership, tackle the problem of pupil discipline, intervene in poorly performing schools and give more flexibility to head teachers (interviews, Jack McConnell and Peter Peacock). But to a substantially greater degree than in England, responsibility for implementing national educational priorities, enhancing standards and tackling persistent weaknesses continued to be vested in educational professionals in both local authorities and schools (Arnott 2005: 254; Issakyan et al. 2008: 8).

Scottish Labour's commitment to the professional model was given fullest acknowledgement in the 2001 McCrone agreement, which was designed to reach a comprehensive settlement with the teachers after years of industrial turbulence. Teachers gained a pay rise of 21.5% over three years, a 35-hour working week, increased rewards for those who demonstrated high teaching standards, a contractual obligation ensuring that all teachers undertook 35 hours of professional development each year, guaranteed support for newly qualified teachers and more support staff affording teachers more time to teach (Scottish Executive 2004: 8). McCrone's objectives were 'to increase standards within the teaching profession, to create a provision for weeding out poor teachers, to establish minimum standards for teachers and overall to raise the status of education' (interview, Jack McConnell). Crucially, though there was a commitment to more flexible working practices, no strict conditions were attached. 'Scottish teachers were given a deal "up front" as an act of faith in their willingness and ability to modernise and enter an era of new professionalism' (Arnott and Menter 2007: 258).

The lack of conditionality provoked considerable criticism. Critics claimed that Scottish Labour was unwilling to stand up to the powerful Educational Institute of Scotland (EIS), by far the strongest teaching union in Scotland, and the educational establishment in general. The blunt-speaking and acerbic Sam Galbraith, Education Minister from 1999 to 2000, who was responsible for negotiating the early stages of the agreement, commented tartly: 'I wouldn't have given them that extra money without a solid agreement to continue professional development. They've not fulfilled their part of the bargain as I suspected. They just took the money' (interview). It was, another former minister opined, 'a big missed opportunity in terms of what was happening in Scottish classrooms. The worst aspect is that it's not been implemented. Even the small changes that it asked for in terms of classroom practice have not been seen through' (interview). McCrone was, such critics contended, above all a political settlement. McConnell, as Minister of Education, was seeking to amass political capital. 'He wanted the credit for solving the problem' (interview, Sam Galbraith). Another former minister (equally unsympathetic to McConnell) claimed:

> Henry's weakness was ruthlessly and very cleverly exploited by Jack [Henry McLeish had recently defeated McConnell for the leadership by an unexpectedly narrow margin]. Jack knew that if he publicly announced that he had done a deal that gave the teachers 25% for no productivity gain whatsoever then Henry wouldn't have the bottle to say 'no bloody way', and of course he was right. It was

a scandal to commit yourself to expenditure worth billions of pounds without ever having put it through the Cabinet. (interview)

For defenders of the McCrone settlement these criticisms were both unfair and one-sided. The agreement, it was contended, included as a centrepiece the annual contractual commitment to Continuous Professional Development, a commitment never previously required of teachers. It also substantially eased the very onerous legal restrictions limiting the ability to dismiss teachers for poor performance and established new flexibilities between teachers and classroom assistants, and also between primary and secondary schools (interview, former minister). Attacks on the settlement, it was also argued, overlooked the broader historical context in which it had been negotiated. For many years under the Conservatives, one MSP commented, there had been 'utter discontent and disarray in the Scottish education system', constant industrial unrest and huge resentment over pay, conditions and other Conservative proposals. 'A period of stability was essential' and the McCrone settlement achieved this. 'It was a pragmatic solution to a difficult issue' (interview). 'McCrone was pivotal', Education Minister Peter Peacock reflected: 'If we hadn't settled in some reasonably good way we were back in industrial dispute and that just wasn't acceptable.' Under the Conservatives, teachers in Scotland had felt 'berated and belittled and demotivated'. The McCrone agreement 'helped create an atmosphere in which for the first time in years some trust was beginning to develop and we were being seen to be prepared to invest in a profession that we needed to invest in if it was to give us the performance that we wanted' (interview).

Whatever the differences within Scottish Labour, on one key point there was a broad consensus: the internal market was not the appropriate strategy for ramping-up standards, and far from narrowing entrenched inequalities (as New Labour claimed), it would exacerbate them. In a competitive system where rewards accrue to schools which obtain a higher place within an explicit hierarchy, there must inevitably be losers as well as winners, irrespective of any overall rise in standards: what matters in a league table are a school's position vis-à-vis other competing schools. Such an approach, Scottish Labour objected, segmented the schooling system as well as giving added competitive advantage to children from more affluent backgrounds. A poor position in the league tables and the application of sanctions via 'naming and shaming', far from operating as an incentive to raise standards, would lower them by damaging morale (interview, Peter Peacock). Competitive systems inevitably stigmatise failure, whether these be individuals (pupils) or institutions (schools). As Jack McConnell reasoned:

If you create a system where there are failures as well as successes, which is the ultimate outcome of the system south of the border, then the kids that go through those failing schools will lose out. In order to see some schools racing ahead we didn't want some schools falling behind. This was not acceptable in Scotland. (interview)

This is why the Scottish Executive announced, in September 2003, the abolition of school league tables – 'central to the discourse of parental choice and the establishment of a market in schooling' (Lingard 2008: 973).[1] As Peter Peacock's ministerial foreword to 'Ambitious Excellent Schools' put it:

No one in Scotland should be required to select a school to get the first rate education they deserve and are entitled to. Choice between schools in Scotland is no substitute for the universal excellence we seek and Scotland's communities demand. (Scottish Executive 2004)

Some observers claimed that improvements in education in Scotland, as measured by exam results, were failing to keep pace with those in England. For advocates of the internal market these findings demonstrated that New Labour's market-oriented strategy was more effective than the collectivist approach preferred by Scottish Labour. But this begged the question of whether the quality and the value of the educational experience could be accurately evaluated in terms of quantitative 'performance outputs'. Scottish Peacock put the matter this way:

I can tell you with absolute confidence now how I could get Scottish exam results to rise. It would become the preoccupation of the system. I would narrow the curriculum in order to give more time to [outcomes that were measured]. I would learn what the examiners very precisely were looking for and I would coach my students to get over the exam hurdle. I might even in the short term incentivise results. But you pay a huge, huge price for that. If you do that you can get exam results to rise but my God, would you have any better-educated kids? I don't think so.' (interview)

Ultimately, this raised the fundamental question of what education was for. Peacock queried:

How come nothing in our education system but the exam result has got a value? This is absurd. We need to create systems of capturing and rewarding and recognising value beyond the narrow academic attainment which is of course important. (interview)

For the Blair Government the prime value of education was in the benefits it conferred on those who acquired it. These benefits were defined primarily in instrumental terms. By investing in education a pupil or student was amassing human capital – skills, capabilities and qualifications – appropriation of which enhanced the possessor's earning power on the labour market.

Education was thus the principal vehicle for individual advancement, the means by which people could satisfy their aspirations by augmenting their capacity to purchase goods and services.

The instrumental aspect of education has long been recognised within the social democratic tradition as vital, since access to high-quality education has always been seen as essential both for achieving greater equality of opportunity and for building a high-skill, value-added economy. But it had always been coupled with another strand, one that stressed the intrinsic aspect of education, something which had value in itself as a means of extending intellectual ability, cultural awareness and human sensibilities. It was this strand that influential voices within Scottish Labour were loathe to abandon. The danger of a very heavily instrumental view of education, with its obsessions with measurable learning and performance, was that it would unduly narrow and distort the whole educational experience, neglecting such vital attributes as the capacity for critical reasoning and problem-solving, the ability to empathise, and the capacity to work with others in a collaborative spirit (interview, Peter Peacock).

The ideal to which the universal comprehensive aspired was that all pupils of all ability ranges and (as far as was feasible) social backgrounds should be taught in schools designed to serve the local community. The commitment to a common schooling experience for all was seen as a means of strengthening social solidarity and community cohesion. This belief remained a cardinal principle of Scottish Labour's approach to education and could not be reconciled with the English-style model of a competitive and increasingly stratified secondary schooling system. Rebuffing Westminster-style ideas for 'beacons of excellence', First Minister Jack McConnell declared, 'I am not interested in a few schools of excellence. I want to see excellence in every school in Scotland. Opportunity for the majority, not the few, must be our guiding principle' (*Sunday Herald*, 3 November 2002).

The internal market would fragment the educational system and would damage the community cohesion sustained by a system which (to some degree at least) exposed pupils from differing social backgrounds to a similar educational experience. As the Scottish Parliament's Education, Culture and Sports Committee reported in its 'Inquiry into the Purposes of Scottish Education', 'Education should seek a balance between cohesion and diversity, but the general view was that promoting social cohesion should be the more important priority. There was no support for specialist models as seen in other parts of the UK' (quoted in Arnott 2005: 255).

Scottish Labour did not object to choice as such. It favoured choice as a generic social value, as a means of tailoring educational provision to the needs of individual pupils. But, crucially, it disconnected choice from competition, in which the ability of parents to choose between competing schools would act (as in the New Labour lexicon) as a driving force for improvement. The mechanical application to the public sector of principles that might be appropriate to the private sector took no account of the major differences of structure and purpose. As the Scottish Executive explained: 'Choice in public services is different from the choice an individual might expect in the private sector where supply outstrips demand, where everything is priced and where the user is constrained by their personal budget' (Scottish Executive 2006: 11).

Critics of Scottish Labour claimed that its tenacious attachment to a traditional collectivist approach to schooling was directly responsible for its lack of progress 'in resolving such intractable problems as stubbornly high rates of illiteracy and innumeracy, especially in the west central belt' (interview, John McTernan). Its resolute opposition to the use of internal market mechanisms, the argument ran, reflected a streak of ideological obstinacy combined with a complacency over the quality of Scottish secondary education, parochialism and a besetting fear of offending powerful producer interests.

A spate of reports that appeared during Labour's second term did indeed suggest that the record of Scottish schooling was decidedly mixed. In 2004, the Scottish Executive conceded that the performance of the poorest-performing 20% of pupils had failed to improve, that leadership was inadequate in about one in seven schools, that poor discipline in some schools distracted teachers and impaired teaching and learning, and that a worryingly high 15% of 16- to 19-year-olds were not in education, employment or training. It also acknowledged concerns among both parents and teachers 'about the volume and nature of assessment and about a cluttered curriculum' (Scottish Executive 2004: 10). A 2007 investigation by Her Majesty's Inspectorate of Education into the McCrone agreement found little evidence that the hoped-for improvements in learning and teaching had as yet materialised (The Herald, 9 January 2007).

Defenders of the Executive's record countered that this overlooked real achievements. One example given was the 'Schools of Ambition' programme. Launched in 2005 by First Minister McConnell, it was designed both to address long-standing problems in Scottish schooling and as a Scottish alternative to New Labour's Academies programme. It aimed to give head teachers more room to innovate, with pump-priming cash available from a national fund to finance imaginative schemes for low-performing schools. Researchers from a team drawn from three universities found that the programme had been innovative, had fostered flexibility, autonomy and professional accountability, and was highly valued by those head teachers who had participated in the scheme (Menter et al. 2010: 47–8).

But former ministers were prepared to accept that progress had been too halting. Though 'there had been significant gain, the gap in educational attainments has persisted, with many working-class children leaving school poorly qualified and educated, resulting in a lack of opportunity, esteem and income. We are still left with a profound inequality' (interview). More could have been done, it was felt, to remove inadequate teachers (around 5 to 7% of teachers in Scotland, according to one estimate) and to devolve management to head teachers. One argument forcefully expressed by former ministers was that the Executive should have invested energetically in a well-funded early years interventions strategy for children in disadvantaged communities. The key to educational performance was the acquisition of reading, writing, mathematical and communicative skills in the decisive early years of a child's life, in nursery and primary education. Steps could have been put into place to ensure that no child should be allowed to leave primary school functionally illiterate (interviews, Frank McAveety, Peter Peacock and others).

However, few believed that succour could be found through competition, diversity of provisions and rigorous performance appraisal on the English model. In part, this was because Scottish Labour were more likely than Blairite modernisers to regard poor educational attainment as, to some degree at least, the product of wider societal problems such as poverty, inequality, poor housing, family breakdown, poor parenting, drug and alcohol misuse and a culture of low educational aspirations. But, more broadly, a consensus persisted that community-based comprehensive education, professional regulation and co-operation were more effective levers for attaining Labour's traditional educational goals than unleashing market forces.

Scottish Labour and Health

Along with education, health was the key area of social policy devolved to the new Scottish Parliament. The Blair Government came to power pledged to unravel the internal market inherited from its predecessors, and under Frank Dobson some steps were taken. However, in 1999 he was replaced as Health Secretary by the staunch Blairite and eager 'moderniser' Alan Milburn who, slowly at first and then with mounting zeal, reversed policy and revived the internal market in England. As in the secondary school sector, it was assumed that competition would have a galvanising effect as producers would be impelled to take note of consumer preferences or suffer loss of custom and revenue. Two major legislative initiatives were the establishment of 'Foundation Trusts', hospitals which enjoyed a considerable degree of 'earned autonomy' in organisation and finance, and Payment by Results, by which the monies flowing to hospitals were to a large degree determined by their activity level, driven ultimately by their ability to win contracts. A league table for hospitals, the so-called 'star ratings' system, was also introduced to facilitate informed choice by healthcare commissioning bodies (Primary Care Trusts) and to foster competition among NHS providers. Competition and choice, it was anticipated, would be rendered more effective by encouraging new entrants to the market – private providers – the third leg of the New Labour reform triangle. The key reform here was the creation of 'Independent Sector Treatment Centres' or ISTCs, whose principal purpose was to 'incentivise' NHS clinicians to work harder and more efficiently by exposing them to competitive pressures.

The ultimate aim – and this was a decisive rupture with traditional social democratic thinking – was the establishment of a 'mixed economy of welfare'. In place of a unified system in which all public services were delivered by the public sector, public authorities would perform the roles of purchaser, regulator and guarantor but not necessarily the direct provider of services. Whether this amounted to privatisation was heatedly debated, but it certainly entailed intensified competition and the purchase of a growing volume of services from the private sector (see Shaw 2007: 108–10).

New Labour-style NHS modernisation rested on two key assumptions: 'that private finance and management is better than its public equivalent, and that markets and more choice represents the key to public sector reform' (Greener and Powell 2008: 629). Even before devolution, it was evident that these assumptions were not shared in Scotland. The NHS in Scotland had never been run by the UK Health Department but by the Secretary of State for Scotland and the Scottish Health Department of the Scottish Office (Baggot 1998: 122). Different legislative instruments applied to Scotland and the organisation of the NHS exhibited distinctive features (see, for example, Webster 1998: 90–3) that operated as filtering devices mediating the impact of Westminster legislation. During the Conservative years, the NHS in Scotland was also reconfigured along more market lines (with a purchaser/provider split), but because of Scotland's distinct organisational arrangements they were less well-entrenched than in England. After Labour's return to power in 1997, its Scottish Office ministers soon made clear their desire for a change of direction. A Scotland Office White Paper, 'Designed to Care' (1997), emphasised a much more integrative approach and signalled that the purchaser/provider divide, in which Primary Care Trusts purchased treatment on behalf of patients in their territorial areas from hospital trusts and other providers, would be gradually phased out. A key role here was played by the Scotland Office Health Minister, Sam Galbraith, a consultant neurosurgeon with a fiercely independent mind who was determined to get rid of what he regarded as the dysfunctional purchaser/provider split (interviews, Sam Galbraith, Margaret Curran).

'Designed to Care' set the line of advance for the devolved Scottish Executive. The Scottish Health Plan, 'Our National Health' (Scottish Executive 2001), continued the dismantling of the internal market by merging trusts into boards whose powers were thereby enlarged. In October 2001, fifteen NHS boards based on geographical areas were established 'to manage local healthcare organisations, give strategic direction and provide clinical governance'. They were charged with allocating funds and for developing local, regional and national health plans (Smith and Babbington 2006: 26). Finally, the 2003 health White Paper,'Partnership for Care', speeded up the process of dissolving NHS trusts, fully scrapped the purchaser/provider split and reversed the trend towards growing reliance on contractual arrangements (Greer 2004: 81). In sharp contrast to New Labour's market-oriented strategy, Scottish Labour favoured a co-ordinated and integrated health system, with the various health boards entrusted with responsibility for strategic planning, governance and performance management (Tannahill 2005: 213). 'The public, patients and staff', 'Partnership for Care' declared, 'expect the NHS at local level to be a single organisation with a common set of aims and values and clear lines of accountability' (SEHD 2003: 57). The White Paper marked a return to the concept of a pact between the state and the medical profession in which the latter, in co-operation with health managers and administrators, retained a key role in the allocation of resources (Greer 2004: 81).

The organisational changes outlined in the White Paper were implemented via the National Health Service Reform (Scotland) Act 2004. The functions of the NHS Trusts were incorporated into the NHS Boards, which were given the task of overseeing primary and secondary care (Robson 2007: 5). But this was not simply the re-creation of the 'top-down' form of NHS management. Rather, an attempt was made to balance centralised strategic decision-making by regional boards with the granting of more autonomy to medical practitioners (Winchester and Storey 2008: 21; Freeman 2007: 92). The aim was 'integrated, decentralised healthcare services' which devolved operational management authority to the front line, while enabling the boards to concentrate on 'strategic leadership and performance management across the entire local NHS system' (SEHD 2003: 58).

Adopting a market-oriented approach never received any serious consideration by Scottish Labour. Unlike in England, there was no appetite for private involvement in the delivery of public services. Indeed, the new private HCI hospital at Clydebank was brought into public ownership. 'The English model was never on the agenda', as one former minister put it. One reason commonly adduced (as with education) was that issues of scale and demography rendered the choice and competition agenda inappropriate. 'We did not believe it was right in Scotland', Jack McConnell explained, 'because of the scale of the communities that were covered. Even in our biggest communities the ability of hospitals to compete without damaging the service would be difficult, whereas in England you had that option, the scale to do it' (interview). Doubts about the value of a market-oriented approach, however, extended (as in education) beyond practical considerations. The central point for Scottish Labour was this: the best way to galvanise and spur forces for sustained improvement was not competition but through partnership with professionals, collaboration and service integration.

'It intuitively feels right', Malcolm Chisholm, Health Minister in the crucial years 2001–4, ruminated, 'that you actually do give a strong role to clinicians' (interview). This belief was reflected in a key innovation, the creation of Managed Clinical Networks (MCNs). These were envisaged as networks of clinical specialists in particular health areas and from primary, secondary and tertiary care who would work 'together in a co-ordinated manner, unconstrained by professional and NHS Board boundaries' to ensure high-quality provision (SEHD 2003: 39). MCNs embodied a strategy that 'sought to combine the advantages of co-operation, delegated responsibility and flexibility by allocating resource flows and activities according to the technical demands of the process rather than by territorial "patches"' (Greer 2004: 82). Thus, while in England policy was geared to nurturing market disciplines, in Scotland the focus was on planning and the development of networks and partnerships to encourage the different constituents of the health service (primary, secondary, differing specialisms, etc.) to co-operate for the common good (Smith and Babbington 2006: 26–7; Kerr 2005: 52).

In the absence of competitive pressures, would there not be a temptation – this was the New Labour critique – for public organisations to relapse into familiar and comfortable patterns of work geared to the benefit not of service users but of the producers, especially with such a powerful elite group as medical practitioners? Without market disciplines how could the major disparities that statistical analysis uncovered between different boards, hospitals and service providers be narrowed? Indeed, the Labour-led Executive did come under pressure to amend its policy as unfavourable comparisons were made in the press with England, where an allegedly more dynamic health service was making more progress in elevating standards and, in particular, reducing waiting times.

In fact, Scottish Labour policy-makers were generally aware of these dangers. Their answer was that reliance on professionalism had to be coupled with a 'really strong regulatory and inspection regime' (interview, Richard

Simpson). Thus, in response to the slow pace of health improvements in 2003, the Scottish Executive announced a new tighter set of targets and stronger statutory powers to grapple with service failure (SEHD 2003: 22–3). It pledged 'rigorous and independent monitoring and inspection, with robust arrangements to investigate and tackle serious service failure' (SEHD 2003: 23). If patients were not treated within the targeted timescale at their local hospital they were given the right to be treated elsewhere in the NHS, in the private sector or, in exceptional circumstances, elsewhere in Europe (SEHD 2003: 27). Two years later, 'Delivering for Health' (2005) laid down a whole range of targets for outpatient and inpatient waiting times (normally 18 weeks) (SEHD 2005: 6). To minimise opposition from within the medical profession, efforts were made to engage clinicians and health boards (representing the local population) as well health service managers in setting targets. Further, in contrast to the New Labour Government, tougher monitoring and inspection and the use of targets and performance indicators were not linked to resource flows. Outlining its proposed Performance Assessment Framework, the Scottish Government was at pains to distinguish it from the English system of star ratings. Far from being part of a competitive project, it pointed out, the Framework 'does not have strong financial or non-financial incentives attached to performance and it does not publish the data in the form of league tables' (Farrar et al. 2004: 35). In short, the assessments were explicitly not to be used as surrogate price signals.

There were some experiments with patient choice but this was largely limited to choice of NHS providers, rarely made explicit and infrequently exercised (Tannahill 2005: 214). There was a slight shift in emphasis in 2004 when Malcolm Chisholm was replaced by Andy Kerr, a more right-of-centre politician who did not share his predecessor's ideological objection to private sector participation. During his period as Health Minister a number of contracts were signed with the private sector, though arguably more as a way of meeting temporary capacity shortfalls than (as in England) to inject contestability into the system (interview, Andy Kerr). The shift was more nuance than substance, with 'reliance on professional networks' remaining 'the core of Scottish health policy' (Greer 2008: 124).

A core concept underpinning New Labour's health modernisation strategy was the extension of consumer choice. Holyrood shared Westminster's concern to foster greater receptivity to patient concerns, 'but the structures, incentives and accountabilities being put in place to establish this end are strikingly different', preferring extending 'voice' rather than 'choice' mechanisms (Tannahill 2005: 213). Voice, in Le Grand's words, 'is shorthand for all the ways in which users can express their disaffection (or indeed their satisfaction) by some form of direct communication with providers' (Le Grand 2007: 30–1).

Labour south and north of the border both used a combination of the two, but while for the former choice was the key mechanism, for the latter it was voice. 'Our vision', the Scottish Executive explained, 'is for personalised public services, which not only view service users as consumers, but also as participants and citizens' (Scottish Executive 2006: 11). It sought improved patient input and feedback channels and greater patient and community participation through a number of institutional changes. These included the establishment of two new bodies, the Scottish Health Council and Community Health Partnerships. The Scottish Health Council, which brought together a number of small local community health councils across Scotland, was charged with securing greater public involvement in NHS Scotland and with ensuring that 'quality improvement is driven by the needs of patients and service users' (SEHD 2003: 43). Community Health Partnerships were designed to encourage the involvement of local communities in the design and delivery of health service by working closely with local authority services and NHS Boards, and acting as a focus for integrating health services at local level (SEHD 2003: 35).

It is beyond the remit of this book to offer a considered view of Scottish Labour's health record. It is certainly the case that, despite substantial improvements, Scotland continues to be characterised (as it has been for many years) by health inequalities and health outcomes that are significantly worse than elsewhere in the UK, indeed than in most parts of the EU. But in his influential report, Professor David Kerr cited as the principal factors responsible for this not the institutional features of the organisations delivering healthcare, but life circumstances such as poverty, poor housing, low educational status, unemployment, smoking, poor diet, lack of exercise, and alcohol and drug misuse. Its main recommendation (accepted by Andy Kerr as Health Minister) was more emphasis on preventative care (Kerr 2005: 48). In sharp contrast to New Labour, market-driven reforms were never seen, by the party in Scotland, as the best way to raising standards of healthcare (Greer 2004).

CONCLUSION

In their survey of Scottish welfare policy, Mooney and Poole concluded that 'political and ideological choices are framed in the context of an overarching New Labour and neo-liberal agenda' (Mooney and Poole 2004: 476). The evidence in this chapter does not substantiate this conclusion. In some ways the greater test case is healthcare, given that the Scottish schooling system has always possessed institutional characteristics which set it apart from the rest of the UK. Here it is worth noting that none of the key institutional innovations introduced by New Labour – Foundation hospitals, star ratings, payment by results, a growing role for private providers, enhanced patient choice and incentivisation – was adopted by Scottish Labour. The whole emphasis remained on promoting unified and integrated healthcare in which different bodies were encouraged to pool resources and expertise by more collaborative working methods. In place of the mixed economy of health favoured by New Labour, Scottish Labour has stood by the traditional social democratic recipe of healthcare provided overwhelmingly by public institutions, free of substantial commercial intrusions. As Keating comments, 'on issues of organisation and delivery, England and Scotland have begun to diverge quite sharply' (Keating 2010: 211). Kerr and Feeley concluded that 'we have two healthcare systems (in Scotland and England)', which having started from the same place, 'have moved in significantly different directions, both in terms of the coding of those values into policies and in terms of how those values have been adapted and revealed in the process of making policy' (Kerr and Feeley 2007: 34). Freeman noted that in contrast to New Labour's preferences for healthcare, Scottish Labour's approach continued to bear 'all the hallmarks of social democratic policy making' (Freeman 2007: 92).

NOTE

1. It should be added that informal school tables, published in the press, circulated widely.

CHAPTER 10

Ideology, Institutions and the Programmatic Trajectory of Scottish Labour

INTRODUCTION

Writing in 2004, Richard Finlay concluded that 'for all the talk of Scotland being more radical than England and of the nation being predisposed towards left-of-centre redistributive politics, these characteristics have not really manifested themselves in any meaningful way. There is little to differentiate between the policies pursued at Holyrood and those pursued at Westminster' (Finlay 2004: 393). In fact, by 2007 it was quite clear that in the key devolved areas of healthcare and education, policy north and south of the border was moving in sharply differing directions. In England, the focus in healthcare policy was on introducing market disciplines and expanding the role of private providers, while in Scotland the internal market was scrapped in favour of planning capacity, networks and partnerships, and a reliance on professional trust (Smith and Babbington 2006: 26; Greer 2006: 20). Equally, in secondary education Scottish Labour's strong commitment to comprehensive schooling, its scepticism about the value of competition and choice, and its determination to sustain a major role in regulating education for professional organisations and local authorities all attested to a drifting apart of the education philosophies of Scottish Labour and British Labour.

How can we account for this? Were policy divergences the consequence of differing institutional, structural and political conditions or did they reflect contrasting ideological dispositions? Since it is a reasonable supposition that both sets of factors were at work, what was the balance between them? This chapter first considers the impact of institutional variables in shaping and constraining policy change. It then turns to the influence of electoral factors and differential strategic challenges. Finally it investigates the extent to which policy divergence is explicable in terms of Scottish Labour's distinctive values, beliefs and policy preferences, and the idea of 'Labour Scotland'.

169

INSTITUTIONAL FACTORS AND THE ROLE OF POLICY COMMUNITIES

Historical institutionalist theory has proved highly influential as a source of explanations of policy choice. It emphasises the importance of the institutional landscape – constitutional division of powers, rules and procedures, policy-making arrangements and policy communities – in the framing and adoption of policy (Campbell 2002: 30). Its central thesis is that such factors engineer a bias towards continuity through the process of 'path dependency'. Policy-making arrangements embody and reflect existing equilibria of power among affected interests, and disturbing them would raise the political costs of policy-making. Given that policy stability is normally politically cheaper than radical innovation, there is an inherent bias towards maintenance of the status quo. Furthermore, policies that are compatible with established ways of tackling problems and that can easily be processed through the existing policy machinery will appear politically more attractive since they reduce the expenditure of time, effort and political capital. As a result, 'once actors have ventured down a particular path they may find it very difficult to reverse course' (Pierson 2004: 10–11). Policy formation typically becomes 'an incremental process in which the weight of existing commitments limits the scope for innovation' (Keating 2001; see also Peter, Pierre and King 2005: 1276).

Institutionalist theories do, however, accept that sharp policy breaks are possible. The normal flow of events can be interrupted or 'punctuated' by 'critical junctures' when a crisis or a radical restructuring of the machinery of state disrupts established power equilibria, deflecting historical developments from the established path (Hall and Taylor 1996: 942). Typically, 'critical junctures' create windows of opportunity in which 'policy entrepreneurs' can exploit new and fluid conditions to promote major policy shifts.

It may be inferred from this that to the extent that institutional complexes, power configurations and policy traditions in Scotland and Westminster exhibited similar characteristics, a high measure of policy convergence post-devolution could be anticipated – and vice versa. Equally, to the degree that post-devolution Holyrood policy-makers found themselves confronting markedly new institutional realities, constraints and challenges, a window of opportunity would open for those who might seek to carve out a distinctive Scottish policy trajectory. Here the block-grant system of funding created propitious conditions for Labour to carve its own trajectory, since it gave Scotland full discretion as to how to spend allotted income (Greer 2004: 195).

What then of institutional legacies? Here one must distinguish between the two areas of secondary education and healthcare. Under the Act of Union in 1707, Scotland retained control over education, and a Scottish Education Department charged with administering primary and secondary education was established in 1872. Devolution did not so much extend the right of Scottish authorities to decide educational policy as to ensure that this right came under democratic control. It built on 'an existing and well-established system of administrative devolution in which each of the component territories had a distinct way of making or adapting policy and delivering services' (Keating 2001). Although healthcare north of the border has long possessed its own distinct institutions, norms and processes, the NHS in Scotland was part of a UK-wide system sharing the same fundamental characteristics and underpinned by the same principles. For this reason, the two policy areas are discussed separately.

THE INSTITUTIONAL COMPLEX OF SCOTTISH EDUCATION

A concerted drive was launched by the Conservatives from the mid-1980s to establish an internal market in English secondary schooling, but only diluted versions were exported to Scotland and even these were implemented at a slower place. This meant that new ministers in the devolved government confronted a structure of secondary schooling markedly different from that facing their Westminster colleagues. As Jack McConnell recalled, 'in England there already was a diverse range of providers, they were building on a system that was already there, different models and a massive private sector. Outside of Edinburgh and maybe Perthshire there is not a big private sector in Scotland and never has been' (interview). South of the border, diversifying the schooling system and deepening and expanding the internal market was running with the grain of inherited policy. In Scotland, a similar policy would have required far-reaching changes and a starker challenge to a pattern of education provision that had deep roots in Scottish culture. There was no disposition 'to rip the system up . . . As Education Minister in 2000 I was very determined that education policy in Scotland was not going down the diverse range of providers route' (interview, Jack McConnell).

Who, Greer asks, 'shapes the cost-benefit analysis and sense of plausibility and feasibility of policy ideas? Who helps or hampers policies and nudges policy ideas and advocates in or out?' His answer is the 'policy community' (Greer 2004: 1). Here the term *policy community* will be broadly defined to refer to a stable network of actors regularly and routinely engaged in the formation, development and implementation of policy in a given area. Typically, in addition to ministers and civil servants, it will consist of experts and representatives of professional bodies and interest organisations who

171

have acquired the status as policy stakeholders and recognised interlocutors, with the right to be consulted and even to participate in the determination of policy. Policy communities, it is widely acknowledged by commentators, play a crucial role in the design, framing and implementation of policy. They influence the repertoire of policies by filtering the flow of ideas, shaping notions of which should be deemed as credible, relevant and realistic, and therefore meriting consideration (Zahariadis 1999: 76; Béland 2005: 8). Equally, they 'determine the nature of coalition-building processes within states by granting societal representatives access to, and participation in, policy formulation in a particular area' (Cortell and Peterson 1999: 182).

Given that the structure of the Scottish education system has always been quite distinct from that in England, it is not surprising that the character of the two policy communities has also historically varied. However, this gap widened appreciably with the major restructuring of secondary schooling which occurred south of the border during the Conservative years after 1979. In England, bodies which had in the past exercised very considerable influence over the determination of education policy – local authorities, trade unions and professional associations – were progressively pushed to the margins. After Labour's victory in 1997, steps were taken to improve relations with teaching unions and local education authorities in England but, as the Government embarked on an increasingly market-oriented course, they never regained the status they had held under earlier Labour governments.

Thus, in Westminster policy-making was increasingly centralised in the hands of a tight coterie of ministers, officials and advisors located in the Department of Education and Science and in particular Number 10. In Scotland, building on pre-existing traditions, habits and practices, the Government inherited and opted to consolidate a more corporatist pattern of policy deliberation, working closely with local authorities, the Educational Institute of Scotland (EIS) and other professional bodies such as the General Teaching Council for Scotland (GTC). The EIS, by far the strongest teaching union in Scotland, has always been closely involved in policy-making as an 'insider' group. The GTC, a majority of whose members are elected by the teaching profession, is charged with the monitoring of professional teaching standards and must, by law, be consulted by the Scottish education minister on matters concerning teacher education (Issakyan et al. 2008: 13–14).

Under the Conservatives, local education authorities were stripped of many of the powers they had traditionally wielded. The New Labour administration was little more enamoured of local authorities than its predecessor and these powers were not restored, indeed even more were forfeited. In Scotland under the devolved settlement, in contrast, the role of local authorities, which had been somewhat abridged under the Tories, revived and they remained central players in the education policy community (Lingard 2008: 972; Humes 2008: 71). As a group of education policy researchers concluded, 'policymaking in education in Scotland still seems to be dominated by a well-networked community with close interconnections and a high level of professional expertise' (Issakyan et al. 2008: 21).

Real political significance was imparted to this by the trenchantly collectivist character of discourse within the Scottish education policy community, a discourse 'characterised by stronger support for comprehensive education, for an inclusive and unified arrangement for post-compulsory education, for public control and professional leadership of education, for stronger and more socially oriented policies for inclusion and for a social partnership approach' (Raffe 2004: 7). This set the frame of reference, the language and arguments that informed the conduct of debates about education policy in Scotland (Arnott and Menter 2007: 253).

Nowhere did the composition and role of the policy communities in the two nations differ more sharply than in the respective status accorded to the teaching unions. In England the influence of teacher unionism had always been weakened by its fragmentation as competing organisations jostled for membership and their often fractious relations diminished their capacity for co-ordinated action. In Scotland, in contrast, the great bulk of teachers were organised in the EIS. In England the role of the unions had been ruthlessly marginalised by the Conservatives, and though relations improved somewhat under Labour the unions – in particular the NUT – were still regarded with misgiving and mistrust and generally held at arm's-length. In contrast, in Scotland, with its long-standing relationship with the Scottish Education Department, 'the EIS was very much a part of the educational establishment' (interview, Sam Galbraith). As one of Galbraith's successors as Education Minister, Peter Peacock, recalled, 'I was always aware of how powerful they were . . . The EIS are the big players and what the EIS says in terms of the inter-union debates within education goes' (interview).

The relationship between Scottish Labour and the EIS was a close and collaborative one. Peter Peacock recalled, 'I got on well with their general secretary [Ronnie Smith] who happened to be from a Labour Party background. So we'd speak to each other a lot. I'd phone him, he'd phone me. We had disagreements but we always sought to manage them' (interview). The head of a major union which was (unlike the EIS) affiliated to the Labour Party reflected that 'the EIS's relationship with the Labour–Lib Dem administration at Holyrood was always far better and deeper than other unions on policy issues. They were treated as a social partner . . . the most successful trade union in doing deals for its members in recent years in Scotland has been the EIS' (interview).

In the eyes of some Labour critics, an excessive regard for the susceptibilities of the EIS had a damaging effect on Scottish education. Sam Galbraith, Education Minister between 1999 and 2000, found his experience of dealing with the union very frustrating. 'If you want to do something they'll give you ten reasons why you can't so it. They were totally resistant to all forms of change. They never, ever produced an idea . . . Until the Scottish Party gets a grip on the EIS and other so-called educational experts they'll never make progress' (interview). The failure of the McCrone settlement to insist on strict conditionality – binding obligations on teachers to make concessions to improve the quality of teaching in return for higher salaries and reduced hours of work – reflected (the argument ran) Scottish Labour's reluctance to grasp the nettle of EIS power, its preference for a strategy of conciliation, or, in some eyes, appeasement (interviews, Sam Galbraith, John McTernan, Rhona Brankin). As John McTernan (who worked both for Tony Blair and Henry McLeish) tartly put it, during the McCrone negotiations Education Minister Jack McConnell's strategy was 'to stuff their mouths with gold' to gain 'peace with the unions' – his 'great political prize' (interview).

For key political figures within the Scottish party, creating a more harmonious relationship with the EIS, and teachers in general, after years of strife, bitterness and demoralisation under the Conservatives, was a wholly legitimate end. They were prepared to acknowledge that union resistance, for example over reforming poor working practice and facilitating the speedier dismissal of inadequate teachers, was at times an impediment to raising standards. Notwithstanding, an improvement in standards could more rapidly be achieved through consensus and partnership with the EIS. It made sense to expend energy on restoring good working relationships with the teaching profession thorough confidence-building measures. 'The way to make progress was not through confrontation but to create alliances for change' (interview, Margaret Curran). Adversarial stances ignored the fact that the teachers the EIS represented had real grievances and, rather than being simply motivated by self-interest, genuinely wanted to do their best for their pupils. Far from being supine, Peacock countered, his strategy was 'to be firm on the things I needed to be firm on, be clear, try and bring them with me, and agree to disagree or to put it off to negotiate another day where we differed. But I never felt I had to dance to their tune' (interview, Peter Peacock).

Whatever the division within Labour's ranks, all felt constrained by the mix of inherited policy traditions, institutions and ideologies that gave rise to an educational setting quite different from that of England. A shift towards a New Labour-style market-based strategy would have represented a much more radical break, a veritable 'paradigm shift', which would have been vehemently resisted by a powerful coalition of forces wedded to a more traditionalist collectivist ethos. It was never on the cards.

THE INSTITUTIONAL COMPLEX OF HEALTHCARE IN SCOTLAND

Scotland has for long had a powerful and highly institutionalised health community. The very high status of the medical profession has traditionally afforded it considerable influence over all aspects of health policy, more so, perhaps, than their colleagues elsewhere in the UK (Greer 2004: 68). The fact that the Scottish Office, responsible for health policy to Scotland, lacked the policy and administration resources available to the Health Department in London had the effect of rendering it more dependent on Scotland's medical elites entrenched in Scotland's hospitals, universities, the British Medical Association (BMA) and the Royal Colleges, for information and advice, and for conferring legitimacy on key policy decisions. Officials relied heavily on a 'powerful, impressive, and high-status set of medical elites to help it make and operate policy and administration' (Greer 2007: 142). These elites occupied a strategic position within the Scottish health community, enjoying 'a respect among policy-makers for professionals in social life and the health services often lacking elsewhere' (Smith and Babbington 2006: 19; see also Cairney 2008: 362).

Their influence was further augmented when the Scottish Parliament was established. What were the policy and political implications of this? The British medical establishment was never very enthusiastic towards market-oriented prescriptions but its Scottish counterpart was even less so. In part this was due to the differentiated interest structure in Scottish and English medicine. In England there had always been (especially in London) a lucrative market for private medicine, and a high proportion of consultant surgeons drew a large (and, for some, a very handsome) slice of their income from private practice. In contrast, the opportunities for private work were lesser in Scotland and most clinicians committed themselves fully to the NHS. Furthermore, the culture of the Scottish medical profession was imbued with a firmer attachment to collectivist notions than in England. The chair of the Scottish council of the Royal College of General Practitioners claimed a 'stronger feeling for the NHS in Scotland, both by the general public and by health professionals', with both 'totally committed' to the institution and its principles (quoted in Stewart 2004: 114) – perhaps a predictable claim, but one accepted by Labour MSPs who were also senior medical practitioners and by no means uncritical of their profession (interviews, Sam Galbraith and Richard Simpson).

In England the health policy community contained experts and corporate representatives who were eager advocates of New Public Management and of a market-oriented NHS reform programme (Smith and Babbington 2006: 19). There were numerous (often part corporate-funded) think tanks and research centres with both the institutional capacity and the enthusiasm to formulate, disseminate and mobilise support for policy proposals that challenged the social democratic/professional consensus. Added to this was the growing presence of private healthcare corporations (many from abroad) who scented tempting commercial opportunities, forged close institutional links with civil servants, ministers and sympathetic think tanks and experts, and lobbied assiduously for a market-friendly approach. In Scotland, in contrast, not only were there few think tanks, but private healthcare corporations, seeing modest commercial possibilities, took little interest in extending their operations northwards.

In short, the collectivist consensus was not exposed to the same powerful challenges as in Westminster. While in England the health policy community was eagerly incubating pro-market ideas, in Scotland political and professional discourse around the delivery of public services continued to be permeated by social democratic perspectives (Smith and Babbington 2006: 19). This discourse drew added strength from the Scottish style of consensual policy-making, with its preference for extensive consultation and the accommodation of the interests and preferences of professional elites (Arnott 2005: 255).

For some this 'cosy consensus' stultified new and imaginative thinking. One senior New Labour advisor opined that Scotland's 'deeply-rooted and long-lasting social and cultural institutions' afforded a 'thickness of the institutional structure' which inhibited new thinking and created a 'great echo chamber for discussion and debate'. As a result, ideas about the future shape of the public services or about 'the role, scope, and ambition of government' remained confined to those consistent with the post-war collectivist settlement (interview, John McTernan). Such views were not confined to those sympathetic to the New Labour script. Education Minister Peter Peacock agreed that 'as soon as you've got consensus you get complacency. There was very little challenge inside Parliament, inside politics, about the policies we were pursuing. On the one hand, we're comfortable and it's quite good because you partly own the argument. On the other hand, over a period of time that can become dangerous because you need challenge' (interview). Further, in education so too in healthcare, the muscle of professional associations and trade unions and their entrenchment in policy communities undoubtedly had a constraining effect on Labour ministers. As one senior minister testified, 'there was a definite reluctance to challenge established interests and challenge the status quo, a lack of political will' (interview).

However, it would be wrong to conclude that Scottish Labour were deterred from challenging the ruling collectivist consensus and experimenting with bolder schemes, along the lines of the public sector reform programme south of the border, by the formidable institutional and political obstacles they would have to navigate. In fact, as will be seen below, these ideas were never on the party's political agenda. Before considering why this was the case, this chapter turns to another set of institutional constraints, those emanating from the pattern of electoral competition.

The Influence of the Party System and Electoral Imperatives

Electoral calculations inevitably intrude in policy-making. Party leaders will always be concerned about the impact of policy proposals on their ability to woo the voters. To what extent was policy divergence between Labour north and south of the border a response to the differing strategic challenges they faced? Here there are two distinct, though related, strands to the argument. The first was that Scottish Labour confronted a more centre-left electorate, the second was that the axis of the party system was tilted more markedly towards the left.

The first point is a matter of some dispute among commentators. McCrone found that 'Scotland remains significantly more left-of-centre as regards private education, educational selection, redistribution of income and wealth, as well as attitudes to poverty, the EU social chapter and the minimum wage' (McCrone 2001: 124). Similarly, Stewart has contended that 'we have a public sector, collectivist ethos and culture in Scotland that markedly distinguishes it from New Labour aspirations and policies and, perhaps, from the currently dominant value system in England' (Stewart 2004: 143; see also Arnott 2005: 246). While English politics and public life (and in particular that of London and the South East) was becoming ever more individualistic in temper, collectivist sentiment remained more solidly anchored in Scottish political culture. Indeed, in reaction to what was perceived as an alien Thatcherite assault, allegiance to more solidaristic values was increasingly seen to define modern Scottish identity (Keating 2003: 433).

Others have argued that differences are in fact negligible. Using data from Scottish Social Attitudes surveys, Bond and Rosie found little empirical evidence to support the thesis that Scotland was more left-wing. They conclude that 'despite common perceptions, social surveys consistently show that, in terms of their broad socio-economic and political attitudes ... people in Scotland are not markedly more social democratic than people in other parts of the UK' (Bond and Rosie 2007: 55; see also Curtice et al. 2009). There is some evidence that those who evince a strong sense of Scottish identity tend to be more social democratic in outlook but the difference is not very pronounced (Curtice et al. 2009: 28).

However, it should be noted that the Scottish Social Attitudes surveys do not investigate attitudes towards the use of market forces and private producers in the public services. The data that *does* exist suggests there are indeed disparities between the two nations. The responses collected for the Scottish Executive's 2002 'National Debate on Education' revealed substantial levels of confidence in comprehensive schools, noticeably more so than in England (Arnott and Menter 2007: 257; Keating 2005a: 458). Similarly, the consultations organised as part of the Kerr investigation into the NHS in Scotland uncovered 'a strong degree of antipathy towards the "market-driven" health reforms which appeared to dominate England's NHS' and a powerful sense that healthcare should be part of the local community. 'People felt they belonged to the NHS and that the NHS belonged to them' (Kerr and Feeley 2007: 33).

But given the scarcity of material, any judgement on the issue has to be cautious and tentative. In particular, the absence of systematic comparative data enabling us to assess variations in the attachment to individualistic or communitarian/solidaristic value constellations in the two countries does not allow firm conclusions to be drawn. Where there does appear to be a difference is that public sector discourse *among the professional middle classes in Scotland* articulates a distinctly more collectivist ethos than in England. The widespread resistance towards the introduction of market forces and private sector mechanisms into the delivery of public services appears to reflect a deeply ingrained belief that the state and not the market should be responsible for welfare provision (Stewart 2004: 143; Arnott 2005: 246, 255).

There is less ambiguity about the impact of party system pressures. Even prior to devolution, the party system in Scotland had acquired characteristics that clearly demarcated it from England's. This was due to two factors: the salience of the constitutional issue which had dramatically changed Scottish politics, and the decline of Scottish Conservatism. The effect was to tilt the ideological axis in Scotland considerably further to the left than that in England. Though the compulsions of a highly adversarial style of politics – which persisted after devolution – prodded all parties to inflate them (sometimes grossly), in reality the differences between the main non-Conservative parties (Labour, the SNP and the Liberal Democrats) were rarely other than matters of tone or emphasis (interview, Malcolm Chisholm). 'Rhetoric apart', another former senior minister commented, 'there's about a 90% agreement and the differences between the parties would be about 10% or maybe even less' (interview). Whereas in England, Labour's main challenge came from the right, in Scotland it came from a party, the SNP, that inhabited broadly the same ideological territory. As one senior political advisor put it, 'Whereas New Labour's opposition were the Tories in Scotland, it's a fight to the death to be the social democratic centre-left party and it just dominates all Scottish politics' (interview, Danny Phillips).

What this meant was that the espousal by Scottish Labour of market-oriented policies on healthcare and education (and in other areas too) would have been immediately and ruthlessly pounced on by the SNP, which was making determined efforts to portray itself as the authentic Scottish custodian of social democratic values. (It would also be at risk of leaking votes to the Greens and the SSP, who between them held thirteen seats in the 2003–7 Parliament). The only advocates of a market-based solution in the public services were likely to be the Conservatives, and their 'brand' was widely seen as being so 'toxic' in Scotland that their support alone would suffice to discredit it in the eyes of the public.[1] In short, whatever Scottish Labour's own predilections, electoral considerations operated as a major inhibitor to any temptation to emulate the New Labour model.

The Ideas and Values of Scottish Labour

Institutional legacies, the composition of policy communities and strategic challenges all operated as factors which favoured the pursuit of more traditional social democratic policies. But does this suggest that the values and ideas – the belief system – of Scottish Labour were irrelevant? The rest of this chapter suggests not. Its point of departure is that institutional variables 'may help to explain why a policy alternative is defeated or enacted but it can seldom account for the reasons why actors conceived and made sense of this alternative in the first place' (Béland 2009: 703).

New Labour claimed to have swept aside ideology: 'what matters is what works'. Their avowed pragmatism stipulated an approach to policy which made decisions on the grounds of the merits of the case, the feasibility of a policy and a careful and scrupulous investigation of its likely consequences. But how is one to determine what is feasible? Do policy-makers have access to sufficiently reliable information and sufficient time to conduct full investigations of the merits of differing policy options? In a complicated, unpredictable and fast-flowing world where information is always imperfect and time pressures are relentless, political actors must inevitably rely on mental maps or frames of reference which impart intelligibility to complex phenomena. Frames can be defined as more or less coherent mental structures that 'select for attention a few salient features and relations from what would otherwise be an overwhelmingly complex reality. They give these elements a coherent organization, and they describe what is wrong with the present situation in such a way as to set the direction for its future transformation' (Schon and Rein 1994: 26).

In the case of the organisation and operation of the public services, Labour Party opinion generally divided between two conflicting frames, which will be called the *competitive* and the *professional*, each with its own distinct diagnosis and prognosis. For the competitive frame, the key to sustained improvement in the quality of public services and the optimal use of scarce resources was exposure to competition. The professional frame, in contrast, contends that, with appropriate safeguards, the best way to ensure the delivery of efficient, responsive and equitable public services is by reposing trust in the judgement of public sector professionals (Le Grand 2007: 18). A fundamental distinction between the two frames arises from their differing assumptions about human motivation. As Le Grand explains, 'Policy-makers fashion their policies on the assumption that both those who implement the policies and those who are expected to benefit from them will behave in certain ways, and that they will do so because they have certain kinds of motivation and certain levels of agency . . . Conscious or not, the assumptions will determine the way that public policies are constructed' (Le Grand 2003: 2). Advocates of the professional frame were convinced that the most effective motivating force was that combination of an adherence to a professional code and a sense of public service known as the 'public service ethos.' It was this frame that had in the past defined and organised Labour's thinking (Plant 2003: 561).

Key New Labour figures were dismissive of the professional frame. They questioned (as the Prime Minister's Strategy Unit put it) 'the reliability of the public service ethic as a motivational drive' and, in its stead, expressed 'a growing conviction that self-interest is the principal force motivating those involved in public services' (Strategy Unit 2006: 59). It was this belief that lay at the root of New Labour's critique of the collectivist philosophy of public service delivery. In the private sector market disciplines impelled self-interested producers to respond to consumer desires, but in the public services monopoly providers had no incentive to respond to the needs or preferences of their users. As a result, public organisations tended to succumb to bureaucratic inertia, a wasteful use of resources, rent-seeking behaviour, weak management and (above all) 'producer control' (Strategy Unit 2006: 50). New Labour's response was three-pronged: to expose providers to competitive challenges (this was known as 'contestability'); to constrain professional autonomy and enforce greater accountability by such means as audits, targets, league tables and performance monitoring; and by introducing 'incentivisation', that is, linking incentives to personal performance (Gleeson and Knights 2006: 280–1; Doig and Wilson 1999: 28).

Scottish Labour, in contrast, retained a broad allegiance to the professional frame, preserving a belief in the capacity of the public service ethos to mobilise the energies of public- sector employees and enhance organisational performance. It saw organisations in the public sector as bound together not by incentive structures but by a shared culture, professional norms and public service. Scottish Labour's reform strategy, Tom McCabe explained, 'is predicated on the belief that we must value those dedicated, and often highly qualified, individuals who ensure consistently high standards of public services are provided to those who need them most' (Tom McCabe, in Scottish Executive 2006: 2). They should be 'incentivised to act as professionals' (Winchester and Storey 2008: 11).

Sam Galbraith, another former minister, highlighted the difference between the two approaches:

> When we said we would abolish the internal market [in the NHS] one of the officials asked what we were going to give as an incentive. I was somewhat flummoxed by that. I said they don't need an incentive – they'll do their best for their patients. You want to be regarded as a high-quality consultant, your results as good as his. In my experience consultants were motivated by just giving patients a good service. There are knaves who are money-driven, but they are in a minority, especially in Scotland, because the private sector is marginal. (interview)

The majority of Scottish Labour ministers endorsed the proposition that 'to deprofessionalise, to distrust professionals and to subject them to crude material incentives and penalties, is merely going to worsen the problem without providing an effective alternative' (Keating 2007: 247). Unleashing market forces and installing arrangements designed to institutionalise a more competitive and instrumental ethos would promote self-interested behaviour and undermine the co-operative relations vital to the effective delivery of public services. A former minister (and GP) elaborated the point:

> There's a genuine belief among the health service professionals, management and politicians that the ethos of the health service in Scotland is of great importance in the way we deliver the service. Efficiency and productivity are important but they are secondary considerations to an ethos of being a good service which actually values the clinicians and values the patients. (interview, Richard Simpson)

Not all Scottish Labour politicians were convinced of the validity of the professional frame. Some were keen to assert their willingness to engage with the private sector and to encourage its involvement in the provision of public services. Several ministers were ardent champions of the Private Finance Initiative (in which private sector consortia build and continue to own hospitals, schools and so forth, which are then contracted out to public authorities), which they believed represented the best way of undertaking major capital projects. If the political conjuncture had differed, such figures may (though this is speculative) have been prepared to contemplate market-based solutions to other public sector problems.

But these were in a minority. Key figures, such as Education Minister Peter Peacock and Health Minister Malcolm Chisholm, were staunch proponents of collectivist policies and would have adamantly resisted New Labour-style public service 'modernisation'. It does not, however, follow that those (the majority) who adhered to the professional model were unaware of or indifferent to the problems to which it could give rise. High status, a very large measure of self-regulation and the possession of valued expertise, it was understood, conferred a large measure of organisational power on professionals, which could have detrimental effects without firm measures of accountability or control. Labour Holyrood ministers knew (from practical experience) that public sector organisations, professional associations and trade unions (the EIS was often named) would seek assiduously to promote their own collective and institutional interests and could act as a break on innovative policy reforms. Some felt (at the time or on reflection) that they had been too solicitous of professional opinion and that more should have been done to challenge them (interviews, Margaret Curran, Tom McCabe).

Notwithstanding, they retained confidence in the essential pillars of the professional model: that a sense of professional obligation, pride in public service and altruism were more effective drivers of effort than competition and 'incentivisation'. As one senior trade union leader commented, 'there was no body of opinion that was willing to create or generate a debate within the Labour movement about public sector reform, that is, the marketisation of public services' (interview).

The differences between Scottish and New Labour were not confined to their attachment to clashing professional and competitive frames. At the heart of New Labour's advocacy of market-oriented public service reform was a 'conception of the modern world being dominated by the practices and experiences of a consumer culture' (Vidler and Clarke 2005: 21). In the words of a resolute Labour moderniser, 'Ordinary consumers are getting a taste for greater power and control in their lives. They expect services tailored to their individual needs. They want choice and expect quality' (Milburn 2007: 8). Scottish Labour, in contrast, preserved more of an attachment to the traditional social democratic image of public services as an expression of collective purposes. The public good, such as community cohesion or equity, could not be reduced to the amalgamated preferences of individual service users, or left to the interplay of supply and demand. There was, for example, a strong sense that a school was very much part of the fabric of the local community, and by providing a common educational experience it helped to sustain communal bonds. As former Education Minister Peter Peacock contended, education was 'not just about gaining a clutch of qualifications. It's also about the social environment of your community. It's about learning about your community, it's about mixing in your community, and it's about strengthening your community. It's about identity as well' (interview).

Linked to this was a sense that co-operative human effort and collaborative service delivery was 'better' than competition. Co-operation was better both in the sense of being more effective – partnership, collaboration and integration were more likely to deliver high-quality public services – but it was also better in a moral sense, reflecting the 'value-based judgement' that 'competition is wrong in principle and that co-operation is right in principle' (interview, John McTernan).

The ethos of Scottish Labour was, in short, influenced by what Paterson called 'social democratic communitarianism'. This envisaged human identity as 'intrinsically social', and affirmed that 'personal fulfilment depends upon our relations with others. The main aim of public policy should be to safeguard and develop the community conditions that help individuals to be fulfilled' (Paterson 2001: 121). Not all, by any means, shared this view, but it did constitute a significant feature of Labour's political culture, manifested in a certain wariness and mistrust about the efficacy, appropriateness and indeed morality of market instruments as means for addressing Scotland's social problems. Whatever the sources of this view – in Scotland's culture, traditions and experiences – the effect was to render Scottish Labour 'uncomfortable with the argument that says that the only way you can create change in the public sector is through market-based reforms' (interview, Margaret Curran).

POLICY DIVERGENCE AND IDEOLOGICAL DIFFERENCE

This chapter has focused on the degree and evolution of policy divergence post-devolution. While noting the importance of policy inheritance and traditions emanating from the existence of autonomous and semi-autonomous Scottish institutions prior to devolution, it found a widening gap between New and Scottish Labour over the two crucial areas of health and secondary education. Why?

The chapter has argued that Scottish Labour's decision to opt for a more traditional social democratic approach to the two crucial policy areas of secondary education and health was the result of a complex interplay of factors. As Bale points out, separating the role of institutions, interests and ideas is ultimately an artificial exercise, since politics 'can only be understood . . . by focusing on the intersection, the relationship, and the reciprocal influence' of all three (Bale 2010: 12). Thus, policy-making processes and policy communities shaped how policy proposals evolved, the obstacles they had to navigate, the interests they have to propitiate and accommodate. Where ministers anticipated that a policy innovation would encounter strong institutional obstacles and provoke intense political resistance, they were reluctant to proceed. The party system and the balance of opinion within the electorate, equally, influenced the party's calculation of the broad programmatic direction it needed to travel to maximise its prospects at the polls. Given (to take one example) the embedded traditions of an autonomous Scottish secondary school system, given the deep roots the notion of the universal, community-based comprehensive had sunk, given the power of the EIS and its close relations with officials in the Scottish Education Department (SED), given, finally, Scottish Labour's unflinching attachment to the concept of comprehensive education, any politician who chose to defy all this, disrupt the consensus and opt for a more marketised system would have been taking very high political risks. As one senior aide who had little sympathy for the New Labour approach observed, 'it wasn't worth a fight, wasn't worth the hassle' (interview, Danny Phillips). Indeed, absent in Scotland was both any driving political and ideological impulse to follow the New Labour route, and a powerful coalition of interests that would have supplied institutional and political muscle to sustain it. The energy, ideas and sheer political determination that propelled public sector reform in Westminster emanated from Number 10. Scotland lacked a similar central control capability and no figure of real weight embraced the marketising project that was the leitmotif of the Blairite programme.

In order to understand decision-making in conditions of uncertainty, we need also to take account of 'the mental models that individuals construct to make sense out of the world around them' and 'the ideologies that evolve from such constructions' (Denzau and North 1994: 4). Reflecting on differing patterns of public service reform north and south of the border, Jack McConnell commented, 'Tony's Government was ideologically committed to market-driven delivery, absolutely committed to that. There was an ideological difference between the two governments' (interview).

What was the essential nature of that 'ideological difference'? There was no real disposition in Scottish Labour to challenge the basic tenets of traditional social democratic thinking. For New Labour it was an exhausted paradigm, a fetter on efforts to revitalise the public services. Scottish Labour, in contrast, was neither intellectually convinced by nor ethically at ease with the notion that the public services could best be revitalised by consumer choice, competition and the entry of private providers. At root it continued to retain faith in the traditional social democratic belief that the public interest would best be served by a public sector grounded in the precepts of professional pride, public service and co-operative effort. Contending that Scottish Labour was 'far less New Labour than the Blair Government', Bogdanor conjectured that its new leaders 'might well have different diagnoses of the problems from that held by the Blair Government' (Bogdanor 2001: 152). This we have found to be the case.

But in a sense the notion of 'ideological difference' is misleading. Scottish Labour's unease with market-oriented policies was instinctive and rarely articulated in clear theoretical ways. Its creed tended to be more a congery of beliefs, notions and principles than a clearly thought out or coherent intellectual construct: it expressed a social democratic 'sensibility' and 'idiom' rather than a developed ideology. This sensibility, reinforced by its proximity to the institutional interests representing the public sector, operated as a bar to the absorption of policy ideas emanating from New Public Management and rational choice theorising. The penetration of market disciplines, a commercial ethos and pecuniary motivations into the fabric of public services were all culturally uncongenial to Scottish Labour.

Scottish Labour was, equally, disinclined to engage in any intellectual or ideological exchange with New Labour. Its justification for moving in a different direction was generally strictly pragmatic: Scotland was different by virtue of size, demography and traditions. It made no real attempt to defend its policies by elaborating its own narrative. Its policies on healthcare and education in effect posed a challenge to Blairite modernisation, but were never presented or elaborated as such. As Keating commented, Scottish Labour seemed 'to be retaining old models of public provision, sometimes by inertia and sometimes by design, but without articulating a rationale or philosophy' (Keating 2007: 244).

All this reflected the essentially empirical, practical character of Scottish Labour, some would say its 'labourist' provenance. The party only engaged very episodically in general discussions of political values and goals – what the party was actually *for* – and even then there was a tendency to regard them as disconnected from real, down-to earth issues. If the merits of rival policies were debated, it was generally in terms of tangible considerations and political exigencies – as will be seen in detail in the following chapter when the case of free personal care for the elderly is discussed.

Indeed, there was a lack of interest in exploring the meaning and significance of the values with which Labour is commonly associated – equality, social justice, solidarity and so forth. Values such as these were frequently invoked, but sustained effort to determine precisely what they entailed and how they could be applied as criteria for policy choice was rare. They were seldom used as an integrative mechanism, linking individual policies to over-arching purposes. If asked to define such values, politicians would usually respond in terms of highly concrete policies (a definition of social justice proffered by one senior figure was 'free bus travel and free central heating'). The terms 'socialist' and 'social democratic' were rarely employed (either in public or in interviews) except for ritualistic or symbolic purposes. Equally, there was little sense of an educative mission. The presumption was that Scotland was Labour's natural territory, the two bonded together in shared norms and values – and, hence, the chief task in elections was to 'get out the Labour vote'.

This reluctance or inability to engage in any systematic and sustained way with New Labour advocates over the philosophical trajectory of the party deprived Scottish Labour of a clear and distinct profile. It exposed it to the criticism that it was ideologically barren and backward-looking, unwilling to embrace the bright new shiny future of modernisation, lacking in vim and energy for the 'Brave New World' of New Labour. It was quintessentially 'Old Labour' in the tendentious New Labour parlance. This failure to chisel out a sharp sense of what it stood for, what it was trying to achieve and what values animated it was to render it electorally vulnerable to a party less inhibited about its social democratic credentials.

Note

1. In fact, the electoral and institutional dynamics contributed in Scotland to pushing all the mainstream parties, Conservatives included, onto terrain which was resistant to the choice and competition agenda in relation to public services. This meant there was no Dutch-style auction of parties positioning and manoeuvring, as has happened south of the border, to appeal to floating voters in marginal constituencies, on the 'choice' agenda.

The Paradox of Free Personal Care for the Elderly

THE POLICY SETTING

'By far the most dramatic case of policy divergence in any field since devolution', Greer has written, 'was the decision by Scotland to fund universal long-term personal care for the elderly' (Greer 2004: 87). The decision to make this a universal entitlement represented a serious challenge to one of the central policy planks of New Labour, the shift towards a more selective (or means-tested) approach to the provision of welfare, and, as such, was bitterly resented in Westminster (Pollock 2001). It seemed to indicate that Scottish Labour had opted for a quite different perspective on 'the role of the State and the boundary between public and private responsibilities in long-term care', one which corresponded far more closely to traditional collectivist thinking (Deeming and Keen 2001: 85). 'Thanks to devolution', The Guardian declared, the UK 'has a constituent state in which social democracy is strong' (*The Guardian*, 27 January 2001). During the 2003 election campaign, Scottish Labour celebrated the policy as their proudest accomplishment.

The paradox of free personal care is that if the decision had been left solely to the party it would never have been adopted. The party was dragged reluctantly to accept it by First Minister Henry McLeish who exploited the new political realities of devolved government to overcome resistance from the bulk of his ministers and the majority of Labour MSPs – and in the teeth of opposition from Westminster. Whatever it tells us about Scottish Labour's philosophy, the story is not a simple one.

Long-term care has been defined as the provision and financing of care over an extended period of time for those suffering from physical or mental ill-health (Osterle 1999: 7). The Labour Government in 1997 inherited a situation seen by many as thoroughly unsatisfactory. The matter was of rapidly growing political importance as the proportion of the population in higher age brackets was steadily rising and the existing mixed state and private family support system was widely seen as unfair and inadequate. Recognising this, in December 1997 the Government set up a Royal Commission into long-term care, headed by Sir Stewart (now Lord) Sutherland, with the remit of proposing 'a sustainable system of funding of long-term care for elderly people' (Royal Commission on Long Term Care 1999).

The central issue was this: to what extent should the cost of care be borne by the bearers themselves (and their carers), and what extent shouldered by the state? Care has conventionally been divided into three types: nursing (medical), personal and 'hotel' (i.e. food and accommodation). Personal care included such matters as personal toilet, dressing, eating and mobility. The Commission's report, 'With Respect to Old Age', published in February 1999, recommended, firstly, that medical care dispensed at home or in nursing homes should be provided for all. Secondly, so-called 'hotel costs' should remain means-tested. The third recommendation was the most controversial: that long-term personal care should be furnished free for all, on the basis of need (Royal Commission on Long Term Care 1999: 6.32). The first two recommendations were accepted by the Government but the third was rejected outright. According to Health Secretary Alan Milburn, this was because universal free personal care would 'consume most of the additional resources we plan to make available for older people through the NHS'. The real reason was that the Government objected to the higher taxation implied by Sutherland (*The Guardian*, 1 September 2000).

The Scottish Executive, led by Donald Dewar, followed suit. In October 2000, Health Minister Susan Deacon announced a three-year investment package, rising to £100 million per year in 2003–4, including funds to help older people remain in their own homes, to speed up discharges from hospital and to implement universally free nursing (medical) care. But personal care would still be means-tested. Before the policy could be implemented, Dewar died and was succeeded by Henry McLeish. He declared that all policies would be reviewed and intimated that serious consideration would be given to free personal care. In November 2000, the Scottish Parliament's Health and Community Care Committee published the results of an enquiry into Community Care. 'The overwhelming message from stakeholders in community care', it found, 'supports the principle of making available personal care services free at the point of use as recommended in the Sutherland Report', and it proclaimed that 'our cross-party committee unanimously supports the principle of free personal care delivery, without means testing individuals' eligibility' (Health and Community Care Committee 2000). This propelled free personal care firmly onto the agenda.

Notwithstanding, when Susan Deacon announced a care package for the elderly on 24 January 2001, it broadly reiterated the position taken by the Dewar Cabinet in October the preceding year. Pensioners' groups were dismayed; opposition parties dismissed the First Minister as a figurehead of Downing Street and he was widely denounced in the press. Within a few days the Executive dramatically reversed its position, stating that it was now 'unequivocally committed to bringing proposals to this chamber that will implement free personal care for all' (Official Report Vol. 10 No. 06, 25 January 2001: col. 697). This decision opened up 'the biggest policy divide yet between Holyrood and Westminster' (*The Guardian*, 27 January 2001). A Care Development Group under the then Deputy Health Minister Malcolm Chisholm was established to investigate how the proposal could be implemented. By this time Scotland was in the hands of a new First Minister – the third since 1999. Jack McConnell had replaced McLeish in November 2001, after the latter had resigned over allegations relating to expenses. Though McConnell was not an enthusiast for the policy, it was too late to turn back and the Community Care and Health (Scotland) Act 2002, passed in July, introduced free nursing and personal care for the elderly. This took effect the following year.

The term 'free personal care' is in fact a little misleading. Payment for personal care for those in care homes was fixed at £145 per week, with an additional £65 for nursing care. Since the cost of an average care home place in Scotland was £427 per week, the balance was deemed to be accommodation costs and was means-tested. Personal care for those living at home was free of charge but subject to a need assessment by the local authority. While the Scottish Executive provided guidance for local authorities on eligibility criteria and levels of quality of service provision, interpretation and implementation was left to individual authorities, but this meant that both eligibility and quality varied significantly (Bowes and Bell 2007: 436; Dickinson et al. 2007: 468).

Problems have continuously dogged the implementation of the policy. Money given to local authorities to fund personal care has not been ring-fenced and critics have claimed that, because need was under-estimated, it has been inadequate. As a result, many councils have introduced waiting lists and there have been disputes over the coverage of the payments. Furthermore, there is some evidence that private care homes have made up the shortfall in funds to cover personal care by over-charging on hotel costs for those who are self-funded (Cairney 2007: 13). The fact that many people appear to be unaware that free personal care does not include residential costs caused some disaffection. However, after an investigation into the operation of the policy the Rowntree Foundation concluded that the 'system is popular and perceived as fair. The biggest beneficiaries have been people on modest means and people with dementia facing high care charges. Costs have not escalated out of control by unleashing limitless demand, as some had feared' (Hirsch 2006). Further, even after the onset of the financial crisis and mass pressure on public spending levels, all major parties (aside from the Tories) remain committed to maintaining the policy.

OPTING FOR UNIVERSALISM

Universal personal care, as noted, would never have been passed if Labour had held a majority in Holyrood. Its passage was partly a matter of chance – the death of Donald Dewar. 'If Henry McLeish had not re-opened the issue', a top civil servant recalled, 'it would have gone away' (interview). This raises two questions: Why did McLeish take this decision? And how – despite the serious reservations of virtually all his Labour ministerial colleagues, the opposition of the majority of Labour MSPs and (as will be seen) the fury of the Blair Government – did he succeed?

As is common in the real world of politics, McLeish's decision was driven by a mix of conviction and calculation. McLeish was a mainstream Scottish Labour politician and had, one close political ally reported, a 'healthy contempt' for the folklore of Scottish socialism. Politically sympathetic to Gordon Brown, he was convinced that Labour had to be modernised along the lines prescribed by the national party leadership (interview). Yet, on this issue, he went his own way. As one well-informed observer commented, 'McLeish instinctively felt free personal care to be right, to be humane' (Taylor 2002: 38). A system which covered fully the cost of treating the victim of cancer but not of Alzheimer's 'in what should be a totally integrated healthcare approach . . . made no sense and created cruel anomalies' (McLeish 2004: 143). The distinction between nursing and personal care was, he maintained, artificial and contrived. Finally, he felt that Labour was ducking the 'huge problem' of how to care for the growing numbers of the frail and elderly, a problem he was hence determined to prioritise (interviews with McLeish aides; McLeish 2004: 144). These convictions were reinforced by the First Minister's second wife, who was a senior social worker specialising in care of the elderly and a staunch protagonist of free personal care (Taylor 2002: 37).

Calculation coalesced with conviction. The new First Minister was looking for a political success to shore up his political position, establish his authority and place a very distinct personal imprint on the new politics of devolved Scotland. 'He wanted to do something that Westminster would not do, that Donald Dewar had not done. He wanted to make his mark' (Taylor 2002: 38).

He arrived in high office with multiple disadvantages. While Dewar had been a highly regarded and eminent politician with a nationwide reputation, McLeish was little known outside Scotland and had only occupied a junior position in the Westminster Government. He lacked political stature and the confidence and respect of many of his colleagues (interview, MSP). He was mocked in the media because of his verbal infelicities and an alleged lack of lucidity, and his unexpectedly narrow win over McConnell indicated a fragile base among Labour MSPs.

McLeish knew free personal care was popular (Health and Community Care Research 2001). He was aware that Scotland had an ageing electorate and that the over-45s were twice as likely to vote as the under-45s. Further, he was keen to demonstrate that devolution worked. One senior colleague observed:

> It was Henry's legacy issue, it was as simple as that. Why did he choose this as a legacy issue? My guess is that Henry was looking for an issue that differentiated him from London, that at least was perceived, even if it did not in reality, as helping more vulnerable members of society. The boxes he was seeking to tick: something big and significant, and that could be portrayed to be about social justice even if it wasn't necessarily in reality and differentiated him from London. (interview)

Opting to make free personal care his personal mission would enable McLeish at a stroke to identify himself with a popular political cause, 'assert independence from London, present himself as the pensioners' hero, break from the Dewar leadership and command his reluctant cabinet colleagues' (*The Scotsman*, 3 September 2001). Aware of the opposition of virtually all ministers, he decided to 'bounce' them into supporting it. Once McLeish as First Minister had declared publicly for universal free personal care, many felt they had little choice but to fall in behind (interview). Behind the scenes McLeish, it was alleged, 'more or less goaded' Parliament to vote against his own government, playing off Liberal Democrats against his own ministerial colleagues (interview, MSP).

But all this was the judgement of an instinctive, somewhat impulsive, politician. No attempt was made to consult the Westminster Cabinet or the Department of Health. There was little consideration given to the problems of finance, of practical implementation or of the serious implications of relations with London. It was, one insider commented, 'policy-making on the hoof' (interview). All this might seem to bear the hallmark of an inept, ham-fisted politician, who was (as his Party critics put it) totally out of his depth. But if he was not a coldly calculating politician, arguably he was an intuitive one. He understood that government was, for the most part, about routine administration and that the ability to make an intervention which actually has a real, tangible effect on politics and on people's lives is very rare – and should be seized if the opportunity occurs. A change had to be swift and dramatic to be noticed – and galvanise the electorate.

Significant as it was, McLeish's advocacy alone – in the face of widespread party resistance – would not have sufficed to place free personal care on the statute book. Party competitive pressures equally had a powerful impact. Scharpf distinguishes between two types of decisional modes: 'single-actor constellations', which are characterised by 'hierarchical direction'; and 'multiple-actor constellations', in which decisions are made via 'mutual adjustment' and 'negotiated agreement' (Scharpf 1997: 46). Westminster followed (broadly) the former model. The Government can force its policies through Parliament via the mechanisms of a disciplined party system sustained by high levels of party cohesion. Not so at Holyrood, which is much closer to the latter model. Initially, the Liberal Democrat ministers (Jim Wallace and Ross Finnie) had endorsed the Dewar line on free personal care – but were forced by backbench pressure to change tack (*The Herald*, 28 January 2001). As a partner in a coalition government, they shared with Labour an interest in its unity and success. But as the junior party they were at risk of diluting their political identity. In free personal care the Liberal Democrats found a policy which was popular, which had majority support in Holyrood, which appeared to differentiate them from a divided Labour Party and for which they could claim the lion's share of credit.

McLeish astutely took advantage of this. He used his coalition colleagues to out-manoeuvre his Labour opponents in the Cabinet. As one of his senior colleagues recalled, 'there was actually a point in which Henry met with the Lib Dem ministers and asked them to keep the pressure on because he was having trouble with the Labour ministers and Labour group. He asked them to make a bit of a racket about it so that would allow him to say that they would go bananas if we pulled out of this' (interview). In McLeish's own words, 'my position was strengthened quite remarkably by the support of other political parties, including the Liberal Democrats . . . this created a natural majority in the Parliament' (McLeish 2004: 141–2).

The 'mutual adjustment' model helped McLeish secure free personal care in another way too. While in the Westminster system backbench and opposition MPs play a negligible role in legislation, devolution was 'deliberately designed to alter the balance of power between the Executive and Parliament' (Taylor 2002: 92). The powers and status of select committees were enhanced by vesting them with the functions of both Westminster's Select and Standing committees and by norms encouraging their members to develop a legislative rather than a purely partisan identity. Thus, while the Dewar-led executive was deliberating on the Sutherland Report, the

Health and Community Care Committee, as noted, conducted its own investigation. It unanimously recommended in favour of universal, free personal care delivery (Health and Community Care Committee, 16th Report, 2000: para. 43). Not only did this lend moral and political weight to the cause of free personal care, it undermined the credibility of those Labour members of the Committee who had signed the report but subsequently (for whatever reason) sought to detach themselves from its conclusions.

One further factor is worth noting. In Holyrood the pattern of relations between government and the organisations of civil society supplied greater accessibility and more entry-points to the welfare lobby than in Westminster. Devolved politics engendered a policy-making structure more open and fluid than either in London or pre-devolved Scotland, and this benefited a lobby that traditionally lacked the intimate insider status of business, financial and professional interests. Equally, the centre-left consensus which defined much of Scotland's party system – and much of its media – has rendered the system more amenable to welfare policy advocates. As a result, Labour MSPs found themselves 'under tremendous pressure' from lobbyists skilfully deploying sympathetic contacts in the media (interviews, Labour MPs and MSPs).

Such were the new institutional realities of a devolved polity. The New Labour leadership in London appeared to appreciate little of this. In public its response was sanguine. Was not the whole rationale of the new constitutional settlement that devolved governments could go their own way? (*The Guardian*, 27 January 2001). In private ministers were incandescent, with Number 10's political advisors 'screaming down the phone to their counterparts in Edinburgh, and McLeish came under intense pressure to back down' (interviews, McLeish aides). The Treasury threatened 'to re-examine the extent of the funding available to Scotland. If the Executive could even contemplate free personal care, it plainly had too much disposable cash' (Taylor 2002: 40). As McLeish recalled, 'they found it so incredible that we would step out of the Westminster net and would come up with something which, if implemented in England, would cost them a fortune' (interview). The First Minister had quite simply gone too far.

Anger in the Blair Government stemmed from two main considerations. Firstly, it felt that McLeish had violated the emergent convention governing relations between Labour ministers in Westminster and Holyrood. This stipulated that both would refrain from any political initiative which might cause political embarrassment to the other without full prior consultation: the rule of 'no surprises'. Any troublesome issues should be quietly resolved by informal, behind-the-scenes ministerial discussion. The springing by McLeish of a major policy reversal with potentially damaging repercussions for the Westminster Government was perceived as a flagrant breach of this convention – and, indeed, of party solidarity (interview, Helen Liddell).

Secondly, what made this apparent breach of convention so provocative was that the issue was politically such a sensitive one. There was widespread dismay in England and Wales that so many homes were being sold to pay for nursing and residential home fees (*The Guardian*, 23 June 1999). According to a BBC poll conducted in February 2002 – to which 150,000 viewers contributed – free long-term care for the elderly was seen as the NHS's top priority (*BBC News*, 20 February 2002). Furthermore, there was a general expectation that the state would and *should* provide for all in old age, that it was a right of citizenship – and puzzlement that personal care should be free for some illnesses but means-tested for others. In other circumstances, the Government would have been able to claim that, whatever people's reservations, its approach was the only realistic and financially viable one: there was no real alternative. The decision of the Scottish Executive to press ahead with free personal care pulled the rug from under its feet. As Age Concern proclaimed, it 'wholly undermines the case which UK ministers have been making' (*The Guardian*, 26 January 2001). The Government was besieged with demands from elderly campaigners that England follow Scotland's lead (*The Guardian*, 27 January 2001; *The Scotsman*, 3 September 2001). The pressure abated, but never disappeared. As many suspected, the Westminster Government's own policy was not sustainable and, in its final year in office, it was still pondering how to reform it. In the end it off-loaded the problem to its successor.

But the Westminster Government did not confine itself to words. It wanted to demonstrate that there was a cost to be attached to a public act of defiance. Prior to the introduction of free personal care, Scottish pensioners had received a non means-tested Attendance Allowance from the UK Department of Works and Pensions, designed to give support with personal care needs due to disability (Bowes and Bell 2007: 437). Universal personal care replaced Attendance Allowance, saving the UK the cost, and the Executive requested that the Department of Work and Pensions transfer the money (some £25 million per annum) to Scotland where it could contribute to defraying free personal care. 'This met with an absolutely firm refusal' (McLeish 2004: 142). The Government claimed that its hands were tied for legal and administrative reasons (interview, Helen Liddell). McLeish disputed this interpretation but to no avail. The real reason was political. The refusal to release the money was 'Whitehall's punishment for introducing free personal care' (*Sunday Herald*, 13 January 2002). McLeish – and Scottish Labour – had to be taught a lesson. It was 'a slap on the wrist', 'a rap over the knuckles' – a warning, perhaps, to act with greater circumspection in the future (interviews).

'Henry', as one MP commented, 'nailed his leadership colours to the mast on it, which then created a dynamic difficult to resist' (interview). He caught his colleagues unaware, he caught his parliamentary party unaware and he caught London unaware – and by so doing forced the issue. In effect, he came close to making free personal care for the elderly a *fait accompli*. He thereby made his mark. But, from a personal point of view, it was a miscalculation: he offended too many powerful figures, forfeited much goodwill and, rather than bolstering his political base, eroded it. When his moment of crisis occurred – within less than a year – and he was assailed with charges of financial mis-demeanours, there were few prepared to lend a hand to the beleaguered and transient First Minister.

THE DEBATE WITHIN SCOTTISH LABOUR

What does this sequence of events tell us about Scottish Labour? The form the debate took within its ranks needs to be explored. There were three main (and interconnected) considerations: the Barnett Formula, sustainability (or long-term affordability) and general principle – the issues of universalism, selectivity and equity.

The first consideration was both financial and political, and revolved around the maintenance of the Barnett Formula for determining the size of the grant delivered by the UK Treasury to Scotland under the terms of the devolution agreement. Already the Executive (under pressure from the Liberal Democrats) had agreed to a system of tuition fees less onerous for Scottish university students than that enacted by London for England. Further, it had just negotiated the McCrone settlement which provided for Scottish teachers better pay and conditions than their colleagues elsewhere in Britain received. Would not free personal care for all the elderly infirm provide ammunition for those within the PLP – notably in North East England and London – who claimed that Scotland was being too generously treated? McLeish recalled that, 'much of the debate was influenced by those who demanded how on earth we could find the money to pay for it . . . If you have the money, then we must be giving you too much' (McLeish 2004: 143). Why, ministers had complained (as a report discussing recently released ministerial files from the period disclosed), play into the hands of Scotland's critics? (*Sunday Herald*, 15 June 2008).

The implications for Barnett were directly linked to the second consid-eration, sustainability. The majority of Labour ministers and backbenchers believed that free personal care was unsustainable, in that the Executive would be incurring costs that it could not afford. Health Minister Susan Deacon (and Department officials) argued forcefully that it would suck in an ever-increasing proportion of the Department's budget. The Sutherland Commission had seriously under-estimated the danger of escalation in the costs of free personal care, notably by taking too little account of demographic pressures – the rising proportion of the elderly – the indeterminacy of take-up rates and the actual costs of providing the service (interview with high-ranking civil servant; *Sunday Herald*, 29 January 2001). This, according to Susan Deacon, was 'a huge issue' (interview). A former senior McLeish aide concluded that for this reason alone the policy was 'a terrible error'. The immediate costs could be absorbed but in the longer term the effort to maintain an open-ended commitment would be a serious drain on the Scottish budget (interview, John McTernan).

The debate over long-term affordability was, in reality, a judgement less about 'the scale of financial costs' than about 'the *opportunity costs* in terms of foregone benefits in spending limited resources in some other way' (Deeming and Keen 2001: 79). Scotland's revenue-raising powers are limited and the UK Government's rejection of the Sutherland Commission's recommendation that personal care should be paid for from general taxation left the Executive with no option but to draw the money from within its current block allocation. Rather than the better-off bearing a disproportionate share, personal care would be funded by re-apportioning spending within the block grant (Pollock 2001: 311–12). As Health Minister, Susan Deacon was deeply worried that more pressing priorities would be sacrificed by having to find the cash to cover the costs of those who were (by definition) not among the (financially) most needy (interview).

The belief that the opportunity costs of free personal care were too high was rooted in normative as well as financial considerations. At issue was the conflict between two conceptions of equity, one expressing itself in support for universalism, the other for selectivity. 'Historically', a leading authority has noted, 'a crucial political divide across the British political spectrum has been over the fundamental aims of the welfare state, with those on the Right . . . seeing its role as predominantly that of poverty relief, while the Left has pushed towards provision of welfare services on a universal basis, not just to the poor' (Hills 1998).[1] Selectivity, or means-testing, from the traditional social democratic standpoint, had a series of disadvantages, such as stigmatising recipients, eroding the principle and legitimacy of social welfare, and piling up administrative costs. Universality, in contrast, embedded social solidarity as 'universal institutions enshrine our common membership of society and equal social status' (Horton and Gregory 2010: 221). Universalism, in short, forges a common interest among all groups in society and both articulates and institutionalises the notion that the nation as a whole has a moral responsibility for the welfare of all (Keating 2007: 252).

The Sutherland Commission opted for the classic social democratic universal formula. 'From a theoretical point of view, the Commission are persuaded that universal risk pooling of some kind . . . represents the most effective way of providing the coverage required' (Royal Commission on Long Term Care 1999: 3.16). Institutions acting on behalf of society had an over-riding obligation to protect the welfare of those of its members who 'unpredictably and through no fault of their own' fall victim to the extreme vicissitudes of life. Since neither the 'incidence nor the scale of care needed' were predictable, it was 'equitable and proper for the state to meet at least one element of these "catastrophic" costs for everyone' (Royal Commission on Long Term Care 1999: 6.32–6.34, 10.13). In short, universalism was 'the best guarantee of equity' (Royal Commission on Long Term Care 1999: 3.15).

New Labour rejected universalism (outside of healthcare and schooling) on two grounds. The first was political. Desperate to shrug off the association in the public mind between Labour and high taxation, it repeatedly pledged not to raise – indeed, actually decreased the standard rate of – income tax and, equally, lowered taxation on the corporate sector. There was a limit to how much income could be extracted via 'stealth' taxes, which meant that free personal care for all could only be funded by cutbacks elsewhere in the welfare budget. Secondly, it believed that targeting, by ensuring that resources go to those least capable of fending for themselves, was the most redistributive of policy options. Indeed, a deliberate expansion of means-testing became 'one of the hallmarks of New Labour's social security policy' (Brewer et al. 2002).

Scottish Labour's problem was that it lacked, for the most part, the capacity to fund universal programmes through progressive taxation and had to meet them from existing resources.[2] For this reason the argument was not about the balance between taxation and spending but about spending priorities. The point that caused most anguish was posed starkly by the First Minister. What was the rationale for providing free healthcare for someone plagued by physical illness while 'if the same person had a debilitating condition, no less harsh in its impact but not classified as "medical", such as those with dementia who need constant attention and physical care, it had to be paid for by the individual or the family. In what should be a totally integrated healthcare approach, this made no sense and created cruel anomalies' (McLeish 2004: 143).

For some this argument was misconceived. If you suffered from cancer, you received medical and nursing care as a right, but not personal care. Why should the same not apply to dementia? (interview, Sam Galbraith). Others were less certain. Dementia was no less incapacitating, no less devastating in its consequences because its manifestations were not primarily physiological. Indeed, Richard Simpson (like Galbraith, a medical practitioner) cast doubt on the genuineness of the distinction between nursing and personal care (Scottish Parliament Official Report, 24 January 2001: col. 503). Doubts about the rationale for differential treatment for those afflicted by mental and physical disease were widespread and caused palpable unease. The result was 'one of the most turbulent debates in the Scottish party's recent history', one which generated 'a huge amount of trauma' (interview, MSP). As one MSP recalled, 'people were torn both ways because it is a strong argument to say that those suffering from Alzheimer's should be treated in the same ways as those suffering from other long-term diseases such as cancer. Why should a person be charged with their care needs because of an incurable brain disease?' (interview).[3]

But the majority concluded that universal free personal care was not the most equitable way of allocating scarce resources.[4] As one MSP observed, free personal care was 'wrong because it wasn't the most deserving in society who were benefiting . . . That money has to be better targeted' (interview, Mike Watson). 'If you've got in excess of a hundred million pounds a year to spend', another MSP queried, 'would you wish to spend it on free personal care from which probably no more than seven thousand people would benefit, or would you prefer to use that to improve care services for the elderly as a whole?' (interview). One senior figure in the party put the matter very bluntly: it was 'at the end of the day a measure that allows middle-class people to stoke up capital that is then inherited by their wealthy kiddos' (interview). Every Labour minister, Sam Galbraith, McLeish's Education Minister, later wrote, opposed the universal option not simply because it was 'unafford-able' but because it was wrong – it was a 'right-wing policy' promoted by the Lib Dems to 'protect their own – the elderly rich . . . Labour governs for all the people, but it is surely not its job to prop up the wealthy' (The Herald, 9 February 2004). For the protagonists of the policy this analysis failed to acknowledge the fundamental unfairness of the existing system: that, in the words of the Care Development Group set up by the Executive, it discriminated 'against older people who have chronic or degenerative illnesses and need personal care' (Dickinson et al. 2007: 462). But, equally, they argued it betrayed a wilful misunderstanding of social realities. As one senior MSP commented:

I don't think enough people had a feel for the level of resentment there is out there among people who'd worked hard, who'd sacrificed, who hadnae just pissed it up against a wall for forty years, who'd actually made a go at it, who wanted to give their children a better platform in life than they had and yet all of a sudden found that when they become unfortunate enough this big monster called the State started to swallow up the thing at a hell of a rate, which it does. (interview)

Free Personal Care and Scottish Labour

So what does the episode tell us of Scottish Labour? Free personal care represented a significant extension of social citizenship, a crucial principle underpinning the social democratic welfare state. It institutionalised a new social right – the right to personal care for all those suffering from all chronic disabling disease, irrespective of their income. By extending the borders of the welfare state, free personal care endowed Scots with social citizenship rights greater than elsewhere in the UK. That this should have occurred in Scotland appears to be consistent with the findings of our previous two case studies: that the social democratic values of social solidarity and universal collective provision were more firmly rooted in the party north than south of the border.

In reality, it was implemented against the will of the majority of MSPs and, overwhelmingly, of ministers. A complex concatenation of circumstances pushed them reluctantly to embrace a policy for which very few had much enthusiasm. 'Being absolutely honest about it', one Labour MSP mused, 'there's many within the party who thought we should not have gone down the route of free care for the elderly' (interview). As has been seen, many feared that the policy would swallow up resources that could better have been targeted on other areas where greater advances would have been made in promoting social justice. Universalism, they reasoned, was redistributive to the extent that universal services are funded via progressive taxation, and this was not an option available to the Scottish Executive.

The Scottish Labour Party thus confronted a different range of choices and constraints in free personal care than in healthcare and secondary schooling. Whatever decision was made would have painful (from a social democratic perspective) consequences. But what is striking is how rarely the argument was conducted in ideological terms. As has been noted, many found it difficult to refute the argument that current policy (and policy as it operates in England) operated unfairly against those afflicted by degenerative mental rather than physical disease. But there was little concern that it breached the concept of a universal welfare state. One Scottish Labour MP dismissed the principle of universality as a totem (interview), and many appeared to accept Gordon Brown's argument that selectivity was *fairer*. Universal personal care was, in one Scottish Westminster MP's phrase, 'a personal care plan for Scotland's rich' (*The Herald*, 15 January 2002). A common response (in interviews) to the point that the same reasoning could be applied to treatment of physical illnesses was a slightly uncomfortable pause, as if the implications of their reasoning had not been fully thought through.

Policy was of course heavily influenced by political circumstances and pressures, as well as by the perceived departmental interests of ministers. But what remains striking is the disconnect of the debate over free personal care from a wider appreciation of the norms structuring the classic social democratic welfare state (see Esping-Andersen 1990). In fact, notions of social solidarity, community and collective responsibility hardly figured in the debate. This seems puzzling, in that Scottish Labour politicians liked to present themselves as more communitarian in outlook than their English colleagues – indeed, as has been seen, this was a consistent theme in the defence of the 'community-based comprehensive'. As one former minister commented, within Scottish Labour 'there was very little consideration given to relating policy to first principles' (interview, Susan Deacon). All this reflects, as argued in the previous chapter, that the idea and 'myth' of 'Labour Scotland' sat alongside its highly empirical cast of mind, its focus on immediate, highly tangible day-to-day issues and its disinclination to conduct debates and formulate policies within a framework of clearly elaborated principles. This is a theme to which the book will return.

NOTES

1. 'What best characterises the Swedish and the other Scandinavian welfare states is most programs are universal, not selective. This means that social programs . . . are not targeted to "the poor", but instead cover the entire population without consideration of their ability to pay' (Rothstein 2001: 218).
2. Though Scotland has the right to vary the standard rate of income tax by 3% either way, the idea that free personal care should be funded by raising the tax was never seriously discussed or even aired.
3. This was the point forcefully made by Sutherland: 'Whereas the state through the NHS pays for all the care needs of sufferers from, for example, cancer and heart disease, people who suffer from Alzheimer's disease may get little or no help with the cost of comparable care needs' (Royal Commission on Long Term Care Report 1999: 65).
4. It was also pointed out that the means-tested element was still applied for the 'hotel' (i.e. food and accommodation) aspect of care for residents of nursing homes.

Part Four
Dynamics of Scottish Labour

CHAPTER 12

Still the People's Party?
Scottish Voting Behaviour and the
Scottish Party System

INTRODUCTION

Scottish politics have been characterised by different eras of party competition and dominance. There was the Liberal era of the nineteenth century, and in the twentieth century a Tory Indian Summer of 1945–55, followed by a period of Labour dominance from 1959 to 2007, and in recent years the emergence of the SNP as the leading party in the Scottish Parliament.

This chapter will provide a brief outline of the main patterns of post-war Scottish politics in relation to voting intentions and the wider party system. It will utilise Lipset and Rokkan's work on political cleavages to understand Scottish politics and Labour's place, examine the influence of possible new alignments and social movements, look at the role of the media in Labour's politics, and address the role of electoral systems. It will conclude with an assessment of party images and the contemporary state of Labour.

First, Scottish politics need to be understood in context. A large part of public conversation about politics is focused on 'the Scottish dimension' without defining it, or addressing its inter-relationship with 'the British dimension'. The former and the latter need to be understood situationally, as constantly changing, and importantly, in a relationship where each influences the other. Johns et al. reflect on 'the Scottish dimension' historically and observe, 'The extent to which the Scottish dimension assumed a positive valence status in Scottish politics is rarely remarked upon, yet it is one of the most enduring and pervasive aspects of UK politics' (Johns et al. 2010: 79).

Second, elections, whether for the Scottish Parliament or Westminster, contain a contest for which party is best seen as addressing Scottish interests. Third, any party which is seen by voters as not sufficiently advocating Scottish interests runs the risk of being seen as 'anti-Scottish', a perception which took deep root about the Conservatives in office during 1979–97. This is not just about party stances on constitutional issues but about wider discourse and how the electorate interpret signals and subliminal messages (see Miller 1981: 165–8; Brand et al. 1994: 219–20; Bennie et al. 1997: 131–41, Brown et al. 1999: 157–8; Paterson et al. 2001: 40–1; Johns et al. 2010: 88–97).

Scotland has not always been Labour. There was a pre-'Labour Scotland': the Liberal Scotland of the nineteenth century, the managed society of the committees of the great and the good with its limited, elite democracy (Hutchison 1986; Fry 1987). The Liberal Party of this period was a powerful force, drawing from the Highlands and Islands, Borders and the Central Belt, urban and rural. Between 1832 and 1910 they won a majority of the popular vote in every one of the twenty general elections, only failing to win a majority of parliamentary seats once in 1900 (Craig 1981).

Labour's electoral breakthrough occurred in 1922, when the party won 32.2% of the vote and finished with the most seats, twenty-nine out of seventy-one, aided by Liberal divisions. This election, which is sometimes seen as the manifestation of 'Red Clydeside', with Labour's historic breakthrough in Glasgow where it won ten of the city's seats to the Conservatives' five, also saw the beginnings of the Conservatives reaching out to new constituencies of support, aided by the collapse of the Liberal vote.

The evolution of Scottish politics in the 1920s saw the emergence of Labour as a national party and chief competitor across the UK with the Tories, forming two minority governments in 1924 and 1929–31 which contributed to the party being seen as able to govern, squeezing the Liberals as an anti-Tory force, and disappointing many left-wing hopes. The Conservatives also gained from the emerging two-party system and challenge from Labour, articulating a broad coalition which was anti-socialist, portrayed Labour as a sectional interest, and began to develop the values of a progressive, modern Conservatism that invoked the ideas of a 'property owning democracy' (in the writings of Walter Elliot and Noel Skelton). Many accounts ignore the fact that the narrative of 'Red Clydeside' was a contested perspective at the time, and a useful mobilising perspective for mainstream Conservatism to win over moderate opinion.

FROM NEW JERUSALEM TO POST-NEW LABOUR

Labour's historic victory of 1945 was marked by some concern in the party with regard to Scotland. Labour made, on first impressions, impressive gains in votes and seats in Scotland, winning 47.6% of the vote and thirty-seven out of seventy-one seats. However, their vote was below the overall UK percentage vote, while the number of seats was only one more than the party won in 1929, and proportionately less (52.1%) than the UK (61.4%).

The party could boast of significant electoral gains across Scotland, with fifteen gains compared to the position at parliamentary dissolution, while the Conservatives lost the same number. Labour gained Edinburgh Central, Leith and North, Paisley, Kilmarnock and the two Dundee seats, and won back Motherwell from Robert McIntyre after his SNP victory months before the general election. Labour failed to make major progress in Glasgow, gaining only one seat across the whole city: Kelvingrove. A Mass Observation diarist at the time reflected on the Glasgow results, 'The most Conservative of the big British cities is – Glasgow! And it did so by staying as it was before. London is far "redder" than Glasgow' (Calder and Sheridan 1984: 225).

More tellingly, Labour was a party lacking in energy and enthusiasm in representation or at the level of ideas. Tom Johnston, Churchill's wartime Secretary of State, had retired from active politics, while the 'Red Clydesider' tradition was exhausted, and the ILP close to folding, finally rejoining Labour with the death of James Maxton in 1946. The mainstream of the party elected to the Commons was middle-aged, male and with little radical intent or ferment.

The Conservatives polled respectably in Scotland, winning 41.1% of the vote, and post-1945 invested time and resources in party organisation, materials and railing against the centralisation of the Labour Government, in effect adopting Scottish credentials (Mitchell 1990). This contributed to the party outpolling Labour narrowly in votes in 1951, and then in 1955 winning 50.1% of the vote – the only occasion in post-war Scotland a party won a majority of the vote.[1]

This new Conservative coalition was impressive in range and depth. Conservative Party membership was estimated to be in the region of 250,000, with Church of Scotland membership hitting 1.307 million in 1955 (*The Herald*, 12 May 2008; Report to the General Assembly 2011).[2] It was also shaped by anti-Catholicism, if not quite as virulent as in the 1920s and 1930s, and the continuation of widespread discrimination. The Tories had deep roots in the Protestant working class as well as middle class, aided by a populist anti-Catholicism in parts of society, pro-union values, the pride of Empire and Scottish credentials. This was a powerful political combination of 'Empire, militarism, "Orangeism" and a Scottish distinctiveness sheltered amicably under the Unionist umbrella' (Seawright 1999: 154).

In three successive general elections the Conservatives won seven out of Glasgow's fifteen parliamentary seats to Labour's eight. This was in folklore supposedly the heart of Scottish Labour's constituency, and yet the Conservatives were able to poll well and win across the city.

The Conservative high point was by its very nature the beginning of their decline, with the then emergence of Labour as the leading party of

Scotland for the next four decades. This was not completely obvious at the time as elections are fought one at a time with longer-term trends tending to be visible after the event. A host of economic indicators and industrial job losses underlined Scottish vulnerability in the late 1950s and early 1960s. While Macmillan talked of 'you've never had it so good' in 1959, Scottish unemployment from the year previous began to rise significantly, reaching 116,000 in May 1959, having risen through the politically sensitive figure of 100,000. Traditional jobs were in decline in manufacturing and mining, and shipbuilding in particular, while new industries were not enough to replace them. There was also cultural change, with the totemic, symbolic heavy work traditionally done by men being challenged by the expansion of services, increased consumerism and women's employment (Finlay 2004: Ch. 4; Macdonald 2009: Ch. 7).

In Scotland in 1959, the Conservative vote declined slightly with them still ahead of Labour by 47.2% to 46.7%, while Labour gained four seats, finishing with thirty-eight seats to the Conservatives' thirty-one, as the UK overall swung to Macmillan and gave the Conservatives a third term.

Scotland began to change significantly at this point. In the 1964 election, Labour won 46.7% to the Conservatives' 40.6% and forty-three seats to twenty-four. In Glasgow, the number of parliamentary seats won went from eight Labour and seven Conservative in 1955 to thirteen Labour and two Conservative in 1964. In 1959, Labour won Craigton and Scotstoun from the Conservatives, while they won Kelvingrove back which Labour had won in a by-election the previous year (following the death of Walter Elliot) (Wright 1960). In 1964, Kelvingrove and Pollok were gained by Labour from the Conservatives, while they retained Woodside which they won in a 1962 by-election. Five of Scottish Labour's nine national gains between 1955 and 1964 were in Glasgow. The changing dynamics of the city's political representation made a big impact on the respective fortunes of Labour and Conservatives.

Underneath parliamentary representation, voting patterns tell a more complex picture. Between 1951 and 1964 the Conservative vote in Glasgow fell by 8.6%, similar to its Scotland-wide fall, but what was different was the rise in Labour's vote in the city of 6.4%. Tory decline was aided by Labour advance, the decreasing population and rising abstentions, the city's electorate falling by 61,000 and abstentions by 100,000.

Edinburgh returned four Conservatives and three Labour for each of the four elections, but saw the Conservative vote fall by 8.0%, while the Labour vote only increased by 1.0%, resulting in the 1964 election in Edinburgh producing a 48.8% Conservative vote to Labour's 44.2%.

Scottish Labour's zenith in popular terms was 1966, winning 49.9% of the

Table 2: Glasgow Voting Figures at Westminster Elections 1951–64

	Labour	Conservative	Liberal	SNP	Others
1951	305,922	272,155	–	–	3,758
1955	257,774	245,449	–	–	6,642
1959	281,184	243,168	2,589	–	5,776
1964	284,113	183,558	7,113	2,366	6,585

Table 3: Glasgow Voting Figures at Westminster Elections 1951–64 (as a percentage)

	Turnout	Labour	Conservative	Liberal	SNP	Others
1951	80.54	52.35	46.57	–	–	0.64
1955	71.50	50.56	48.14	–	–	1.30
1959	75.52	52.78	45.65	0.48	–	1.09
1964	72.83	58.73	37.95	1.47	0.49	1.36

Source: Scottish Unionist Association, *The Year Book for Scotland*, 1951, 1955, 1959, 1964.

vote and forty-six seats to the Conservatives' 37.7% and twenty seats. This was also at the cusp of Scottish politics beginning to change radically, and the Labour–Conservative duopoly to fragment and crumble. The SNP were, the following year, sensationally to win Hamilton, leading eventually to their first national breakthrough in October 1974, winning 30.4% of the popular vote.

Scottish politics were dramatically changed in a number of ways by the arrival of the SNP as a serious electoral force. One obvious point was that Scotland was no longer a two-party system where both blocs won near to 50% of the vote, as had happened throughout the 1950s, and that this reflected a society which had become less class polarised and more individualised. The Conservative decline continued inexorably, while the SNP went up and down but remained a permanent fixture in Scottish politics. These changing party dynamics and fortunes for a period aided Scottish Labour, for the Conservatives had proven formidable adversaries in votes and seats in the immediate post-war period, whereas their decline and emergence of the SNP reinforced Labour on a minority vote in an increasingly multi-party politics, being the leading party in votes and winning most of the parliamentary seats.

From 1974, and even more from 1983 onwards with the forming of the Liberal-SDP Alliance, multi-party politics in Scotland in a FPTP system hugely benefited Labour. The party's winner's dividend, the difference between votes and seats, continued to rise and reached new levels in 1987 and then 1997. A contributory factor was the dramatic decline of the

Scottish Conservatives in the West of Scotland. Glasgow, after the brief respite of the Tories winning Pollok in a 1967 by-election, pre-Hamilton, thanks to the SNP taking Labour votes, saw Teddy Taylor lose Cathcart in 1979 (the only Tory loss in the entire UK), and then Roy Jenkins' win at Hillhead in the 1982 by-election. The latter made the city entirely Tory-free, and subsequently George Galloway's defeat of Jenkins in 1987 made Glasgow a completely Labour city in parliamentary terms. The Conservative vote, which had held up until the 1960s, collapsed in the city, while Labour seemed increasingly unassailable, both the Liberal-SDP Alliance and SNP compromised by years of poor organisation and unable to make a break-through except in high-profile by-elections.

The SNP breakthrough in 1974 was not immediately built on, the party finding devolution as problematic and challenging as Labour did in the 1970s, and they fell back significantly in 1979 and then again in 1983. Post-1979 political developments are dealt with in detail elsewhere in this book, but suffice to say in this period the SNP positioned themselves unambiguously to the left of Labour, as the two parties competed to provide the most convincing alternative to Thatcherism.

The 1979–97 period saw Labour entrench their position as the leading party, holding off the challenge of the Liberal-SDP Alliance in 1983, and the SNP in 1988–9 post-Govan with, in 1997, Labour winning 45.6% of the vote and a record fifty-six seats, while the SNP displaced the Conservatives in second place with 22.1% and the Conservatives with 17.5% won no representation. Labour's victory led to the establishment of the Scottish Parliament, which dramatically changed the contours of Scottish politics. The first elections confirmed Labour and the SNP as the principal two parties seeking office, and while they both lost votes and seats to smaller parties in 2003, in the 2007 election the SNP finished ahead of Labour in votes and seats and formed a minority government, four years later winning an emphatic victory and forming the first majority government.

The geography of the 2011 election showed the SNP winning across Scotland, taking Labour FPTP seats, winning in traditional Labour areas such as Glasgow, Lanarkshire and Ayrshire, and reshaping the political map of Scotland in what to all intents looks like a re-aligning or 'critical election', namely, an election which fundamentally alters the contours and dynamics of party competition (Evans and Norris 1999).

The extent of the SNP victory and Labour's rejection can be gauged by Glasgow voting figures. Leaving aside the SNP five constituency gains from Labour – Anniesland, Cathcart, Kelvin and Shettleston, along with the 'notional' Southside seat – the Nationalists' victory in the city was the first time in a national election that they finished ahead of Labour. Examining the regional vote list from 1999–2011, the cumulative fall in the Labour vote can be seen over the course of the four elections, along with the challenge of the SNP, and long-term and continued decline of the Conservatives.

This last phenomenon saw the Tories get a Glasgow vote in actual numbers running at 4.7% of their peak vote. Labour managed significantly better, but the scale of their decline in their once impregnable heartland is dramatic: Labour's 1999 vote was 36.8% the size of their peak vote in 1951, and their 2011 vote down to 23.9%. Both Tory and Labour decline has continued inexorably between 1999 and 2011, the Tory vote down 37.0% and the Labour vote down 35.1% (the SNP being up 27.1%).[3] This underlines the argument put, even before the 2007 and 2011 defeats, that the strength of the Labour vote in their heartlands was hollowing out through low turnout and disillusion, leaving Labour in a vulnerable position should a credible opposition emerge; so it has proven (Saren and McCormick 2004).

Table 4: Glasgow Voting Figures 1999–2011: Scottish Parliament Elections Regional Vote

	Labour	SNP	Con	Lib	SSP*	Green	Others
1999	112,588	65,360	20,239	18,473	18,581	10,159	10,948
2003	77,040	34,894	15,299	14,839	31,116	14,570	16,520
2007	78,838	55,832	13,781	14,767	8,574	10,759	24,116
2011	73,031	83,109	12,749	5,312	6,972	12,454	15,085

Table 5: Glasgow Voting Figures 1999–2011: Scottish Parliament Elections Regional Vote (as a percentage)

	Turnout	Labour	SNP	Con	Lib	SSP*	Green	Others
1999	48.28	43.92	25.50	7.90	7.21	7.25	3.96	4.27
2003	41.27	37.71	17.08	7.49	7.26	15.23	7.13	6.80
2007	43.17	38.15	27.02	6.67	7.15	4.15	5.21	11.67
2011	40.76	34.99	39.82	6.11	2.55	3.34	5.97	7.23

* SSP 1999–2003, Solidarity 2007, Respect 2011
Sources: 1999 figures, Hassan and Lynch 2001; 2003, 2007, 2011 figures, Denver 2011b; Electoral Commission 2011.

CHANGING SCOTLAND: VOTER ALIGNMENTS AND THE PARTY SYSTEM

How can we make sense of these voting changes in post-war Scotland? A persuasive analysis of voting alignments and their relationship to party competition and systems is provided by Lipset and Rokkan's work addressing different cleavages (1967). They offer four distinctions:

> Two of these cleavages are direct products of what we might call the National Revolution: the conflict between the central nation-building culture and the increasing resistance of the ethnically, linguistically, or religiously distinct subject population in the provinces and peripheries: the conflict between the centralising, standardising, and mobilising nation-state and the historically established privileges of the Church. Two of them are products of the Industrial Revolution: the conflict between the landed interest and the rising class of industrial entrepreneurs; the conflict between owners and employers on the one side and tenants, labourers and workers on the other. (Lipset and Rokkan 1967: 14)

These four cleavages can be summarised as centre–periphery, religion, urban/rural and that of class. How do we find each of these in Scotland? A central–peripheral cleavage can be found in the dominance of the Central Belt and the different political cultures evident in the Highlands and Islands, North East and Borders. The influence of religion has played a role in shaping society and political attitudes different from the rest of the UK. An urban–rural divide can be found in Labour's powerful hold over Scotland's cities and their identity as an urban party. And lastly, the issue of class has been a major influence on Scottish politics.

Lipset and Rokkan identify a 'hierarchy of cleavage bases' and explore how the relationships between different cleavages change over time and cross-fertilise and influence each other. Can we understand the patterns of post-war Scotland with reference to this? First, the era of Conservative popularity can be seen as one where a politics of class identity was affected by the issue of religion. This period with its class and cross-class currents (Protestant working-class Tories, Catholic middle-class Labour) made it nearly impossible for third parties, whether Liberal or SNP, to make their mark.

Second, the age of 'Labour Scotland' saw class come to the fore, with issues of national identity very much secondary. This began to change post-1979 with a politics of class and national identity complementing and reinforcing each other in a politics which emphasised difference from the rest of the UK. The 1979–97 Conservative Government saw increasingly a Scottish social democratic and nationalist politics face a British centre-right unionist politics; on the one side were Labour, SNP and the Lib Dems, and on the other the Conservatives.

Third, the emergence of the Scottish Nationalists has reinforced this intersection of class and national identity, with the latter coming to the fore in more recent times, as the SNP post-2011 attempt to emphasise the catch-all nature of their party and emphasise that they are a truly national party in appeal, while also holding on to their centre-left credentials. This will be a precarious balancing act in the medium to longer term. There is also a powerful case to be made given the 'hierarchy of cleavages' that this inter-weaving of class and national identity has its roots in the evolution of politics in the 1960s and 1970s shaped by concerns about economic growth, indus-trial policy, unemployment and devolution, seen in such cases as Linwood, Longannet, UCS and North Sea oil (Phillips 2008). This argument does not detract from but strengthens an understanding of the long revolution which has led to the current configuration.

The Shock of the New: Social Movements and Labour

Lipset and Rokkan situate their analysis of voter alignments and party systems in the historical context of changes in industrial capitalism and the nation-state, and thus recognise that new cleavages and alignments will con-tinually emerge, rise and fall, reflecting economic and social trends. This can be seen in the work of Inglehart and others, who addressed the issue of 'post-materialist values' (1977). Another is the emergence of new political and social movements which have been extensively written about post-1968 and the hopes of 'the new left'. How have these affected and influenced Scottish Labour and how have the party responded?

The rise of new political movements has reshaped large aspects of political life across the West and, in particular, centre-left politics. A whole literature has arisen pondering the nature of such movements and their implications for Marxist and socialist politics (Laclau and Mouffe 1985; Melucci 1989). The impact of such movements has been more limited in the UK, aided by the monopoly of Labour and Conservatives in British politics until recently, and their impact seems similarly restricted in Scotland.

The development of an environmental movement in Scotland has been more cautious, non-governmental organisation (NGO)-orientated and pro-fessionally run and focused, developing politics around lobbying and influ-encing rather than mass campaigning, and therefore posing less of a direct challenge to conventional power and politics. Organisations such as Friends of the Earth and the World Wildlife Fund in Scotland seem to have been content to gauge their impact on making incremental change and not sys-temic or wider political change, and in many respects succeeding in influenc-ing the intentions of, for example, the Labour–Lib Dem Executive of Jack McConnell (see Scandrett 2011).

Environmental politics contributed to the rise of the Scottish Greens, who achieved their biggest success by winning 7% of the regional list in the 2003 Scottish Parliament elections. This did not contribute to environmental issues becoming a new cleavage, with the support of the Greens falling back in 2007 and 2011. More crucially, the Scottish Greens did not position themselves as an anti-system party or as part of a wider radical movement in the way the German Greens did, allowing green issues to be incorporated into mainstream political concerns (Bennie 2004).

A similar but different picture can be found in the reach of feminism, women's politics and lesbian and gay rights. For a long time, Scottish Labour was deeply resistant, indeed hostile and dismissive, to both of these perspectives, seeing them even more than Labour did elsewhere as not 'real politics' and as 'middle class diversions'. There was more to it than this. The wider trade union and labour movement pre-Labour had in places such as Dundee, with high levels of women's employment, a significant women's politics and radicalism along with male attempts to control it (Gordon 1991). The ILP's early years drew from these traditions, giving sustenance to a whole generation of Labour women campaigners that was mostly lost when the party disaffiliated from Labour (Smyth 2000: Ch. 5; Civardi 1997).

Scottish Labour has, for most of its existence and post-ILP, on such issues articulated a deep-seated voice of conservatism, drawing on a culture of unenlightened prejudice and a lack of understanding of the need to make a stand against sexism and homophobia. The party represented an unashamed masculinised politics that interpreted the interests of organised labour in a very narrow sense as synonymous with the interests of organised male trade union members. 'Left' arguments were used to marginalise the need for women's representation and for championing women's issues (McCrae 1991).

For most of Labour's history, until very recently, the party had a very poor record of electing women as MPs, or in prominent party positions; local government provided more opportunities for women's representation. Three women Scottish Labour MPs were elected in 1945; over thirty years later in 1979, the party elected a solitary woman, Judith Hart. It took until the election of 1997 for this to change in any major way, with nine women Scottish Labour MPs elected (Mackay 2004). Jean Mann represented Coatbridge, then Coatbridge and Airdrie, from 1945 to 1959 and stated that 'Labour women are more handicapped than Tory women' and treated as outsiders:

> Labour men, particularly in the unions, meet together often. Friendships are made, sometimes around the bar; introductions to those who have influence in the safe seats follow. Men have an 'old pals club' whilst women stand out in the cold. Men gang up and push each other into positions. Who ever heard of women doing this or joining the men in a pub or hotel bar? (Mann 1962: 45)

However, major changes occurred from the 1980s onwards, reflecting a general push in the British party to improve women's representation. The drive to achieve gender equality in Scottish Labour was spearheaded by the campaign for 50–50 representation in the proposed Scottish Parliament, which became Scottish Labour and STUC official policy in 1991. Key groups in this change were the LCC (Scotland) Women's Committee and Scottish Labour Women's Caucus, prominent members including Margaret Curran, Johann Lamont and Roseanna McCrae. This push played a major part in aiding the breakthrough in women's representation in Labour in the Scottish Parliament (Mackay 2004: 112–20).

Lesbian and gay issues faced even more hostility, decriminalisation of male homosexuality not occurring in Scotland along with England and Wales in 1967 due to the entrenched conservatism of Scottish Labour MPs and the Church of Scotland (Keating 1975); decriminalisation did not occur until 1980.

Long into the 1980s and 1990s, the era of the GLC and English tabloids berating 'loony left' political correctness, lesbian and gay issues did not enjoy the support or prominence in Scottish Labour they enjoyed south of the border. A contributory factor was the view of religious leaders, and even in present times the Catholic Church's pronouncements continue to make Labour politicians nervous. This played into a moral conservatism of Labour which was given validation by concerns about Catholic voters and church leaders, from abortion to Section 28 and contemporary concerns about same-sex marriage. Scottish public opinion slowly liberalised post-1999 on lesbian and gay issues, but it was a particularly 'quiet revolution', not led by political leaders or championed by a lesbian and gay politics, but part of a wider cosmopolitan changing of Scottish society (see Park 2002).

What the above illustrates is a wider set of observations about the nature of Scottish Labour. The party, for longer than most other parts of British Labour, were influenced by the power and hold of a very narrow, economistic, trade union-based, labourist politics that did not feel the need to accommodate or change in response to other political pressures. In the Scottish Parliament elections of 1999 to 2011, Labour felt they could win with a core vote strategy, just speaking to their base and doing so each time with diminishing returns. Therefore, Scottish Labour have not felt for most of the post-war era that they needed to be more supportive in how they dealt beyond a politics of class and labour with emerging new social movements.

One movement that did emerge and did significantly influence Scottish Labour was the politics of nuclear disarmament. This caused many repercussions in British Labour, and in Scotland was magnified by the siting of nuclear weapons in the West of Scotland near to Glasgow with the 1961 arrival of US submarines at Holy Loch and 1963 stationing of Polaris missiles at Faslane (Erickson,1969; Chalmers and Walker 2001). Nuclear disarmament

became a major issue at the start of the 1960s and an early point of controversy between Labour and SNP, with a host of senior Labour politicians such
as George Robertson and Brian Wilson, first being in the SNP, attracted to
them by their anti-nuclear stance. The modern SNP logo adopted at this
time was a conscious combination of the St Andrew's Cross, thistle and CND
logo (Wolfe 1973: 46–7).

Nuclear disarmament re-emerged on the political agenda in the 1980s,
with the decision of the UK Government to purchase Trident as a replacement for Polaris, with the submarines situated at Faslane. British Labour
annual conferences in the early 1980s supported unilateral nuclear disarmament, while Scottish conference did likewise. What made this different in
Scotland was that this did not leave Labour isolated, but as part of mainstream anti-nuclear opinion, along with the SNP, Scottish churches and a
host of campaigning groups.

Despite this, nuclear weapons have never been a major mobilising
issue in an election. Even after Labour post-1997, the UK Government
became unapologetically pro-nuclear and pro-military. However, in Scottish
Parliament elections, nuclear weapons have been an important defining
point of difference between Labour and the SNP, a reinforcing reference for
the Nationalist argument that Labour has 'sold out' the anti-nuclear traditions in the party.

SCOTTISH LABOUR'S FOURTH ESTATE NO MORE: THE ROLE OF THE MEDIA

A significant though often unexplored factor in the sustenance of Scottish
Labour's popular base has been its relationship with the media. The Scottish
press, television and radio all have significantly different characteristics compared to the rest of the UK. Newspapers sometimes with the same titles north
and south of the border can be very different, significant parts of television
and radio are different; some are completely the same, Channel 4 and BBC
Radio 4 being two examples.

The Scottish media played a crucial role in the development and sustenance of Scotland as a distinct 'communicative space', a place where different kinds of political conversation and exchange take place (Schlesinger
et al. 2001). There has been a distinct regional dimension to the Scottish
press, with *The Herald* in Glasgow and the West, *The Scotsman* in Edinburgh
and Lothian, *The Courier and Advertiser* in Dundee, and *Press and Journal* in
Aberdeen. This has become less pronounced in recent years with the rise
of the *Daily Record*, then *The Sun*, and the Scottish-ing of titles such as the
Daily Mail and *The Times*.

214

The *Daily Record* surpassed the *Scottish Daily Express* in sales in 1973, and for the 1980s and most of the 1990s had a healthy, comfortable lead over its main competitor, *The Sun*. In 1976, the *Daily Record* sold 676,000 copies a day compared to *The Sun*'s 155,000. By 2006 the *Daily Record* was down to 384,000 copies, while *The Sun* had risen to 394,000, aided by an aggressive price-cutting promotion, a lead it has subsequently maintained and widened (Hutchison 2008: 67).

The *Daily Record* had a critical role in disseminating the Labour message, and its dominance from 1973 to 2006, without for long periods facing serious challenge, contributed to a feeling of complacency and almost smugness, which could be seen to mirror Scottish Labour's own sense of itself over the same period. The *Daily Record*'s surprise, shock and panic were plain to see with the decision of *The Sun* to come out for the SNP and independence in 1992 (*The Scottish Sun*, 23 January 1992).

The relationship between the *Daily Record* and Scottish Labour has been a pivotal one in the years of their respective dominance. There was a close relationship between *Daily Record* journalists and Labour Party politicians, and a revolving door between newspaper staff and Labour advisors. Helen Liddell went from being General Secretary of the party to being Robert Maxwell's Head of Corporate Affairs from 1988 to 1991, witnessing first-hand the demise of Maxwell's empire after his death. Tom Brown worked for the *Daily Record* as one of its highest-profile columnists and went from that to advising Henry McLeish as First Minister. Paul Sinclair was political editor of the *Daily Record*, later becoming a political advisor to Douglas Alexander then to Prime Minister Gordon Brown and subsequently Scottish Labour leader Johann Lamont.

The *Daily Record* oscillated around power during the Labour years of dominance. Mike Watson reflected that 'the one paper no Labour MP or MSP can afford to ignore is the *Daily Record*' (Watson 2001: 59). A former MSP went further, saying, 'The *Record* gives you an insight into the mind of a typical Labour voter, and gives you a way of understanding that perspective and directly communicating with it' (interview). Helen Liddell developed the point: 'The *Daily Record* was of enormous importance. It was selling 800,000 copies and it would be read by two and a half people for each copy, so keeping the *Daily Record* on side was of critical importance and I spent a lot of time with the *Record* because they became our mouthpiece into communities' (interview).

Tensions between Labour and the press boiled over in the first Scottish Parliament elections in 1991. Donald Dewar was reported as calling *The Herald* 'an out and out nationalist newspaper' and the party was exposed threatening the newspaper with withdrawing up to £100,000 of election advertising (Ritchie 2000: 91, 104–5). Further problems emerged post-election with the *Daily Record*'s coverage of Scottish politics, and in particular Section 28, under the editorship of Martin Clarke, with Alastair Campbell calling the *Daily Record*'s coverage 'complete fiction' (*The Herald*, 14 March 2000).

The *Daily Record* came back into the fold post-Clarke and was as pro-Labour loyalist as it could be in the 2003, 2007 and 2011 Scottish Parliament elections. On polling day in 2007 it declared:

> Today's election is not about war in Iraq. It is not about Tony Blair. It is about who will run Scotland. It is about schools, hospitals and law and order. Do not sleep-walk into independence. Do not let a protest vote break up Britain. Think about it. (*Daily Record*, 3 May 2007)

The Sun returned to the Labour fold for the 1997 election. In 2007 it pronounced on its front page on polling day, 'Vote SNP and Put Scotland's Head in the Noose', and went on in typical no-nonsense *Sun* style to give '10 Reasons to Be Fearful of the SNP'. These were, 'Out of NATO, Income Tax Up 3p, Super-rich will pay nothing, £5000 bill per family, Brain drain, Independence, . . . And its price, Westminster conflict, Jobs on the line, Public services threat' (*The Scottish Sun*, 3 May 2007).

In 2011 *The Sun* returned to supporting the SNP, but not independence. In a rather different media environment, the *Daily Record* found its pro-Labour stance a rather lonely one, as many other papers came out supporting the Nationalists, including *The Scotsman*, *Sunday Herald*, *Scotland on Sunday* and *News of the World*.

Scottish television and radio are also important in how politics is conducted. BBC Scotland and STV offer significant coverage of Scottish politics. BBC coverage in particular is seen by some as politically sensitive, with BBC Scotland's position in the UK-wide BBC, and allegations concerning political bias, either for Labour or the Nationalists (see McAlpine 2011). There have also been concerns about what some believe is the Anglocentric nature of much of the BBC's output, and its failure to come to terms with devolution and post-devolution Scotland in particular (BBC Trust 2008; Fraser 2008).

LABOUR'S LAST DEFENCE? THE ROLE OF THE ELECTORAL SYSTEM

A final major factor in Scottish voting intentions and party competition is the electoral system. The Westminster FPTP system has historically over the post-war era worked increasingly in Labour's favour and given it a false sense of its support and dominance of Scottish politics. The high point of proportionality was 1955 at the peak of Conservative–Labour dominance, while the low point of proportionality was Labour's victory in 1997.4 That year Labour won 45.6% of the vote and was rewarded with 77.8% of the seats. At the same election, the SNP won 22.1% of the vote and 8.3% of seats, the Conservatives with 17.5% of the vote no seats, and the Liberal Democrats with 13.0% of the vote 13.9% of representation.

This has increasingly been the pattern of Westminster elections since the 1950s, and even more so since 1987, 1983 being the last point in Scotland when the Conservatives won more representation proportionately than their vote. Since then the pattern has solidified into a distinct four-party system of Labour over-representation, the Lib Dems achieving proportionately the same number of votes and seats, the SNP and, in particular, the Conservatives being under-represented.

Labour was less rewarded by the Scottish Parliament electoral system, with its Additional Member System (AMS) element. However, such has been Scottish Labour's dominance of FPTP seats that the first three Scottish elections saw Scottish Labour win more seats proportionately than their vote because the AMS seats were not enough to counter this. The 2011 Scottish elections, with the rout of Labour FPTP seats, saw this all change, the party becoming for the first time more reliant on list MSPs and winning fewer seats than votes.

What the Westminster FPTP system did was make parts of Scottish Labour believe that their idea of 'Labour Scotland', a minority nation in terms of votes and reach, was an all-powerful, all-encompassing force which spoke for all of Scotland. This was a crucial misjudgement, overstating Labour's popularity and at the same time not having any real grasp or recognition of other Scottish traditions and progressive cultures, from the radical traditions of the Highlands and Islands which managed to sustain a Liberal Party even in the 1950s, and the North East bases of support for the SNP and Liberals.

IMAGES OF SCOTTISH LABOUR AND THE SCOTTISH NATIONALISTS

Labour have then for most of their existence represented and reflected a very partial account of Scotland. At the same time significant sections of the party, in local government, trade unions and the Westminster party, have chosen, consciously and unconsciously not to understand this, and to believe that the Scottish Labour vision is one which is inclusive and welcoming to all. This was the world where Jim Sillars said of South Ayrshire in the 1960s and 1970s, 'it was a welcoming, wonderful, rich world, a place of self-education, discussion and debate', which did not reflect how exclusive it appeared to outsiders (interview).

217

Labour have been for most of their history a very male party, urban and geographically concentrated in the Central Belt and West of Scotland in particular. One of the main arguments used with great effect in the 1979 devolution referendum was the fear of the non-Labour parts of Scotland being governed by 'Labour Scotland', with significant parts of the electorate and elite groups feeling more comfortable with Westminster rule (Bochel et al. 1981). The by-words of rule by 'Glasgow cooncillors' or 'Strathclyde Region writ large' struck fear into the hearts of many. By the 1997 referendum this had nearly completely changed, and concerns about Westminster rule replaced these (Denver et al. 2000).

The SNP's breakthrough in the 1974 elections dramatically changed politics and challenged Scottish Labour assumptions. Labour believed the SNP were opportunistic, 'tartan Tories', 'separatists' and undermining the prospect of economic and social justice. Scottish voters have never seen the SNP in that light, viewing the party as a positive force for good and for standing up for Scotland. Miller, looking at the 1974 Scottish Election Survey, found that 'the overwhelming majority of Scottish electors felt that the SNP's existence and electoral success had been "good for Scotland"' (Miller 1981: 92). Nearly all SNP voters subscribed to this view, but so did three-quarters of Labour and Conservative voters; it would take their party leaderships a lot longer to acknowledge this reality.

Scottish voters' perceptions of Labour in the 1980s and early 1990s illustrate that the party's problems did not escape the notice of voters. In 1992, 66% of Scottish voters thought that Labour were divided, while 52% believed that they were not capable of strong government. By 1997, these figures had transformed, with 91% of Scots voters thinking Labour were capable of strong government, while 66% thought they would keep their promises (Surridge 2004: 78).

Detailed survey evidence shows what Scots voters thought of New Labour in relation to social class, unions and business. In 1997, 93% thought New Labour looked after working-class interests very or fairly closely, but by 2001 this fell to 61%. In contrast, the figures for looking after the middle class over the same period dropped from 88% to 80%, indicating a sizeable shift in voter perceptions about New Labour's attitudes to the middle and working classes. One interesting finding in terms of Labour's traditional core vote was that in 1997 94% of working-class respondents thought New Labour looked after working-class interests, but by 2001 this had fallen to 52%. Similarly, in 1997 89% thought New Labour looked after trade union interests, but this had fallen to 67% in 2001; in 1997, New Labour were thought to look after big business interests by 75% and this rose to 85% in 2001 (ibid.: 72–3, 75).

The 1999 Scottish Parliament elections found little difference in how voters saw Scottish Labour and SNP in relation to social class: 63% of respondents thought Scottish Labour looked after working-class interests, while 66% thought this of the SNP. When asked about looking after middle-class interests, 71% thought Scottish Labour did this very or fairly closely, as opposed to 65% for the SNP. However, when we come to perceptions of the parties in relation to how they look after Scottish interests we find a more differentiated picture. Only 42% thought New Labour looked after Scottish interests, compared to 63% for Scottish Labour and 72% for the SNP (Paterson et al. 2001: 58). These findings pointed towards the crucial terrain of party competition in future Scottish Parliament elections: an alignment of working-class interests and Scottish national identity.

The Scottish Election Survey of 2007 found that the SNP had maintained and built on their reputation to look after Scottish interests, while Labour had fallen back. When asked how well they thought each of the main parties looked after Scottish interests, 74% thought the SNP very closely or fairly closely did, while 26% thought they did not very closely or not at all closely. This gave them a clear advantage over the Lib Dems with a 55:45 rating, Labour on 50:50 and the Conservatives on 26:74. This led the authors to conclude that Labour was in potential danger of being seen in a way 'more resembling that of the Conservatives – a party criticised as anti-Scottish – than that of the SNP' (Johns et al. 2010: 88–9).

The Scottish Election Survey of 2011 found that one of the most crucial factors in the SNP victory was the reputation of competence gained by the SNP Government over the course of the previous four years, and the comparison with Labour. When asked to evaluate the performance of the SNP in office, 56% of respondents rated them very or fairly good compared to 20% who rated them very or fairly bad. This contrasted with an evaluation of 33% very or fairly good if Labour had been in power versus 45% very or fairly bad, giving the SNP a +36 rating versus -12 for Labour. Respondents were also asked to rate parties in relation to how closely they looked after Scottish interests from a rating of four for 'very' to one implying 'not at all': the results were SNP 3.5, Labour 2.5, Lib Dems 1.3 and Conservatives 0.75 (Carman et al. 2011).

The differing perceptions of the parties allowed the SNP to be perceived as standing up for Scotland, and to neutralise the independence question, while all the other parties struggled on the terrain of the Scottish dimension. Labour for four successive Scottish elections had articulated an anti-Scottish Nationalist negative message which was cumulatively less and less effective. The 2011 election pointed to the need for a new strategy for Scottish Labour, embracing a distinct Scottish agenda, and coming to terms with the SNP as a normal political party and competitor.

CONCLUSION

Scottish politics has changed dramatically over the post-war era, which should not surprise anyone given the scale of transformation of Scottish society. Political parties have radically altered; some of the names remain the same, while some have undergone change such as the Conservatives and different variants of the Liberal Party. More crucially, voters no longer think and act the way they used to, with far-reaching consequences for the nature of party competition.

The alignments and cleavages that shape politics are different. Centre–periphery factors have weakened with the decline of Labour across Scotland; religion has clearly declined; urban/rural divisions are not of great importance; class alignments have weakened, while at the same time a subjective sense of class alongside national identity has increasingly defined politics and is likely to for the foreseeable future. New political movements and alignments have not reshaped and reconfigured Scottish politics as much as elsewhere, and Scottish Labour in particular has demonstrated that it has not adapted to new currents and the possibility of a more pluralist, diverse, different politics, while its old norms and approaches have been working less effectively.

Two major factors in how Labour strengthened their support in Scotland were their media relations and the way FPTP worked in Westminster elections (along with how it worked in local government). For many years the party had a close, intimate relationship with large parts of the Scottish media, gaining favourable coverage, and protecting them from the kind of attacks Labour experienced south of the border in the 1980s. That media–party management now looks much less possible, and Labour will have to come to terms with a more hostile media environment. And while FPTP still exists for Westminster, Labour will have to deal with boundary changes for the second time post-devolution, reducing the number of Scottish MPs. The party's defeat in the 2011 Scottish Parliament election has dramatically altered the geographies of party support and removed any FPTP bonus the party gained.

Where does Scottish Labour go in terms of voting intentions, party competition and how they addresses their image? The party have to recognise that they have been in recent years out-manoeuvred, out-positioned and out-resourced by the SNP, to an extent many would have thought unthinkable pre-devolution. The SNP have positioned themselves as a catch-all party with national appeal, leaving Scottish Labour as a party of a declining Scotland.

Scottish Labour will need to undertake radical action if they are to change these fundamentals, addressing how they represent Scottish interests, and who they look to speak for. It is not very clear after two election defeats which Scotland Scottish Labour politicians see themselves as representing, and what vision and future they aspire to have for the country. The Scottish Labour Party have a long and proud history, but for the moment their immediate future looks likely to be one which will be challenging and less comforting than previously.

NOTES

1. In the 1955 general election the Conservatives, besides winning a majority of the Scots vote (50.1%), also won a majority of the English vote (50.4%) and the Northern Ireland vote (68.5%). They only failed to win a majority in Wales (26.7%), which prevented them winning a majority of the popular vote across the United Kingdom. Therefore, while the Scottish Conservatives reached a high point of popularity in 1955, it has to be seen in the context of the enormous popularity across the UK of the Conservatives, Wales excepted.
2. Church of Scotland membership fell from 1.307 million in 1955 (25.5% of the population) to 660,954 in 1997 (15.5%) and 464,000 in 2010 (9%) (Church of Scotland 2011). At the same time the number of churchgoers was even lower with for the first time in 2005, according to analysis by Christian Research, the number of Catholics going to church exceeding the Church of Scotland by 215,000 to 208,400 (*Scotland on Sunday*, 24 May 2008).
3. A significant part of the decline of Labour and the Conservatives in Glasgow between 1951 and 1964 and 1999 and 2011 is the decline in numbers on the electoral register, reflecting the decline in Glasgow's population and the fall in turnout. Glasgow's electorate in 1951 was 725,539 and turnout was 80.54%; in 2011 the city's electorate was 511,944 and turnout 40.77%. The Conservative and Labour votes in Glasgow have declined in number because the city has got smaller, but have also taken a smaller share of the vote remaining.
4. The index of proportionality in an electoral system totals each party vote and representation. The figures below are for the 1997 election:

Table 6: Index of Dispropotionality Votes/Seats 1987

	% Vote	% Seats	Difference
Labour	45.6	77.8	+32.2
SNP	22.1	8.3	−13.8
Conservative	17.5	–	−17.5
Lib Dem	13.0	13.9	+0.9
Others	1.9	–	−1.9

Sum Total = 66.3
Deviation from proportionality = 33.15
In comparison, the deviation from proportionality in 1955 was 1.8.

CHAPTER 13

The Evolution of Scottish Labour

THE ORGANISATION OF SCOTTISH LABOUR: THE FORMATIVE YEARS

'A party's organisational characteristics', Panebianco has argued, 'depend more upon its history, i.e. on how the organisation originated and how it consolidated, than upon any other factor' (Panebianco 1988: 50). The organisational origins of political labour in Scotland lies in a somewhat obscure body, the Scottish Labour Party, founded by Keir Hardie in 1888. It survived a mere five years before being merged into the UK-wide Independent Labour Party (ILP), set up by Hardie and others in 1893. From this point on, the development of Labour in Scotland becomes enmeshed with nationwide trends. In 1900, the ILP together with other socialist bodies (the Social Democratic Federation and the Fabian Society) joined up with a number of trade unions to form the Labour Representation Committee, renamed the Labour Party in 1906.

The progress of the Labour Party in the years leading up the outbreak of the First World War was, in Scotland as elsewhere in the UK, modest and unimpressive. Their fortunes, even more than south of the border, were transformed by the turbulent war years as the impact of wartime mobilisation and events such as the Glasgow rent strike and mass industrial unrest on the Clyde energised and radicalised the Scottish working class. In Britain as a whole, the scene was set for the post-war emergence of Labour as the Tories' main competitor for power, with the promulgation of universal male and partial female franchise, a massive expansion of union membership and organisation, and the rupturing of the Liberal party – Scotland's leading political formation – between the adherents of Lloyd George and Asquith.

Crucial to the organisational trajectory of a party, Panebianco has suggested, is its mode of expansion in its formative years. This can take either of two forms: 'territorial penetration' or 'territorial diffusion'. 'Territorial penetration occurs when the "centre" controls, stimulates, or directs the development of the "periphery", i.e. the constitution of local and intermediate party associations. Territorial diffusion occurs when development results from spontaneous germination: local elites construct party associations which are only later integrated into a national organisation' (Panebianco 1988: 50). Prior to 1918, Labour were an alliance of institutions (trade unions and socialist societies) with no direct membership and no systematic pattern of UK-wide organisation. This changed at the crucial 1918 party conference when the party instituted a national membership scheme and established the constitutional framework for a nationwide network of constituency and branch parties which developed in the 1920s.

The first small step in organisational building in Scotland had already occurred with the appointment of a Scottish Secretary in 1914, followed by the establishment of a Scottish Advisory Council in 1915. Despite a formal commitment to Scottish devolution, the constitutional status of the Scottish party – significantly its formal title was (until 1994) the Scottish Council of the Labour Party – was that of a 'region' and, like other regional councils, it possessed little by way of resources, responsibilities or autonomy. The regional organisations, which were established in the 1920s, were effectively 'central offices located in the regions for administrative purposes rather than autonomous regional units'. In the late 1930s, this administrative tier was supplemented by (indirectly elected) regional councils 'to act as a representative mechanism for the party in the regions' (Lynch 1996b: 564).

Party-building north of the border (as elsewhere) therefore seemed to conform closely to the pattern of 'territorial penetration' rather than 'territorial diffusion'. Appearances, however, were deceptive. Notwithstanding Labour's decision at the 1918 conference to establish a centralised, nationwide machine, the ILP retained their own separate organisation, membership and leadership. Indeed, in Scotland, a major bastion, they continued to expand, reaching their peak in 1925, being home to around a third (307) of all ILP branches. In 1923, a trade union delegate to the Scottish Labour conference claimed that the previous year's election gains were 'mainly due to the ILP which had undertaken the spadework . . . and also provided the funds for most of the elections' (quoted in Wood, I. 1989: 38). The ILP were also responsible for the propagation of the Labour and socialist message, organising a formidable range of propaganda and cultural activities. *The Times* reported in 1922 the existence of 'Socialist study circles, Socialist economic classes, Socialist musical festivals, Socialist athletic competitions, Socialist choirs, Socialist dramatic societies, Socialist plays . . . Socialist Sunday schools . . . [and] Socialist newspapers' (quoted in Knox 1999: 239). Most of Scotland's growing band of Labour members were active and prominent members of the ILP. All but one of Labour's sixty-eight candidates at the 1929 general election were ILP members, thirty directly sponsored, while at the 1928 party conference, three-quarters of party speakers were ILP activists (Knox and McKinlay 1995: 175). In short, the ILP were primarily responsible for party expansion in the decisive decade when Labour rose to be the major opposition to the Conservatives, supplying much of the personnel, energy and idealism. This meant that the Labour Party in Scotland were a far more pluralist and decentralised organisation than a brief inspection of the party's rulebook would suggest (see Brown 1981).

The problem was that the relationship between the Labour Party and the ILP was an unstable and uneasy one, defined by overlapping responsibilities, constitutional ambiguities and intensifying political tensions. It markedly deteriorated from the 1920s when the ILP lurched to the left, with their leadership by the end of the decade in the hands of radical socialists, notably the Scot James Maxton. During the short-lived and unhappy minority Labour Government of 1929 to 1931, under the premiership of former ILP stalwart Ramsay MacDonald, relations between the two parties became increasingly fraught.

The 1931 election was an unmitigated disaster for Labour in Scotland as elsewhere and as a result, and compounded by the narrative of the 'MacDonald betrayal', the party swung sharply to the left. But this did nothing to bridge the widening rift with the ILP, which culminated in 1932 in the ILP's disaffiliation from Labour. Within a decade it was clear that this was a self-destructive decision as the ILP dwindled into an ever-shrinking band, but the impact on Labour in Scotland was also profound. As Arthur Woodburn, appointed as Secretary of the Scottish Labour Party in 1932, reflected, 'there was practically no Labour Party in Scotland. The Labour Party was still a federated body and the real drive was in the ILP . . . my job was practically to build from scratch' (quoted in Knox and McKinlay 1995: 175). The party north of the border slowly reconstructed themselves but this time the process emphatically took the shape of territorial penetration. It is clear, in retrospect, that the 1930s were the formative decade for Scottish Labour, the years when crucial decisions were taken that moulded both the organisational shape of the party (including their relations with the party centre) but also, as we see in more detail later, their ethos and mentality.

Prior to ILP disaffiliation, Labour in Scotland may have appeared to be a subordinate piece of machinery in the party's centralised structure, but the key role of the ILP, effectively a party within a party, imparted to them a powerful and vigorous life of their own. The size, energy and influence of the ILP in Scotland had *de facto* created a devolved form of territorial politics.

Disaffiliation eliminated this and replaced it with a much more centralised territorial scheme. According to party rules, the Scottish party 'was not autonomous but is part of the national machinery of the Labour Party', and this is emphatically what they became. The constitutional status of the Scottish party was now unambiguously that of a region, and although regions had their own conferences and executive committees, these had slender powers. Regional conferences were strictly debarred from discussing, much less formulating, policies on matters of general national and international interest. Speaking on behalf of Labour's NEC, Rhys Davies MP told the 1927 Scottish Labour conference that its remit was restricted to 'dealing with Scottish aspects of public, legislative and administrative affairs' (Wood, I. 1989: 35). This may have mattered little prior to 1932, since the ILP afforded a more than adequate arena for vigorous debate and dissent, but with disaffiliation this was lost.

For the generation after the Second World War, the Scottish party conference was an uninspiring affair, dominated by discussions over the Scottish economy, housing and education, cramped by the restrictions on what it was allowed to discuss. The policy role of both the Scottish Labour Executive (SEC) and conference was confined to framing advice on Scottish policy and to issuing 'a programme to meet specific Scottish requirements', but – as a further illustration of their lack of autonomy – they were required 'to support NEC decisions and national Conference pronouncements'.[1] Scottish conference's limited remit meant that its debates were often dull, bland and parochial, which inevitably diminished media interest, minimised its profile and marginalised its influence. It made Scottish Labour seem 'an unappealing provincial backwater for ambitious party members. The real political action was at national conference or at Westminster' (Lynch 1996a: 11).

The Scottish party had very little say over staff appointments and its senior figure, the Scottish Secretary, was selected by the NEC and under the direction of the London-based General Secretary. The SEC was entrusted with relatively modest functions. The Scottish Secretary, Arthur Woodburn, described it as 'a piece of internal machinery providing the movement with advice on Scottish affairs, and the movement in Scotland with a coordinating authority to review, advise and cooperate [sic] the membership and organisation' (quoted in Knox,1999: 242). With its fingers burned by the ILP experience and confronting constant efforts by a small but highly disciplined Communist Party to infiltrate Labour's constituency machinery, the national leadership instituted a tough managerial regime. 'From 1931 the NEC consciously used Labour's regional organisation to police constituency politics. The Scottish executive was thus left with little discretion in policy or organisational matters' (Knox 1999: 241–2).

The Scottish Council of the Labour Party operated as the regional arm of the national party, with its rather meagre staff charged mainly with organisational tasks such as candidate selection, membership recruitment and election campaigning. Keir Hardie House (later John Smith House) was an integrated part of Labour's national organisational structure, and while its officials enjoyed a fair degree of discretion they were charged with carrying out the directives of the party centre. Though secretary to the SEC, and therefore something of an intermediary between the Scottish and national levels of organisations, the Scottish Secretary (later called the Scottish General Secretary) was, in essence, a national party official acting as a territorial manager for London. He or she was, a senior party official explained, the eyes and ears of the UK party leader, charged with maintaining close and regular contact with the national Head Office (interview). He or she was expected to perform the role of a bridge-builder: representing Scottish party interests in the British party, while also having to articulate and advocate British Labour decisions and processes in the Scottish party – the personification of the dual identity and role of Scottish Labour. While in appearance Labour in Scotland seemed to have all the paraphernalia of an autonomous party, with their own conference and executive committee, in practice these were largely insipid and lacklustre institutions. In effect, Labour in Scotland were nationalised and incorporated into the British party: in the early 1960s Magnus Magnusson referred to them as 'just a branch office' of the British Labour Party (Wood, F. 1989: 102).

All this would appear to indicate that Scottish Labour, from the 1930s onwards, were little more than a satrap of the national party, a regional organisation that possessed neither the constitutional authority, resources or perhaps even the desire to forge their own distinctive political identity. However, such a view is a partial and somewhat misleading one because it overlooks Labour's hybrid constitutional structure. The party's NEC was entrusted with full control (subject to conference ratification) over party organisation, discipline, funding and rule-making. But this unitary structure was coupled with a confederal dimension in which a key role was played by affiliated trade unions in policy-making, candidate selection, leadership recruitment and campaigning. Trade union leaders were power-brokers in their own right, controlling organisations, political networks and funds that limited the political leadership's control capability, imparting to the party a pluralistic character.

This applied no less to the Scottish wing of the party. Not only were affiliated trade unions represented in all sections of the party, but union organisation assumed an autonomous form in Scotland. The influential Scottish Trades Union Congress (STUC), to which most unions were affiliated and which well into the 1980s had a massive membership, was not a regional section of the TUC but a wholly independent body with a tradition of being led by astute, capable and highly influential figures. As we note below, in resource terms Scottish Labour was always heavily dependent on its union affiliates, with relations between the party and union elites assuming the form of mutual inter-dependence. This meant that whereas constitutionally Scottish party officials and the SEC were subordinate to the party centre, in practice national influence was muted by the need to co-operate with powerful local interests in Scotland.

Organisational change is frequently set in motion by the need to respond to powerful external challenges. The subordinate position of party institutions in Scotland remained largely unquestioned until the emergence, after two decades of easy electoral dominance, of a new challenge from an increasingly energetic, confident and professionally run SNP. In the two 1974 elections, the SNP secured a sizeable number of seats and, with Labour returned to power with only a wafer-thin majority after the October election, it feared that any further SNP advance would be at its expense. The party leadership hurriedly persuaded a reluctant Scottish party to back proposals for the establishment of (what was then called) a Scottish Assembly, but the upsurge in SNP support also brought in its wake pressure for some devolution of power within the party's own institutional structure, to which the NEC felt it had to some degree to accede. The rule limiting the Scottish conference to specifically Scottish matters (first challenged in 1968) was lifted in 1972, and it was allowed to debate all domestic (though still not international) issues. In addition, the Scottish party's policy capability was strengthened with the formation in 1975–6 of a range of policy sub-committees and working groups. However, these organisational modifications were relatively minor and did not alter the fundamental shape of inter-party relations.

A sustained campaign on 'party devolution' only really got underway in the early 1980s, largely as a result of the rising influence of the Labour Co-ordinating Committee (LCC) (Scotland), the Scottish affiliate of an energetic left-wing ginger group established in 1978. With a leadership composed of a cohort of young, determined and ambitious figures and with the help of allies among the more left-wing trade unions, by the early 1980s LCC (Scotland) had dislodged the centre-right party establishment on the SEC. It sought not only to radicalise the Scottish party but to win for them much greater control over their own affairs – to couple the party's commitment to constitutional devolution with 'party devolution', including greater powers for the Scottish party over policy-making, finance and organisation.

In 1980, in its evidence to the NEC's Committee of Enquiry into party organisation, the Scottish Executive called for responsibility for formulating policy matters which fell within the jurisdiction of the Scottish Office to be entrusted to the Scottish conference and for a much greater say over the content of Labour's Scottish manifesto.[2] The British Labour leadership was not responsive, insisting that (in the words of the Party's National Agent, David Hughes), 'in a unitary party there could be only one policy-making body'.[3] In response to further pressure, the party warned of the 'danger of policy fragmentation'. If the Scottish Party was given the right to determine policy on matters deemed to be Scottish then 'other sections of the party – such as the Welsh Party, other regional parties, Women's Conference and local government Conference – could all begin to demand similar rights. And this may be difficult to resist'.[4] After prolonged and sometimes acrimonious discussion, a compromise, which provided for a larger Scottish input into the party programme, was reached. In addition, a Joint (sometimes called 'Scottish') Liaison Committee was set up (in 1981) as a mechanism of co-ordination and consultation between the NEC and SEC (from whom its members were drawn).[5]

The drive for enhanced autonomy for the Scottish party was taken up after the 1987 election by Scottish Labour Action, a left-wing pro-devolution body which replaced LCC (Scotland) as the main group on the left (with there being co-operation between the two and a cross-over in members). Under the influence of both bodies, the SEC pressed for control by the Scottish party over staffing, work priorities and resources, but made a serious miscalculation.[6] It submitted proposals to the Scottish Party conference in Inverness in March 1989 without properly consulting Scottish party staff, who feared that party devolution would jeopardise their conditions of pay and employment. This convinced unenthusiastic trade unions who believed, in the words of an engineering union (AEU) official, that 'the Scottish party is not a separate party, it is part of the national party', to cast their votes against the SEC's proposals, which were overwhelmingly defeated by 550,000 votes to 151,000 (*The Glasgow Herald*, 13 March 1989). This thoroughly deflated the moment for party devolution. Despite, by the 1990s, an unequivocal commitment to devolution, it was clear that the party leadership was not prepared to relinquish control over its own organisation north of the border: the unitary nature of the party would remain intact.

THE PARTY ON THE GROUND

In the classic social democratic organisational tradition, party-builders 'sought to create cohesive class-based communities whose overlapping activities would reinforce a collective political identity' (Scarrow 1996: 4). A mass membership was regarded as vital. It was seen as the means to embed the party within society, enabling it to penetrate sympathetic social groups, operate as a conduit for their grievances, concerns and aspirations, and thereby forge a strong collective political identity. Social democracy's 'ability to mobilise voters was always closely linked to its large reservoir of party members, committed activists and associated institutions (above all, the trade unions). These core groups, in turn, created momentum and support for social democratic policies and ideas' (Cramme, Diamond and Liddle 2009: 8). In short, in the mass social democratic party model a large membership was seen to enhance the party's profile, enabling it to disseminate its message and operate as a key agency of voter mobilisation.

The Labour Party in Scotland never conformed to this mass party model. Writing in 1989, Scottish Secretary Murray Elder noted that the party in Scotland was 'a low membership Party' with a weak organisation and limited resources.[7] This picture would have been all too familiar for virtually the whole history of Scottish Labour. Indeed, we can speak of the paradox of Scottish Labour: for most of its decades of dominance in Scottish politics both the quality of its organisation and the size and activism of its membership have consistently been among the poorest of any region of the Labour Party in Britain.

As has been seen, the ILP was the main engine of membership activity until its disaffiliation. The membership of the Labour Party itself rose from around 11,000 in 1929 to 25,000 in 1935, at which level it stuck for a number of years. In 1939, Arthur Woodburn, the Scottish Secretary, declared that, measured by constituency, Scottish membership was the lowest of any region with an average of 423 compared to 754 for English counterparts (Harvie 1983: 921, 925).

After the Second World War figures become progressively less reliable as minimum affiliation levels became the basis of calculating party membership. In the 1950s, CLPs affiliated on a minimum membership of 240, rising to 800 in 1960 and then to 1,000 in 1963 – which meant that the gap between official figures and reality steadily widened. According to the official figures, membership stood at 57,567 in 1952 (CLP average 810), rose to 70,240 in 1953 (989) and fell heavily to 51,773 in 1955 (729). With the figures artificially inflated by the minimum affiliation of 800, the figure was 66,904 in 1963 (942) and increased again, with the minimum now set at 1,000, to 79,054 in 1965 (1113), at which point it hovered till the scrapping of the affiliation rate in 1979. Hereafter actual membership figures were reported.[8]

In reality, membership was almost certainly falling from the 1950s onwards, though perhaps with some oscillations. It has been possible to compile more accurate figures from internal reports submitted to the Organisation Sub-committee of the NEC. In 1952, 1953 and again in 1955, it was reported that of the ten Labour Party regions, membership in the Scottish was the lowest (per CLP and absolutely) and well below the average. An especially high proportion of CLPs had below 1,000 members.[9] In 1965, the Organisation Sub-Committee was told that of seventy-one Scottish CLPs, sixty-one had below the minimum membership, the highest proportion in Britain (though with Wales and the North East, also Labour strongholds, not that far behind). In contrast, in London only eleven out of forty-two CLPs had below the minimum.[10]

From time to time, enquiries produced more detailed analyses of the state of party membership and organisation. For example, the following figures were provided in 1958:[11]

Table 7:   Scottish Labour Membership 1958

Leith	418
Edinburgh Central	511
Edinburgh East	1,115
Motherwell	approx. 800
Kelvingrove	177
Craigton	721
Scotstoun	1,076
Woodside	488
Provan	approx. 800
Lanark	approx. 5,000
Bothwell	400
North Lanarkshire	3,600
Stirling and Falkirk	1,060

The pattern of membership throughout Scotland was uneven. One consistent theme running through many reports was the deplorably low membership scores in the party's staunchest urban bastion, Glasgow. Indeed, it is precisely because of the poor state of organisation in the city, provoking a series of NEC investigations, that more information is available. In 1951, after eighteen years of continuous Labour control of the council, it was estimated that total party membership only stood at 5,000. Seven of the city's fifteen CLPs affiliated on the minimum 240 (which meant that real membership could be much lower) and a further five on under 500 (Hutchison 2001: 89). In 1961, an unusually detailed and rather revealing report on the state of party organisation in the Glasgow Labour Party was submitted to the Organisation Sub-committee by NEC member Arthur Skeffington MP.[12]

The 1960s did not register any improvement in the overall state of party organisation. Despite the fact that the party was tightening its grip on Glasgow's parliamentary representation, efforts to generate more cash and inject more life into the city party – for example, by establishing a social club –

Table 8: Glasgow Labour Membership 1961

Constituency	Membership	Active workers
Shettleston (Labour held)	given as 200	20
Springburn (Labour held)	given as 200	40
Scotstoun (Labour held)	given as 1,000	50
Maryhill (Labour held)	983	50/60
Cathcart (Con held)	no figures	30
Craigton (Labour held)	370	24 No AGM for two years.
Govan (Labour held)	400	60 A serious split over defence.
Woodside (Con held)	450	40 Very poor organisation.
Central (Labour held)	130	8/10
Hillhead (Con held)	30	5 Shocking state.
Provan (Labour held)	given as 354	70
Kelvingrove (Con held)	80	60
Bridgeton (Labour held)	250	20
Gorbals (Labour held)	given as 350	20
Pollok (Con held)	no figures	25 Organisation very poor.

failed ignominiously (Hutchison 2001: 128). The NEC was so perturbed that in 1969 it launched an enquiry headed by the Scottish Regional Organiser, Willie Marshall, and the party's most senior organising official (the National Agent), Reg Underhill. It offered a bleak portrait of the state of the party. The total individual membership in the fifteen constituencies was 1,786. Nine constituencies had less than a hundred members, and of these six less than fifty. Only one constituency had more than three hundred members. Executive committees met regularly in less than half the constituencies and attendance at General Committee meetings was frequently very thin. Other forms of activism were equally unimpressive. In some constituencies, the enquiry reported, 'a small number of members have been doing their best to carry out limited educational propaganda activities'. In a number of wards, the local election campaign team consisted mainly of a few of the candidates' friends, and some candidates were forced to pay their own election expenses. In general, it concluded, constituency activities were spasmodic, and in some areas 'only the devoted work of two or three people had prevented a complete collapse of organisation'. Equally, the committee reported, the financial position was 'very serious'. In November 1968, a 'politically disastrous situation' was only avoided when an affiliated organisation (presumably a trade union) donated sufficient funds to enable the Glasgow city party to pay its outstanding 1967–8 rates bill. The income of most constituency parties was 'totally inadequate' and a number were in considerable arrears in affiliation fees to Head Office.

The conclusions of the report were damning. Lamenting 'the deplorable rundown state of the Party organisation', it noted that though individual party membership in Glasgow had never been high, it had now 'reached the lowest position for very many years'. The organisation in most constituencies was 'woefully inadequate'. Councillors and MPs were criticised for permitting matters to drift and the city party condemned for the complete absence of any effective field organisation.[13] Two years later, little had changed in the Labour stronghold of Glasgow Shettleston CLP, where the party was found to be in a 'shockingly bad state of organisation', with individual membership totalling no more than a dozen.[14]

Although there was general agreement that party organisation and membership was particularly poor in Glasgow, there is some evidence that affairs were little better elsewhere. Aberdeen, for example, in the early 1970s had only two hundred members, the lowest ratio of party members to voters in Scotland (Knox 1999: 303). An inquiry into Paisley CLP in 1960 reported that only three out of eight wards had any real organisation. It was 'a shocking state of affairs. It would appear that the affairs of the party are largely controlled by a small group.'[15] Writing in the aftermath of Wilson's 1966 landslide, Marwick bemoaned a party and movement in a state of atrophy and decline. Local Labour parties were 'largely inactive, except at elections', with 'a general apathy or inertia', while 'propaganda, whether by the spoken or the printed word, declined; Fabian Societies in a few centres served as almost its only organ, speaking to the converted few' (Marwick 1967: 113).

The late 1960s and the 1970s were politically difficult years for the Labour Party in Scotland, but the picture does not appear to have improved in any substantial way in the 1980s, a decade in which Labour was very firmly entrenching itself in Scottish politics. Writing in 1988, Keating found that in Glasgow money from membership fees was so low that frequently constituency parties were unable to pay their national affiliation fees and hence were not allowed to send a delegate to the annual national conference (Keating 1988: 12). In 1982, Labour's Scottish Organiser, the capable and outspoken Jimmy Allison, described membership as 'a disgrace', with membership levels especially sparse in Labour-held seats.[16] Membership in Scotland, he reported the following year, 'has never been at a satisfactory level. Anyone who indicates otherwise is deliberately misleading the public and the party.'[17] Little had improved by the early 1990s.[18]

Even in those few areas where membership totals seemed impressive, they were not uncommonly inflated by the existence of 'Labour clubs', that is drinking clubs owned by the local party selling cheap alcohol, membership of which required taking out a party card. For example, Jimmy Allison noted that Glasgow Cathcart boasted a membership of 1,500, but the vast majority had affiliated via the Labour social club. Prior to its establishment, constituency membership was approximately 120.[19]

Nor did a sudden surge in membership and attendance in meetings neces-sarily indicate swelling political interest or activity. Big selection battles, as ambitious party members sought to fill a vacancy or dislodge the incumbent, not infrequently led to an influx of new members, especially when new membership carried the immediate right to participate in selection contests (interview, Anne McGuire). 'Nothing stimulates political activity', Allison caustically commented, 'more than an empty seat waiting to be filled' (Allison 1995: 52). These new members not uncommonly vanished as quickly as they had appeared.

Recent decades have not witnessed any substantial and sustained improvement in membership. Membership was listed as 19,708 in 1993, rising to 30,770 at the end of 1998, before falling to 21,524 in 2001 (Lynch and Birrell 2004: 181). Glasgow, as usual, recorded (in 2001) dismal totals: Shettleston and Springburn CLPs with less than two hundred members and Baillieston and Pollok just over. But the pattern was repeated elsewhere, with Greenock and Inverclyde and Paisley North notching up less than two hundred, and Aberdeen North, Ayr, Central Fife, Dumbarton, Falkirk East and West Renfrewshire all less than 250. Even these may have been over-estimates. Before 2000, members' subscriptions fifteen months in arrears continued to appear on the rolls, though this was cut to six months in 2000, and a shift in 2002–3 to monthly direct debits improved accuracy. After 2003, as a result of the Iraq war, membership slumped further, as elsewhere in the country (Whiteley 2009). By 2010, though Scottish Labour claimed a membership of over 20,000, the number of ballot papers sent out to party members in Scotland for the UK leadership election in September 2010 suggested the total was a rather meagre 13,135 (*Caledonian Mercury*, 29 September 2010). This is explored further in Chapter 8.

Why Does Scottish Labour Have Low Membership and Activism – and Does it Matter?

Writing in 1989, at the end of a decade in which Labour had acquired a position of dominance in Scottish politics, Scottish General Secretary Murray Elder noted, 'The decade to 1988 was a period of political rather than organisational ascendancy. Our political and electoral success did not imply great organisational strengths or a strong membership base.'[20] This begs the question, why, even when circumstances were propitious, with firm partisan loyalties buttressed by social class and denominational affiliations, forging strong connections with the party, did Labour fail to extend its membership and activist base?

Membership size, it can be argued, is affected by strategic decisions on a range of questions. What is the electoral value or utility attached to a mass membership? How actively does a party seek to enrol new members? How much effort and energy is it prepared to expend? To what extent do its organisational structures render it accessible to new members – or are there barriers to entry?

The general pattern (not confined to Scotland) was that members (and levels of activism) tended to be lowest in areas where Labour was – electorally – strongest. FPTP, by creating political monopolies, removes a key incentive to recruit a mass membership, with the lack of political competition often breeding a certain complacency. While Scottish membership figures were, one MP observed, 'an embarrassment, the Scottish party could always say, "but we deliver"' (interview, Anne McGuire). The outcome could often be the effective atrophying of the local party as an electoral machine. Writing in 1988, Keating noted the fitful nature of electioneering in Glasgow local elections, with little door-to-door canvassing and little activity on the streets. Indeed, the party experienced difficulties in recruiting candidates not only for unwinnable seats, but increasingly for winnable ones 'where the Labour Party nomination is tantamount to election' (Keating 1988: 54). A report into the Paisley North and South by-elections in 1990 noted that, even among the handful of members showing a willingness to engage in electioneering, enthusiasm 'was less than wholehearted'.[21]

In contrast, membership tended to be larger and more active in electorally more competitive areas, for example in Edinburgh (interview, party organiser). Jack McConnell, leader of Stirling Council in the early 1990s, recalled Stirling CLP (a highly marginal constituency with tight contests also for control over the local council) as having 'a high level of political debate', including a vigorous political education programme (interview). Another party staffer described the party in electorally competitive Dundee in the 1980s as 'incredibly active' (interview). There were even spurts of activity in Labour areas. Bill Butler MSP recollected Glasgow Garscadden in the 1980s as a large and active party with keen political discussion (interview).

Outside the Labour heartlands, there is some anecdotal evidence of a growth of party membership and activism in the late 1970s and 1980s, with an influx of younger, more radical elements, often university educated and with a public sector middle-class background. The intense factional struggles in this period often encouraged political participation and mobilisation. Three major groups contested for control of the party: the right, the mainstream left (LCC (Scotland) and Scottish Labour Action) and the far left (mainly the Trotskyist Militant Tendency). Debates were heated, votes closely fought, 'there was a battle of ideas and it seemed to really matter if you turned up'

234

(interview, Sarah Boyack). Factions such as the LCC (Scotland), SLA and Militant all played a role in enlisting, organising and energising members in a bid to strengthen their influence. 'It was a period of quite genuine political ferment within the party' (interview, Bill Butler MSP). Whatever the positive effects of the lessening of intra-party tensions and the weakening (and, in the case of Militant, the exclusion) of factional organisations, it also led to the removal of one spur to political activity.

Yet such examples of vibrant political engagement were relatively rare and driven by the enthusiasm usually of small numbers of dedicated local activists. At national (Scottish) level the party lacked the means to mount sustained recruitment drives or engage in systematic party-building. As the Scottish General Secretary observed, 'far too often the organiser's time is taken up solely by policing activities on behalf of the National Executive and increasingly the re-selection round which will be immensely time-consuming . . . The limited organisational resources mean that there is too little time, . . . for the organisers to get out to the constituencies and ensure that the parties are modernising . . . in short to do the work of organisers'.[22] Inevitably, in these circumstances the responsibility for recruitment devolved onto constituency and branch parties. Where passions in the party ran high, as rival groups or factions fought for control over the local council or battled fiercely for rival candidates in parliamentary selection contests (as happened from the late 1970s to the late 1980s), larger numbers of people might be drawn into party activity.

It was precisely for this reason that, in Labour strongholds, local elites often had an incentive to keep membership low. As Labour's control of local government tightened, it was not unusual for local parties to be run by councillors (and their family and friends), and they were loathe to imperil their power bases by an influx of newcomers. In some areas, the party's senior organiser, Jimmy Allison, recalled, 'there was a deliberate policy of people being kept out in case they upset the balance of power within the local constituency' (Allison 1995: 40). The very fact that it was easier to de-select a councillor than an MP gave incumbents an interest in conserving local party control. As Henry McLeish, former Fife Council leader, explained, 'a lot of the councillors had very small branches – for their own survival. Branch would have the magic seven members, maybe four of the family and a couple of buddies. Nobody had a big interest in building up the membership' (interview). Nor were there many party members imbued with the old ILP spirit of active proselytising for socialism. Some areas where worse than others: 'You needed a blood-test to get in to Glasgow Govan', Anne McGuire recalled (interview). Not infrequently potential recruits might be discouraged (at a time when local parties had responsibility for membership) by the sheer difficulty in joining the party, the result not of policy but of a combination of lethargy, indifference and the absence of efficient methods to process applications for membership.[23]

It should not be forgotten that recruitment is time-consuming and often discouraging work, and it is for this reason that central animation, direction and co-ordination are important. But this involves the commitment of resources and, as the Scottish General Secretary complained in 1989, the party had 'few resources scattered very generally over all Scotland and with organisers whose current workload means they are badly overstretched'.[24] In fact, recruitment was never seen as a high priority, which could justify diverting significant resources from other tasks. A key reason for this was the absence of what was for most social democratic parties a prime motivation for building up a mass membership – the need to secure a reliable source of income. Lacking access to the more ample funding to which parties with a strong base in the more affluent sections of the community have access, parties of the left have traditionally relied heavily on subscriptions and the voluntary unpaid work of a mass membership. For the Labour Party, however, there was an alternative. From its inception a high proportion of its income was supplied by trade union affiliation, income generously supplemented at election times by donations. Resource dependence on the unions was particularly pronounced in highly unionised areas, such as the more heavily populated areas in Scotland. Referring specifically to the 1950s, Hutchison reported that 'with an enfeebled organisation Labour drew very heavily upon the commitment and support given by the trade unions throughout this period' (Hutchison 2001: 93) and stated:

> It was the funding supplied by the unions which permitted any Scottish central administrative and organisational framework to survive. Unions paid affiliation fees on their members in Scotland, but also put up additional sums at elections. They also frequently released their Scottish officials to assist Labour in contesting elections, serving as agents in constituencies where the local party could not provide. Above all, since numerous constituencies could not finance running a candidate, it was not unusual for a member of a prominent local trade union (frequently an official in the union's bureaucracy) to secure the nomination through the guarantee of sponsorship. (Hutchison 2001: 94)

If anything, this dependency subsequently intensified. Union affiliations rose more rapidly in Scotland than in England and Wales: the figures from 1952 to 1978 were 48% compared to 17%, which meant a bigger relative rise in subscription income. Indeed, Hutchison suggests that this rise in trade union cash and help played a key role in enabling the party to fend off the SNP challenge in the 1970s (Hutchison 2001: 135). In addition, it became a well-established practice to contribute directly to Labour's electoral machinery by agreeing to second full-time officials to key constituencies for the duration of elections. At all levels of the party, party and union office-holders worked closely together. Indeed, the party's access to manpower and resources, and to a whole network of local connections that the unions placed at its disposal, helps explain why it was able to sustain its political hegemony despite persistently low levels of membership and activism, and the often ramshackle state of its constituency organisation. In the party stronghold of Fife, for example, 'Unions and Labour were very, very close. Unions were very active and supportive in terms of finance, sponsorship, and foot soldiers. The Labour Party was small in membership and the unions were large, and when it mattered they were there' (interview, Henry McLeish).

A low membership and a thin layer of activists would appear to suggest a party that had signally failed to penetrate the social fabric. But the impression of Scottish Labour as a weak and unrepresentative organisation dominated by narrow self-serving cliques of councillors disconnected from the wider society is, at best, a half-truth. It reflects a model which assumes a contrast between three discrete groups – activists, members and voters – and assumes that the party's ability to mobilise and solidify support was primarily a function of the number of its committed members. Seyd and Whiteley point out that a flourishing membership acts as testimony 'to the fact that a party has support in the community and is rooted in the concerns and values of real people. In this sense, members are "ambassadors in the community"' (Seyd and Whiteley 2004: 361). Such ambassadors could 'multiply votes through their willingness openly to declare, and even to explain, their personal political allegiances' (Scarrow 1996: 43).

However, this crucial role of 'ambassadors in the community' could be performed by relatively small numbers if they were well known, involved in manifold social activities in their local communities, well regarded and enjoyed the status of community leaders. There is some evidence (though it is mainly anecdotal) that within local Labour parties, especially in working-class communities, there were a small but significant number of party activists, many of them councillors, who honed their skills as effective street-level politicians. Many, a long-standing party organiser recalled, were respected members of their local communities, embedded in social networks and well known as 'Labour men' who could be approached more or less informally to cope with the concerns and grievances of their constituents (interview). As another experienced party organiser recollected, 'they were involved in the community councils, they were involved in the residents' associations, the tenants' associations, the schools council, the elderly clubs, the boxing club, they were all connected' (interview). Most of them were primarily interested in local politics, the day-to-day practical issues that were the staple diet of the local councillor, and might evince only a passing interest in broader political debates. A former Glasgow MP and then MSP recalled those Glasgow councillors who 'looked after their wee patch, got what they could for their constituents, never seeking high office nor with any set agenda. These are the people (though not the majority) who hold the party together . . . keeping us going, solid, local activists' (interview, Sam Galbraith). Active members (especially elected representatives) formed a hub which reached out to many who broadly identified with the party and could be mobilised to troop into the polling stations. Informal conduits of influence and connectivity, in short, replaced formal party ones. 'People in Scotland don't need to join the party to show their commitment to Labour – I used to hear that all the time', Anne McGuire recollected: '"We know our people"' (interview).

The survival of these informal networks with their intricate and multiple connections in local communities depended both on the existence within the party of a cohort of members suitably equipped to act as effective 'ambassadors in the community' and of cohesive communities where the main electoral task was simply to mobilise the Labour vote. By the 1970s, as the then South Ayrshire Labour MP Jim Sillars recalled, 'the self-sustaining, supporting world of Labour was slowly eroding and disappearing' (interview). The process of party de-alignment and attenuating class–party solidarity, together with a rising challenge from the SNP, increasingly meant that activation of dormant Labour supporters was ceasing to suffice. It did not help that by the end of the 1980s the party had become 'a bit lethargic. We cocooned ourselves from the outside world. We became increasingly insular' (interview, Henry McLeish).

Yet, did low levels of membership in Scotland actually matter? Membership levels may have ranged from the modest to the paltry but the party continued to win votes and seats. At times complaints about low membership seemed genuine enough, at other times formulaic, but little ever improved. Perhaps there was no real need?

Decisions about the most effective deployment of the usually very limited resources available to a party are influenced by its organisational strategy, that is, its assessment about what combination of methods and techniques is most likely to win votes and seats (Scarrow 1996: 49). Was the expense and effort entailed in attracting and retaining members actually justified by the electoral benefits? Increasingly, especially from the mid-1980s, new techniques of mass communication and persuasion, mainly imported from the US and very effectively exploited by the Conservatives – key Labour strategists came to believe – had greatly reduced the value of grassroots electioneering. What mattered was the ability to transmit one's message via the mass media. This required the building up of a powerful, sophisticated and highly professional communications capability, staffed by qualified public relations experts, publicists, marketing and advertising executives, that could project an appealing image of the party and its leaders (for a detailed discussion, see Shaw 1994: 54–67, and for a classic exposition of the underlying reasoning by one of Labour's top strategists, see Gould 1998).

Indeed, for the party 'modernisers' bruised by the internecine battles of the 1980s, party activists, far from being an asset, were actually a liability. They tended to be disproportionately on the left and (it was felt) more interested in fettering the party with vote-losing policy commitments than in burnishing its image. Thus it could be argued 'that the opportunity costs of organizing and maintaining the party membership exceed any potential benefits which could be provided by these members' (Scarrow 1996: 41).

Such was the received wisdom, both within the party and among many commentators. But in the 1990s this orthodoxy was increasingly challenged by empirical investigators. Denver and Hands concluded from a survey of constituency electioneering that local parties fulfil key electoral functions, such as communicating party information, political persuasion and voter mobilisation (Denver and Hands 1997). Research increasingly indicated that 'constituency party organisation and the efforts of party members at the local level do matter'. Not only was 'more intense campaigning . . . associated with higher constituency turnouts', but 'variations in the intensity of Labour and Liberal Democrat campaigns have been clearly associated with variations in party performance across constituencies in all three elections studied' (Denver, Hands and MacAllister 2004: 303). The evidence increasingly pointed to a direct correlation between the number of active constituency campaigners and electoral performance (Seyd and Whiteley 2004: 361). 'Particularly in close-fought contests, an effective and energetic local campaign can make the difference between winning and losing' (Pattie et al. 1994: 479).

In short, the failure of Scottish Labour to build a strong membership mattered. Its dwindling membership and contraction in the number of its activists meant that it had fewer 'ambassadors in the community' and formed a diminishing part of civil society in Scotland. To staff its electoral machine it became increasingly reliant on parliamentary aides, party officials, local councillors and trade union officials, reinforcing an ageing cohort of voluntary workers. Where conditions were conducive – when the political weather was fair – this might not be too damaging. But given the evidence that local campaigning 'played a very important role in influencing the vote' (Whiteley and Seyd 2003: 320), the fragility of its constituency presence spelled danger when the political weather turned stormy. As a leading expert on party membership concluded, it is hard to see how parties can function effectively in the wider community without their voluntary organisations' (Whiteley 2009: 254). Scottish Labour – Labour in general – ignored a fading membership very much at its peril.[25]

THE PARTY MENTALITY

Political parties, Moschanas has written, 'are in some sense condemned to store their previous states in their memory and despite their demonstrable capacity for evolution, they cannot readily, at will, transcend – and escape – their distinguishing qualities and characteristics. Each party is the bearer of its own tradition, and these traditions, sometimes strongly institutionalized, are embedded in the parties' identities and self-conceptions' (Moschanas 2002: 243). These distinguishing qualities, characteristics, identities and self-conceptions compose, to use Durkheim's phrase, a party's 'collective consciousness', its pattern of 'acting, thinking and feeling' (Durkheim 1982 [1895]).

It has long been recognised that British Labour's 'collective consciousness' and self-identity differs sharply from that of its continental sister parties. The classic social democratic party was what Epstein called a 'program-matic' party, a party inspired by a vision of the good society which evolved its polices through an articulated framework of principles. From this vantage point, policies were 'part of a settled long-range programme' derived from an 'intellectualized perspective' and closely tied to 'a long-range social purpose' (Epstein 1980: 262). Forrester summarises this mindset as 'educative, ideo-logical, principled, intellectual' (Forrester 1976: 35). It amounted, at its most rigorous, to an orientation to politics that 'concentrate[d] on broad social and moral principles' and tended to 'argue deductively from general political or social or economic theories' (Putnam 1971: 656).

Unlike its sister parties, the British Labour Party was formed by the unions, inherited their traditions, and imbibed many of their characteristics, customs and habits of thought. It saw itself as as 'the instrument of the labour inter-est rather than as the vehicle for any ideology' (Marquand 1991: 16–17). Drucker went as far as to argue that 'the spirit of the party, its traditions, its habits, its feel' were all largely a product of its ties with trade unions (Drucker 1991: 244; see also Drucker 1979). As with the unions, so in the party: prece-dent, tradition and established custom and practice and experience were seen as more reliable guides to action than abstract intellectual schemes (Minkin 1980: 118). This has given rise to a distinctive mindset – sometimes labelled 'labourist' – which Forrester characterised as 'reflective, empirical, pragmatic, evolutionary' (Forrester 1976: 35). Labour, Marriott explains, 'emerged as a pragmatic response to new challenges, and subsequently developed through political expedience. From the outset its commitment to Labour representation was characterised by an incipient logic of empiricism, evolutionism, compromise and defence' (Marriott 1991: 4).

Scottish Labour has always had a strong sense of a remembered past – one of tenacity, of heroic struggle and defiance – but this idealised view had little tangible effect on its essential cautions and pragmatic temperament, one heavily suffused by the practical, down-to-earth labourist mindset. As with the party nationally, so too in Scotland the culture of the party exhibited an indifference to broad intellectual currents and a 'deep scepticism towards all political schemes which diverge from everyday common-sense and experience' (Fox 1978: 5). Though 'masked by a language of political debate based upon concepts of working class solidarity and drawing on the myths of Red Clydeside . . . Labour had become the local political establishment, the path to municipal power and parliamentary careers' (Keating 1989: 93–4). Most of the energies of local party organisations and activists were expended in running local government, which meant that a high proportion of its upper layer (excluding Labour MPs) were absorbed in the practical details of municipal administration. In local parties a large percentage of the (usually rather modest number) of active party members was local councillors, and meetings were dominated by council reports and by organisational and electoral matters. The prime purpose of the party on the ground (one seasoned senior party figure recalled) was to act as 'an electoral machine to get people elected to the political battlefronts' (interview, Henry McLeish). As a result, the bread-and-butter issues of local politics – housing, education, the pay and conditions of municipal workers and so forth – increasingly dominated the political agenda and set the intellectual horizons of Scottish Labour. 'Pragmatism and management became ingrained in Scottish Labour's post-war outlook' (Finlay 2004: 32; see also Hutchison 2001: 95). The era of the Clydesiders and ILP evangelists, the radical, fervent and idealistic earlier generation, had receded well into the past. Keating summed up the ideology of the Labour Party in the largest by far of Labour-run councils, Glasgow, as 'municipal labourism', that is, 'a concern with a limited range of policy issues with an immediate impact on their constituents – notably housing matters – but little consideration of wider policy issues'. These wider issues – such as public ownership and the structure of the welfare state – 'were taken for granted but their contemporary meaning rarely debated'(Keating 1988: 12–13).

Labour's hold on large parts of the political life of Scotland was not coupled by any sustained efforts or even interest in promoting a distinctive set of ideals and beliefs. By the mid 1970s, John Mackintosh MP, one of the party's few intellectuals, reported that Labour in Scotland had 'aged and lost dynamism. Its one absorbing interest has been jobs (saving rather than creating jobs) and capital projects such as schools and houses. But the original idealistic vision of a kind of society socialists wanted, of the point of building schools and houses, tended to fade out and now the social purpose of the party is far from clear' (quoted in Knox 1999: 303). When, a decade or so later, the first systematic survey into the values and beliefs of Labour Party members was undertaken, it found, notwithstanding the Scottish party's radical traditions and self-image, Scottish Labour members' ideological placements were almost identical to the average for Labour members in general, and to the right of members in the East Midlands, the South, the South West and Greater London (Whiteley and Seyd 1992: 130).

The empirical rootedness of Scottish Labour did have some undoubted advantages. Many of the cohort of politicians who were to fill the ranks of its Holyrood group had practical experience derived from work in voluntary organisations, trade unions, the public sector and council services; a decided advantage when they came to engage with policy-making on devolved matters. The Scottish party was rarely agitated by highly abstract theorising, which lent such an unreal air to deliberations of such parties as the French Socialists. The focus on concrete issues, equally, helped keep Labour in touch with its constituents.

If Scottish Labour was 'ideology lite', the myth of its radical past did nevertheless have consequences for the way it conducted itself. It encouraged what could be called a dual level of political discourse within the party – perhaps particularly marked in the West of Scotland. Few were inclined to dissent from what might be regarded as totems of the left, such as support for unilateral nuclear disarmament, the unions and the collective provision of public services – what could be called a rhetorical 'Clause Four socialism'. Thus a certain left language or terminology deemed as appropriate to the public expression of opinion in Labour Party meetings would be deployed, though it might signify little real commitment. Helen Liddell (General Secretary of the Scottish Labour Party from 1977 to 1988), recalled that 'often the people who lionised Tony Benn were quite pragmatic as local councillors – a lot of the ideological argument was more a romantic one than a focused one' (interview). But this rhetorical radicalism did have some practical consequences: it supplied a fund of symbols, myths and reference points which was available for mobilisation by more left-wing elements in the party to block New Labour initiatives, complicating (for example) its efforts to secure support for the abolition of Clause Four of the party constitution at the 1995 Scottish Labour conference.

The combination of this rhetorical radicalism with the rootedness of Scottish Labour in traditional ways of 'acting, thinking and feeling' – an inherited reluctance to query the assumptions and principles underpinning its own behaviour – rendered it less receptive to the New Labour 'modernising' project. This resistance was bolstered by its relative electoral success in the 1980s and early 1990s, which meant that (unlike Labour in England) there were no electoral shocks to galvanise the party into questioning long-standing tenets of belief. For advocates of 'the project', this could be very frustrating – 'politics in aspic' in the words of one senior advisor (interview, John McTernan). Equally, and from a different perspective, Scottish Labour's disinclination to frame policies within a broad canvas of meaning, deliberate about the ultimate aims and purposes of its political activities or formulate any 'vision of the good life' left it ill-equipped to carve out for itself a distinct political identity and profile and, hence, vulnerable when another political force emerged to challenge its monopoly claim to the mantle of social democracy.

NOTES

1. Memo from Helen Liddell, Scottish Secretary, to SEC 3 April 1981, Scottish Council of Labour Party Minutes, Mitchell Library Box TD 1384/2/1/2.
2. GMWU Evidence to Scottish Council of the Labour Party (henceforward SCLP) for Labour Party Commission of Enquiry, March 1980. SCLP Minutes, Mitchell Library Box TD 1384/2/1/1.
3. Meeting of SEC with the National Agent, A, 24 September 1980. SCLP Minutes, Mitchell Library Box TD 1384/2/1/1.
4. Home Policy Committee Devolution of policy-making to Scotland: *A note from the Research Secretary*. RD: 3103/September 1984.
5. Meeting of Representatives of the NEC and SEC, 17 January 1984. SCLP Minutes, Mitchell Library Box TD 1384/2/1/4. Minutes of the Meeting of the Joint Liaison Committee, 19 June 1984. SCLP Minutes, Mitchell Library Box TD 1384/2/1/4. Murray Elder, Office Note to members of the Joint Liaison Committee, Report of meeting with JLC and NEC, 3 March 1987. SCLP Minutes, Mitchell Library Box TD 1384/2/1/6.
6. JLC, 16 February 1989. SCLP Minutes, Mitchell Library Box TD 1384/2/1/10.
7. M. Elder, Scottish Council Report to the Organisation Sub-Committee (henceforward Org. Sub.) of the NEC, 6 March 1989.
8. Org. Sub., 23 April 1952; NEC, 28 June 1954; Org. Sub., 18 April 1956; Org. Sub., 18 March 1964; Org. Sub., 17 May 1966.
9. Org. Sub., 23 April 1952; Org. Sub., 15 April 1953; Org. Sub., 18 April 1956.
10. Org. Sub., 17 May 1966.
11. Report by Scottish Regional Organiser Willie Marshall, Org. Sub., 28 February 1958.
12. Inquiry into Party Organisation in Glasgow, Org. Sub., 14 February 1961.
13. Inquiry into Party Organisation in Glasgow, NAD, 14 February 1969 by Janey Buchan, C. Donnnett, R. Stewart, W. G. Marshall, H. R. Underhill, NEC, 26 February 1969.
14. Report into Glasgow Shettleston CLP. NAD/1/1/71 CLP, NEC, 27 January 1971.

15. Org. Sub, 19 July 1960.
16. SEC, 9 October 1989, SCLP Minutes, Mitchell Library Box TD 1384/2/1.
17. Labour Party Scottish Conference Report, 1983.
18. SLC, 2 March 1993, GS:33/3/93.
19. SEC Org. Sub., 1 November 1982, 1989. SCLP Minutes, Mitchell Library Box TD 1384/2/1.
20. M. Elder, op. cit.
21. DO/32(b)/12/90, NEC, 19 December 1990.
22. M. Elder, op. cit.
23. New recruits might also find branch and (especially) constituency party meetings alienating experiences. Jimmy Allison, one of Scottish Labour's most capable organisers, recalled that when he began attending ward meetings in the 1960s, 'to my dismay . . . I found them totally boring . . . I had gone along expecting a political debate on issues such as nuclear disarmament but instead we spent our time talking about trivial matters such as street lighting or the state of the pavements' (Allison 1995: 40).
24. M. Elder, op. cit.
25. Peter Hain MP noted that 'one of the key lessons to be learnt from the 2010 election is that, in those places where we worked closely with the local community, embedded ourselves as part of the local political and social landscape, Labour candidates bucked the national trend and held their seats' (Hain 2011).

CHAPTER 14

The Internal Politics of Scottish Labour

Parties are not homogenous organisations but typically contain a wide range of members with differing beliefs, goals and interests. Internal party groupings naturally arise because members can only pursue their goals – whether they be matters of ideology, policy or personal advancement or, more commonly, a mixture – by acting in association with others. As Hume pointed out, 'men have such a propensity to divide into personal factions, that the smallest appearance of real difference will produce them' (Hume 1742). Competition among these factions – or, less pejoratively, groups or combinations – is an irreducible feature of party life. Party actions cannot be understood if these internal conflicts are ignored, and the nature of internal alliances and coalitions has to be appraised to make any sense of party behaviour.

This chapter addresses a range of questions: How can one define and characterise intra-party groupings within Scottish Labour? What role did these groupings play? To what extent has the scale, nature and role of group activity within Scottish Labour changed over the years? And what does this tell us about Scottish Labour?

Party ginger groups or combinations can be defined as associations of the like-minded bound by some commonality of objects and with some capacity for collective action. Party members are animated by a diverse range of goals when they form combinations. On the basis of their motivational structure, commentators have distinguished between three ideal types: of principle, of patronage and of personality. Principle-based combinations are oriented towards the pursuit of collective goals, their members inspired by purposive incentives, that is, 'intangible rewards that derive from the sense of satisfaction of having contributed to the attainment of a worthwhile cause' (Wilson 1995: 34). They include both issue-based groupings and ideological ones where groups differ over 'a broad range of problems' and where 'attitudes are held together by a more or less coherent political philosophy' (Rose 1973: 321).

Patronage-based combinations refer to 'self-seeking groups primarily concerned with the accumulation and distribution of selective and divisible goods, such as party posts, campaign funds, government appointments and contracts' (Boucek 2009: 465). Their aims may be couched in terms of policy or ideology but these tend to be used as cloaks or legitimising devices for the accrual of selective benefits. Personality-based combinations refers to groups 'that form behind different political leaders primarily on the basis of the leaders' personal attraction' (Janda 1980: 122).

In real life, of course, internal party groupings will be motivated by a range of considerations. As Hume pointed out, factions 'are seldom found pure and unmixed, either of the one kind or the other'. But notwithstanding they can be characterised 'according to that principle which is predominant, and is found to have the greatest influence' (Hume 1742). The key factor determining which principle becomes predominant is the prevailing form that intra-party cleavages take, 'i.e. whether they are about power and careers, policy issues and ideologies, or different sectional interests' (Köllner and Basedau 2005: 13). For this reason, the nature and basis of intra-party struggles tell us a lot about the nature of a party and what it values.

Party combinations also vary according to their organisational characteristics. Here three classes of combinations can be distinguished. The least organised is the *tendency*, which Rose defined 'as a cluster of attitudes . . . held together by a more or less coherent political philosophy' but lacking an organisational structure. A *faction*, in contrast, is 'self-consciously organised as a body with a measure of discipline and cohesion' (Rose 1973: 320). Defined principally by its developed organisational structure, it will generally have a name, a formal membership, rules, a decision-making structure and a recognised leadership (Beller and Belloni 1978: 425, 427). A *network* lies somewhere in between the two. Consisting of party members with shared interests or goals, it lacks a formal organisational structure, rules and procedures, but does have the capacity to pursue its purpose through concerted action. This action typically will be informal in nature, operating primarily through personal ties and connections, and generally shunning publicity. Tendencies by definition will be principle-oriented, but both networks and factions may be ideological-, patronage- or personality-based – or some combination of all three.

Analysis of internal party dissension has tended to focus more or less exclusively at the national level, which overlooks the fact that not only does much party work take place within the framework of local politics but that control over local authorities is a major prize for politicians not least because of the access it affords to public office, prestige and material rewards. As will be seen below, the fact that Scottish Labour usually controlled local authorities

246

(especially in the west Central Belt), often over long periods of time, gave it the capacity to appropriate resources which it lacked (until 1999) at Scottish level. Hence, it could be expected that the nature and role of internal party combinations and the form factional activity took would differ at national (Scottish) and local levels. The next two sections explore the role of internal party combinations respectively at these levels. The final section discusses internal party alignments at the national (Scottish) level since the advent of the Scottish Parliament.

PARTY ALIGNMENTS AT THE SCOTTISH LEVEL PRE-DEVOLUTION

For all the historical echoes of 'Red Clydeside' that many in the Scottish party were prone to invoke, Scottish Labour was for many years a stronghold of loyalism (McLean 1990a). This particularly applied to its parliamentary representatives. 'Hardly any Scottish MPs were identified with the various internal left-wing revolts of the era – Victory for Socialism, the Bevanites and the Tribune Group' (Hutchison 2001: 95), and for much of the post-war era ideologically-rooted factionalism was relatively rare. Thus there is little evidence of organised and sustained factional activity for membership of the Scottish Executive Committee (in contrast to the National Executive Committee) until the late 1970s.

The relative quiescence of the Scottish party ended in the 1970s, which saw the emergence of two types of cleavages, one constitutional, the other ideological. The Scottish party had been (notionally) committed to home rule until 1958, when it was formally abandoned at a special Scottish Labour conference (Keating and Bleiman 1979: 146–7). The years 1958–74 saw Labour embrace the virtues of British centralism and oppose any form of Scottish devolution. However, the mounting challenge of the SNP from the late 1960s forced a re-appraisal. The party leadership's rather hasty and ill-thought-through response to the SNP upsurge in the two elections of 1974 was to revive the party's traditional but almost forgotten commitment to home rule for Scotland. Due to entrenched resistance from many within its ranks, the result was that throughout the 1970s the party was bitterly divided between pro- and anti-devolution wings, with the former encouraged by the party's national leadership for reasons of electoral expediency. A large segment of the Scottish party opposed devolution in the 1979 referendum, including a significant part of its local government base who feared displacement by any Scottish Assembly (Hassan 2002a; 2002b).

The 1979 referendum was soon followed by Labour's electoral defeat and the outbreak of the most virulent and uninhibited bout of factional strife that the party had ever witnessed. Rival left- and right-wing bodies were locked in combat over a wide range of issues – over policy, principles, strategy and party organisation. Inevitably this spilt over into Scotland. A whole range of party pressure groups had sprung up in the 1970s within British Labour, supplementing the already existing (and parliamentary-based) grouping Tribune on the left, and (more recently) the Manifesto Group on the right. These included the Campaign for Labour Party Democracy (CLPD), the Labour Co-ordinating Committee (LCC) and the Campaign Group of Labour MPs on the left, the Labour Solidarity Campaign on the right and the Militant Tendency and Socialist Challenge on the far left. Of these, the LCC was by far the most successful in Scotland. The LCC had been formed by a group of MPs and activists in 1978, including Michael Meacher, Stuart Holland, Chris Mullin, Tony Banks and Peter Hain, and rapidly emerged as the most influential pressure group on the mainstream left. It appealed to a cohort of young, predominantly university-educated, often ambitious radicals eager to make a mark on Labour politics. In Scotland, it recruited an impressive cadre of young activists such as Bill Speirs, Mark Lazarowicz, Mike Connarty, George Galloway and Bill Gilby – indeed, Scotland became a key LCC stronghold. It operated as a fully fledged faction with its own membership, formal rules and procedures, an elected leadership and decision-making structures. It rapidly gained influence in a number of urban centres, such as Glasgow, Edinburgh, Dundee and Stirling, though it made much less headway in solidly working-class areas in Lanarkshire (interview, Helen Liddell). It gained extensive representation on Labour's SEC, making an almost clean sweep of the constituency section and, with help from sympathetic trade union members, developed as the paramount force (interviews, Helen Liddell and Bob Thompson).

For LCC (Scotland) the existing Scottish Labour establishment was conservative-minded, detached from the concerns of ordinary people and lacking verve, drive and inspiration. Its object was both to promote more radical policies and to transform Labour in Scotland into a more campaigning, outgoing party. One member recounts that LCC (Scotland) sought 'to redefine what political campaigning is about, what power is about, why we want it, to broaden out the number of people involved in the political conversation and search out the issues that really mattered to people. It was about making politics much more representative and authentic' (interview, Margaret Curran MSP). It offered, Jack McConnell, another adherent, recalled, 'a modernising, political perspective and an innovative and realistic approach to politics' (interview).

Though LCC (Scotland) did have an impact and helped to revitalise Scottish Labour politics, by the late 1980s its energy and influence ebbed and some of its younger members joined with others in 1988 to form Scottish Labour Action. SLA founder member Jack McConnell maintained that by 1987 'LCC (Scotland) had become too close to the party establishment and insufficiently committed to a radical Scottish agenda' (interview). It differed from the older body mainly in the priority it assigned to devolution, support for which was rapidly gathering momentum as the perceived depredations of Tory rule had revived the popularity of schemes for constitutional reforms. The crushing of Labour's hopes in the 1987 election coincided with a revival of the party's fortunes north of the border, while the Conservative decision to introduce the hugely unpopular poll tax there first fuelled the resentment of those who claimed that it lacked any mandate in Scotland. The SLA's founding statement advocated 'obstruction and civil disobedience in the implementation of the poll tax' and enunciated 'the dual mandate' theory which contested the legitimacy of Conservative rule given its dwindling vote. 'It became, almost overnight, the most influential grouping in the Scottish Labour Party', according to Iain Macwhirter (*Sunday Herald*, 12 September 1999). It played a prominent role in persuading Labour to participate in the Scottish Constitutional Convention, in agreeing to tax-varying powers for a Scottish Parliament and accepting a system of proportional representation for elections to the Parliament – though the party was not prepared to accept the 'dual mandate' theory. Equally, as has been seen, the efforts by SLA to promote 'party devolution' (more control by the Scottish party over policy, staffing, finance and organisation) made little headway, partly because of opposition from the NEC but also from Scottish Labour officials fearful of its detrimental impact on their job security, pay and conditions. All impetus for reform evaporated when union opposition led to an emphatic defeat for SLA-sponsored SEC proposals for enhanced autonomy at the 1989 Scottish party conference (for more details, see Chapter 3).

A third group, which worked closely with both LCC (Scotland) and SLA, was the Scottish Labour Women's Caucus (SLWC). It campaigned for equal gender representation in the selection of Labour candidates to the Scottish Parliament, an extended women's voice in party bodies, and for more emphasis to be given to issues of particular concern to women – achieving a very large measure of success on all counts and in a party that traditionally had not been very receptive to women (Mackay 2004: 112–16).

LCC (Scotland), SLA and SLWC all emanated from the mainstream left of the party. The Trotskyite Militant Tendency was of a quite different order. With its roots in revolutionary politics, Militant first emerged as a significant factor in Labour grassroots politics in the late 1970s. A tightly organised and highly disciplined faction, it adopted an 'entryist' political strategy to build a base within the party by infiltrating its constituency structures (Shaw 1988).

In some areas of the country, most notably in Liverpool, Militant embedded itself in the internal life of the party, gaining some notoriety. It never acquired the same influence in Scotland, though it did gain some footholds, such as Glasgow Pollok. It concentrated its efforts in winning parliamentary seats, at a propitious time since the introduction of mandatory re-selection (under which all sitting MPs had to compete to win re-nomination as the party's candidate) rendered incumbent parliamentarians more vulnerable to challenge. Militant made a number of determined bids to seize candidatures in what were a series of fraught, acrimonious and furiously fought contests. Party officials, in particular the formidable organiser Jimmy Allison, laid aside neutrality and threw their energies into foiling Militant (Allison 1995: 64–70). Resistance to the Trotskyists was marshalled not only by the bitterly hostile right of the party but also by the staunchly anti-Militant LCC. In Edinburgh the Militant-sympathising leader of the council, Alex Wood, was driven from power by a centre-left alliance led by leading LCC member Mark Lazarowicz, who replaced him as council leader.

By the second half of the 1980s, Militant had been officially proscribed and its leading cadres were expelled from the party. The party in Scotland followed suit and in successive waves Militant activists were purged in areas where it had acquired some influence, such as Pollok, Cathcart and Springburn in Glasgow, and Cumbernauld and Kilsyth (The Herald, 23 May 1990). The best-known casualty was Tommy Sheridan, a leading figure in the anti-poll tax campaign, who with others abandoned the entryist tactic and formed an independent organisation, Scottish Militant Labour, which merged with other bodies in 1998 to form the Scottish Socialist Party. This terminated the problem of extreme left factionalism in Scottish Labour.

Factional organisation has been rarer on the right of the party than on the left, primarily because it normally occupied the seats of power. This was certainly the case by the mid-1990s, when the party apparatus was firmly in the grip of the new leader, Tony Blair. But while Labour's National Executive was reduced to docility, its Scottish counterpart remained independent-minded and left-inclined, as it soon demonstrated.

In 1996, without consulting the SEC, Blair announced that a devolution referendum would be held, inviting people to pronounce on whether they favoured a Scottish Parliament and whether it should be granted the power to vary the standard rate of income tax. Many on the SEC were incensed and objected vehemently, and it was only with difficulty that it was brought into line. This convinced Blair that a less recalcitrant SEC was needed.

A second factor also weighed heavily on him. By 1996, Labour was actively preparing for devolution and a key task was to devise a set of procedures for selecting candidates for the new Parliament. It was, for Labour, a delicate matter since, for political reasons, the national leadership did not wish to be seen directing the process. Hence, authority for designing and operating the new system was formally devolved by the NEC to the SEC. But the row over the referendum raised real doubts about the 'reliability' of the Scottish Executive. Blair was 'determined', John Alridge wrote, to 'seize control of the Scottish executive to ensure that an Edinburgh parliament does not pursue an old Labour agenda' (*New Statesman*, 14 February 1997). In early 1996, a group aptly called the 'Network' – which exhibited the characteristics of a political network as defined above – was quietly established. A key role was played by the staunch Blairite Jim Murphy, a party staffer (to be elected an MP in 1997) with a reputation as a deft political operator. Funded by the AEU, he was appointed 'Special Projects Officer', formally responsible for election preparations and setting up the new policy machinery (the Scottish Policy Forum), but also charged with assisting the Network. The Network assembled a number of prominent figures on the party's right and centre, including Rosemary McKenna (soon to be an MP and a central figure over-seeing the selection process for the Scottish Parliament); Bobby Parker, the Scottish Secretary of the GMB; Bill Tynan (later an MP), a senior AEU official; Allan Wilson (subsequently an MSP), a Unison official; John Glass, an USDAW official; and Rhona Brankin (also soon to be an MSP). Douglas Alexander, then a Brown advisor, was briefly associated with the group. Jack McConnell, the Scottish General Secretary, was supportive but kept a discrete distance.

The Network's prime objective was to secure control of the SEC. In a document leaked to the press, it explained its objects as:

- Co-ordinating 'support within the movement for the Labour Government and its policies'.
- Undertaking political education 'in support of the party project'.
- Ensuring that 'those who hold office in the party have a healthy relation-ship with the Labour Government'. (*The Scotsman*, 29 January 1997)

In practice, its work entailed compiling a database of sympathetic figures, drawing up a slate of candidates for the annual SEC elections, mobilising support from prominent figures in Labour councils, trade unions and CLPs, seeking to influence the choice of delegates at the Scottish party conference and, not least, targeting left-wingers who it wanted to be removed from membership of the Executive. In this last object it was almost wholly successful. The political complexion of the Executive was transformed, with seven out of eight targeted left-wingers losing their places and the loyalists securing a solid majority (*The Herald*, 10 March 1997). At the same time, the rules governing the composition and role of the SEC were altered. To curb the influence of grassroots activists, members of the constituency section were in future to be elected by one member one vote (rather than by general committees). The size of both the trade union and constituency sections was reduced, with new places created for MPs, MEPs, councilors, MSPs and Holyrood ministers (when elected). Key officials including the party chair, vice-chair and treasurer were no longer to be elected by conference but appointed by the executive (*The Herald*, 10 March 1997; Scottish Labour Party Rules and Standing Orders). Shortly after, its work complete, the Network was dissolved. The new SEC could now safely be entrusted with the task of formulating selection rules for Labour candidates in the Scottish elections due in 1999.

The dysfunctional effects of factions within political parties – deepening and inflaming divisions, diverting their energies, producing policy deadlocks and tarnishing their public image – has been frequently documented (Boucek 2009: 477). Some of these negative effects were evident when left–right struggles were at their peak in the 1980s. Discussions on the SEC between the LCC (Scotland)-led left and the right were at times rancorous but the most keenly fought battlegrounds were (as ever) parliamentary selection contests. George Robertson, twice challenged in re-selections, recalled 'a God-awful time. Party meetings were constant battles, no holds barred. People were vilified. There was total warfare, which sapped energy' (interview). However, extremes of factional conflict that ruptured the party in some areas in England (Manchester, Liverpool and various London boroughs) were rarer in Scotland.

Despite the opprobrium which attaches to the word 'faction', a number of commentators have pointed to the positive effects of what can be called less pejoratively party combinations or pressure groups. Thus it has been claimed that they foster intra-party democracy by facilitating contests for internal party elections, promoting new ideas, stimulating debate, operating as a platform for dissenting and minority opinion, and holding the leadership to account (Boucek 2009: 479). LCC (Scotland), SLA and the Women's Caucus all performed these roles. Elections to the SEC, especially in the constituency section, became much more competitive, with active campaigning and the circulation of formal and informal slates which, by structuring and simplifying choice, encouraged higher turnouts. As a long-time member of the Scottish Executive recalled, 'you felt that win, lose or draw there was a kind of energy getting onto the SEC. You had to fight your corner to get election.' Nowadays, she mused, it was difficult even to attract enough candidates to fill all the seats (interview, Anne McGuire). Further, through their efforts to mobilise support, these groups encouraged discussion, critical debate and the germination and dissemination of new ideas. As a former Party General

Secretary recollected, 'there was quite a lot of animosity but out of that animosity came some positive change, and it did mean that the party was having to go through a process of questioning and re-invigoration' (interview, Helen Liddell).

Finally, LCC (Scotland), SLA and the Women's Caucus helped to rejuvenate the party by bringing in new cohorts of activists, drawing within their orbits ambitious and capable young politicians and expediting their election to positions within the party (e.g. within the SEC) and representative political office. As Macwhirter put it, SLA had 'provided a bridge for the radical outsiders of one decade to become the political establishment of the next' (*Sunday Herald*, 12 September 1999).

From the mid-1990s onwards, throughout the Labour Party ideologically structured cleavages waned. LCC (Scotland) and the Scottish Labour Women's Caucus had all but disappeared and in 1997 SLA decided to disband, its supporters focusing on selections and the campaign for a Scottish Parliament, as Chapter 3 describes.

Party Alignments at the Municipal Level

Until the establishment of the Scottish Parliament, the only direct source of power available to Scottish Labour was at municipal level. Claims about wipespread patronage, 'jobs for the boys' and rampant careerism have for years been levelled against Labour's Scottish urban strongholds. 'Cronyism, factionalism, junketing, petty corruption, favouritism, sectarianism, incompetence', one of Scotland's top political commentators, Iain Macwhirter, wrote, 'have been all too common a feature of local Labour life for decades' (*Scotland on Sunday*, 9 February 1997). The party, he contended, had forged a veritable patronage-based 'Labour state' encompassing a network of 'councils, quangos and apparatchiks' where 'membership of the party is a precondition for personal advancement in most aspects of public life – an essential career accessory. Factionalism, rather than democracy, becomes the organising principle of politics' (Macwhirter 2002: 27, 28).

Unfortunately there has been very little research and data is difficult to gather, with much of the limited coverage in the press taking the form of sporadic reports rarely followed through in any systematic way. Furthermore, the accusations are often couched in very general terms which blur the difference between outright corruption and misappropriation of public funds on the one hand, and the milder forms of patronage always found as consensus-building devices in all political parties. All this renders claims about Labour's 'patronage states' difficult to assess. However, there is a certain amount of material available which, supplemented by interviews, does shed some light on two Labour citadels where such allegations have been rife – Glasgow and Lanarkshire. Each will be discussed in turn.

The character of internal party combinations and alignments is shaped not only by the motivations of party members but by the opportunity structures in which they operate. For example, parties which are in a position to control or regulate access to public goods or resources – jobs, contracts, planning permission or whatever – are more likely to give rise to a spoils system. Nowhere have accusations about a patronage-ridden Labour politics been more loudly voiced than in Glasgow, lambasted by Ian Bell as 'cadre government, administration by cabal, inveterate patronage' (*The Scotsman*, 17 December 1999). Since Labour first won a majority in 1933, the party controlled Glasgow with increasingly large majorities, until the introduction of STV in 2007. In his study of Labour in Glasgow in the 1980s, Keating found that, 'in the areas of the city where Labour was best established (the older working-class areas), political "machines" had developed with local bosses able to control council nominations and, to some extent, other forms of patronage (jobs in council departments for teachers and manual workers, trade union positions)' (Keating 1988: 11). 'People would join the Labour Party', the then Scottish General Secretary Helen Liddell recalled, 'to get good jobs in the council' (interview). Inevitably this had an impact on city-wide Labour politics. 'If you trace what was happening in the party in the '70s', Liddell continued, 'a lot was based on the hegemony and power in local government. There was a lot of powerful, strong local government figures but there were also some who were pretty near to the bone and there were problems right across the West of Scotland with corruption, sometimes genuine corruption, sometimes just sailing close to the wind, and a lot of it was because of the power that existed at a local government level' (interview).

The term 'factions of personality' has been used to describe intra-party groupings 'that form behind different political leaders primarily on the basis of the leader's personal attraction' (Janda 1980: 122). Hume labelled them factions from *affection*, that is to say those 'founded on the different attachments of men towards particular families and persons, whom they desire to rule over them' (Hume 1742). To a considerable degree intra-party politics in Glasgow comprised a blend of personality- and patronage-based factionalism. Throughout the 1980s and running into the 1990s, there was a long-standing struggle between rival groups headed by Jean McFadden and Pat Lally. Lally, an ambitious, highly experienced and wily politician, challenged McFadden for the leadership in the mid-1980s on a platform mildly to the left, a more combative attitude to the Tory government and a more inclusive and de-centralised style of leadership. Whether there was any real and genuine policy disagreements was, in fact, problematic. As

Frank McAveety, a later leader of Glasgow City Council, commented, 'Pat organised under the auspices of the Tribune Group but it bore no relation to the politics of the Tribune Newspaper . . . because essentially it was, it was a vehicle for the organisational running of the council and the committees by a very strong leadership' (interview). As a council leader he was highly pragmatic and collaborated closely with business in his attempts to regenerate Glasgow. He was also a highly skilled political in-fighter, and in Allan Massie's words a 'crafty operator, adept in the working of machine politics' (*The Sunday Times*, 22 February 1998). A further layer was added to this conflict by the decision of the Conservative Government in 1986 to dismantle the regional authorities and opt for single-tier local government. This led to an influx of Labour councillors from the Strathclyde regional authority onto Glasgow City Council who formed a caucus under the leadership of the former Strathclyde boss, Bob Gould. What followed was a three-way power struggle between what were largely three 'factions of personality and patronage', in which Gould won leadership of the Labour group and hence the council.

In 1997 an usually detailed insight into factional strife in the Glasgow Labour Party was afforded by the sudden and highly publicised eruption of infighting among the rival groups. In February, exasperated by fellow Labour councillors' reluctance to agree to a programme of cuts, Gould alleged that in the past votes had been 'traded' for foreign trips. This provoked a blaze of unfavourable publicity which angered the Labour leadership in London, in the process of waging an election campaign in which denunciations of 'Tory sleaze' featured prominently. As soon as the election had been won, the NEC launched an enquiry into the Glasgow party which appeared to confirm allegations of a tainted 'patronage state'. While finding no evidence for the 'votes for junkets', it concluded that 'The promise of political patronage and the threat of loss of existing patronage has been used, in our view, to promote certain individuals to group positions and this has been disruptive and to the disadvantage of other Labour group members' (*The Sunday Times*, 7 September 1997). Jim Murphy MP (and close to Blair) added that 'the truth is that a minority have abused their power and influence. Among other things, they have used the trappings of power, such as committee positions, as trinkets to be given in return for support from fellow councillors' (*The Scotsman*, 24 September 1997). The NEC suspended nine councillors – including Gould, and Pat Lally, then Provost of the city – pending the drawing up of disciplinary charges (Labour Party NEC 1997b). One party investigator exclaimed: 'What we uncovered almost defied belief. It was the very thing we have criticised the Tories for in the past. It must stop now' (*The Guardian*, 24 September 1997).

The systematic leaking by party sources of 'hints of sleaze, scandal, graft, corruption, misuse of public funds' (*The Sunday Times*, 28 September 1997) was designed, Brian Deer suggested, 'to make people believe the worst' of Glasgow Labour, in order to 'demolish the biggest power base of old Labour in Scotland' (*The Sunday Times*, 25 January 1998). In fact, the precise charges levelled against the suspended councillors were unclear and many of the more lurid allegations could not be substantiated. The accused resorted to legal redress and at the Court of Session in February 1998 they won the right to have their suspensions lifted pending judicial review. It soon became evident that the NEC's own legal advice placed a question mark over the adequacy of the party's disciplinary procedures and in due course it decided to lift the suspensions of the nine councillors and drop all charges (*The Herald*, 30 June 1998). Glasgow, predictably, proved to be a harder nut to crack than Labour's leadership had anticipated.

For years commentators had pointed a finger at the so-called 'Lanarkshire mafia', often seen as emblematic of Scottish Labour in its urban heartlands. As Macwhirter wrote, 'rightly or wrongly, Lanarkshire has been associated with factionalism, sectarianism, bureaucracy, jobs for the boys, votes for trips – the kind of politics that has thrived in the one-party states which have dominated local Scotland for the last century' (*Sunday Herald*, 3 December 2006). Claims about the existence of a powerful 'Lanarkshire mafia' linked together two threads said to typify the way in which Labour conducted itself in its west Central Belt heartland – religion and patronage. These claims exploded onto the political scene during the Monklands East by-election caused by the untimely death of Labour's leader, John Smith. During what was a very bad-tempered by-election (narrowly won by Helen Liddell), there were widespread allegations that a narrow clique of councillors in Labour-controlled Monklands Council had for years engaged in nepotism, sectarian discrimination and a range of other abuses.

Within Monklands Council in Lanarkshire there were two major centres of population, largely Catholic Coatbridge and largely Protestant Airdrie. Public disquiet was at such a level that the council agreed to commission an independent report from Edinburgh University's Professor Robert Black QC. It investigated a series of allegations, including that in investment projects the Labour council had given preferment to Coatbridge over Airdrie, and in employment practices, the placing of contracts and access to council housing had discriminated in favour of both Catholics and of friends and relatives. Black's report found evidence in favour of many of these allegations and Labour's national leadership responded by suspending the Labour group.

However, the matter did not rest there. In the wake of the furore caused by the Black Report, the (Conservative-run) Scottish Office announced it would mount an investigation to be headed by Sheriff (later Lord) Nimmo Smith QC, a prominent advocate. The 83-page report that was published in December 1995 reached quite different conclusions from the earlier Black report. It found no evidence to substantiate charges of sectarian favouristism, nepotism or a spoils system within the council or to support claims that Labour Party connections had a material effect on appointments. Instead, the report maintained problems had arisen from 'the insensitive exercise of power' which gave rise to 'a sense of exclusion' and allowed allegations to gain currency (*The Herald*, 21 December 1995).

Subsequently, Labour's NEC conducted its own investigation into the Monklands party. Its report echoed Nimmo Smith's conclusions. It noted that all independent inquiries had found 'absolutely no evidence' to support claims of religious discrimination, though it acknowledged 'an under representation of non-Catholics in both the Group and the wider party in the area which is an issue which must be addressed'. To the allegations that party membership, family ties and religion had all influenced appointment and promotion decisions, it cautiously judged that 'with the evidence available to us we would have had difficulty in reaching firm conclusions' (Labour Party NEC 1996). As Anne McGuire, who helped conduct the NEC's investigation, later recalled, there were 'some unsustainable practices' and although no evidence of systematic corruption emerged, there 'certainly was an unhealthy situation where most councillors and many officials seem to come from one [i.e. Catholic] background' (interview, 2009).

LABOUR, PATRONAGE AND 'MACHINE POLITICS'

Reaching a judgement on this tangle of accusation and conflicting reports is difficult because of the paucity of reliable evidence. But part of the problem is conceptual, reflecting differing meaning attached to the term 'patronage'. An example of one usage is Ian Bell's blistering portrait of Scottish Labour as a party which was 'scarcely accountable, rarely transparent, rank with nepotism, cronyism and freeloading', operating in a system in which full-time Labour councillors depended on local government for their livelihoods, rendering them reliant 'for their pay cheque' on 'whoever runs the Labour group' (*The Scotsman*, 17 December 1999). From this perspective, Scottish Labour had been transformed into a political conduit through which resources (jobs, contracts, public facilities, etc.) could be extracted by illicit or unseemly means from the public for the benefit of faction members. But the term 'patronage politics' can also refer more loosely to the distribution of rewards (honours, jobs, positions) in exchange for political support or loyalty.

To which model of patronage did Labour in key municipal strongholds most closely conform? It is difficult to reach any hard and fast conclusions because of the paucity of hard evidence. George Robertson, a senior figure in the Scottish Labour establishment for many years, remarked, 'there were endless problems about Monklands' but 'every time you tried to grab it, like mercury it went away. It was all so nebulous' (interview). As has been noted above, a series of investigations in those areas – Glasgow and Lanarkshire – where such accusations proliferated found little solid evidence of systematic nepotism, corruption or discriminatory practices. In short, the wilder allegations of a 'Labour state' conspiracy engaging in the sustained and single-minded exploitation of public resources for its own gain cannot be substantiated. It may well be that the more overtly corrupt form of patronage became less common from the late 1970s, for legal and institutional reasons, as rules governing the activities of local councils became tighter and firmer controls were instituted over discretionary decision-making by local councillors (e.g. over the allocation of council housing, and the hiring and promotion of public sector employees). However, patronage politics in the second, weaker, sense of the term does appear to have been (and may well still be) far more common. Here there is evidence that divisions grounded in the competitive pursuit of access to elected offices and other tangible forms of reward rather than ideologically or policy-based conflicts tended to define internal party life, with a key mechanism for consolidating power the ability to dispense patronage to putative faction members.

The patronage opportunities available to local authorities declined in the 1980s, but there is some evidence that patronage-based politics staged a revival in the last decade in Glasgow, with the establishment of Arm's Length External Organisations (known as ALEOs). ALEOs were organisations entrusted with functions – culture and leisure, catering, parking, construction and maintenance services, and so forth – previously discharged by the council itself and now outsourced. Under the leadership of Stephen Purcell (who resigned in March 2010), these arm's-length bodies proliferated. While a number of Scottish councils used the ALEO model, only in Glasgow were councillors paid to sit on their boards. In April 2011, nineteen Labour councillors occupied paid positions (normally £6,335 per year, though over £10,000 for chairmen). Of these nineteen, six had positions on two ALEOs and one on three.[1] It was claimed that ALEOs formed an extensive web of patronage utilised by Purcell to solidify his power base (*The Herald*, 26 April 2011; *The Herald*, 1 April 2010; Gray and French 2010). After a review, the Scottish Local Authorities Remuneration Committee (SLARC) pressed Glasgow City Council to axe the system, and Purcell's successor as Glasgow Council leader, Gordon Matheson, pledged to end 'the culture of cronyism' –

though by the following year it did not appear that much had changed (*The Herald*, 26 April 2011).

How widespread patronage-based factionalism was, and how deeply embedded in the structure and culture of municipal Labour, is difficult to ascertain in the absence of much more systematic research. Three brief points can, however, be made. Firstly, the more highly charged portrayals of corrupt Labour machines 'rank with nepotism, cronyism and freeloading' have rarely been supported by hard facts. Secondly, the evidence does suggest that entrenched and effectively monopoly one-party government at local level does lend itself to 'factionalism' of personality, patronage, status and power. Thirdly, the advent of proportional representation (in the form of the single transferable vote) is demolishing one-party local government, introducing much more competitive systems and thereby eroding the basis of the patronage-driven 'local Labour state'. This is likely, in due course, to affect the character, texture and feel of internal Scottish Labour politics.

PARTY ALIGNMENTS POST-DEVOLUTION

One of the striking features of the Scottish Parliamentary Labour Group since its establishment in 1999 was the absence of the 'factions of principle' which have been such a perennial aspect of Labour parliamentary politics. This absence can largely be attributed to a dual process of 'de-factionalisation' and 'de-ideologicalisation'. The former refers to the decline of institutionalised factions, that is, groups that possess a distinct profile, a common identity, a degree of organisation and a formal membership. Thus in Scotland no organisations have appeared to fill the vacuum left by the disappearance of bodies such as LCC (Scotland) and SLA. The only ideological or issue-based grouping which has survived was the Campaign for Socialism, formed in 1994 as part of the campaign to retain Clause Four of the Labour Party Constitution, but it has few members, little organisational presence and has had a negligible influence on the direction of the party. 'De-ideologicalisation' refers to the abating of ideological disagreements, that is, the emergence of a broad consensus over values and policies, and the development of a more pragmatic and managerial approach to policy. 'De-factionalisation' and 'de-ideologicalisation' in combination changed the nature of intra-party struggle at national (Scottish) level, with differences over programme and principles playing a diminished role in structuring intra-party political competition and debate.

Given that political actors always combine to advance their ends, it was inevitable that some form of groupings or alliance networks would emerge. As noted, a key factor influencing the form that internal party competition takes is the structure of incentives and opportunities in the political setting a party inhabits. The creation of a new tier of government, in which until 2007 Labour was the ruling party, made available a supply of selective benefits, especially ministerial positions, whose distribution the First Minister largely controlled. To some degree patronage is an inevitable part of party politics. All competing power-brokers seek to acquire, retain and consolidate their power by distributing jobs and key positions. One MSP and former minister reflected:

> There's a certain level at which in every political organisation you've got to dis-tribute enough jobs to keep enough people happy, not just to represent different parts of your party and different perspectives but also to make sure that you've got enough people who are prepared to support you out of loyalty. That sounds a bit cynical but look at every form of political organisation – to some extent, greater or lesser, that'll happen. (interview, Peter Peacock)

The central issue is the extent to which support is mobilised, coalitions built and intra-party cleavages defined principally by the appropriation and distribution of 'selective' or of 'collective' (policy or ideological) benefits. In the Scottish Parliamentary Labour Group, in the absence of significant con-flicts of principle, cleavages primarily took the form of competition between coteries organised around the key dispenser of patronage, the existing or aspiring candidates to be First Minister (after 2007, party leader). A notable example was the contest between the followers of Henry McLeish and Jack McConnell, often intense, at times ill-tempered but rarely about significant matters of principle: the currency of politics was 'loyalties, obligations and rewards' (interview, Peter Peacock). Clashes were 'about leadership: who you would support and who would support you – who got jobs, positions, junior ministerial positions – about power, about patronage. In terms of policy it meant nothing' (interview, party official). In the past, factional conflict would at the very least be wrapped up in ideological terms. Now these were much diminished in importance. As a seasoned political operator reflected, 'Now you haven't got the label so it's a conflict of personalities . . . A lot of it was, well, you got promoted and you didn't get promoted, I am out of your camp, I'm into that camp' (interview, Helen Liddell). These personality-based networks were loose and often subsumed within themselves smaller, almost clan-like, groups based on kinship, friendship or on territorial or municipal affiliations, notably in Glasgow and Lanarkshire.

There were, of course, divisions over policy – notably the impassioned split over free personal care, and even here attitudes were influenced by loyalty (or lack of it) to the author of the policy, First Minister Henry McLeish. But while there were divisions of opinion on specific issues, there have been no real fault-lines over major matters of principle, or divisions into rival ideology-based camps. This reflected a general shift to a less factional, less polarised and more pragmatic style of politics which diffused throughout the party in the 1990s and well into the new millennium.

Labour's defeat in the 2010 general election and the election of Ed Miliband as party leader refashioned, at the UK level, internal party alignments, dividing (in broad terms) the centre-left of the party from the Blairite right. Whereas the split between Blairites and Brownites was fundamentally between two power- and patronage-based factions, the new alignment structure is rooted, to some degree at least, in differences of principle. So far a more ideological pattern of politics and party alignments has not surfaced within Scottish Labour politics, with the competition for the leadership of the party in 2011 much more a matter of personality than principle. But the internal politics of the party are at present fluid, with the election of many new and untested MSPs, and the future pattern is difficult to predict.

NOTE

1. Eight SNP councillors and one Liberal Democrat were also board members.

CHAPTER 15

Power and Policy-making

SCOTTISH LABOUR'S POLICY PROCESS: THE FORMAL STRUCTURE

A crucial function for any political party is the formulation of policy. As a party wedded to the canon of internal party democracy, the responsibility for determining Labour's programme has always been entrusted to its representative institutions as embodied in the theory of conference sovereignty (Minkin 1980: 5). Practice, of course, fell far short of theory and throughout its history the principles, procedures and practices of internal party decision-making have been the subject of perennial controversy. By the 1990s there was widespread disaffection with the established policy machinery and hence much support for a radical overhaul of the way in which Labour framed its programme and manifesto. Added impetus to change was given by the election of Tony Blair to the leadership and the process of internal party reform, already underway, was accelerated. The outcome, agreed in 1997, was the 'Partnership in Power' project, which witnessed the most sweeping transformation of Labour's policy-making machinery since the advent of the party (Labour Party NEC 1997a).

For the authors of 'Partnership in Power', the traditional system of policy determination suffered from numerous defects: it was ineffective, archaic and cumbersome; it afforded few opportunities for grassroots participation; institutionalised and exacerbated a fractious relationship between the parliamentary leadership and the wider party; and magnified internal divisions. The central aim of 'Partnership in Power' was to foster a culture of partnership and trust between the parliamentary leadership and the wider party by creating a 'stakeholder' model of policy-making where all constituent parts enjoyed 'shared involvement and ownership' of the party and a 'shared responsibility for maintaining good communications, upholding mutual respect and securing careful co-ordination'. Under the new system the National Policy Forum (NPF), composed of representatives of constituency parties, unions and other 'stakeholders', was charged with developing a rolling policy programme that would form the basis of the election manifesto. The detailed elaboration of policy was undertaken by Policy Commissions, while the Joint Policy Committee exercised strategic oversight over the whole process. All proposals were presented to the annual conference whose approval, as the party's sovereign body, was still required (Labour Party 1997).

With devolution on the horizon, consideration had to be given to adapting the party's new policy-making institutions to devolved government. Provision was made for a specifically Scottish input into policy development on 'reserved matters' (including economic, foreign and many aspects of social policy). Scotland was allocated eight members on the NPF (two from the Scottish Labour Party, five representing local constituency parties and one from local youth sections) out of a total of 180. In addition, the four officers of the Scottish Policy Forum (SPF) were also members of the NPF. Responsibility for devolved policy issues was entrusted to the SPF, created in 1998, whose rationale, composition, structure and responsibilities broadly paralleled the national body.

Like the national body, the SPF was intended to represent all party 'stakeholders' and was divided into three divisions.

> Division I – CLPs. This consists of 36 constituency party representatives, with four elected by each of the eight Scottish Parliament electoral list areas by one-member-one-vote amongst Scottish party members plus four elected by a ballot of all Young Labour members in Scotland. (Following a rule change at the 2008 Scottish Conference there is now one member for every two constituencies with constituencies being twinned plus 6 members from Young Labour.)
> Division II – Trade unions and affiliates. This consists of 25 members from national affiliated organisations, 22 from affiliated trade unions, two from affiliated socialist societies and one from the Scottish Co-operative Party.
> Division III – Elected Representatives. This consists of 25 members; 5 Scottish Parliament ministers/Shadow Cabinet ministers, five from the Scottish Parliament Labour Group, 6 members of the Scottish Executive Committee, the Westminster Scottish Secretary (or Shadow Secretary), two members of the (Westminster) Parliamentary Labour Party, one representative from the European Parliamentary Labour Party and 5 representatives of Labour local government elected by ballot amongst all Scottish members of the Association of Labour Councillors. Finally, Scottish members of the National Policy Forum are ex-officio members of the Scottish Policy Forum (Scottish Labour Party Standing Order 11).

The new policy forum model was designed to extend the rights of members 'to engage in policy development through a more deliberative and extended procedure' (Labour Party 1997). The main conduit for the articulation of rank-and-file views were the local policy forums, ad hoc gatherings organised by constituency parties and the Scottish Head Office (John Smith House) convened to discuss reports on specific subjects circulated via the Policy Forum process. According to the party, in the run-up to the framing of the 2003 manifesto fifty CLPs (almost three-quarters of the total) participated in 256 local policy forums. In addition, over three hundred written contributions commenting on draft documents were submitted by CLPs and other party units (Scottish Labour Party 2003a).

The SPF operated on a two-year cycle. In the first year it considered submissions and produced consultation documents for comment by CLPs and affiliated organisations on a wide range of questions. In the second year there was a focus on the fuller and more systematic elaboration of policy ideas. The detailed development of policy proposals was the responsibility of policy commissions. Composed of three government ministers, three members of the SEC and four elected members of the Scottish Policy Forum, they were charged with discussing and filtering policy submissions and drafting policy reports. These were then transmitted to the SPF for consideration and amendment. If a minority viewpoint attracted over 25% of the vote, it qualified as an 'Alternative Position' which conference was required to debate and vote on alongside the relevant SPF reports (Scottish Policy Forum, 10 May 2008).

In addition, constituency parties and affiliated organisations were entitled to submit one motion on a topic which, according to the judgement of the Conference Arrangements Committee, 'is either not substantively addressed in the reports to Conference of either the SPF or the SEC or which has arisen since the publication of these reports' (Labour Party Standing Order 3c). The Scottish party conference was (on devolved issues) the sovereign body determining – by a two-thirds majority on a card vote – which policy proposals drawn from the SPF process would form the party programme and therefore be available for inclusion in the Scottish manifesto. The vote at the conference was divided equally between affiliated organisations (mainly trade unions) and CLPs. Approved SPF reports and agreed amendments were then conveyed to the Scottish Joint Policy Committee (SJPC), responsible for strategic oversight of policy development. Chaired by Labour's parliamentary leader (until May 2007 the First Minister), it was composed of the party's deputy parliamentary leader, three ministers/shadow ministers, the chair and two vice-chairs of the SPF, the chair, vice-chair, treasurer and three additional members of the SEC, the chair of the SPLG and two other Labour MSPs, the Secretary (or shadow Secretary) of State for Scotland, two members of the Scottish Trades Union Labour Party and two elected CLP delegates to the SPF. It was authorised to frame the manifesto on the basis of the materials submitted to it. A joint meeting of the SEC and a committee of the SPLG then decided which items from the party programme would be included in the manifesto.

The Distribution of Power in Scottish Labour's Policy Process

The aims of the new system were to democratise the system of policy-making, to render it more inclusive and to promote the consideration of policy in a reasoned and harmonious spirit (interview, MSP). To what extent did it achieve these goals? It is widely acknowledged that at the UK-wide level 'Partnership in Power' arrangements have had relatively little impact on policy development (Russell 2005). From 1997 to 2010 the formulation of policy was the preserve of ministers and political advisors, and (with the partial exception of the unions) the party on the ground had negligible influence. What of Scotland?

There are influential theories that contend that elite control over party policy-making is inexorable. Almost a century ago, Michels propounded the view that, whatever their claims and aspirations, oligarchy within mass parties was inevitable. To become effective claimants for power, parties must develop elaborate, bureaucratically ordered and functionally specialised structures. A career leadership served by an ever-expanding administrative apparatus composed of an increasingly professionalised staff has access to a wealth of knowledge, expertise and experience which the rank and file cannot match. Efficient organisation, functional differentiation and the need for swift, centralised decision-making divests the membership of their rights. Whatever the formal guarantees for democratic decision-making, in practice the growth of leadership power is ineluctable (Michels 1962).

More recently, scholars have argued that in fact in the past a modicum of democratic control persisted – but is now finally unravelling. The process of bureaucratisation identified by Michels as a cause of oligarchy is now reinforced by professionalisation. The weakening of traditional political allegiances coupled with the all-pervasive reach and impact of mass communications has impelled parties to transform (or 'professionalise') their campaigning and communications strategies. Party campaigning and voter mobilisation now emanates from the centre, with the spotlight relentlessly on national party leaders. Image-projection through the mass media has dwarfed other campaign activities and 'strengthened the affirmative mechanisms of identity and loyalty building at the expense of traditional or new forms of political participation' (Puhle 2002: 69). Further, 'professionalisation' has greatly enhanced the weight attached to the specialist skills of political professionals, opinion pollsters, press officers, and public relations and marketing experts. Campaign professionals are employed by and accountable to the parliamentary leadership to whom they owe primary loyalty, hence professionalisation expands the power capabilities available to the leadership (Moschanas 2002: 124). In contrast, the contribution of the mass membership is seen as increasingly obsolete.

Furthermore, much-publicised measures intended (ostensibly at least) to democratise parties by bolstering the power of the ordinary rank and file at the expense of the activist layer have had the practical effect of actually reinforcing oligarchical trends. By reducing the powers and limiting the functions of the 'organised party on the ground', the capacity of the grassroots to mount a challenge to the leadership is weakened (Katz and Mair 2002: 128). Activist leverage over policy is indeed seen as dysfunctional as it curtails the ability of leadership to respond swiftly and flexibly to the shifting winds of public opinion. For these reasons Katz and Mair concluded that mainstream parties 'have now been transformed simply into parties in public office, and that the other faces of the party are withering away' (Katz and Mair 2002: 126). In practical terms, parties are run by elites composed primarily of parliamentary leaders.

There is certainly evidence in the experience of Scottish Labour to substantiate these theses. Formally the Policy Forum process represented a major advance in intra-party democracy, furnishing multiple opportunities for rank-and-file members to contribute to policy deliberation. Consultation documents were circulated to all CLPs and branches, revised in light of comments made and then distributed for more discussion. Further, the forum itself was structured on an admirably democratic basis, with all key party stakeholders represented. But there was a major gap between formal representation rights and effective participation. While it is true that many local parties (for example, in Aberdeen and Edinburgh) participated eagerly in the SPF process, organising local policy forums and submitting documents, Labour ministers were well-placed to filter the flow of inputs into the SPF system and effectively manage the process. Although responsibility for drafting documents formally lay with policy commissions, it was mainly carried out by ministers, their advisors in collaboration with party staff and (as will be seen below) union officials, enabling them to establish the parameters for policy debate, identify the policy options deemed to merit more detailed exploration and shape perceptions of what was deliverable, politically feasible, electorally attractive and affordable. The drafters, in short, had a great deal of power (interviews, MSPs, political advisors).

Whatever the notional formal equality of all SPF members, ministers inevitably were able to assemble and utilise resources which ordinary delegates lacked. Labour's Scottish Executive Committee was the custodian of the wider party but had a minimal policy staff. Most of the research capacity available to the party took the form of parliamentary assistants employed individually by MSPs or collectively in the form of the Labour Resource Centre, a body designed to service the Scottish Parliamentary Group as a whole. While Labour was in office, ministers in addition had the huge advantage of the support of the civil service, though of course this resource had to be used with a little discretion in internal party bodies.

Further, there was an inevitable major imbalance of power between well-briefed ministers with easy access to information and specialist knowledge on the one hand, and the mass of constituency delegates on the other. The authority, prestige and access to expertise and information conferred by ministerial status gave the 'party in office' a considerable advantage over 'the party on the ground'. As one minister commented, constituency members lacked 'the wherewithal and the capacity' to formulate proposals and to engage in any detailed consideration of policy (interview, Andy Kerr). The one exception to this (aside from the unions, considered below) was representatives of local authorities, particularly the larger Labour-controlled ones. Not only did council leaders and other local government notables dispose of significant resources, they could also concert their activities either through informal networks or via COSLA (Council of Scottish Local Government Authorities). Local government had traditionally operated as a powerful lobby within the Scottish Labour Party and this continued to be the case post-devolution, with senior councillors always consulted either via the SPF process framework or informally on any relevant policy matter. On only one, though highly contentious, issue was the combined view of Labour's municipal lobby over-ridden – the introduction of PR for local government elections – forced through by the party leadership as the price after 2003 for continuing the coalition with the Liberal Democrats.

The exertion of policy influence is, in part at least, a function of the availability of choice. As noted above, SPF members had the right to comment on policy drafts and to offer 'textual amendments', and if more than 25% of SPF members agreed, to develop 'alternative positions' which could be submitted to conference alongside majority SPF reports. In practice, although amendments were not uncommon, the formulation of alternative policy positions was rare. This was for a number of reasons.

Firstly there were strong pressures for accommodation. SPF procedures were designed to facilitate conflict resolution by promoting dialogue and give-and-take. Continuous effort was made within policy commissions and the forum itself to discourage the development of entrenched positions and negotiate compromises. Not only was the process structured in such a

267

way as to defuse the potential for divisions, but the norms of party solidarity operated to temper open disagreements which could be exploited by a media avid for stories about 'splits' (interviews with policy forum members).

Secondly, the influence of CLP delegates at the SPF (as at the NPF) was undermined by a range of factors. One was the dwindling of party membership and activism. Initially, as the Labour Party crested on a wave of popularity, party membership in Scotland as elsewhere had surged, but by the first years of New Labour in office there was a plateau and then, after the Iraq war, a precipitous descent. The consequence was an unprecedented hollowing out of the party as few members attended meetings, which themselves became more irregular and spasmodic, at branch and constituency level. In many parts of the country, party organisation was becoming moribund. A falling membership inevitably reduced the ability of constituency SPF delegates to present themselves as ambassadors of party opinion, as did the looseness of the institutional links that bound CLP Forum members to the areas they ostensibly represented. The net result was that constituency input into the policy-making process was very modest. A senior aide to one of Scotland's First Ministers reflected that in his experience 'the Scottish Labour Party Policy Forum process didn't contribute a great deal' to policy development, with a 'limited impact on the manifesto' (interview), while Jack McConnell's political advisor remembered 'feeling pressure from backbenchers, from unions, from the voluntary sector, from ministers, [but] I don't remember feeling much pressure from CLPs' (interview, Danny Phillips).

But one should not infer from this that the party elite dominated the policy process in disregard of rank-and-file beliefs and preferences. In fact, such evidence as we have suggests a large measure of genuine consensus. As has already been noted, there was in Scotland (in sharp contrast to Westminster) little dissent over the broad direction of policy in the two key areas of devolved policy-making, education and health. Where there *were* sharp divisions, they tended, as will be seen, to be between the unions and the leadership, with the latter often *backed* by the constituency rank and file (as with the controversy over the Private Finance Initiative: see below).

While, further, it is difficult to find any example of pressure from constituency delegates causing a significant shift of policy, it does not follow that the SPF process was a meaningless exercise. The very fact that ministers felt they had to attend meetings of the SPF and the policy commissions was an acknowledgement that they could not simply be ignored. Such bodies were instruments of both consultation and accountability, with ministers required to argue their case, listen to constituency views and engage in debate. Rank-and-file influence was limited but there was notwithstanding a degree of mutual adjustment, and real elements of reciprocity in the system.

The Unions and the Scottish Policy Forum

What of the unions? The role of Labour's affiliated trade unions has always been, and continues to be, contentious, with many commentators regarding the 'block votes' wielded by 'trade union barons' as a major impediment to both party democracy and effective policy-making. This was very much the view taken by Blair, who from the moment of his election was determined to curtail union influence – indeed, this was one of the main aims of 'Partnership in Power'. As Robert Taylor noted, New Labour's 'modernisation project' 'deliberately sought to develop a positive and intimate relationship with business and a more arm's-length and unsentimental one with trade unions' (Taylor 2001: 246). Under the Blair Government the old sense of collaboration in a common project binding together what used to be called 'the political and industrial wing of the movement' to a large extent disintegrated, to be replaced by a more hard-headed, pragmatic relationship.

In Scotland, trade unions have long been an inseparable part of the party – more so than in many parts of England – and this has remained the case. Under devolution a dual form of trade union representation evolved, one oriented to government, the other to party structures. From Holyrood's inception, Labour ministers encouraged a constructive engagement with the unions, in sharp contrast to the reticent, mistrustful and at times even hostile attitudes of their colleagues in London. What Grahame Smith, General Secretary of the STUC, called 'a bilateral social partnership arrangement' (interview) rapidly took root and this was formalised in April 2002 in the 'Memorandum of Understanding' between the Executive and the STUC. Signed by Jack McConnell as First Minister and David Bleiman, President of the STUC, it acknowledged the important role of the unions 'in sustaining effective democracy in society' and committed ministers to promoting 'effective trade unionism, fair employment practice, and greater partnership between employers and trade unions.' It pledged the Executive to maintain a continuing dialogue with the STUC and its individual affiliates, 'as a means of ensuring an effective trade union input to the development and implementation of the Scottish Executive's policies and priorities' (Scottish Executive/ STUC 2002). The outcome, as has been seen in the case of health policy and education, was a continuous dialogue, which involved union officials in regular discussions with both civil servants and ministers from the early stage of policy development to implementation (interview, Grahame Smith).

The unions were even more deeply implanted in the party's policy-making arrangements. As well as being represented on the Scottish Executive Committee, the unions had twenty-two members on the SPF and normally a minimum of three members on the various policy commissions. In addition, the affiliated unions set up the Scottish Trade Union Labour Party Committee (STULP) to co-ordinate their efforts. Consisting of representatives from trade unions in Scotland affiliated to the Labour Party, it defined its purpose as 'to seek to co-ordinate all matters of policy relevant to the affiliated unions and to liaise with the Scottish General Secretary of the Labour Party and the appropriate ministers in Westminster and Edinburgh'.[1,2] It provided a forum where SPF issues could be discussed, briefing papers exchanged and co-ordinated action arranged.

Unlike constituency delegates, union participants in the SPF process had access to a level of research and administrative resources which, although slender, contrasted with their virtual unavailability to most constituency members (except those linked to pressure groups or voluntary organisations). Well-established communications networks facilitated a degree of inter-union co-ordination that CLP delegates were rarely able to emulate. Further, to a greater extent than most CLP delegates, union members of the SPF were (like ministers and their advisors) seasoned political operators, familiar with Labour's rules, procedures and practices and experienced in deal-making. As a minister put it, they 'know how to speak to people, they know how to get involved in the policy process' (interview, Peter Peacock).

Party policy-making was in reality a dual process. On the one hand, there was the formal edifice of the SPF, the local policy forums, the policy commissions and so forth in which ministers, trade union representatives, constituency delegates, members of Labour's Scottish Executive Committee and MSPs all deliberated. On the other hand, there was the informal system where the real bargaining took place between ministers and union leaders – the 'side meetings', in the words of one senior trade unionist, in which agreements were hammered out (interview).

Unions and ministers would often engage in tough and hard-nosed bargaining sessions, but instances of overt and publicised conflict over matters of principle were rare. The crucial exception to this was over the decision by the Scottish Government to make extensive use of the Private Finance Initiative. Under PFI (a policy instrument originated by the Conservatives and massively expanded by New Labour), private sector consortia agree to build and run schools, hospitals and other infrastructure projects, typically over thirty years, in exchange for a stream of payments from the public purse. A radical departure from traditional public procurement, under Gordon Brown's eager tutelage PFI became a cornerstone of the New Labour 'modernisation' programme. The Scottish Executive decided to follow suit and a major wave of PFI projects, in education, the NHS and the prison service, was set in motion.

In Scotland, as in England, opposition from the unions (spearheaded by

Unison) was vociferous. PFI contracts, they contended, cost billions more than conventional public procurement, both because of the higher borrowing costs for public as against private bodies and because of the need to divert funds towards profits and dividends. The result was that public organisations were accumulating huge liabilities which were contractually protected, so not only were scarce resources being wastefully used but if cuts had to be made in public spending they would fall disproportionately elsewhere. To the extent that savings were made – herein lay a crucial union objection – it was through a deterioration in pay and conditions. More efficient use of resources could have been made through refurbishment, an option rejected by private contractors because much larger profits accrued from new builds (interviews, trade union officials).

These objections were rejected by Labour ministers who regarded PFI as a highly effective means for re-invigorating decaying public capital infrastructure (especially new schools and hospitals), with Glasgow's school-building programme the biggest PFI project in the UK. Two major arguments were advanced. Firstly, PFI was the only feasible option, 'the only game in town'. Holyrood did not have borrowing powers and could not therefore finance capital investment projects through conventional public procurement (Keating 2003: 435). As one high-ranking trade union figure acknowledged, 'ministers had very, very little room for manoeuvre. They had no borrowing powers, they had no opportunity to fund major capital works other than that route and really the enemy was Westminster, that's where the power rested' (interview) – and on this issue Westminster (Brown in particular) was not prepared to budge. The choice for Labour ministers was between a smaller number of new schools and hospitals built through conventional procurement or a once-in-a-lifetime opportunity to renew the public infrastructure (interviews, Scottish Parliament ministers).

That said, the stance of most Scottish Labour ministers was not reluctant acquiescence but enthusiastic advocacy. They were convinced that PFI was more efficient than traditional methods of public procurement, guaranteeing a higher quality of schools and hospitals and other public projects at a lower cost and with far fewer delays (interviews, Sam Galbraith, Frank McAveety, Andy Kerr). 'It afforded ready and immediately available funds for ambitious capital development projects, notably in hospitals and schools. Its virtue was that it removed the capital constraints that had persistently impeded new capital projects, such as the endlessly delayed Edinburgh Royal Infirmary, in the past' (interview, John McTernan).

There were lively debates in the policy forum process and the unions sought to dissuade the party from approving PFI projects, but compromise proved elusive. The main public sector unions then took a dramatic step at

271

the 2002 Perth conference by casting their combined votes against three key policy documents in which approval for PFI figured. Such a move was highly unusual since outright rejection by conference of reports accumulating two years' work would have inflicted considerable public embarrassment on the party – and in any case the leadership would never have agreed to include opposition to PFI in the 2003 election manifesto. After a rather acrimonious debate, the reports were approved by 58% to 42% – indicating that the great mass of CLPs had swung behind the leadership.

The unions did in fact extract some concessions, notably a commitment to end the two-tier workforce and protect workers who transferred from the public to the private sector (Scottish Labour Party 2003b). But few in the union movement were satisfied and union leaders concluded that they had not maximised their influence. Long-standing personal and institutional rivalries, divisions between left and right and the weakness of the machinery to co-ordinate union positions had all, it was felt, deflated potential union power and greater efforts had to be made to develop unified policy stances. These efforts were facilitated by the departure of a number of senior figures (for example, John Lambie from Unison, Bobby Parker from the GMB, Danny Carrigan from Amicus), not all of whom had worked well together. This afforded a window of opportunity to those, like Dave Watson and Richard Leonard, the capable political officers of Unison and the GMB, who were keen to streamline unions' operations in the party. Sustained efforts were made to reconcile differences and thrash out a common set of policy demands, which came to be dubbed the 'workforce agenda'. Unions worked closely together within the SPF process via STULP and (more importantly) in informal meetings with ministers, with Watson, Leonard and other officials playing major roles in the preparation of both the 2007 and 2011 manifestos.

Union influence was reflected in a significant modification in the party's stance on PFI. Outright rejection of PFI, it was accepted, was not a realistic option, so the unions pushed, on the one hand, for solid legislative guarantees protecting workers affected by PFI agreements and, on the other, for changes in contractual terms that effectively reduced the potential for future PFI deals (interview). They sought to achieve the latter by the phasing out of hidden subsidies and, more controversially, by securing the exclusion of (usually very profitable) facilities management services from future PFI contracts. Ministers came under some pressure to resist the latter demand from Gordon Brown's Treasury officials, worried that the removal of facilities management from PFI deals would depress their profitability and discourage private sector interest – which, of course, was the intention. The unions (led by Unison) were adamant, warning that they would vote against any manifesto that failed to formulate an acceptable compromise (interview). After some tough negotiating they got their way. The 2007 manifesto stated that 'Scottish Labour will review the approach to PPP [Public Private Partnership – another phrase for PFI] to ensure a level playing field between PPP and conventional capital procurement and will have the aim of excluding soft facilities management services from future PPP contracts' (Scottish Labour 2007: 90). Given the limits of what was realistically attainable, the unions were content with the outcome. As one senior trade union official reflected, 'the 2007 manifesto process was much better organised from our point of view . . . we got all the things or most of the things we wanted' (interview).

Not that union reservations about PFI had dissipated. As one leader commented, 'we still recognised that we were just storing up financial disaster' (interview). Indeed, in 2011 two major House of Commons reports, by the Treasury and the Public Accounts Select Committees, contained damning criticism of PFI, fully substantiating these reservations (*The Guardian*, 19 August, 1 September 2011; *The Observer*, 4 September 2011). The case against PFI as a highly expensive way of renewing the public capital infrastructure had been in fact steadily mounting (see Shaw 2007: 80–94). Yet few Labour ministers in Holyrood appeared to be aware of this and, if they were, preferred to disregard it. Nor was there any evidence that the party grassroots evinced any interest, though in effect it amounted to a major programme of privatisation. If the unions had not raised the issue, and invested considerable efforts in seeking to dilute or mitigate the effects of the policy, it seems probable that PFI would never have been seriously questioned. This places a large question mark about the vitality and effectiveness of the SPF process.

The fact that policy did shift, however, reflects the scale of union leverage. As noted in an earlier chapter, the Scottish Labour Party has always relied heavily on trade union funding and other staffing and material contributions, and remains so, and arguably this dependency has intensified post-devolution as the party's electioneering and campaigning needs have grown. Unlike New Labour under Blair (and, more recently, the SNP), Scottish Labour has not been able to entice donations from wealthy benefactors. The shrinkage of the party's activist base and the ossification of its machine in many parts of Scotland, as elsewhere in Britain, has meant that if anything the unions supply a growing proportion of the manpower and other resources required for electoral mobilisation.

One should, however, beware of exaggerating trade union influence. Impressive though their research and administrative resource base may have seemed compared with those available to constituency parties, when set against those (while Labour was in power) at the disposal of ministers they were very limited. The need to husband their resources meant that they had to focus on a limited range of policy priorities impinging directly on the interests and concerns of their members. In opposition, however, the power balance has shifted in favour of the unions as the leadership can no longer tap public resources.

But one should be cautious about seeking to elucidate the nature of the party–union relationship simply in terms of power. In truth, there was a high measure of consensus between the party leadership and the unions. The dispute over PFI was a rare case where the two were at loggerheads over a major issue of principle. In terms both of culture and institutional practices, unions and party were in Scotland inextricably entangled. Union involvement in party decision-making was not regarded as the intrusion of some outside force but as rightful participation by organisations who were an essential part of the Labour family. As one MP put it, 'I actually do believe in the old Jack Jones adage, when asked about the relationship between the trade unions and the Labour Party, "murder you can imagine, divorce never"' (interview, Anne McGuire). In short, and in striking contrast with the Blairite mentality, there was, deeply ingrained in the ethos of Scottish Labour, a continuing (if somewhat weakened) attachment to the concept of a 'labour movement' in which unions and party combined to pursue shared interests and ideals.

CONCLUSION

An earlier assessment of the Scottish Labour policy-making system concluded that it was 'essentially oligarchic in nature with power residing primarily with the Scottish leadership' (Clark 2002: 6). It was certainly the case that the leadership rarely encountered major problems in securing acceptance of their policy agenda from the party grassroots. The Scottish Policy Forum and conference performed useful consultative and legitimating functions, but with the exception of those issues where the unions have chosen to assert themselves they have not operated as the major motor of policy – certainly not while Labour was in office. The constituency parties, the traditional power bases of the left, have been quiescent, stripped of much of their capacity to act as a counter-vailing power to the party establishment, reflecting the serious decline in grassroots activism characteristic of the party right across Britain (Hassan 2002a; 2002b).

It is worth noting preparations for the 2011 Scottish election and manifesto, with the party in opposition having the time and opportunity to develop a more inclusive, less top-heavy consultative process. The SPF undertook a two-year process, setting up four policy commissions – A Prosperous and Sustainable Policy Commission, A Scotland of Opportunity Policy Commission, A Safer Scotland Policy Commission, and A Caring and

Healthier Scotland Commission – and over the course of its two years took 171 submissions, of which thirty-eight came from CLPs, trade unions and Labour MSPs. The rest came from a narrow sector of the Scottish voluntary sector (SCVO, SAMH) and from national bodies. What was missing was policy expertise that was not about lobbying and special interests. There were few independent research agencies or think tanks (Policy Studies Institute being the exception) and an absence of academics and policy experts. Overall, the process underlined the narrowness of the Scottish policy community and the disconnection of large parts of it from policy deliberations. Labour, on the evidence of this, still had little idea about how to draw on the best resources and widest engagement possible.

Margaret McCulloch, SPF Chair, called it 'the most exciting and ambitious policy process that Labour has ever embarked on' (Report of the Scottish Policy Forum 2010: 5). The truth of the 68-page document was rather more mundane in that it was lacking in any real landmark policies or positions, and as Labour approached the 2011 election it had to reverse its opposition to several of the SNP's main policies, such as freezing the council tax and opposition to tuition fees, to have anything noteworthy to say. These decisions were taken by a small coterie around the leader, Iain Gray, with minimal consultation (interview, party staffer). Although the need to respond nimbly to campaigning pressures was understood, such short-term decision-making rested uneasily with the party's claims to have evolved a democratic and inclusive policy process. After decades of being Scotland's leading party, learning how to use opposition effectively was clearly going to take some time.

But it does not follow that SPF procedures were little more than the rubber-stamping exercise that its UK counterpart tended to be. While at Scottish (as at UK) level there were tensions between those for whom the prime purpose of the policy forum system was to establish a more participative model of policy-making and those for whom it was a device for managing the wider party, the general view of people with experience of both institutions was that policy-making in the Scottish party was more open (interviews). Scottish parliamentary leaders could never command the patronage, resources or allegiance of their British counterparts (in the era of Blair and Brown). Further, a 'prime ministerial' style of government never evolved in the years Labour was in office, where a more collegial decision-making approach prevailed, while out of office leaders have experienced real difficulty in establishing their authority.

The key difference with British Labour was that the unions were more solidly embedded in Scottish Labour's policy-making system and, indeed, in its organisational fabric as a whole. Policy proposals championed by the larger unions (and, as noted, they increasingly worked in concert) could not, unlike those that sprang from other sources, be disregarded. As long as trade unions remained an integral part of the policy machine the leadership could never secure the monopoly over organisational, political and communications resources which alone furnishes the basis for a enduring pattern of elite domination. As one minister reflected on the events leading up to the 2007 manifesto, 'an awful lot of time was taken up in internal processing, squaring people off and working out what's going to be acceptable to certain groups or interests . . . the kind of Blairite comparison would be we're just doing this and here's the reason why. It's very difficult to do that in a Scottish context' (interview, Peter Peacock).

Notes

1. However, it should be noted that elsewhere the response was patchy and policy forums in a number of areas were slow to take root (interview, party official).
2. http://www.scottishlabour.org.uk/trade-unions.

CHAPTER 16

Power in the Scottish Labour Party: The Case of Candidate Selection

INTRODUCTION

Candidate selection represents 'one of the highest stakes in any internal struggle for control of a party's leadership and policy' (Ranney 1965: 10). The importance of the method used by political parties for recruiting candidates for elected offices has long been recognised by scholars of political parties (see, for example, Gallagher and Marsh 1988; Hopkin 2001; Lovenduski and Norris 1993; Ranney 1965; Rush 1969). It raises crucial issues of representation, power and democracy. Where many seats do not change hands, those who select often elect a candidate; and where the executive is drawn from the legislature, those who are empowered to pick a candidate also influence the composition of the governing elite. Those who can shape selection procedures and decisions can, hence, indirectly influence policy formation. Further, since they have prime responsibility for expounding their party's policies, 'a party's candidates in large measure define and constitute its public face in elections'. By helping to shape its 'ideological and sociological identities' they project an image of what a party is and what it stands for (Katz 2001: 277).

Candidate selection is about power. In recent years the capacity of the rank and file in political parties to directly influence policy, always rather restricted, has tended to shrink further. Traditions of intra-party democracy have waned as voter-oriented parties have placed a premium on the capacity of their leaders to adjust policy to shifting electoral and campaigning requirements – thereby allowing them to arrogate to themselves a decisive role in shaping the party programme. Given the structural and technical barriers that limit a party's grassroots ability to participate in any substantial way in the formulation of policy or to compel governments to implement party policy, candidate selection survives as one of the few effective ways in which they can assert a measure of control over the party leadership (Katz,2001: 285).

By the same token, party leaderships have strong incentives to optimise their control over the selection process. Facing the problems and constraints of government, a grip on the machinery for recruiting candidates, enabling them to secure preferential treatment of candidates sharing their general ideological outlook, affords a means by which they can guard against the 'unrealistic' expectations of the rank and file. Furthermore, the way in which candidates are selected – and de-selected – has consequences for parliamentary cohesion and the ease of party management. Parliamentary representatives will be most sensitive to the views and demands of those on whose approval they depend for the continuation and elevation of their parliamentary careers, so the relative capacity of the rank and file and the leadership to influence selection outcomes will have a significant impact on their behaviour. In light of these considerations it is not surprising that where there are divisions within a party they will often be at their most intense in the arena of candidate selection. As Ranney put it, 'what is at stake . . . is nothing less than control of the core of what the party stands for and does' (Ranney 1981: 103).

For this reason, the issue of selection procedures has for long been a matter of controversy within the Labour Party, a key battleground in the struggle between left and right, the activists and the parliamentary leadership. This reached boiling point after the defeat of the Callaghan Government in 1979, when the left sought to enforce a greater degree of PLP accountability to the rank and file by instituting a system of 'mandatory re-selection' of MPs. Under this scheme, in place of their more or less automatic re-adoption, sitting MPs would face competition from other contenders, thereby rendering them more vulnerable to pressures from constituency activists. This was narrowly pushed through in 1980, but was never accepted by the leadership or by the majority of centre-right Labour MPs. Both were convinced that weakening the hold of constituency activists over selection was vital if a major impediment to Labour's 'modernisation' was to be swept aside, but union opposition meant that initially the leadership proceeded cautiously. In 1987, the right to decide selections was transferred from the constituency general committee to an electoral college in which a minimum of 60% of votes were allocated to local party members and a maximum of 40% to affiliated organisations, mainly unions (Norris and Lovenduski 1995: 64). But this was only a stopgap. By 1993, at his last party conference as leader, John Smith overcame union resistance and finally pushed through a full one member, one vote (OMOV) system. This had the effect of diminishing the role both of activists and of affiliated trade unions, who formed a large proportion of General Committee members.

Ostensibly (and indeed to some degree in practice), OMOV was all about democratising a key party function. But it also had a very tangible political purpose: to weaken the hold of more left-oriented party activists by enfranchising the more passive – and, it was assumed, more moderate – members (that is, those who were not members of constituency general committees) and thereby facilitating the leadership's centrist political strategy. In another significant move, the rules governing selection were modified, with mandatory re-selection ceasing to be automatic. In future a sitting MP could only be challenged if a majority of branches and affiliated bodies agreed to hold a ballot of members which would then set in motion a full selection contest. Further rule changes occurred in the mid-1990s as a result of the decision to establish elected bodies for Scotland, Wales and London. These are discussed below.

In what follows, a range of questions are addressed. Who were the key players in influencing the selection process? What roles were played by key institutional actors, such as party officials, senior party politicians and affiliated trade unions? Who exerted most control? The first section focuses on the organisation of selection procedures for the first Holyrood elections, discussing, in particular, the introduction of a vetting procedure, but also considering two other innovations, the twinning of constituencies and the organisation of the regional list. The angle of vision is then widened to encompass both Holyrood and Westminster selections. The chapter proceeds to analyse, in turn, the role and capacity to affect selection outcomes of 'the party machine', affiliated trade unions and locally based networks. It concludes with a consideration of what the candidate selection system tells us about the distribution of power within Scottish Labour.

SELECTION PROCEDURES FOR SCOTTISH PARLIAMENT ELECTIONS: VETTING CANDIDATES

Some while ago, Ranney noted that tension between national and constituency organisations in the Labour Party was endemic. However, he concluded that, because of an entrenched culture favouring constituency autonomy, the actual influence wielded by the centre over candidate selection was 'substantially weaker than their formal supervisory powers allow' (Ranney 1965: 270, 272). In fact, formal powers were largely confined to responsibility for ensuring that selections were conducted according to the rules, and while the NEC did have the right to withhold endorsement from an adopted candidate, almost invariably (from the 1960s) this was only invoked where serious irregularities had occurred.

The limit in practice to NEC power is illustrated by its minimal influence over the pool from which candidates could be drawn. There were two lists from which constituencies could (though were not required to) choose. The so-called 'A List' consisted of potential candidates who had been placed on trade union-organised parliamentary panels, in effect those union members who would receive some form of financial support if adopted as parliamentary candidates. A 'B List of Available Candidates' existed but this was simply a roster of political aspirants who were eligible for nomination, compiled from nominations received from CLPs and affiliated organisations, and it carried no imprimatur of approval.

The rules revision process in 1996–7 provided the opportunity for a comprehensive review of candidate selection procedures. The aims of the new procedures, agreed in 1997, were enumerated as follows:

- Widening the pool of good-quality candidates and certifying that they possessed the relevant qualities and experience for the job;
- Increasing the diversity of candidates;
- Maximising membership involvement; and
- Establishing a fair, impartial and transparent system. (see Shaw 2001)

The new rules applied to the new devolved legislative bodies as well as to Westminster. They were fleshed out (in Scotland) by Scottish Labour officials operating under the aegis of the SEC and in close co-operation with headquarters staff (subsequently, in 2001, responsibility for formulating more detailed rules and procedures for Holyrood were delegated to the SEC, though the NEC retained control over Scottish Westminster selections). The crucial reform – and one which broke most sharply with traditions of constituency autonomy – was the establishment of a formal parliamentary panel, membership of which was a prerequisite for proceeding further in the selection process. Under the new rules, anyone with the requisite two-year membership was invited to nominate themselves. Those who did so received a job description, a 'person specification' which listed the qualities aspiring candidates were expected to possess, and an application form.[1]

As Chapter 5 covered, in the case of selections for the first Holyrood elections, of the 534 who returned nomination forms, 326 were chosen for interview, the next stage in the process. Responsibility for scrutinising the applications and for conducting the interviews was given by the NEC to a specially convened selection board of twenty members, drawn from the NEC, the SEC, 'detached' MPs and outsiders with professional experience of appointment procedures. It was headed by Rosemary McKenna MP and divided into five selection committees of four people each. Selection board members were charged with 'compiling a diverse and dynamic panel of quality potential candidates, representing a wide cross section of the Party's membership and support', including a fair balance of 'gender, age, experience and background'.[2]

Those called for interview by the selection committees were given five minutes to present their case, questioned for about twenty-five minutes, then grilled in a five-minute role-playing 'press conference'. The rules stipulated that candidates were assessed 'against the standard selection criteria, using an agreed scoring mechanism'.[3] Points were awarded on the basis of performance in the interview, understanding of party policy, the possession of designated skills and a demonstration of 'a commitment to party policies' (Bradbury et al. 2000: 54). On completion of the interview schedule, the full selection board, on the basis of recommendations from the selection committees, drew up the final panel, membership of which was a condition for selection as a parliamentary candidate. Of the 326 interviewed, final approval was given to just 166 (of whom sixty-nine were women), a small number given the 129 places to be filled, with one successful appeal (Susan Deacon). Scottish CLPs were left to choose from a pool from which to recruit their shortlists both for the constituency and regional list seats of 1.3 candidates per seat, while Welsh CLPs had nearly three approved candidates for every seat.

Since those selected and elected would form the first cohort for a new Parliament, it could be expected that their composition would have a major impact on Labour parliamentary representation for a considerable time. In any circumstances, the methods chosen were likely to be controversial but, given their novelty, their break with tradition in instituting a much greater degree of central regulation and, most of all, their consequences, the effect was to light a political tinder box.

What were the new rules intended to achieve? There was widespread concern within the leadership (in particular on the part of Donald Dewar) that established notables in Labour's local government strongholds, whose longevity in office was not always matched by their talents, would win too many places in the new Parliament. A more meritocratic system was required to improve the calibre of candidates and this had to be spearheaded from the centre. As Rosemary McKenna MP, perhaps undiplomatically, put it, it was essential to sweep away 'the cronyism, the smoke-filled rooms and the mutual scratching of backs' which had too often intruded in Labour's selection contests in the past in favour of a more professional 'criteria-led selection' (*The Scotsman*, 25 May 1998).

While no doubt some of those who failed to make the grade lacked the requisite qualities, the number, standing and calibre of those who failed the vetting procedure was surprising, as Chapter 5 sets out. The most controversial case was the exclusion of the Westminster MP for Falkirk West,

Dennis Canavan, an outspoken left-winger but widely regarded as a first-class constituency MP. Others eliminated beside the MPs Ian Davidson and Mike Connarty (who withdrew) included a wealth of talent and skills which the party was to find to its later cost it could ill afford to exclude (for more details, see Chapter 5, pp. 86–8).

Left-wing critics charged that an 'ideological cull' had occurred – that perfectly sound applicants had been rejected on the basis of their political views and independence of mind. It was certainly puzzling why so many apparently well-qualified applicants were screened out of the process – not least because many (even within Labour's ranks) queried the quality of those who were approved (Taylor 2002: 145). In their research, Bradbury et al. found that 'all stages of the selection process were marred by perceptions of heavy central party manipulation to promote candidates loyal to the New Labour project and to screen out dissidents', with even significant minorities of *successful* candidates agreeing that the procedures were neither fair nor democratic (Bradbury et al. 2000: 59; emphasis in the original).

The party establishment in Scotland countered that the process had been highly professional and rigorous, that applicants were excluded from the panel either because they lacked the appropriate aptitudes or had not interviewed well (this was said to be the case of Murray Elder, former Scottish General Secretary of the party and subsequently ennobled, a long-standing friend of Gordon Brown), or had failed to treat the process with proper respect (interviews, Rosemary McKenna MP and party officials). It was also pointed out that a number of well-known left-wingers *were* successful and were subsequently nominated, including Malcolm Chisholm MP, Cathy Jamieson and John McAllion MP.

Another explanation for what happened was that some of the unexpected exclusions from the panel decisions reflected less political motives than the unanticipated effects of basic flaws in the system. For example, most applicants assumed that the information they had supplied in the written application would be taken into account and therefore did not refer to it in their interview answers. If no mention was made by interviewees of their experience, accomplishments and abilities as detailed in their application, these were simply discounted. In addition, performance was assessed in a very mechanical way, with scores being allocated according to responses to set questions (interview, MSP). This imparted a rigidity to the process which distorted the outcomes. This factor may well have accounted for some of the more inexplicable decisions, but it is clear that there were also political factors at work.

In fact, evidence suggests that precisely how the several selection committees responsible for overseeing the process discharged their responsibilities tended to vary. Some were professional and impartial in their approach, evaluating applicants according to their knowledge, experience and competence. Others took a less detached view. Thus, in some cases questions were used to ascertain the political leanings of aspiring candidates, for example by probing their attitudes to controversial policies such as the Private Finance Initiative and Trident, and asking them to attest their commitment to 'New Labour'. A number of interview panels were chaired by Ernie Ross MP, an unswerving loyalist (though once a left-winger). Rosemary McKenna was closely associated with the pro-Blair 'Network' group and indicating that her objectivity had its limits, she averred that 'it is important for the party to be comfortable that the people who represent them will be loyal to the party in the future' (*The Scotsman*, 25 May 1998).

However, inevitably political judgements were always being made by board members who were for the most part experienced operators with sharp political antennae. Much depended on the contacts applicants had, the extent to which they had the ear of party and union influential figures, and on their general standing. For example, rejecting the left-wing Cathy Jamieson would have risked seriously alienating her union (TGWU). However, those who were regarded as both unsound *and* lacking such connections found their hopes of securing adoption thwarted.

There is some ambiguity about the precise role played by Dewar. A senior MSP close to Dewar dismissed as 'mythology' the notion that 'Donald fixed all the selections'. Others disagreed. George Foulkes, a former MP and subsequently a member of both the House of Lords and the Scottish Parliament, maintained that 'Donald had a tight grip on who was not on the list – making sure that Rosemary McKenna and Ernie Ross did his bidding. He wanted a Parliament in his own mould and his own people' (interview). Rosemary McKenna herself recalled that 'he made it quite clear that he wanted it to be a new Parliament, he didn't want Westminster politicians' (interview). This view was echoed by other interviewees.

Certainly there was a lack of enthusiasm about accepting responsibility for the vetting system. There were widespread and embarrassing accusations of 'control freakery' in the media as well as in the party (see Shaw 2003). Nor was the exercise hugely effective. 'If there was a concerted effort tae influence' a party official observed, 'it failed' (interview). One left-wing applicant rejected for the list in 1998 but later approved and elected MSP (for Dewar's seat) later recalled, 'it wasn't very subtle nor was it very sophisticated, nor was it very successful' (interview, Bill Butler).

After the furore in 1998, there was a loss of political will to intervene so heavily in the selection process. Given the rancour, ill feeling and resentment the vetting system provoked, given the rash of critical press stories –

most notably over the rejection of Dennis Canavan – many concluded that the game was no longer worth the candle. McConnell's short-lived successor as General Secretary, Alex Rowley, recalls being told by Dewar, 'we really got that one wrong, Alex' (interview). A party official sympathetic to the system conceded that it 'was too draconian and insufficiently transparent, which bred suspicions' (interview). The vetting procedures were effectively abandoned and the party in Scotland reverted to the more laissez-faire system that had prevailed throughout most of Labour's history.

A parliamentary panel survives but entry is more or less automatic for those who meet the basic requirements for standing as a Labour candidate. Interviews for membership of the panel are conducted by the SEC, but there is now no systematic vetting, and efforts to filter the flow of candidates have been discontinued. As one party official explained, 'there's very little control, you don't get grilled and it's . . . very unlikely that somebody might not get on for political reasons'. Indeed, he complained that 'It's gone too far the other way . . . there's a slackness or a lack of rigour in the panel interviews . . . there are people who quite frankly should not be candidates . . . you only have to look at Jim Devine' (interview).

By combing out people of a less tractable disposition, the leadership prob-ably did secure a parliamentary group more manageable than it might other-wise have been. But the cost was high. The installation of a vetting system in Scotland (and Wales) was part of a broader effort to intensify leadership control over the party, which included equally controversial episodes, notably the ill-fated efforts to block the election of Rhodri Morgan as Labour's leader in the Welsh Assembly and Ken Livingstone as the party's candidate as London mayor. All proved embarrassing failures, which generated a rash of damaging media coverage that helped to discredit 'control-freakery': 'we fucked up', as senior Blair advisor Jonathan Powell candidly admitted to Chris Mullin (Mullin 2009: 80). With fingers burned, senior figures in Labour's hierarchy in both London and in Scotland were subsequently more guarded and circumspect about seeking to impose their will.

TWINNING AND THE LIST

The vetting procedure was not the only means by which the party establish-ment could intercede in Holyrood candidate selections. Two other institu-tional arrangements supplied opportunities for management of the process: twinning arrangements and the compilation of a regional list.

Twinning was designed to achieve gender parity (which it did, very effec-tively). Constituencies were paired on the basis of geographical proximity and 'winability', one selecting a male and the other a female candidate. The two constituency executives met to shortlist a maximum of eight candidates from those who secured the most nominations, four men and four women. A joint selection conference was held in which the highest-scoring male and female candidates were chosen on the basis of one member, one vote.[4]

Deciding which constituencies were to be twinned was in many cases reasonably straightforward (for example, where there were two seats in a borough, as with Dundee). But this was by no means always the case and it could be a highly political exercise. Decisions about which constituencies to pair could affect selection outcomes because they determined who would be battling whom. If, for example, there was a strongly favoured male candidate in one constituency it would be highly unlikely that another male in a paired constituency could be selected. For example, Cumbernauld and Kilsyth was initially to be twinned with Airdrie and Shotts, but it was decided to twin it instead with Strathkelvin and Bearsden, thwarting the candidature of Ian Smart, a well-known left-winger, who could not hope to beat Sam Galbraith, the constituency's sitting MP.[5] Another tactic was to link one 'reliable' CLP with a large membership (large almost invariably because it had a Labour club) with another judged as more 'flaky', so its votes would be swamped. There is some evidence that such adjustments were made to twinning decisions after consultation with Donald Dewar's office (interviews, party officials). However, it should be added that there were fine calculations to be made and with so many uncertainties it was by no means unusual for the best-laid plans to go awry with the 'wrong' candidate slipping in by default.

As part of the effort to maximise support for devolution, Labour supported the election of the Scottish Parliament by a form of proportional representation. The additional member system (AMS) was chosen which meant that seventy-three of the 129-member Parliament were elected by FPTP from each of the existing Westminster constituencies (Orkney and Shetland were given two seats) and fifty-six according to party votes for lists in regions based on the eight former European Parliament constituencies. The 'closed' regional list was used, under which voters choose between rival party lists but not between individuals. A candidate's fate was, therefore, a function of his or her ranking on this list. Regional lists were compiled after aspiring candidates addressed an electoral conference attended by constituency representatives. Responsibility for ranking candidates was entrusted to an electoral board, comprising four members of the SEC, the Scottish General Secretary, the Secretary of State or his/her representative and two members of the NEC. Constituency parties could accept or reject their recommendations but not alter the ranking, and the final word lay with the board, which provoked further charges of excessive central control. Lists were imposed on both Glasgow and the Highlands and Islands against the wishes of constituency representatives, but since few seats were expected to be gained via the lists (actually just three, from the Highlands), the protest was more muted than it could have been (Bradbury et al. 2000: 55).

In response to heated criticism about these impositions it was decided in future to open out the process and allow party members, voting by postal ballot, to determine the rank ordering of the various regional lists. The issue of the list and its composition has recently (and unexpectedly) acquired much greater importance when, as a result of a haemorrhage of constituencies to the SNP, for the first time in 2011 the majority of Labour MSPs were elected via the list.

The Power of 'the Machine'

Instituting the vetting system in 1998 was only one aspect of a long-standing debate, both within the party and among commentators, about power and the selection process. As Russell has observed, 'no question has been more central to the debate about the internal democracy of the modern Labour Party than that of how candidates and leaders should be selected' (Russell 2005: 34). The rest of this chapter will contend that the answer to the commonly asked question, 'Who controlled the selection process in Scotland?' is that no one did. Power in the Labour Party for much of its history (though much less so in the Blair/Brown era) has been apportioned among various 'stakeholders', that is, groups and organisations endowed with the constitutional right to act within it, including affiliated trade unions, co-operative and socialist societies (such as the Fabian Society) and Labour council groups. They constituted political networks, groups of people with some sense of shared identity, norms or interests and with a capacity to act in a co-ordinated way to promote their goals. It was, it will be argued, through the operations of these networks that the crucial resources required to affect selection outcomes – political information or intelligence, connections and access to resources – were mustered and flowed. Three networks over-shadowed all others: party officialdom, trade unions and local-based networks. All these are discussed in turn.

Much has been made of the power of the 'party machine' (see Bradbury 2009: 135) and it is true it controlled resources that rendered it strategically placed to influence selection contests. Through day-to-day administrative work, party officials inevitably accumulated a wide range of contacts within the constituency parties and were well-informed about the intricacies and vagaries of internal constituency politics and personalities as well as future selection openings. As one official commented, 'you get information and a feel for things . . . you can give advice on conditions and on key players [in the constituencies]' (interview).

It was not at all unusual for Scottish party officials from the General Secretary downwards to be approached by aspiring candidates seeking advice and help. Officials would be receptive to the extent that they felt a candidate would make a useful addition to Labour's parliamentary contingent, and their action would be approved by their political superiors. As one senior official acknowledged, 'Did the Labour Party hire the party machine to deliver in certain areas? Yes we did' (interview). This included providing briefings about particular constituency parties, suggesting contacts and other forms of unofficial help. But the decision to intervene would only be taken after a careful weighing of the costs, risks and benefits, and officials would act with prudence and discretion.[6]

There were definite limits to the influence of 'the machine'. The 'machine' was (and is) in practice a small, under-staffed, usually over-stretched team barely able to keep up with the demands placed on it. Officials had a wide range of responsibilities, such as routine administrative tasks, engaging in election campaigns (local, Scottish, Westminster and European), advising various party bodies about rules and procedures, organising meetings, overseeing the policy forum process and helping smooth disputes. As one official reflected, 'the level of resource in the Scottish party is relatively small, the amount of work they have to do is heavy. They're covering fifty-nine, sixty parties, heaven knows how many branches, thirty-two local authority groups, MEP regions, regional list areas, all with structures built around them. Sometimes party officials get the reputation that they're up to something. In fact they're just far too busy wading under a thousand and one different priorities' (interview).

Furthermore, selection contests could be extremely stressful and time-consuming. Local members were always suspicious of any attempt to 'fix' a contest and if anything went wrong it would be the officials who would have to take responsibility (interview, party official). Minor irregularities could be shrugged off but more important ones, and those where powerful groups were involved, would have to be investigated. This was an eventuality that party officials dreaded. He or she would think, 'I've got too much to do . . . You are running up to an election, you are doing a thousand and one things, the biggest priority is winning constituencies, you don't want to get wrapped up in sideshows about . . . somebody wanting to appeal to the NEC. Then you've got to spend hours and hours doing paperwork' (interview, party official). Fear of precipitating such distracting investigations was a powerful deterrent to party officials acting in ways that could be construed as favouring one candidate over another. Added to this was the unwanted attention of the press always sniffing round for a 'scandal' – particularly after the heavily publicised Canavan affair rendered 'control freakery' so newsworthy. In short, there were limits to the capacity of an under-staffed party administration to shape selection outcomes.

The party administrative apparatus was not the only conduit through which senior figures sought to influence selection outcomes. Comments were often made in the press about the role of Scotland's most powerful politician, Gordon Brown, and his 'fiefdom' in the Scottish Labour Party, though these were rarely backed by solid evidence. Immersed in his onerous responsibilities in Number 11 and then Number 10 Downing Street, one can assume that he had relatively little time to expend on Labour's internal politics in his homeland. But if Scotland was never a Brown 'fiefdom', he did exert a considerable degree of influence through a wide network of contacts, particularly with senior trade officials (notably in Unite). He had, one very senior figure in the Scottish party recalled, an 'amazingly powerful personal influence' (interview). This was occasionally deployed to promote the candidatures of protégés, for example Des Browne and Douglas Alexander in the safe Westminster seats of Kilmarnock and Loudoun, and Paisley South, and Brian Fitzpatrick for the Scottish Parliament seat of Strathkelvin and Bearsden in a 2001 by-election. It is difficult to establish how pervasive was Brown's reach. Much depended on the willingness of senior union officials to act on his behalf, which it appears they were surprisingly willing to do despite substantial policy differences. Precisely why is unclear.

THE UNIONS AND CANDIDATE SELECTION

The second major network in Labour's selection process was that formed by the unions. Prior to 1987, selection was the responsibility of the constituency general committee, which consisted of delegates from local branch parties and from affiliated organisations. These included co-operative and socialist societies, but by far the most numerous affiliates were trade union branches. Attendance at general committees by many trade union delegates tended to be sporadic, except when a parliamentary selection was in the offing, when delegates rarely seen might suddenly materialise in large numbers. Most of them could be marshalled (though not mandated) to rally behind their union's preferred candidate. Union support would also normally guarantee a candidate sufficient nominations to ensure a place on the shortlist. Not least, union-backed candidates usually came with a 'dowry'. Unions could sponsor a candidate, which meant not only that the sponsoring union could defray up to 80% of the constituency's (legally limited) election expenses but could be expected to contribute in other ways such as the provision of manpower, offices, transport and other facilities (Minkin 1991: 243). Obviously this was tempting to cash-strapped CLPs.

The capacity of unions to affect selections was greatest where a single union was dominant (as in mining areas) and a seat was virtually regarded as a union benefice. Where a number of unions were affiliated locally, much would depend on the ability of a candidate to obtain the support of a bloc of powerful unions. George Robertson, then a young GMB official, recalled attending the STUC when a parliamentary seat became vacant. He lobbied a number of senior union officials 'and by the end of the week I had it pretty sewn up or at least a sporting chance' (interview). However, where unions had rival candidates they could cancel each other out and allow a non-union-supported candidate to slip through, such as John McFall in Dumbarton and Lewis Moonie in Kirkcaldy in the 1987 election.

It should not be supposed that the party (in Scotland at least) resented trade union influence. Party officials understood that their tasks would be considerably eased if trade unions assumed a significant share of the responsibility for financing constituency electioneering and supplying much-needed organisational assistance. This encouraged them to cultivate good relations with their counterparts in affiliated trade unions. Top party officials such as Willie Marshall, Jimmy Allison, Helen Liddell and Lesley Quinn worked closely with the regional (or Scottish) organisers of the larger unions, such as the NUM, TGWU (later Unite), GMB, the engineers and NUPE (later Unison). Key figures here included Hugh Wyper, Regional Secretary of the Transport and General Workers Union, and Jimmy Morrell, Regional Secretary of the General and Municipal Workers Union, in the 1970s and early 1980s, and John Lambie, a senior figure in NUPE and subsequently Unison, in the 1990s and early 2000s (interviews with Jimmy Allison, Helen Liddell). The relationship between party and union officials was, as one party official reflected, 'a close, continuing and long-term one in which people had invested effort and which operated according to the norms of compromise, mutual accommodation, mutual support and give and take' (interview).

One curious feature was the role played by union officials who were members of the Communist Party, including Hugh Wyper of the TGWU and Mick McGahey of the NUM. Helen Liddell recalled, 'it wasn't really until I became Scottish Secretary that I became really aware of the full extent of the Communist influence' (interview). But this was not perceived to be a problem. Right-wing Labour politician George Robertson saw 'people like Hugh Wyper and Jimmy Milne' (General Secretary of the STUC from 1975 to 1986) as 'much more mature in their politics then the Bennite left. They had a calming influence. They hated Militant and thought the Bennite left irresponsible.' Helen Liddell agreed, commenting that one of the reasons why Militant failed to secure a foothold in Scotland was because of the activity of Communist union officials who 'were very, very useful in keeping Militant at bay . . . They kept the Labour Party freer of infiltration' (interview). The level of co-operation between Communist union leaders and party officials is less unusual than it might appear on the surface when it is understood that in practice little separated Communist unionists in outlook, goals and priorities from their more left-of-centre Labour colleagues.

In 1993, as noted, OMOV was introduced. This had the effect, as intended, of significantly curtailing trade union influence, which was further reduced when, as a result of the Nolan Report on party funding, traditional sponsoring arrangements were phased out. Trade union aid continued to be a useful asset. It still helped in the garnering of nominations. Though the focus of attention for aspiring parliamentary candidates was now the membership, the amassing of nominations helped create momentum and 'street credibility' (interview, Anne McGuire). Further, a candidate with a significant number of nominations could not be denied a place on the shortlist, though after this stage the number of nominations mattered little. Where trade union help really counted was in the provision of resources, political intelligence and connections. A union-backed candidate would have access to union funding and office equipment to help finance promotional material, while officials could provide briefings and arrange contacts. Finally, the fact that a union-supported candidate would be well placed to call on union resources in the election campaign remained a factor which would weigh with some party members, especially in more marginal constituencies.

Estimating precisely how much influence the unions wielded is difficult. They played a significant role at all stages in the selections for the 1999 Scottish Parliament elections. In many areas their chosen candidates won selection against higher-profile people. In Motherwell and Wishaw, the party's retiring General Secretary, Jack McConnell, only narrowly defeated Bill Tynan, a senior figure in the engineering union AEU (later Amicus, later absorbed into Unite), after a very hard-fought contest. Some candidates who may otherwise have fallen foul of the vetting procedures were effectively pro-tected by known union backing. However, it is noticeable that a high propor-tion of Labour candidates for the elections were either former union officials or had strong union connections, with Unison especially well-represented.

The unions took an even more pro-active role in the 2001 Westminster elections, in part because there were an unusually large number of eleven Labour seats vacant (plus Tommy Graham's seat pending his expulsion).[7] In some of these a candidate had been lined up well in advance, but in a bid to maximise their influence in the rest the major unions arranged, as one senior union official put it, to 'divvy them up' by selecting an agreed candi-date for each constituency, with all unions pledging to throw their weight behind that candidate (interview). The arrangement was hammered out in collaboration with Gordon Brown, who was keen to see as many potential 'Brownites' elected as possible. In virtually every case the unions succeeded in securing the adoption of their agreed candidate (interviews, Anne McGuire, Rosemary McKenna).

Not all went entirely to plan. There was a controversial and bitterly fought contest for Strathkelvin and Bearsden which had been 'allotted' to John Lyons, a Unison official. Despite extensive support from his union he was beaten in a nail-biting finish by airline pilot Doug Maughan, by one vote. Almost immediately there were complaints from Unison about procedural irregularities. A key role was played by Unison's Political Officer, John Lambie, a tough, highly experienced and deft operator with a formidable reputation as a political fixer in the Scottish party. After a bout of energetic lobbying, when Maughan's candidate came to the NEC for endorsement (this was normal procedure) the committee decided, controversially, to declare the contest void and ordered a re-run. The grounds for the decision were never made entirely clear, but as the party official present (as NEC representative) at the contest commented, 'If Lyons had won in the first contest, no way that selection would have been re-run' (interview). In the second selection contest Lyons won by a solid margin.

Paradoxically, Strathkelvin and Bearsden indicates the limits as well as the potency of the trade union role. Doug Maughan was unusual in that he was not linked to any of the major networks or circuits of influence within the party. Lyons was the agreed union candidate for the constituency and an official in the strongest union in Scotland. Notwithstanding all this, he (initially) lost and was only rescued by the willingness of the NEC to engage in an imaginative interpretation of the rules. The episode suggests that while trade union influence remains substantial it is less formidable than it once was. A major factor here was the shift to OMOV but there are other factors too. The proportion of the party membership who are also members of affiliated unions is falling, reflecting the increasingly public sector middle-class composition of the party: many members belong to non-affiliated unions such as the various teacher unions and associations. The general trend was for union influence, though still considerable, to gradually ebb. It is worth noting that Richard Leonard, Political Officer for the GMB and one of the most capable and respected union officials in Scotland, only very narrowly won the contest for what was thought to be the safe Labour seat of Carrick, Cumnock and Doon Valley (it was lost to the SNP in 2011).

What were the unions seeking to achieve? The classic object was to promote working-class representation but already by the 1980s this was losing importance. The proportion of union-backed candidates who were former officials steadily fell and there was an increasing tendency to co-opt onto parliamentary panels young, bright politicians with tenuous occupational links with the unions, but who were seen as standard bearers both for their union and more generally for the party. Thus John Smith was sponsored by the GMB, Donald Dewar and Robin Cook by the NUR and Gordon Brown and John Reid by the TGWU. What unions were really concerned with – aside from a symbolic demonstration of their own influence – was securing access to the legislative process. A senior union leader spelled this out:

> Access gives you the ability to put the case. It doesn't guarantee you will win your case but it at least gives you the guarantee that you get a chance to put your point of view over and that's not insignificant . . . I don't have to go begging for a meeting or anything of that nature, I just have to make a few phone calls . . . it gives you access in a way that lobby companies would charge you hundreds of thousands of pounds for. (interview)

The existence of a cohort of sympathetic MPs and MSPs also afforded unions a direct input into the legislative process:

> If we need an MP to put down an amendment to a bill . . . to ask the appropriate question, that sort of thing, . . . it's not difficult. I do it much more in the Scottish Parliament . . . if we need an amendment I will draft the amendment . . . I will produce essentially a brief which says this is the amendment, this is the case for it, this is why we want to do it this way, so much so that . . ..you sometimes find civil servants will ring you up and say are you likely to be preparing an amendment on this? Can we talk about it? (interview)

Chapter 15 catalogued the extensive degree of influence unions were able to exert over Labour's policy-making. However, unions did not expect that union-backed MPs and MSPs would in any rigorous way be accountable to them, nor that they should toe the union line where this conflicted with party (or Government) policy. Anne McGuire recalled that as a Westminster minister she had 'really brutal and quite hurtful fights with the union [GMB] but I remained part of the group. You still have an affinity with your union but they don't buy you body and soul' (interview).

So far we have discussed the selection of MPs and MSPs. What about de-selection? This was a hugely controversial issue in the 1980s after the passing of the constitutional amendment in 1980 that required all sitting MPs undergo a selection contest before each election. This was eventually diluted when the 'trigger mechanism' was introduced. A sitting MP could only be challenged if an adverse vote was passed by the constituency executive committee, on which each branch possessed one vote. In effect this placed affiliated unions in a powerful position to precipitate (or block) a full-blown selection contest. While unions could affiliate as many of their branches as existed within the constituency, the number of party branches was constantly (and sharply) dwindling because of a Head Office-sponsored process of amalgamation. This meant that in most constituencies union-affiliated branches would out-number, often by a large margin, the number of party branches.

Mandatory re-selection was an acutely sensitive issue because the threat of de-selection was the most potent weapon a constituency could wield against its MP. One party official, recalling the 'rage' that many party members in Scotland felt about the Blair Government's decision to commit British troops in the Iraq war, suggested that the existence of structures that 'make it difficult to get de-selected' probably relieved some of the pressure on MPs who backed the Government in the crucial House of Commons debate immediately prior to the war (interview).

However, the unions (certainly in Scotland) were overwhelmingly critical of the war and could have urged their affiliated branches in constituencies with pro-war Labour MPs to threaten to use the trigger mechanism to instigate a challenge to those MPs. But they did not. This might seem puzzling to those many commentators in the press who regard trade unions simply as power-brokers – 'trade union barons' in the sloppy and prejudicial parlance – out to further their personal and institutional interests. But as Minkin has amply demonstrated, the nature of the union relationship to the party is far more complex than this. How unions behave is a function of what they deem appropriate, with the notion of what was appropriate being shaped by 'unwritten understandings and a strong sense of the protocol of rule-governed behaviour' (Minkin 1991: 27). One such rule that had emerged was that unions should, except in very exceptional circumstances, refrain from participating in or supporting any move to de-select a sitting MP or MSP. As one union official observed, unions 'certainly have the power to save an MP and they have done so numerous times' (interview).

The most publicised and politically inflamed case occurred in East Lothian, where Anne Moffat, a former president of Unison and a member of Labour's NEC, was narrowly selected for the 2001 general election (against airline pilot Doug Maughan, again attempting to win selection) with the energetic assistance of her union. It soon emerged that she was not a popular choice among party members and, over the years, hostility mounted. Not only had she acquired the reputation of being abrasive and somewhat intemperate in manner, she was regarded as elusive, rarely in the constituency and very seldom spoke in Parliament. In 2006 it was disclosed that in 2003–4 she had accumulated the highest travel bill of any Westminster politician (*The Herald*, 20, 24 November 2008). Indignation within the constituency party finally erupted in 2007, when four out of the six local party branches voted to de-select her, but this was blocked by affiliated union branches. In October 2007, an investigation by Scottish General Secretary Lesley Quinn uncovered anomalies with the selection process, but the NEC the following January voted to back the MP. In September the constituency passed a motion of no confidence in Mrs Moffat. The NEC's riposte in September was to suspend the constituency party. This became a source of huge embarrassment for the party, not only because of the MP's extravagance over travel and other expenses but because the MSP for (broadly) the same constituency was Iain Gray, then Scottish Labour leader. The long and bitter dispute continued and in January 2010 the dogged constituency party voted again to remove their MP (*BBC News*, 22 January 2010). At this point the NEC's prolonged and (for many within the local party) increasingly inexplicable defence of the MP – who was also suffering serious health problems – was reversed and it agreed to uphold the vote (*BBC News*, 23 March 2010).

There seems little doubt that the MP survived for so long because of Unison's efforts, supported by some other unions, to protect her (though on issues like the Iraq war – of which she was a fervent supporter – her views were at odds with her union). As one union leader commented, union votes 'can sometimes be used to save people who maybe shouldn't be saved' (interview). This was partly due to her position of seniority within the union and her membership of the NEC, but also reflected the convention in favour of sustaining sitting parliamentarians. There were solid political reasons for this convention. Unions understood the need for party cohesion and parliamentary discipline and were sensitive to any accusation that they might be using their position within the party to influence the behaviour or undermine the position of parliamentary representatives selected with their support. Further, establishing a rule or convention that normally it would not challenge an existing MP or MSP afforded some insulation for a union (like Unison) with strong left-wing elements clamouring for more pressure to be put on parliamentarians. The very fact that the ability to threaten or actually de-select MPs and MSPs was a potent lever was a problem because if used it would attract negative media attention which might be electorally harmful for the party. In short, there was doubt about the legitimacy of union mobilisation against sitting parliamentarians – 'opening up a can of worms', as one official put it (interview).

LOCAL NETWORKS

The third main circuit of influence in candidate selection is what can be loosely called the local network. Writing in the 1990s, Norris and Lovenduski found that, especially in safe seats, local influence networks mattered a great deal and this influence has persisted (Norris and Lovenduski 1995: 54). Such networks could take a variety of forms. The most common were those spawned by local government. A well-established local figure, such as a local council leader, would have a wide range of contacts and a sound grasp of the views, interests and personalities of local activists. John Hendry, a former leader of Stirling Council and a councillor for over thirty years, in seeking the Stirling nomination for the 2011 Holyrood elections had 'gone round every door, talked to everybody, he built up his base, got his people on side, they advocated for him, he got promises and he worked out who was support-ing him and got all his pledges' (interview, party official). He was selected but failed to defeat the SNP's sitting MSP Bruce Crawford. Council leaders in Labour's local heartlands, with their sometimes considerable powers of patronage, were particularly well placed to construct a web of supporters among fellow councillors and others who could be relied on to rally behind them in selection contests.

Another power base in some (though a declining number of) constituen-cies was the Labour Club. Joining the Labour Party was normally a condition of membership of Labour Clubs (with their economically priced alcoholic beverages) and – as in Cathcart, Tranent or Ayrshire, or infamously in George Galloway's period as Secretary/Organiser of the local party in Dundee in the early 1980s – they could substantially boost the size of the local party, supplying a large reservoir of members whose support could be crucial to the outcome of a selection contest. Sitting or retiring MPs and MSPs could also furnish valuable support. Most parliamentary representa-tives made a point of establishing for obvious reasons a local power base, utilising paid parliamentary aides, researchers and constituency workers, and these could also be activated to help an aspiring candidate who enjoyed their support. For example, Pamela Nash MP worked for three years as John Reid's parliamentary assistant before being selected to succeed him as a youth-ful Labour candidate for the safe seat of Airdrie and Shotts. Claims were made that constituency workers employed by Ochil and South Perthshire MP Gordon Banks were involved in organising his daughter's selection campaign for the (mostly overlapping) Holyrood seat of Clackmannan and Dunblane. (Eventually, amid some controversy, she withdrew from the contest.)

As noted previously, most selectorates were quite small (usually between 150 and 300) and hence it was feasible for a contender to contact every member, either by phone or personally. One candidate (who enjoyed a high public profile in the constituency), recalled, 'though the time was short, I phoned every member – mostly at least twice or one visit' (interview, MSP). Given the waning of ideological divisions within constituency parties, the ability to make a favourable impression on party members was crucial. Contacting all members, sometimes more than once, could be extremely time-consuming. The increasingly widespread use of postal votes made personal contact all the more vital, since fewer now attended hustings or selection meetings, conferring a considerable advantage to those embedded in local networks.

CONCLUSION

'The nature of the nominating procedure', according to Schnattschneider, 'determines the nature of the party; he who can make the nominations is the owner of the party. This is therefore one of the best points at which to observe the distribution of power within the party' (quoted in Gallagher and Marsh 1988: 3). So what does candidate selection in Scottish Labour tell us about the distribution of power within the party?

This debate about who exercises more control over the candidate selection (see, for example, Hopkin and Bradbury 2006; Bradbury 2009: 136) overlooks the possibility that no one actually exercises effective control and that power itself plays a rather smaller part in the process than often assumed. This account has suggested that the capacity to affect who is selected derives mainly through the exercise of *influence*, that is, the ability to induce others to alter their behaviour through persuasion, the exchange of favours or through the activation of a sense of shared identity, values and interests. Influence flows through networks through which the means to effect selection outcomes – political intelligence, contacts and resources – can be appropriated and mobilised. Three such networks are of particular importance – those operated by party officialdom, by the unions and those rooted in the localities (though there are other, less significant ones). It was rare for any one single institutional actor or network to be in the position to deliver seats, though in the 2001 Westminster selections, trade unions acting in a co-ordinated and organised fashion had a high success rate. One official summarised how selections worked as 'slightly chaotic with several influential players, none of whom can consistently be decisive influences in any given circumstance' (email communication).

The prevailing pattern of selection outcomes at any one point was the reflection of the shifting balance of contending forces and interests in a party whose internal processes were much more pluralistic than oligarchical in character. But, equally, they did not conform very closely to the strict canons of organisational democracy. Securing selection was always a struggle, but a struggle among a relatively small number of actors and interests. Candidate selection was a restricted process in two ways. Firstly it was network-driven, in that aspiring parliamentarians had only a slight chance of adoption unless they were attached to one of three major networks or circuits of influence.[8]

Even then, such a candidate must be able (ironically for the Labour Party) to command substantial personal resources. As one MSP remarked, 'If you are a candidate without resources, either personnel or money, then you are in trouble' (interview).

The process was also restricted by the size of the selectorate. OMOV had expanded the franchise to all party members, but as the party's membership (always modest in Scotland) continued to decline this meant that, in the bulk of constituencies, only small numbers were involved in the selection process. The result, Paul Hutcheon of the *Sunday Herald* claimed, was that for the 2011 Scottish elections, 'Scottish Labour maintained its long tradition of selecting members of whichever clique dominated local constituency parties' (*Sunday Herald*, 8 May 2011). This is too sweeping, not least in that it was rare for a single 'clique' to dominate CLPs. But it is true that the small size of most of the party's selectorate both makes the process easier to manage and imparts to it an insular character. Added to this was a rarely noted feature: a de-ideologisation of the process. The abating of ideological differences in the party meant that rival policy stances were of diminishing importance in selection contests, with candidates increasingly chosen on the basis of the personal qualities and political connections. The effect of this was to enhance the importance of those able to marshal network resources, rendering the pattern of political recruitment yet more enclosed.

NOTES

1. Labour Party NEC, Labour Party Selections for Scottish Parliament/Welsh Assembly elections, DO 24 January 1998.
2. Labour Party Rules and Standing Order, Appendix clauses 1 and 2, 2001.
3. Labour Party Rules and Standing Order, Appendix clause 3.9, 2001.
4. Labour Party NEC, Labour Party Selections for Scottish Parliament/Welsh Assembly elections, DO 24 January 1998.
5. Similarly, on the east coast the twinning of Midlothian and Edinburgh South was deemed to be risky since another prominent left-winger, Bob McLean, seemed likely to defeat a favoured Blairite from Edinburgh South. The solution was to set McLean against the sitting MP John Home Robertson by twinning Midlothian with East Lothian (*Tribune*, 19 June 1998; interview, party official). According to one official involved in the process, 'most twinning decisions – about 75% - were right, but there were some glaring mismatches. The result was to only exclude four or five who would otherwise have been selected' (interview).
6. As a senior party official noted, the key operators in seeking to mobilise support for a favoured candidate would not be 'full-time party staff but people that full-time party staff can trust'.
7. The 2001 number of Labour retirements was to be nearly excelled in 2005, with thirteen retirements (although boundary changes and the reduction in Scottish seats

reduced the number of Labour vacancies), and 2010 with nine retirements (plus two, Jim Devine and Anne Moffat, prevented from standing).

8. Mainly by squeezing through the middle on second-preference votes between network contenders.

CHAPTER 17

The Territorial Dimensions of Labour

INTRODUCTION

Devolution raised a whole series of questions for the territorial politics of the Labour Party. How should Labour, as a traditionally centralised party system, adapt its institutions to the post-devolution territorial settlement and to multi-level electoral competition? What degree of de-centralisation (if any) of party structure was required to enable it to discharge its functions as (it was supposed) the natural governing party of a devolved Scotland, as well as to hold off the challenge from the SNP? How should it seek to balance competing pressures for party unity and territorial autonomy? Further, what role should the Scottish party have in policy deliberations on reserved matters at UK level? How, in short, has a traditionally centralised party adapted to new territorial challenges in the post-devolution era?

In 1999, Matthew Taylor, a top Downing Street aide, claimed that 'ever since the referenda in 1997 made devolution to Scotland and Wales a reality the Labour Party has studiously avoided the central question it raises: should a political party devolve as much autonomy to its members in Scotland and Wales as Westminster has done to the Scottish and Welsh people?' (*The Guardian*, 11 May 1999) This chapter explores this question, investigating the extent to which Labour remains a centralised party, that is, 'one which features the concentration of effective decision-making authority in the national party organs' (Janda 1980: 10), or has become more de-centralised with more power exercised by the Scottish party.

In pursuing this theme the chapter distinguishes between a range of centrifugal and centripetal forces. In the former category one can discern three impulses which can be called 'the logic of constitutional de-centralisation', the 'logic of territorial party competition' and 'the logic of party management'. In the latter category one can identify two impulses, which can be labelled the 'logic of institutional inheritance' and the 'logic of party discipline'. This chapter suggests that the nature of Labour's post-devolution territorial settlement is largely a function of the interplay of these forces.

The logic of constitutional de-centralisation

It seems reasonable to suppose some sort of causal link between a country's constitutional design and the vertical organisation of state-wide parties. By its very nature constitutional de-centralisation, when it takes the form of the devolution of policy competences to a new sub-national elected body, would seem to imply a corresponding transfer of powers within parties. Thus Mitchell and Seyd hypothesised that devolution would 'produce centrifugal pressures within the Westminster parties, and ... more differentiation of policy within the parties in response to the particular needs of the regions ... Distinct policy agenda will be followed' (Mitchell and Seyd 1999: 109). More specifically, it has been argued (for example, Thorlakson 2009) that the precise impact of devolution on internal party arrangements will vary according to the form that the territorial re-organisation of competences takes. Where there are many overlapping policy jurisdictions, a high degree of policy co-operation between different territorial levels of government will be needed to ensure policy cohesion. Where the same party is in power at both levels, this will give the national party leadership a strong incentive to retain as much control as possible. Thus, Deschouwer contends that the greater the jurisdictional or functional overlap, the stronger the pressures on a state-wide party elite to reduce centre–periphery differences in policy and electoral strategy (Deschouwer 2003: 222). By the same token, where there are few overlapping policy jurisdictions, centrifugal pressures will be released. As Thorlakson explains, 'Extensive areas of exclusive sub-national legislative jurisdiction, which create legislative autonomy for sub-national governments, give the regions greater scope to develop independent policy stances, therefore making sub-national levels of the party more likely to demand the autonomy to allow them to pursue their own interests' (Thorlakson 2010). Not only would office-holders in the new tier of government be granted fresh powers, but they would also enjoy the legitimacy than only popular election can confer and this, too, will intensify pressure for 'party devolution'.

The logic of territorial party competition

Here the assumption is that the party system per se is a major variable affecting the distribution of power within parties operating at multi-territorial levels. The logic of territorial party competition hypothesises that in multi-level political systems, what can be called the 'regional' branches of state-wide parties require high levels of strategic and policy autonomy to compete effectively in the 'regional' electoral arena. The greater the disparities between party system structures at different territorial levels – and (hence) the more varied the range of strategic and political needs of different territorial units within a party – the greater the pressure for party de-centralisation (Laffin, Shaw and Taylor 2007: 94). This will in particular be the case where the state-wide party faces competition from a pro-independence party which will inevitably seek to portray it as subservient to the centre. As a result, pressure will build up for the party centre to re-distribute power internally in favour of regional elites (Hopkin and Bradbury 2006: 136). As Hopkin argues, party leaderships have a strong incentive to bolster the electoral appeal of their regional branches by 'allowing regional party organisations to adopt differentiated party programmes, discourses and campaigning strategies in an attempt to develop an ethno-regionalist "face"' (Hopkin 2003: 232).

The logic of party management

This derives from an appreciation of the coalitional character of political parties. Parties, especially in multi-level governmental systems, Eldersveld contends, are coalitions of ideological, social and geographic interests characterised by a high level of inter-dependence but with competing and potentially disruptive demands that need to be managed. In the effort to sustain a reasonable level of party cohesion and to find a formula which facilitates interest and policy accommodation, parties will adopt a 'stratarchical' pattern of power (Eldersveld 1964: 9). Under this system, power is diffused and stratified among a multiplicity of groups at various levels and in different locations, but with the leadership seeking to retain a strategic control capability (Eldersveld 1964: 9). Conflicts can be contained and managed by assigning to differing, spatially based, elites their own territorial jurisdictions, with overall party unity protected by fostering a culture in which inter-elite differences can be regulated and reconciled.

Balancing these centrifugal dynamics are centripetal ones, which we call the 'logic of institutional inheritance' and the 'logic of party discipline'.

The logic of institutional inheritance

Hopkin and Bradbury argue that 'politicians may have incentives to behave in certain ways to enhance their power, but they generally do so within political organisations that have their own histories, ideological traditions, formal rules, [and] standard operating procedures' (Hopkin and Bradbury 2006:

301

136). Patterns of behaviour and the repertoire of available strategies, in short, are structured by established organisational formats. The trajectory of institutional evolution, Panebianco maintains, 'is strictly conditioned by the relations that the party establishes in the genetic phases', how it originated and how it consolidated in its formative years (Panebianco 1988: 20). As noted above, party-building varies according to whether it principally takes the form of territorial penetration or territorial diffusion. Territorial penetration, to recapitulate, occurs when organisational construction at the 'periphery' is directed and shaped by a party's central authorities, territorial diffusion when the initiative is taken by local groups or elites that are only later integrated into a national organisation (Panebianco 1988: 50). Once a set of structures has acquired a definitive form, subsequent organisational changes are (in the absence of major crises) likely to be path-dependent, with any proposals for radical innovation encountering serious resistance. De-centralising reforms, it follows, are likely to be inhibited in parties (like Labour) characterised by territorially centralised arrangements.

The logic of party discipline

This arises from the dynamics of professionalised political campaigning, with its strong emphasis on disciplined communication and the delivery of a single, cohesive message. The 'professionalisation' of political communications prescribes the centralised management of all communication processes, with the focus on the production and transmission of a few core messages articulating what the party stands for (its 'brand') and to which all members of a party are expected to adhere. Disciplined communication is rendered even more important by the all-pervasive influence of the media eager ruthlessly to exploit any sign of internal party disagreements or 'splits'. Being 'on message' is seen as vital in that it is assumed that 'divided parties lose elections'. From this perspective the ability of sub-national party organisations to devise their own programmes and campaign appeals needs to be curtailed if this poses any risk of undermining or detracting from the national party 'brand'.

How did Labour respond to these competing centrifugal and centripetal dynamics? Devolution led to the creation within the Labour Party of new roles and institutions, including (as has been seen) the Scottish Policy Forum, the Scottish Parliamentary Labour Group, the Scottish Parliamentary Labour Group and frontbenchers in office and opposition. These new roles and institutions were inserted within the traditional structure of the UK-wide party, with authority invested in a range of institutions including the leader, the NEC, the National Policy Forum and conference. The rest of this chapter will trace the shifting territorially defined institutional order within the party by investigating the division of powers and functions between its national and Scottish institutions in the following three key areas of programme development, candidate and leader selection, and party administration and finance.

How institutions operate and interact with each other are not solely a function of the powers allotted to them, or the ambitions of those who hold positions of power and authority, but of the encompassing culture. Minkin first drew attention to the impact of culture – or what he called (in inverted commas) the 'rules' – in regulating the conduct of key actors in the Labour Party (Minkin 1991). A party's culture can here be defined as 'the unique configuration of norms, values, beliefs, ways of behaving and so on that characterise the manner in which groups and individuals combine to get things done' (Eldridge and Combie 1974: 89). A party's organisational culture includes conventions that structure and regulate the way in which decisions are made and expectations as to how roles should be performed. Precisely what these norms and conventions are, and how they should be interpreted and applied, has always been a matter of debate within a party such as Labour which incorporates within itself a broad range of views, values and interests. Devolution added a further dimension, with the inevitable potential conflict between centre and periphery. A key to understanding the re-shaping of power relations within the party was the emergence in response to the new devolved settlement of a new set of territorial 'rules' or territorially based 'party accord'. The term 'political accord' refers to an 'underlying pattern of norms that governs and regulates the relationships among territorially-defined party units and which spells out their rights and responsibilities' (Carty 2004: 21).

POLICY DEVELOPMENT

As has been noted in Chapter 15, Labour's internal policy-making system was re-organised in 1997 to take account of the devolution settlement, with the Scottish Policy Forum and other party institutions empowered to formulate proposals in those policy arenas falling within the Scottish Parliament's remit. Responsibility for formulating policy in these devolved areas was hived out to Scotland, with little UK oversight. Limited policy overlap meant that for the key policy areas devolved to Scotland, only a relatively modest degree of interaction and co-ordination between the two levels of government was required. In both education and health, the pursuit by Scottish Labour of its own distinctive, more collectivist trajectory could in large part proceed unhindered, since there was no institutional requirement or political pressure

303

to align it with the British Labour 'modernisation' agenda being implemented in England.

The British Labour leadership's response to policy divergence in these areas was largely one of more or less benign detachment. This stance reflected the first principle or convention of the 'territorial party accord', 'subsidiarity'. The practice of subsidiarity, if not its language, meant that Scottish Labour should be left free to determine policy within areas clearly assigned to the Scottish Parliament, with minimal central intervention (except if there was a knock-on effect). Labour was responsible for the new devolved arrangements and plainly had a vested interest in consolidating them by ensuring that they worked effectively. 'The logic of constitutional de-centralisation' suggested that where there were extensive areas of exclusive regional legislative jurisdiction, it made a great deal of both institutional and political sense to devolve legislative power to the corresponding level of party organisation. Although, as has been seen, in the key areas of health and education the Labour–Lib Dem Scottish administration pursued policies which deviated, in some respects quite markedly, from Westminster, no formal attempt was made to restrain it. 'I never felt pressure from Westminster on any of our devolved responsibilities', Jack McConnell observed (interview). Post-devolution the UK Labour Government sought territorial stability and had no wish to commit, nor did it see any profit in committing, political capital or institutional resources to centralised territorial management. As McConnell's political advisor noted, broadly speaking the British Labour leadership was content to allow Scottish Labour to discharge its responsibilities as it saw fit. 'They just didn't want to get involved, they had bigger fish to fry' (interview, Danny Phillips). The fact that there were few (exceptions are discussed below) overlapping policy jurisdictions facilitated a broadly hands-off posture.

The 'logic of territorial party competition' stipulates that where a party is competing for power at different territorial levels, it will benefit from devolving power to lower-level units to allow maximum flexibility. The party below state-wide level is likely to be better equipped to develop appropriate electoral platforms than central authorities, especially where (as in the UK) there are major disparities in the structures of party competition at different territorial levels. For Westminster elections the main axis of party competition is between Labour and the Conservatives, and the exigencies of the electoral system place a premium on the ability to capture floating voters in marginal constituencies. In Scotland, in contrast, the axis tilts much more to the left, with Labour's main competitor the social democratic SNP and with additional threats posed (at least between 2003 and 2007) by other parties occupying broadly similar ideological territory such as the Greens and SSP.

In such circumstances, empowering Scottish Labour to etch out for itself its own distinctive policy profile made a great deal of electoral sense.

There was one major exception to this hands-off policy. As has been seen above (see Chapter 11), the decision by Henry McLeish to adopt the Sutherland Report and institute free personal care for the elderly infuriated New Labour ministers, who demanded that the First Minister change tack. Pressure from the centre and Downing Street proved – quite predictably – futile. A broad coalition of support in the Scottish Parliament favoured the policy, so that even if McLeish had yielded to UK demands the policy would have been enacted. Indeed, what is instructive about the episode was London's slowness to grasp the damaging effects if it had forced a policy U-turn. The credibility of Scottish Labour as an independent voice of Scotland would have been seriously damaged, its leadership humiliated, relations with its coalition partners impaired and the SNP would have been exultant.

How then can we account for the UK Government's flat-footed intervention? The main reason was that indignant ministers – notably Brown and Milburn – felt that McLeish had brazenly flouted the second principle of the territorial party accord – the 'no surprises' convention. According to this, Labour leaders at the two levels of government would refrain from any action likely to cause cross-territorial political difficulties without full consultation, with any troublesome issues resolved quietly by discreet, behind-the-scenes discussions. The launch by McLeish of a major policy innovation with potentially damaging repercussions for the Westminster Government was perceived as a flagrant breach of this convention (interview, Helen Liddell) and a source of acute political embarrassment since it undermined Westminster's justification for rejecting free personal care as financially unaffordable.

But the row had de-stabilising effects and was the only real open rupture in relations between the two governments between 1999 and 2007. It demonstrated (in intra-party terms) the limits of devolution for a leadership – Blair and Brown – already acquiring a reputation for top-down party management and centralising policies. As one former Scottish Parliament minister commented, in London 'people couldn't, can't get their head round the idea that the whole point of devolution was about things being done differently' – even if it did cause 'political embarrassment' (interview). However, London Labour's failure to deflect McLeish from his path and the counter-productive nature of its effort to do so did drive home and it never again sought to muscle into an area that fell squarely into the ambit of the Scottish Parliament.

The Scottish party also drew its own lessons from the episode and in exploring these one can see opposing centripetal forces at work. Its brief period of assertiveness under McLeish was not repeated under his more wary successor, Jack McConnell, who made great efforts to maintain a collaborative relationship with the Blair Government. Thus he abandoned any effort to claw back the Department of Work and Pensions' Attendance Allowance funding which the UK Government pronounced had been forfeited when Scotland adopted free personal care, depriving Scotland of money that could have been used to defray part of the cost of the programme. Equally, he avoided Welsh First Minister Rhodri Morgan's rhetoric about 'clear red water' dividing Westminster and Wales.

But if a stance of mutual restraint was adopted there were, perhaps inevitably, clashes beneath the surface. The most notable was the dispute in early 2007 over the nurses' pay award. The UK NHS pay review body had recommended a 2.5% pay increase for all nurses. This had been accepted by the Westminster Government but it had – to the anger of the unions – decided to phase in its implementation. In contrast, the Scottish Executive promised immediate implementation of the pay award which, it stated, was affordable within the existing health budget. This caused political difficulties for the New Labour Government, with the unions clamouring that it follow the precedent set by the Scots. Publicly the Treasury refused to be drawn on the Scottish settlement, insisting it was a matter for the Scottish Executive (*The Herald*, 13 March 2007). In private, heated words were exchanged. As one insider recalled, 'Gordon Brown went utterly mental and phoned up Jack bawling and shouting at him' (interview). But McConnell, Andy Kerr the Health Minister and Finance Minister Tom McCabe, the three key figures who had taken the decision, stood firm and Brown had to swallow the decision.

The key factor here – aside from the fact that immediate payment *was* affordable – was electoral. This was in the run-up to the Scottish elections and the SNP would obviously have exploited the failure of the Labour–Lib Dem Executive in Scotland to pay the whole increase immediately. As a senior union leader recalled, 'we've just watched *Sky News* and there's [Health Secretary] Patricia Hewitt announcing that she's phasing the pay award . . . Andy [Kerr] was furious, absolutely steaming and he said this is bloody outrageous. I said it's a devolved issue Andy, you don't have to do what Patricia Hewitt does. I said you've got the budget . . . you can go and pay it anyway' (interview). And he did.

This episode affords an example of two logics in conflict with each other: that of territorial party competition and that of party management. On the one hand, passively following Westminster's lead over the nurses' pay settlement with an election imminent would have been a hostage to fortune; on the other, breaking with it inevitably caused it severe political strains on an always contentious and emotive issue. The British party made appeals to

306

party solidarity: 'you've got to behave yourself, boys', Douglas Alexander, the Scottish Secretary of State, admonished trade union leaders at a Scottish Trades Union Labour Group meeting (interview, trade union official), but not surprisingly in the circumstances, such appeals did not wash.

A second source of tension was over 'dawn raids in Dungavel'. Despite the few areas of clear policy overlap, in practice 'there is a high degree of functional dependence between devolved and reserved questions' (Keating 2001). An illustration was the operation of policy over immigration and asylum-seekers, a matter which falls within the responsibility of Westminster. The Dungavel Detention Centre was established in 2001 to accommodate removed, failed or illegal asylum-seekers and their families. A row exploded in the summer of 2003 over the forced internment of the children of asylum-seekers at Dungavel and 'dawn raids' by Home Office and Immigration officials to deport asylum-seekers from the UK. The issue generated an outcry in Scotland, with demands that the Executive intervene to stop the detentions and deportations. Scotland's Children's Commissioner, deploring the raids and the detainment of children as breaches of the Children Scotland Act, pointed out that while immigration and asylum were reserved matters, services relating to the care of asylum-seekers and their families – healthcare, education, housing and so forth – were not (Mooney and Williams 2006: 620). Though representations were made in private, despite mounting pressure, McConnell studiously avoided any comment that might be construed as criticism of colleagues in London.

The controversy highlighted tensions over Labour's territorial accord. Scottish Labour ministers defended their refusal to be drawn into the debate on the grounds that constitutionally the issues raised were unequivocally reserved but, as they were well aware, Westminster's actions had contaminating political repercussions in Scotland. London appeared unaware of or unconcerned about the fact that Scotland had responsibilities for the education and welfare of children held in Dungavel. As the relevant Scottish minister recollected, 'It was horrifying to deal with the Home Office. It was an absolute shock about how completely they didn't get things in Scotland. They just had no concept whatever of what we are contending with in terms of the politics of it all' (interview, Peter Peacock). Scottish Labour incurred much odium from the episode, a matter to which British Labour appeared ignorant or indifferent.

All this suggests that the 'territorial party accord' was ill defined and to a degree differentially understood. This point can be further amplified by making a distinction between two roles enacted by the Scottish party. The first is its *government function*, as a main contender for office in Holyrood and delivering policy on devolved policy questions. The second is its *intra-party function*, where it can act as the voice of Scottish Labour on reserved issues. In the former the British party accepted that policy areas that fell within the jurisdiction of the Scottish Parliament should equally (with the caveats identified above) fall within the remit of its Scottish wing. But it was more reluctant to accede the same latitude to the *intra-party function*, the freedom of the Scottish party institutions to articulate its own view on reserved policy.

The issue of the second role sprang up in the most dramatic of ways in 2003, as the Scottish party conference in March that year coincided with the imminent outbreak of the Iraq war. CLPs and trade unions had submitted emergency resolutions to the conference opposing British military intervention, but the British Labour leadership (with support from among the Scottish party leadership) went to extraordinary lengths to exclude them from the agenda. Although they would have no constitutional standing, such resolutions, if passed (as was quite possible), would have been politically damaging, highlighting serious internal party opposition to Blair's policy. Party officials (under prompting from London) ruled that since foreign policy was outside Scottish jurisdiction, conference had no right to debate the issue. One MP recalled, 'Suddenly someone started saying that the Scottish conference should only be discussing Holyrood matters. This was new to us' (interview, Ann McKechin). In fact, the constitutional position was much more ambiguous: while the right to *determine* foreign policy matters was vested in the British party, there was no obvious reason why the Scottish conference should forfeit its right to *discuss* them. But, as a former minister put it, 'we were reluctant to step out of line. McConnell was virtually told to back Blair over Iraq' (interview). Unions who had moved the emergency resolution reacted angrily and a compromise was hastily cobbled together in which discussion was allowed (see Chapter 7 for reflections on the debate). Crucially, the leadership succeeded in avoiding a vote so the Scottish party was debarred from expressing a view on a question of vital national concern.

Constitutional matters, though integral to the devolution settlement, were also reserved and here too the British party could be heavy-handed. For example, when the Scottish party indicated that it wished to insert into the manifesto for the 2007 Holyrood elections proposals to expand the powers of the Scottish Parliament, the then Scottish Secretary, Douglas Alexander, objected on the ground that the issue was reserved. He only relented when reminded that the British Labour leadership had not demurred when similar proposals had appeared in the Welsh manifesto (interview, senior trade union official).

A politically much more serious instance of tensions and ambiguities over future constitutional change occurred in May 2008.[1] The SNP Government had been elected as a minority committed to bringing forward a parliamentary bill on independence later in their first term. In May 2008 (as discussed in Chapter 8) Wendy Alexander, with the words 'Bring it on', abruptly shifted Scottish Labour into supporting an independence referendum. This had not been adequately discussed or agreed in the Scottish Labour Group of MSPs, let alone among the Westminster Labour Group of Scottish MPs. However, copies of a paper written by the leader's office contemplating a reversal of Scottish Labour's stance on the referendum had been circulated to both Gordon Brown and his predecessor, Tony Blair. The latter had replied (in positive terms), but not the former. Impatient with the delay and noting that Charlie Whelan (an unofficial Brown spin doctor) had briefed the Scottish papers indicating sympathy for a referendum, Wendy Alexander decided to seize the bull by the horns and made her declaration. She was promptly disowned by Brown and became the butt of 'a lot of vicious briefing. The great clunking fist had landed', as one Labour staffer put it. Alexander was left seriously discomfited, her authority badly eroded, and the issue of who had the strategic and political power to advance such a policy position left in total disarray.

What do these examples tell us about the nature of the party's territorial accord? Firstly, the impact of the 'logic of party discipline'. New Labour strategists insisted that only tightly disciplined parties with highly cohesive electoral messages could win elections. Membership of the party involved, a senior New Labour advisor maintained, 'acceptance of its core political identity . . . A party's integrity depends on it embodying a single set of values, principles and core policies regardless of where it operates.' This 'core political identity' was set by the New Labour creed, or 'brand'. While the question of the degree to which Scottish and Welsh Labour could adopt different policies was an appropriate matter for 'negotiation', what was not in question was the right 'to redesign the political platform of each party' (Taylor, 1999). Any questioning of 'the brand', any public display of disagreement – so the argument ran – would be seized on by a ravenous media with an insatiable appetite for exploiting party 'wrangles'. This thinking, underpinned by the pull of party solidarity, deeply permeated the Scottish party, whose leaders were exceedingly chary about any public utterances that could be interpreted as criticism of Labour in Westminster. 'We were so loyal to Labour and did not want to see splits because splits bring down governments and that's what the media would have loved, north and south of the border' (interview, Peter Peacock).

What of 'subsidiarity'? The party's 'territorial accord' revealed itself to be rather lop-sided in practice. Under McConnell, Scottish Labour always trod lightly to avoid any potential embarrassment to Labour in London, eschewing (unlike Rhodri Morgan) the language of 'clear red water'. It persisted with its own distinctive policies but these were always justified as 'Scottish solutions to Scottish problems' and not as any challenges to the New Labour 'brand'. There was, former First Minister Henry McLeish recalled, a tendency 'to constantly look over our shoulder to Westminster' to avoid 'rocking the boat' (*The Sunday Times*, 10 August 2008). McConnell chose 'to cleave closely to the New Labour Government, carefully avoiding criticism or comment where things were done differently in England, and maintaining a strict ban on ministers making their views known on reserved matters' (Keating 2005: 127).

The problem was that this was not always fully reciprocated, as the examples of Dungavel, nurses' pay and 'Bring it on' illustrate. Scottish (and Welsh) elections were regarded as 'second order' elections and hence did not figure very prominently in British Labour's strategic calculations. What really mattered was the impact of dissension on the *national* image of the party – the reverse was less important. The British Labour leadership did not fully appreciate the 'logic of territorial party competition', the need for the Scottish party to project its own distinctive profile. As Jack McConnell recalled, 'my problems with Westminster were with their management of their responsibilities and the impact on Scotland – the political fallout in Scotland' (interview). Too fearful of trampling on toes or causing the centre offence, the result was, as Tom McCabe put it, all too often Labour found itself resorting to the 'obscure language of prevarication' (*Sunday Herald*, 3 August 2008), depriving the Scottish party of the clarity and sharpness of message it required to compete with the SNP.

CANDIDATE SELECTION AND LEADERSHIP ELECTION

Control over candidate selection is a crucial determinant of the internal balance of power in a party. For this reason some have argued that control over the process would be a power lever that the British party leadership would be reluctant to relinquish. Thus, van Biezen and Hopkin anticipated that 'if sub-national tiers of government wield significant power, national leaders will be similarly concerned to ensure that the "right" candidates are selected for elections to regional and local institutions' (van Biezen and Hopkin 2006: 16). This has not proved to be the case in Scotland. Although the NEC retained (until the rule changes of 2011) the overall right to set the rules regulating all internal party activities, including candidate selection, it has delegated responsibility for drawing up, administering and making detailed procedural arrangements for selection to Holyrood to the Scottish Executive Committee. The candidate selection process for the first elections to Holyrood (as discussed in chapters 5 and 16) was highly contentious. but the territorial cleavage was not a significant one and it was over-shadowed by others, political, ideological and institutional.

'The logic of party management' asserts that a stratified system of power will ease the task of party management in territorially diversified parties by relieving the burden on the party centre of managing conflict. Not only had candidate selection – where personal ambitions intersect with broader conflicts over power, democracy and ideology – always been a perennial source of contention in the Labour Party, but equally it had been a time-consuming and onerous activity for over-worked and under-resourced party officials. Thus it made sense for the British party to devolve responsibility to the Scottish party. Intervention by British Labour, either by shaping the rules and procedures or through involvement in local selection contests, would have embroiled it in conflicts and it is not clear what benefits would have accrued. As one party official explained, if a problem arose the General Secretary in London was likely to tell Scotland 'you deal with it, I just don't want to get involved, I don't want to stick my nose in, I'll just get my head bitten off'. Even if a Scottish official sought advice from Head Office officials on the interpretation of rules, 'they would rather not get involved' (interview). As it was, the NEC retained responsibility for Westminster selections, some of which proved quite troublesome and distracting enough without heaping on added burdens.

A party can also centrally exercise control over regional-level parties through influencing the election of regional leaders. Dewar, uniquely of all the holders of the position of Scottish parliamentary leader,was a major power-broker in his own right. His emergence as first leader of Scottish Labour MSPs was in effect a coronation. The McLeish–McConnell contest in 2000 was close and some commentators have detected the hand of Gordon Brown in the former's success, but he clearly had strong support within the Scottish parliamentary party. When McLeish resigned just over a year later, initially Wendy Alexander considered standing but in the event McConnell was elected unopposed. When McConnell resigned, he was replaced by Wendy Alexander in September 2007, but again without a contest. The following June she resigned and Iain Gray emerged triumphant after a three-cornered fight with Andy Kerr and Cathy Jamieson. Overall there is little evidence of any concerted effort by the leadership of the British party to influence any of these elections – not surprisingly, since such intervention would have carried costs for no palpable benefits.

However, on one important point the British party was, until recently, obdurate. The figures mentioned have all occupied the post of leader of the Scottish Labour Parliamentary Group and not of the Scottish Labour Party, a position formally occupied by the British party leader. This mattered both symbolically and practically, because it undermined the authority and reach of the person who led the party in the Scottish Parliament and, even more when Labour was in opposition, diminished the status of the post. It meant that Scottish Labour lacked a leader empowered to run the party and exercise full responsibility for its policy direction.

Election defeats, particularly if massive and unexpected, have always acted as an engine of party organisational change, and so it proved in this instance. Shortly after the election the party established a working group led by Jim Murphy MP and Sarah Boyack MSP which reported four months later (September 2011). The report was unanimously endorsed by the Scottish Executive Committee on 10 September 2011 and by the UK party conference later that month. It was finally debated and approved by a special Scottish Labour Party conference on 29 October 2011. A major rule change was to create the post of leader of the Scottish Labour Party, the holder of which would be entrusted with responsibilities for the organisation, management, programme and strategy of the party.[2]

PARTY ORGANISATION AND FINANCE

Responsibility for policy formation, candidate selection and leadership election had been largely transferred to the Scottish party, but finance and staffing remained under the authority of the party centre. Control over the administrative apparatus confers the ability to apportion funds, organise campaigns, manage internal communications and allocate staffing resources. There have been some small moves towards party devolution. After 1994 the Scottish General Secretary (previously appointed by the NEC) was selected by a joint board of the SEC and NEC. (Colin Smyth was appointed in 2008 by a panel with three members of the SEC and two members from the NEC; party communication.) This change enlarged the Scottish General Secretary's Scottish mandate but he remained ultimately answerable to the centre.

'The organisational level that controls the allocation of funds', Janda states, 'is in a powerful position to set priorities for the attainment of party goals' (Janda 1980: 111). The ability to determine how funds are dispensed can be used to shape party priorities and influence the behaviour of those whose salaries depend on central funding decisions. The Scottish party has traditionally been poorly resourced and financially heavily reliant on the British party. This meant it could call on London to help finance an administrative support machine and a range of campaigning activities that it could not afford if reliant on its own resources, but it did create a relationship of dependency. Equally, the SEC not only lacked any significant research or policy-making capacity but also the means to run effective campaigning and communications operations.

However, the balance of responsibilities between the centre and Scotland was altered by rule changes approved by the British and Scottish party conferences in autumn 2011. In Jim Murphy's words, 'we are completing the devolution of the Scottish Labour Party. From now on, whatever is devolved to the Scottish Parliament will be devolved to the Scottish Labour Party.' The Scottish party was given full responsibility for all organisation matters, including the rules for Scottish Parliament selections, Scottish leadership elections and local government processes and selections.[3] However, the implications of this for financial arrangements and organisational structures have yet to be spelled out.

CONCLUSION

How can the power relationship between the British and Scottish party be summed up? To what degree and over what areas has power been devolved to the Scottish party? This chapter identified three centrifugal forces, the logics of constitutional de-centralisation, of territorial party competition and of party management; and two centripetal forces, the logics of institutional inheritance and of party discipline. It suggested that the shape of Labour's post-devolution territorial settlement would be configured by the interplay of these forces as, in turn, moulded and embodied in the party's territorial accord.

The centrifugal logics anticipated that the party's most rational response to the devolved settlement would be to allow the regional levels of party organisation the latitude to meet their governing and electoral challenges by adopting policies and campaign strategies geared to local conditions. This in large measure occurred (Laffin and Shaw 2007: 65). On matters of devolved policy, the British party has accommodated itself to a functionally based re-distribution of powers and responsibilities within a loose framework of policy consensus. The Scottish party acquired the ability to formulate its own distinctive policies and for the most part British Labour acknowledged the need for flexibility and discretion. The imbroglio over free personal care taught the lesson, if such was needed, that anything that smacked too overtly of central imposition was politically quite counter-productive. The British party leadership on the whole thereafter adopted a permissive attitude to policies pursued in Scotland – as long as they did not threaten to cause it major political problems. It recognised that the combination of different electoral and party systems coupled with the need for coalition government confronted Scottish Labour with a different set of pressures and strategic choices to which it had to respond (Laffin, Shaw and Taylor 2007: 105).

313

The national party elite has recognised that devolved power and functional autonomy afforded the most effective way of sustaining overall party
cohesion, but with an important caveat: there should be no open challenge
to the New Labour 'brand'. 'To suggest', a senior New Labour advisor opined,
'that devolution to the Scottish Parliament means that Scottish Labour
politicians have free rein to redesign the party's values and core policies is to
deny the very definition of a political party' (Matthew Taylor, *The Guardian*,
11 May 1999). This did not prevent Scottish Labour from pursuing policies,
notably in health and education, that embodied values quite different from
those that animated New Labour, but it did inhibit it from advertising the
fact. This reticence helped the SNP in its efforts to depict Scottish Labour
as 'London Labour', a powerful polemical political point which significantly
hurt and restricted the Scottish party.

A distinction was made between Scottish Labour's governing function,
its responsibility for formulating policy on devolved matters, and its intra-
party function, the task of acting as the voice of the party in Scotland on
reserved matters. This latter task has at best been weakly developed. As
Jack McConnell later reflected, 'Scotland had a distinctive political identity
and the Scottish party should have the right to reflect the opinions of party
members in Scotland on reserved matters, which should be heeded by UK
leadership.' Unfortunately 'the national party doesn't recognise this' (interview).

What of other areas of party activity? Some commentators anticipated that
the selection process would become a cockpit of the struggle for supremacy
between national and sub-national elites (van Biezen and Hopkin 2006:
16). This did not happen. To the extent that the centre intervened it was
with the active collaboration of powerful members of the Scottish Labour
establishment. Equally, there is no solid evidence that the British leadership
ever made any serious efforts to swing outcomes in elections for the leadership of the Scottish Labour Parliamentary Group. But British Labour did
retain control over the party organisation and staffing, and the Scottish party
remained dependent on the centre for adequate funding, which counter-
vailed de-centralising trends.

Until 2011 only piecemeal changes had occurred in structural relations
within the party, with any strategic, post-devolution re-shaping of Labour's
institutional machinery avoided. The logic of institutional inheritance
coupled with the logic of party discipline had contained and restrained any
pressure for a radical alteration in Labour's internal relationships, even after
the party's ejection from office in 2007. But the status quo did not and could
not survive its crushing defeat four years later. As noted, in September and
October 2011 the British and Scottish conferences approved a series of rule

change which re-defined the relationship between the two parties, creating the new post of Scottish party leader, extending the powers for the Scottish party and re-drawing constituency party boundaries to follow Holyrood rather than Westminster lines. Sarah Boyack MSP declared that 'Labour used that Scottish Parliament to deliver important reforms for Scotland, but we didn't reform ourselves. Now we need to make devolution a reality within our party too.'[4]

Notes

1. This paragraph is based on interviews.
2. MPs as well as MSPs were eligible to compete for the post, though they must commit to seek election as an MSP and First Minister.
3. http://www.scottishlabour.org.uk/new-position-of-scottish-labour-leader
4. Ibid.

CONCLUSION

The Forward March of Scottish Labour Halted?

INTRODUCTION

At the beginning of this book we posed the range of questions that we aimed to address, examining a series of political, policy and socio-economic factors. In this concluding chapter we set out to explore a number of key areas which have emerged throughout the book, namely, the context of Scottish Labour as part of British Labour and the impact of the British state, the existence and evolution of a distinct Scottish social democracy, the internal dynamics and cultures of the party, and from this its future challenges and prospects.

SCOTTISH LABOUR AND BRITISH LABOUR IN A UNION STATE BRITAIN

The British constitution in traditionalist accounts is characterised as a unitary state representing one central authority with little limits on its power, a degree of standardisation, and parliamentary sovereignty meaning that political power is meant to sit absolutely and unconditionally with the UK Parliament (King 2007). Such constitutional arrangements, so the reasoning runs, have constrained Labour's own structures and internal operations. The centralism implicit in parliamentary supremacy fashioned 'the way the party goes about its business: a centralised party for a centralised system' (Sharpe,1982: 150). Unitary politics meant that there could be no middle ground between the Westminster status quo and Scottish independence; Dalyell argued with a certain logic that devolution was not possible in a unitary state (Dalyell 1977). In the House of Commons in a 1977 parliamentary debate on Scottish devolution he stated: 'Would it not just be more honest to admit that it is impossible to have an Assembly – especially any kind of subordinate Parliament – that is part, though only part of a unitary state?' (House of Commons, Vol. 939, cols 78–9, 14 November 1977).

However, increasingly this is recognised by political analysts and commentators as folklore and myth. For example, it has been clear for nearly four decades, since the UK joined the then EEC, that parliamentary sovereignty in the old-fashioned Diceyian sense is no longer applicable in today's world. Instead, the argument is now increasingly put that the UK is a 'union state', one with significant degrees of de-centralisation, diverse arrangements and, importantly, in relation to Scotland, the retention of pre-union rights (Rokkan and Stein 1982; Mitchell 1996).

The union state account of Britain can explain the multi-dimensional nature of the UK; the fact that, post-1707, Scotland, Wales and Northern Ireland all developed their own territorially distinctive politics long before the most recent devolution proposals. Vernon Bogdanor, the respected British constitutional theorist, understood that the union state reflected the nature of the UK:

> It was precisely because Britain was a territorially differentiated union state, as opposed to a unitary state, that governments were able to react with some flexibility to the challenges posed by the demand for Scottish and Welsh autonomy. (Bodganor 2009: 273)

Meanwhile, union state thinking has further developed, suggesting that the UK is evolving into 'a state of unions' whereby the emerging territorial politics and creation of distinct political spaces and voices are developing a politics where the relationships of the different unions come to the fore (Mitchell 2009).

This analysis is apposite and relevant to the experience and dynamics of British Labour. The party's constitution on first reading seems straightforward and unambiguous: this is a centralist, unitary party that shadows and has the same undiluted sense of power as the British constitution. However, this interpretation is as misleading for Labour as it is for the UK as a whole. While it is true that under Blair and Brown the leadership sought to impose a highly centralised system, this represented a break with tradition. Indeed, it was precisely because of its disparate and pluralistic character – rendering it so often difficult to manage – that the founders of New Labour were so keen to install a centralised command structure. This was less than successful, as witnessed by rebuffs over leadership of the Welsh Labour Party, the London mayoralty and the first Holyrood selections – not to mention the rising tide of House of Commons rebellions (Cowley 2005). Not surprisingly, Labour found it had to adapt, evolve and develop different party positions, values and traditions in different parts of the UK, whatever Blairites and New Labour advocates think. A union Labour politics exists explicitly in Scotland and Wales, and can even be seen embryonically in the increasingly territorial politics of the London mayor and Greater London politics.

Devolution was a product of the dynamics and pressures of the increasingly divergent politics across the UK in different nations, city regions and regions, and it aided the explicit emergence of a union politics which had always been implicit in the UK since its establishment as a state in 1707. Post-devolution union politics in the UK posed significant challenges to most British political philosophies. One basic issue was that after 1999 the British Labour leadership in part effectively forgot about Scotland, only snapping to attention when some crisis or election defeat seemed imminent, or when policies pursued there threatened to cause political embarrassment (see below). This mattered because the British political centre, Westminster, Whitehall and its surrounding policy communities, still impacted on Scotland and Wales in terms of legislation, funding and what the British state did in their names.

The Westminster understanding of the UK post-devolution did not evolve into embracing a more diverse, pluralist, de-centralist politics and state. Instead, there was a visible degree of retreat and retrenchment, as the state did not embark on a new phase of comprehensive constitutional reform at the centre that changed fundamentally its character. The political centre post-1997 regressed into embracing a unitary state interpretation of the UK; in some analyses the Blairite desire for a new fulcrum of power, a 'Presidential' Number 10 and a centre operating as an advocate for corporate and business interests (Allen 2003; Hassan and Barnett 2009).

Much of this is not that surprising and needs to be seen in the longer time-frame of how Labour has traditionally understood the UK and the British state. While throughout Labour's history there have always been differing accounts and alternatives, such as the ILP ethical socialists and guild socialists in the party's early years, the main, dominant account from the 1920s was one of unconditionally celebrating the British state as a 'neutral' entity which could, with the right political instructions, be a force for good, progress and radical change (Greenleaf 1983a, 1983b; Dennis and Halsey 1988). This version drew from Fabian thinking and was given validation by Labour's victory and achievements in 1945 and after; this took succour from buying into the Whig version of British history and the state, and seeing it as having the potential to be adapted for progressive goals and ends.

This perspective fed into and informed a much wider, inclusive Labour story of Britain which was meant to be a counter-story to the powerful, confident, establishment-focused Tory version, but which was uncritical of large aspects of 'the Conservative nation' (Gamble 1974; Aughey 2001). Labour's account was a people's story of these isles, of the power of the state, of collective action and organised labour; a politics that while it can be over-sentimentalised or over-criticised, did connect and have a relevance to millions of people across the UK. This political perspective had numerous strengths, giving Labour an over-arching purpose and sense, in Harold Wilson's words that 'the party was a crusade or it was nothing', but it did have major weaknesses such as its lack of understanding of the need for greater democratisation in public life, its innate conservatism, and its failure to understand the character and nature of the British state (Marquand 2008).

British Labour's historic and contemporary attitude of advocating a conventional and conservative order version of the UK has significantly posed problems for Scottish Labour (and Welsh Labour as well). Even more, it has limited the radical potential of a different kind of British politics and statehood, one more fluid, flexible and diverse, relevant to the early twenty-first century of shared sovereignties and multiple, overlapping identities. Instead, British Labour was still hidebound to the Westminster traditions and myths of parliamentary sovereignty. This increasingly produced a disjuncture between the politics as understood by the centre, and the political dynamics and developments in the nations and regions of the UK.

A union politics or state of unions – and not a unitary state – was implicitly what Scottish Labour, along with Welsh Labour, represented pre-devolution, and explicitly post-devolution. Whether and to what extent the Labour leadership accommodates the new dynamics of territorial power will become a crucial issue in the near future for both Scottish and British Labour.

A Scottish Social Democracy?

A major theme in this book has been an exploration of what Scottish Labour stood for. What, if any, were its distinctive doctrines, beliefs and vision, its animating spirit? For some commentators it was little different from New Labour in Westminster (for example, Mooney and Poole 2004: 476; Law 2005). Our analysis of Scottish Labour policy on key issues such as education, healthcare and long term care for the elderly emphatically does not support this claim. It did not share New Labour's enthusiasm for choice, competition and an enhanced role for the private sector. Instead it favoured partnership, co-operation and unified and integrated service provision while, in education, it cogently defended the comprehensive school, derided by New Labour spin doctors as 'bog standard'. Equally, whereas New Labour disparaged public sector bodies as 'producer interests' – a fixation which allowed for no understanding of the power of 'corporate interests' in public life – Scottish Labour consolidated its alliance with professional Scotland, its policy communities and institutional interests – indeed, for some, rather too cosily.

Scottish Labour's decision to cleave to a more traditional social democratic public services strategy was the product of a complex interplay of factors (Hassan and Shaw 2010). These included embedded traditions and institutional structures, professionally dominated policy communities and 'a cultural, administrative, and political climate and tradition that favour . . . public rather than private provision of welfare' (Stewart 2004: 146). Further, to any Labour minister tempted by New Labour-style 'modernisation' of education and health services, the contemplation of stiff and vociferous resistance from the party, the unions and professional associations, not to mention within public organisations themselves, would have had a powerful inhibiting and deterring effect. Added to this was the absence in Scotland of any powerful corporate lobby that favoured the marketising route. Finally, and not least, the party was well aware that the SNP would ruthlessly exploit any signs that Scottish Labour was vacating traditional social democratic territory.

However, there was more to it than this. Politicians are not hapless puppets flung hither and thither by wider structural and institutional forces. Nor are they simply calculating machines obsessively computing how best to advance their careers. Policy, as we have seen, is also shaped by ideas, values and ingrained traditions. Scottish Labour was intellectually unpersuaded and ideologically uncomfortable with New Labour's marketising reform programme. It did not share its conviction that the key to greater efficiency and improved quality of service was through choice and market disciplines. Rather, it retained confidence in the traditional social democratic policy repertoire of partnership, collaboration and the motivating force of the public service ethos. As New Labour pursued its 'modernising' agenda with mounting vigour, Scottish Labour became more ideologically distinct. 'Might it even be the case', Stewart wondered, 'that Scotland is moving more towards a social democratic welfare regime while England further pursues the Anglo-American model?' (Stewart 2004: 146).

This statement needs to be qualified. Perhaps the single most striking example of policy divergence between Labour north and south of the border was the adoption of free personal care for the elderly, a major expansion of the principle – which lay at the heart of the social democratic welfare state – of social citizenship. But the story of the only really significant legacy of the brief McLeish administration is a paradoxical one. In successive elections Labour laid claim to free personal care as one of its greatest accomplishments, but, in truth, if the decision had been solely in Labour's hands it would never have been enacted. Almost all Labour ministers and the majority of MSPs were opposed, fearing that resources would be diverted from programmes which could have promised more rapid advances towards reducing poverty and meeting pressing need and that the policy would prove to be financially unsustainable. It was a combination of McLeish's populist (if controversial) tactics and external circumstances which eventually induced a reluctant Labour Party to acquiesce in universal care for the elderly, not any belief that this was, in principle, the right action to take.

In contrast, Labour ministers displayed genuine enthusiasm for the use of the Private Finance Initiative mechanism for organising and financing the building of hospitals, schools and prisons. Both instances reflect the essentially pragmatic temper of Scottish Labour, its reticence about evolving policies within clear intellectual frameworks and (institutionally at least) its general indifference to ideas and theoretical debate. Scottish Labour's social democracy, we suggested, was less a coherent intellectual construct than an 'idiom' or 'instinct'. This rendered it less willing to contemplate the introduction into the public services of market disciplines and pecuniary motivations. But it also meant that policies were generally developed in an ad hoc and instrumental manner and disconnected from any wider public vision. This became increasingly evident.

Thus the first year of the Scottish Parliament saw an impressive, energetic, potentially radical programme of legislation launched, which some thought at the time could be the emergence of a 'new Scottish social democracy' (interview). But this never really materialised. Senior figures (like Wendy Alexander and Jack McConnell) later complained about the lack of think tanks and pressure groups in which new ideas could germinate and innovative policies be formulated. The problem was that neither institutionally nor culturally was Scottish Labour configured to invite wide-ranging debate about big issues, such as the respective role of the state and the market, of competition and co-operation and the impact of globalisation. With devolution the range of tasks entrusted to Labour politicians multiplied and they found themselves, as one of McConnell's special advisors explained, 'constantly grappling with practicalities of things and how you do things and make them better' (interview, Danny Phillips). Wrestling with day-to-day problems, immersed in detailed policy issues, the party (as one former minister reflected) became increasingly 'managerial' in outlook. It lacked any narrative, any capacity to weave together its various policies into a coherent whole. In fact, it took pride in its pragmatism, its focus on delivery, its ability to manage policy.

THE LEADERSHIP DIMENSION

We also need to address the issue of why Labour leaders struggled so obviously when the Scottish Parliament was set up and failed to articulate fully a vision or demonstrate the range of skills required to introduce a nuanced set of innovative and achievable policies. Donald Dewar, Henry McLeish and Jack McConnell as Labour First Ministers all had political skills and yet all of them in different ways floundered in setting out a positive agenda and running government with a strategic direction.

What this points to is a much longer-term Labour problem with public leadership. Pre-devolution the Labour models of leadership on offer were those of council leaders who usually worked in committees and were barely public, and the networked state of public agencies and institutions. It is not surprising all three Labour First Ministers had difficulties since there was no appropriate set of archetypes, of an idea of what a modern Scottish Labour leader should look like, or how they should sound and act. Dewar and McLeish in their short reigns found their authority contested, while McConnell went on the path of least resistance. Wendy Alexander challenged many of the shibboleths of what a Scottish Labour politician is meant to be and suffered for it, while Iain Gray developed an approach that was cautious and conservative. The New Labour model of leadership, of charismatic authority and an ideological and practical outsourcing of expertise to the big accountancy and consultancy firms – as in Arthur Andersen's pre-1997 'Preparing for Government' work with future Labour ministers – was not a road the Scottish party wanted to go down.

Scottish Labour pre-devolution did not spend any significant time preparing for and planning for how it could develop a public leadership culture, one with both individual and collective styles. And it is interesting to note that the SNP's transformation into a party of government has seen it adeptly develop a leadership culture around Alex Salmond and collectively, and this was aided by the SNP having a sense of vision and purpose.

The result was that Scottish Labour signally failed to develop a clear sense of what it wanted and where it was going. 'Where', Henry McLeish pondered, 'are the ideas, where is the ideological discussion, where is the vision stuff?' (interview). This failure to carve out a sharp sense of what it stood for, what it was trying to achieve and what values animated it, rendered it electorally vulnerable to a party more confident about its social democratic credentials. A decade ago, McCrone predicted that the future shape of Scottish politics would be heavily influenced by which of the nation's two largest parties 'best expresses the prevailing social democratic mood of the electorate' (McCrone 2001: 125). The responses supplied by the two elections – of 2007 and, especially, 2011 – to this question were unpalatable ones for Labour (Johns et al. 2010; Carman et al. 2011).

THE INTERNAL POLITICS OF SCOTTISH LABOUR

What of the internal politics of the party, the quality and character of its inner life? Some media commentators have been coruscating. Macwhirter lambasted Labour's local states, where patronage was rampant, party membership 'an essential career accessory' and factionalism 'the organising principle of politics' (Macwhirter 2002: 27, 28). Evidence about Labour's municipal politics is in short supply because of the almost complete absence of research. What material we have been able to assemble suggests, on the one hand, that allegations of systematic and pervasive corruption, nepotism and venality cannot be comprehensively substantiated. However, on the other hand, it does indicate that patronage and clientelism have been a notable and long-standing feature of the internal politics of the party, particularly in such strongholds as Lanarkshire and Glasgow.

At national level, Scottish Labour's internal politics has mutated. In the 1980s and much of 1990s, political alignments essentially followed left–right divisions, with ginger groups such as the LCC (Scotland), Scottish Labour Action and the more shadowy Network playing major roles. Since the establishment of the Scottish Parliament a dual process of 'de-factionalisation' and 'de-ideologicalisation' has occurred. Disagreement over principles has been replaced by a broad programmatic consensus. In the absence of significant differences of principle, the major pattern of conflict within the Scottish Labour Parliamentary Group has been personality and patronage based. For example, the often acrimonious clash between the followers of Henry McLeish and Jack McConnell had little, if anything, to do with policy and was more about (as one minister put it) 'loyalties, obligations and rewards'. None of the various debates and positionings, along with one full contest and one mini-contest for the Scottish Parliament Labour leadership in the first decade of devolution, can be characterised for all the subtleties and nuances of difference as anything other than programmatic and idea-free zones.

What of Scottish Labour's power structure? How is power distributed within its ranks? A number of images of Scottish Labour have circulated in the media: as a 'party machine' specialising in the politics of patronage; as a subservient regional outlier of a highly centralised New Labour apparatus; and (its own self-image) as a democratic party run by its own members. Our survey of key internal party processes, including its policy-making, candidate selection and leadership elections, uncovered a more complex pattern.

Responsibility for formulating policy on devolved matters belongs to the Scottish Policy Forum, subject to conference endorsement. Our study indicates that policy-making was not a top-down structure in which (as happened in the UK-wide party) the leadership defined the major parameters of policy, but a process characterised by bargaining and mutual adjustment between the major power-brokers. These included the parliamentary leader (First Minister when Labour was in office), other frontbenchers and the affiliated trade unions, with the latter (unlike in the British party) fully integrated into the process. In fact, many key policies were in effect hammered out, often informally, in discussions between Labour's parliamentary leaders and trade union officials. The constituency rank and file, in contrast, for the most part lacked the capacity to engage in any informed and sustained way in detailed policy discussions and its influence was, at best, modest.

This brings us to the issue of the quality of Labour representatives. A study of Labour MPs from 1945 to 1970 shows that the party had a tendency to select middle-aged, male councillors; this group comprised 53% of all Scottish Labour MPs in the period. This was even more pronounced in Glasgow, where the figure over the same timeframe was 83% (twenty-four out of twenty-nine MPs) (Keating 1975). The promotion patterns in the 1945, 1964 and 1974 Labour governments reveal a paucity of Scottish ministers bar the Scottish Office. Glasgow stands out even more dramatically in this; in the entire era from 1945 to 2010 only two Labour MPs – Bruce Millan and Donald Dewar – served in the Cabinet or Shadow Cabinet, and neither of them was a former councillor. Since the 2010 UK election Ann McKechin and Margaret Curran, both Glasgow MPs, have each served as Shadow Secretary of State for Scotland, indicating a significant degree of change from the past.

There was in the 1970s, and even more so in the 1980s, a Labour Indian Summer whereby the quality of some of the Scottish Labour MPs changed dramatically. One consequence of this was that the first Blair Government elected in 1997 had six Scottish Labour MPs serving as Cabinet ministers. A number of facts contributed to this: namely the Scottish public service tradition more aligning with Labour (aided by the decline of the Tories), and related to that the Glasgow University Debating Society of politics which gave Labour the likes of Donald Dewar and John Smith. Then there was the expansion of further education leading to a rising 'polyocracy' and emergence of a generation, part of which was influenced by the new left, seen in figures in the early parts of their careers such as Robin Cook and Gordon Brown. This shift in Scottish Labour representation now seems to have exhausted itself, but Labour cannot go back to the old patterns of recruitment and selection, leaving huge issues about where Labour's future talent and new voices will emerge from.

Candidate selection, it is widely recognised, is a crucial vantage point from which to assess the distribution of power within a party, and this has been shown to be of paramount importance in terms of Labour's performance and fortunes in the Scottish Parliament. Although much of the discussion in the literature revolves around the question of the respective control capabilities of the central and Scottish leaderships (see, for example, Hopkin and Bradbury 2006; Bradbury 2009), we suggest that the concept of control is itself misleading. Rather the evidence suggests that power is diffused among three competing political networks, those operated by party officialdom, by the affiliated trade unions and those rooted in the localities, whose influence largely derived from their capacity to tap into political intelligence, contacts and resources.

The existence of influential trade union and local networks (usually based in municipal politics) meant that the party machine – which itself was over-stretched and under-staffed – lacked the means even if it had the will to control the selection process. This both reflected and helped to sustain a pluralistic balance of power within Scottish Labour. But a network-dominated selection system also reinforced its rather insular and confined character. A small membership (in most constituency parties) meant that few were involved in choosing a candidate, which facilitated management by network-affiliated contenders. Unless the dwindling of the membership can be reversed, this is bound to undermine the democratic legitimacy of the process.

THE DEVOLUTION CHALLENGE

Devolution has posed a series of challenges to what may be called the territorial politics of the Labour Party. To what degree and over what areas has power been devolved to the Scottish party? Our evidence substantiates neither the image of a completely autonomous 'Scottish Labour Party', nor that of the creature of the Westminster Labour establishment, 'the London Labour' of Nationalist rhetoric. Both of these versions of the party have elements of truth in them, but they are ultimately caricatures, and unhelpful to understanding Scottish Labour. The Scottish party has operated in a manner which displays Scottish characteristics and differentiation, while also responding to and locating itself in a wider set of British circumstances.

On matters of devolved policy, we found that for the most part the Westminster leadership adopted a permissive attitude. The bitter row over the enactment of free personal care for the elderly was the major exception, when Henry McLeish came under intense pressure to abandon the central plank of his administration. Westminster was furious because a policy initiative which caused it acute political embarrassment had been sprung on it. Scottish policy diverged equally sharply from Westminster Labour's on

325

other issues – for example, healthcare – but the key difference was that free personal care had major political repercussions in England. The mask of more or less benign indifference then slipped, and British ministers demanded that McLeish fall into line – a demand that politically could not be met. After this episode Labour north and south of the border became more circumspect, with the British party accepting that on devolved policy issues the Scottish party should be left to go its own way – if only because heavy-handed interference would be a gift to the SNP. Notwithstanding this, other instances that followed, such as friction over the Dungavel asylum centre and the NHS pay award in 2007, suggested that the New Labour leadership had yet fully to come to terms with devolution.

Some, as we have seen, have argued that the problem for Scottish Labour has been Brown's alleged dominance of Scottish Labour from the early 1990s to 2010. In this thesis, Brown and his main Scottish supporters saw Scotland as his 'heartland' and sought to run the party, promote supporters and block opponents and developments they did not like. In fact, there is little evidence to support this too simple and caricatured argument. However, there *was* a perennial tension between Westminster and Holyrood parliamentarians, with a large swathe of the former regarding any distinct action by the latter as a threat to their position, status and influence. Indeed, there was much resentment among Scottish Labour MPs about MSPs' much higher public profile in the Scottish media, a sense that their representative role was no longer sufficiently acknowledged. Discernible among such MPs was a kind of 'entitlement culture' aided by the ethos of the UK Parliament, and the age, background and, until recently, overwhelming maleness of representatives. Labour has as yet to develop a collective mindset to transcend these conflicting jurisdictional claims and ambitions. What was clear was that the power of the 'myth' of 'Labour Scotland' had influenced a whole generation of Labour politicians in Westminster, but that this was less influential to a new generation in the Scottish Parliament. This produced two very different interpretations of Scotland, one a majoritarian 'Labour Scotland', the other of Scottish Labour as one minority among many; parts of each could barely at times comprehend the other.

On organisational issues such as candidate selection and leadership elections there is little solid evidence of a determined drive or any particular inclination by the British leadership to assert its will. To the extent that the centre intervened (as it did in the selections in the run-up to the first Holyrood elections) it was with the active collaboration of powerful members of the Scottish Labour establishment. But the national party *did* retain (until the rule changes of 2011: see below) ultimate responsibility over the party organisation, finance and staffing, with ultimate control over party rules still vested in the NEC, and thereby constrained the Scottish party's control over its own affairs.

Broadly speaking, the British party leadership understood that the imposition of tight control was both impractical and dysfunctional. This reflected its appreciation that the Scottish party faced different strategic challenges and required discretion to evolve its own priorities. But there was an important caveat: there should be no open challenge to the New Labour 'brand', no exposition of its own policies in such a way that might imply criticism of those being pursued in London. The Scottish Labour leadership certainly internalised this injunction as a restraint and inhibition, and no attempts were made to draw 'red lines'. Indeed, some have seen this as reflecting a self-denying ordinance against transgressing or challenging Westminster and British Labour, which had the effect of reinforcing a limited, cautious politics. It is the case that no sustained thought was given to re-casting Labour's internal arrangements to take account of devolution, other than some pragmatic adjustments. There was no real 'party devolution'.

The shock of the 2011 election defeat changed everything for Labour and provoked much soul-searching. A package of measures, based on a review chaired by Sarah Boyack MSP and Jim Murphy MP, was formally adopted by the party in the autumn of 2011. The most important was the transfer to the Scottish party of full responsibility for all its internal operations, and the upgrading of the post of leader of the Scottish Parliamentary Labour Group to that of leader of the party in Scotland. According to Murphy, this was all about completing 'the devolution of Scottish Labour' and transforming it into 'Scotland's Labour Party'.

Scottish Labour faced these challenges with significant voices of Westminster dissent warning that the party was appeasing Nationalism; Michael McCann, MP for East Kilbride, complained that Labour was 'moving on to Tory and Nat territory', while one MP stated, 'We seem to be offering the Holyrood party what it wants and getting nothing in return' (*The Scotsman*, 13 September 2011). It is highly unlikely that such views will carry much weight. Whatever the future contours, Scottish Labour's post-2011 watershed was like that for all the other pro-union parties, having to come to terms with the new environment which also threw down huge challenges to the Scottish Tories and Lib Dems about Scottish distinctiveness and autonomy.

THE FUTURE FOR SCOTTISH LABOUR

Scottish Labour will have to do more than modify its structure. There are at least three dimensions relevant to the party's future prospects – the Scottish,

British and international dimensions – each of which will continue to inter-lace and interact with each other. It is more than likely over the next few years that the Scottish agenda of the party will come to the fore, but that British interests and the wider state of social democracy and global politics will play a role.

Labour faces a series of multiple crises across the UK: the trials and tribula-tions of Scottish Labour after its 2011 defeat, while in 2010 British Labour suffered its second-worst election defeat in terms of votes since 1918; and the wider predicament of Scottish and British social democracy and what direc-tion the party takes after New Labour in an era defined by globalisation, the retreat of social democracy from its high-water mark, and the challenge of neo-liberalism and market fundamentalism. Scottish Labour may try to draw succour from its 2010 electoral triumph in comparison to its 2011 humilia-tion, but in truth the party, atrophying, declining and disorientated about its purpose and direction, cannot be confident about its future prospects.

We need to widen the angle of vision even further. As the new millen-nium opened, social democratic parties dominated government in most of the European Union. In recent years they have suffered a catalogue of defeats and notably have signally failed to derive any benefit whatsoever from the financial crisis of 2007–8 which so graphically demonstrated the vacuity of neo-liberalism. Put in this perspective, the impasse of Scottish (indeed British) Labour is an aspect of a much wider social democratic predicament arising from a host of unfavourable circumstances, political, economic and cultural. The 'Third Way' model of social democracy is clearly – post the financial crash – intellectually and politically exhausted, but its replacement is as yet struggling to be born. This is as evident in Britain as elsewhere. Currently the party, both at Scottish and UK levels, finds itself shorn of a clear mission, purpose, vision or voice. It may in future find these again (and there are indeed signs that the British party is slowly beginning to do so under Ed Miliband), but it will have to start from a recognition of the challenging circumstances it finds itself in, and the need to develop a distinct and new approach to how it does politics.

These are huge questions which need to be at least acknowledged and addressed, but several of which are beyond the scope of this survey. There are a series of multiple and intersecting crises that affect Scottish Labour to which the party has to turn its attention if it is to have a viable future. The first is, as we stated, the demise of 'Labour Scotland', a bereavement which leaves the party needing to develop a completely different politics from the one which characterised its post-war dominance of politics and society at a time when it has scant resources and ideas. The decline of the 'myth' of 'Labour Scotland' leaves the party without a persuasive mission, purpose and connection of its past to the future. Second, within this was what could be called the party's soul and modus operandi, namely the story of Scottish Labour, of a party which saw itself as distinct, with a different set of values and traditions from British Labour, and which saw no contradiction in its bridge-building and advocacy of Scottish and British interests. That story has now exhausted itself and become discredited, and somehow the Scottish party needs to find itself a convincing new story to give it a sense of mission and purpose. The demise of the Communist Party, the weakening of the STUC and the decline of the trade union movement have all contributed to this state.

Third, there once was, as we have also stated, a powerful, potent Labour story of Britain that Scottish Labour and Scotland fitted into. It was a collective story of the power of the Labour movement as a force for progress and good, making Britain a fairer, more decent society with better opportunities for working people. That Labour version of Britain has, like the traditional Tory account, withered and declined through a variety of factors: the changing nature of the UK, Thatcherism, the emergence of Scottish and Welsh nationalist parties, and the impact of New Labour. The eventual demise of this Labour vision does not necessarily lead to Scottish independence, but what it does necessitate is a strategy that is more sensitive and aware of territorial politics. And this will require Labour to come up with a different vision of Britain that has more pronounced Scottish, Welsh and English dimensions. Nothing is inevitable in politics, but we can conclude that 'the forward march of Scottish Labour' has indeed been halted and reversed, and that for the party to counter this it needs to understand the environment and long-term factors we have outlined.

The first major signs of the party beginning slowly to come to terms with the new Scottish political environment were evident in a major speech delivered by Douglas Alexander in October 2011. In it he conceded that the traditional Scottish Labour story had now passed its sell-by date and that 'some of the old Labour "hymns" were increasingly unfamiliar to an audience without personal knowledge of the tunes' (Alexander 2011). He argued that Labour needed to tell 'an alternative story', 'a renewed story' and 'a new statecraft for this decade' (ibid.). This was the start of Scottish Labour hesitantly recognising the reality of a changed Scotland and a new political dispensation. Alexander was strong on critique, but weak on future action, and appeared to be still reluctant to acknowledge the SNP not as the bogeyman of yore but instead as a rival occupying what had once been Labour's unchallenged social democratic territory. It was an analysis shared by all the Scottish Labour leadership contenders, with Ken Macintosh, at the outset the bookies' favourite, declaring, 'Most of us in the Labour Party haven't forgotten our values, but maybe we have forgotten to talk about them'; Johann

Lamont observed, 'I welcome Douglas's speech because I have long believed that a strong economy and a strong society are different sides of the same coin' (*The Scotsman*, 14 October 2011).

Scottish Labour passed the recommendations of the Murphy–Boyack review unanimously at a special conference in Glasgow on 29 October 2011 (*Sunday Herald*, 30 October 2011). Nominations for the leadership and deputy leadership were announced on 16 November 2011. For the leadership, Johann Lamont had the support of twenty-seven MSPs, MPs and MEPs, twelve unions and affiliates and fourteen CLPs, Macintosh had twenty-six parliamentarians, five unions and affiliates and ten CLPs, and Tom Harris had thirteen parliamentarians and one CLP. For the deputy post, Anas Sarwar had forty-four parliamentarians, seven unions and affiliates and eighteen CLPs, Lewis Macdonald had thirteen parliamentarians and two CLPs, and Ian Davidson had eleven parliamentarians, five unions and affilates and three CLPs (*BBC News*, 16 November 2011).

On 17 December, Johann Lamont was elected leader of Scottish Labour and Anas Sarwar became deputy (see Table 6). Lamont won 51.77% of the overall vote but won with 65.4% of the trade union and affiliates section, while Ken Macintosh defeated her in the individual membership by 53.1% to 36.5%.[1] In her victory speech in Edinburgh, Lamont stated that in the 2011 Scottish Parliament election campaign Labour had come across to people as 'a tired old politics machine which was more about itself than it was about them'. The party needed to realise that Scotland had changed: 'If anyone has ever deluded ourselves into thinking that Scotland was really a Labour country – last May must have finally shaken us out of that delusion' (*BBC News*, 17 December 2011).

What Alexander's prognosis failed to address was that in the pre-devolution era Scottish Labour's combination of Scottish and British interests was a huge statement of strength, allowing the party to marginalise the Conservatives of the Thatcher and Major era as 'anti-Scottish' and inflexible on the union, while painting the Nationalists as old-fashioned and irrelevant. Post-devolution this state of affairs has completely altered. Now Scottish Labour's combination of Scottish and British interests, the fact that it is neither completely 'Scottish Labour' nor 'London Labour', has become a problem. It has allowed the Nationalists to take hold of the agenda of Scottish interests and social democratic values, leaving Labour unsure and wrong-footed. The solution for Scottish Labour is to begin to understand its own predicament, to resist caricaturing its Nationalist opponents, and to emphasise its Scottish credentials to help make the case for a different British politics.

That is a tall order when the political environment is an increasingly hostile one and will entail addressing three problems: the legitimacy of the

Table 9: Scottish Labour Leadership Contest 2011 (as a percentage)

	MSPs, MPs & MEPs	Individual Members	Trade Unions & Affiliates	Total
Leadership				
Johann Lamont	17.778	12.183	21.807	51.77
Ken Macintosh	13.778	17.707	8.797	40.28
Tom Harris	1.778	3.444	2.730	7.95
Deputy Leadership				
Anas Sarwar	22.222	20.342	8.531	51.10
Ian Davidson	4.444	8.472	20.366	33.28
Lewis Macdonald	6.667	4.519	4.436	15.62

Source: *BBC News*, 17 December 2011

UK Tories to govern Scotland; who does Scottish Labour speak for?; and the issue of British Labour. The first of these takes us back to the Kilbrandon (previously Crowther) Commission and the evidence it took from Scottish Labour. The delegation was asked whether the Scottish Labour Party would prefer a UK Tory Government to a Labour-run Scottish Assembly; this is the exchange of more than forty years ago:

> Lord Crowther: Suppose as has happened in the past, there were to be another thirteen years of Conservative rule in Westminster. Suppose further that that led to the strengthening of anti-socialist policy and the demolition of the structure of socialism in this country, would your view still be the same?
> John Pollock: It would, though one of the two essentials we have stipulated in our evidence to make a success for Scotland is first of all that the United Kingdom economy should be controlled by socialists.
> Lord Crowther: If you cannot achieve that would you still conclude that Scotland's problems are best tackled within a UK framework?
> John Pollock: Yes ... What we fear is that, if one starts with any form of Assembly with substantial legislative devolution, that is the slippery slope towards total separation, or at least a form of separation which would set up divisions within the United Kingdom. We believe that would be disastrous for Scotland, because it would lead to Scotland becoming a separate small nation economy instead of remaining part of a major economic unit. That would be so disastrous in the long run that even the hypothetical situation of another Conservative Government ruling in Great Britain would be preferable. (Commission on the Constitution 1970: 32, quoted in McLean 1990b: 19–20)

This was the situation Scottish Labour was to find itself in for the eighteen years of Conservative rule under Thatcher and Major, and despite devolution this problem still acutely affects the party given the potent power of anti-Toryism in Scotland. This issue also has further importance because it taps into the issue of who Labour speaks for, and a belief in some parts of Scotland that the party does not have the autonomy or courage to stand unconditionally for the national interest. And this touches on the character of British Labour, and its lack of understanding and interest in the politics of devolution, the territorial dimensions of the UK, and the nature of the political centre. British Labour are portrayed in many accounts as being 'control freaks' or 'anti-Scottish', but what they are is a product of British political culture, and a political tradition which often, sometimes for the best intentions, forgets about Scotland and the character of the UK. This is part of a longer story about the nature of the British Labour Party and British left, but what it does underline is that Scottish Labour's fate is not entirely in its own hands. This is of course always the case with political parties, but more so today for Scottish Labour, with the rise of the SNP as a party of Scottish government, the combining of the Scottish dimension with centre-left values, the continued issue of the Tories' legitimacy in Scotland, and the nature of how British Labour understands the concepts of country, nation and state in the UK.

These are uncharted waters for Labour and especially for Labour in Scotland, and are not easily understandable from the vantage point of any one political perspective or narrative. We hope that this book is taken as a contribution to aid this debate, one that has a distinct Scottish agenda, but also wider British and global relevance. Scottish Labour's story and experience in recent decades has been the product of many factors, Scottish, British and international, and its future state and prospects have wider consequences and impact. After the 'myth' of 'Labour Scotland', the party needs to find a new plausible and popular modus operandi which can come to terms with the very different politics, society and culture it now finds itself in.

NOTE

1. Labour Party sources claimed a 67% turnout among individual party members, 96% among parliamentarians and 12% among trade unionists and affiliates. In the 2008 Scottish Labour leadership contest, the party claimed a 58% turnout among individual party members (*Scotland on Sunday*, 18 December 2011; private information to the authors).

References

Achur, J. (2011), *Trade Union Membership 2010*, Department for Business, Innovation and Skills.

Aitken, K. (1997), *The Bairns O'Adam: The Story of the STUC*, Polygon.

Alexander, D. (2011), 'A Better Nation', John Williamson Memorial Lecture, Stirling University, 13 October, http://www.labourhame.com/archives/2202#more-2202.

Alexander, W. (2005), 'Foundations, Frustrations and Hopes', in W. Alexander (ed.), *Donald Dewar: Scotland's first First Minister*, Mainstream.

Alexander, W. (2008), Speech to Scottish Labour Annual Conference, 28 March, http://www.wendyalexander.co.uk/2008/03/28/speech-to-labour-party-scottish-conference-by-wendyalexander/.

Allen, G. (2003), *The Last Prime Minister: Being Honest about the UK Presidency*, Imprint Academic.

Allison, J. (1995), *Guilty by Suspicion*, Argyll Publishing.

Arnott, M. (2005), 'Devolution, territorial politics and the politics of education', in G. Mooney and G. Scott (eds), *Exploring Social Policy in the 'New' Scotland*, Policy Press.

Arnott, M. and Menter, I. (2007), 'The Same but Different? Post-devolution Regulation and Control in Education in Scotland and England', *European Educational Research Journal* 6 (3).

Ashdown, P. (2001), *The Ashdown Diaries: Volume Two 1997–99*, Allen Lane.

Aughey, A. (2001), *Nationalism, Devolution and the Challenge to the United Kingdom State*, Pluto Press.

Baggot, R. (1998), *Health and Healthcare in Britain*, Macmillan.

Bale, T. (2010), *The Conservative Party from Thatcher to Cameron*, Polity Press.

BBC Trust (2008), *BBC Network News and Current Affairs Coverage of the Four UK Nations*, BBC Trust.

Béland, D. (2005), 'Ideas and Social Policy: An Institutionalist Perspective', *Social Policy and Administration* 39 (1).

Béland, D. (2009), 'Ideas, institutions, and policy change', *Journal of European Public Policy* 16 (5).

Beller, D. C. and Belloni, F. (1978), 'Party and Faction: Modes of Political Completion', in F. Belloni and D. C. Beller (eds), *Faction Politics: Political Parties and Factionalism in Comparative Perspective*, ABC-Clio.

Benn, T. (1992), *The End of an Era: Diaries 1980–1990*, Hutchinson.

Bennie, L. (2004), *Understanding Political Participation: Green Party Membership in Scotland*, Ashgate.

Bennie, L., Brand, J. and Mitchell, J. (1997), *How Scotland Votes*, Manchester University Press.

Bettcher, K. E. (2005), 'Factions of Interest in Japan and Italy: The Organisational and Motivational Dimensions of Factionalism', *Party Politics* 11 (3).

Blair, T. (2004), 'Speech at The Guardian Public Services Summit', 29 January, http://www.guardian.co.uk/society/2004/jan/29/comment.publicservices.

Blair, T. (2010), *A Journey*, Hutchinson.

Bond, R. and Rosie, M. (2007), 'Social Democratic Scotland?', in M. Keating (ed.), *Scottish Social Democracy: Progressive Ideas for Public Policy*, Peter Lang.

Brewer, M., Clark, T. and Wakefield, M. (2002), *Social Security Under New Labour: What did the Third Way mean for Welfare Reform?*, Institute of Fiscal Studies.

Bochel, J. and Denver, D. (1970), 'Religion and Voting: a critical review and a new analysis', *Political Studies* 18 (2).

Bochel, J. and Denver, D. (1983), 'The 1983 General Election in Scotland', in D. McCrone (ed.), *The Scottish Government Yearbook*, Unit for the Study of Government in Scotland.

Bochel, J. and Denver, D. (1988), 'The 1987 General Election in Scotland', in D. McCrone and A. Brown (eds), *The Scottish Government Yearbook 1988*, Unit for the Study of Government in Scotland.

Bochel, J. and Denver, D. (1991), 'The Regional Elections of 1990', in A. Brown and D. McCrone (eds), *The Scottish Government Yearbook 1991*, Unit for the Study of Government in Scotland.

Bochel, J., Denver, D. and Macartney, A. (eds), *The Referendum Experience: Scotland 1979*, Aberdeen University Press.

Bogdanor, V. (2009), *The New British Constitution*, Hart Publishing.

Boucek, F. (2009), 'Rethinking Factionalism: Typologies, Intra-Party Dynamics and Three Faces of Factionalism', *Party Politics* 15 (4).

Bowes, A. and Bell, D. (2007), 'Free Personal Care for Older People in Scotland: Issues and Implications', *Social Policy and Society* 6 (3).

Bradbury, J. (2006), 'British Politics Parties and Devolution: Adapting to Multi-level Politics in Scotland and Wales', in D. Hough and C. Jeffery (eds), *Devolution and Electoral Politics*, Manchester University Press.

Bradbury, J. (2007), 'Territorial Politics in the United Kingdom after Devolution and Regional Reform', Paper to the 'Britain after Blair' conference of the

British Politics Group, American Political Science Association Annual Meeting.

Bradbury, J. (2009), *Devolution and Party Organisation in the UK*, in W. Swenden and B. Maddens (eds), *Territorial Party Politics in Western Europe*, Palgrave Macmillan.

Bradbury, J., Denver, D., Mitchell, J. and Bennie, L. (2000), 'Devolution and Party Change: Candidate Selection for the 1999 Scottish Parliament and Welsh Assembly Elections', *Journal of Legislative Studies* 6 (3).

Bradbury, J. and Mitchell, J. (2002), 'Devolution and Territorial Politics: stability, uncertainty and crisis', *Parliamentary Affairs* 55 (2).

Brand, J. (1978), *The National Movement in Scotland*, Routledge and Kegan Paul.

Brand, J., Mitchell, J. and Surridge, P. (1994), 'Will Scotland come to the aid of the party?', in A. Heath, R. Jowell, J. Curtice and B. Taylor (eds), *Labour's Last Chance?: The 1992 Election and Beyond*, Dartmouth.

Brown, A., McCrone, D., Paterson, L. and Surridge, P. (1999), *The Scottish Electorate: The 1997 General Election and Beyond*, Macmillan.

Brown, G. (1981), *The Labour Party and Political Change in Scotland 1918–1929: The Politics of Five Elections*, University of Edinburgh Ph.D. thesis.

Brown, G. (1994), 'John Smith's Socialism: His Writings and Speeches', in G. Brown and J. Naughtie (eds), *John Smith: Life and Soul of the Party*, Mainstream.

Brown, G. (2000), 'Donald Dewar's Funeral', in Stationery Office (ed.), *Donald Dewar: A Book of Tribute*, Stationery Office.

Brown, G. and Alexander, D. (1999), *New Scotland, New Britain*, Smith Institute.

Brown, G. and Alexander, D. (2007), *Stronger Together: The 21st century case for Scotland and Britain*, Fabian Society.

Bruce, M. (1990), 'PR and Democracy', *Radical Scotland*, April–May.

Bryce T. and Humes, W. (2008), 'Scottish Secondary Education: Philosophy and Practice', in T. Bryce and W. Humes (eds), *Scottish Education*, Edinburgh University Press, 3rd edn.

Bulpitt, J. (1983), *Territory and Power in the UK*, Manchester University Press.

Butler, D., Adonis, A. and Travers, T. (1994), *Failure in British Government: The Politics of the Poll Tax*, Oxford University Press.

Butler, D. and Butler, G. (2005), *Twentieth Century British Political Facts 1900–2000*, Palgrave, 8th edn.

Cable, V. (2009), *Free Radical*, Atlantic Books.

Cairney, P. (2007), 'Governance and Public Policy in Britain since Devolution From Divergence to Implementation', Paper to the Political Studies Association Conference, Bath.

Cairney, P. (2008), 'Has Devolution Changed the "British Policy Style"?', *British Politics* 3 (3).

Calder, A. and Sheridan, D. (eds) (1984), *Speak for Yourself: A Mass Observation Anthology 1937–1949*, Jonathan Cape.

Callaghan, J. (1984), *British Trotskyism: Theory and Practice*, Blackwell.

Cameron, E. (2010), *Impaled Upon a Thistle: Scotland since 1880*, Edinburgh University Press.

Campbell, A. (2010), *The Alastair Campbell Diaries: Volume One: Prelude to Power 1994–1997*, Hutchinson.

Campbell, A. (2011a), *The Alastair Campbell Diaries: Volume Two: Power and the People 1997–1999*, Hutchinson.

Campbell, A. (2011b), *The Alastair Campbell Diaries: Volume Three: Power and Responsibility 1999–2001*, Hutchinson.

Campbell, J. (2002), 'Ideas, Politics and Public Policy', *Annual Review of Sociology* Vol. 28.

Campbell, J. (2003), *Margaret Thatcher Volume Two: The Iron Lady*, Jonathan Cape.

Campbell, M. (2008), *Menzies Campbell: My Autobiography*, Hodder and Stoughton.

Canavan, D. (1989), 'Sovereignty of the People', in O. Dudley Edwards (ed.), *A Claim of Right for Scotland*, Polygon.

Canavan, D. (2009), *Let the People Decide*, Birlinn.

Carman, C., Johns, R. and Mitchell, J. (2011), 'Scottish Election Survey 2011', University of Strathclyde, http://www.scottishelectionstudy.org.uk/data.htm.

Carty, R. (2004), 'Parties as franchise systems: The stratarchical organizational imperative', *Party Politics* 10 (1).

Chambers, M. and Walker, W. (2001), *Uncharted Waters: The UK, Nuclear Weapons and the Scottish Question*, Tuckwell Press.

Checkland, S. G. (1976), *The Upas Tree: Glasgow 1875–1975*, University of Glasgow Press.

Church of Scotland (2011), *Report to the General Assembly of the Church of Scotland*, Church of Scotland.

Civardi, C. (1997), *Le Mouvement Ouvrier Ecossais 1900–1931*, Press Universitaires de Strasbourg.

Clark, A. (2002), 'The Location of Power in Scotland's Post-Devolution Political Parties: An Exploratory Analysis', Paper to the Political Studies Association Conference.

Clark, A. (2004), 'The Continued Relevance of Local Parties in Representative Democracies', *Politics* 24 (1).

Clark, I. and Berridge, J. (1998), *Scotland Votes: The General Election 1997 in Scotland*, University of Dundee/Grampian Television.

Cleland, A. (2006), 'The Antisocial Behaviour (Scotland) Act 2004: Exposing the punitive fault lines below the children's hearing system', *Edinburgh Law Review* 9 (3).

Commission on the Constitution (1970), *Minutes of Evidence: Volume Four: Scotland*, HMSO.

Communities Scotland (2008), *Scottish Housing Tenure Data*, unpublished paper.

Conservative Research Department (1987), *The Conservative Campaign Guide 1987*, Conservative Research Department.

Cook, R. (1988), 'Pragmatic Politics: An Interview with Robin Cook', *Radical Scotland*, December–January.

Cortell, A. and Peterson, S. (1999), 'Altered states: explaining domestic institutional change', *British Journal of Political Science* 29 (1).

Cowley, P. (2005), *The Rebels*, Politico's Publishing.

Cowling, D. (1997), *An Essay for Today: Scottish New Towns 1947–1997*, Rutland Press.

Crafts, N. (2004), *High quality Public Services in Scotland*, Fraser of Allander Series.

Craig, C. (2010), *The Tears That Made the Clyde: Well-Being in Glasgow*, Argyll Publishing.

Craig, F. W. S. (1981), *British Electoral Facts 1832–1980*, Parliamentary Research Services.

Cramme, O., Diamond, P. and Liddle, R. (2009), *Challenging the politics of evasion: The only way to renew European social democracy*, Policy Network.

Crewe, I. and King, A. (1995), *SDP: The Birth, Life and Death of the Social Democratic Party*, Oxford University Press.

Crick, M. (1984), *Militant*, Faber and Faber.

Crick, M. (1985), *Scargill and the Miners*, Penguin.

Crossman, R. H. S. (1977), *The Diaries of a Cabinet Minister: Volume Three*, Jonathan Cape.

Crummy, H. (1992), *Let the People Sing! A Story of Craigmillar*, Craigmillar Communiversity Press.

Curtice, J., McCrone, D., Marsh, M., McEwen, N. and Ormston, R. (2009), *Revolution or Evolution? the 2007 Scottish Elections*, Edinburgh University Press.

Curtice, J. and Steed, M. (1992), 'The Results Analysed', in D. Butler and D. Kavanagh (eds), *The British General Election of 1992*, Macmillan.

Dalyell, T. (1977), *Devolution: The End of Britain?*, Jonathan Cape.

Damer, S. (1990), *Glasgow: Going for a Song*, Lawrence and Wishart.

Davidson, L. (2005), *Lucky Jack: Scotland's First Minister*, Black and White Publishing.

Deacon, S. (1990), 'Adopting Conventional Wisdom: Labour's Response to the National Question', in A. Brown and R. Parry (eds), *The Scottish Government Yearbook 1990*, Unit for the Study of Government in Scotland.

Deeming, C. and Keen, J. (2001), 'The Politics of Long-term Care', *Health Care UK*, London, King's Fund.

Deer, B. (1997), 'The Public Life and Death of a Political Man', *New Statesman*, 14 November.

Dennis, N. and Halsey, A. H. (1988), *English Ethical Socialism: Thomas More to R. H. Tawney*, Clarendon Press.

Denver, D. (2003), 'A "Wake Up!" Call to the Parties? The Results of the Scottish Parliament Elections 2003', *Scottish Affairs* 44.

Denver, D. (2007), '"A Historic Moment"? The Results of the Scottish Parliament Elections 2007, *Scottish Affairs* 60.

Denver, D. (2010), 'Swimming in a Different Direction: The 2010 General Election in Scotland', *Scottish Affairs* 72.

Denver, D. (2011a), 'Another "Historic Moment": The Scottish Parliament Elections 2011, *Scottish Affairs* 76.

Denver, D. (2011b), Private communication with authors.

Denver, D. and Bochel, J. (1995), 'Catastrophe for the Conservatives: The Council Elections of 1995', *Scottish Affairs* 13.

Denver, D. and Bochel, J. (2007), 'A Quiet Revolution: STV and the Council Elections of 2007', *Scottish Affairs* 61.

Denver, D. and Hands, G. (1997), *Modern Constituency Electioneering: Local Campaigning in the 1992 General Election*, Cass.

Denver, D., Hands, G. and MacAllister, I. (2004), 'The Electoral Impact of Constituency Campaigning in Britain, 1992–2001', *Political Studies* 52 (2).

Denver, D. and MacAllister, I. (1999), 'The Scottish Parliament Elections 1999: An Analysis of the Results', *Scottish Affairs* 28.

Denver, D., Mitchell, J., Pattie, C. and Bochel, H. (2000), *Scotland Decides: The Devolution Issue and the Scottish Referendum*, Frank Cass.

Denzau, A. and North, D. (1994), 'Shared mental models: Ideologies and institutions', *Kyklos* 47 (1).

Deschouwer, K. (2003), 'Political parties in multi-layered systems', *European Urban and Regional Studies* 10 (3).

Devine, T. M. (1999), *The Scottish Nation 1707–2000*, Allen Lane.

Dewar, D. (1987), 'Scotland: The Way Forward', in J. Willman et al., *Labour's Next Moves Forward*, Fabian Society.

Dewar, D. (1994), 'Tribute', in G. Brown and J. Naughtie (eds), *John Smith: Life and Soul of the Party*, Mainstream.

Dickinson, H., Glasby, J., Forder, J. and Beesley, L. (2007), 'Free Personal Care in Scotland: A Narrative Review', *British Journal of Social Work* 37 (3).

Doig, A. and Wilson, J. (1998), 'What Price The New Public Management?', *Political Quarterly* 69 (3).

Dowle, M. (1988), 'The Year at Westminster', in D. McCrone and A. Brown (eds), *The Scottish Government Yearbook 1988*, Unit for the Study of Government in Scotland.

Drucker, H. M. (1977), *Breakaway: The Scottish Labour Party*, Edinburgh University Student Publication Board.

Drucker, H. M. (1979), *Doctrine and Ethos in the Labour Party*, Allen and Unwin.

Drucker, H. M. (1991), 'The Influence of the Trade Unions on the Ethos of the Labour Party', in B. Pimlott and C. Cook (eds), *Trade Unions in British Politics*, Longman.

Dudgeon, P. (2009), *Our Glasgow*, Headline.

Dudley Edwards, O. (ed.) (1989), *A Claim of Right for Scotland*, Polygon.

Duncan, R. (2005), *The Mineworkers*, Birlinn.

Durkheim, E. (1982 [1895]), *The Rules of the Sociological Method*, Free Press.

Duverger, M. (1964), *Political Parties*, Methuen.

Eldersveld, S. (1964), *Political Parties*, Rand McNally.

Eldridge, J. E. T. and Combie, A. D. (1974), *A Sociology of Organisations*, Allen and Unwin.

Electoral Commission (2011), Private communication with authors.

Enston, M. (1990), 'Implementing the Unthinkable: The First Community Charge', in A. Brown and R. Parry (eds), *The Scottish Government Yearbook 1990*, Unit for the Study of Government in Scotland.

Erickson, J. (1969), 'Scotland's Defence Commitment: Some Problems of Cost, Capability and Effectiveness', in J. N. Wolfe (ed.), *Government and Nationalism in Scotland*, Edinburgh University Press.

Epstein, L. (1980), *Political Parties in Western Democracies*, Transaction Publishers.

Esping-Andersen, G. (1990), *The Three Worlds of Welfare Capitalism*, Princeton University Press.

Evans, G. and Norris, P. (eds) (1999), *Critical Elections: British Politics and Voters in Long-Term Perspective*, Sage.

Exworthy, M. (2001), 'Primary care in the UK: understanding the dynamics of devolution', *Health and Social Care in the Community* 9 (5).

Fairley, A. (1988), 'The Community Charge and Local Government Finance in Scotland', in D. McCrone and A. Brown (eds), *The Scottish Government Yearbook 1988*, Unit for the Study of Government in Scotland.

Farrar, S., Harris, F. and Scott, T. (2004), *The Performance Assessment Framework: experiences and perceptions of NHS Scotland*, A Report to the Scottish Executive Health Department.

Farrell, F. and Arnott, M. (2008), 'Devolution and Policy Delivery – Education in Scotland and Wales', Paper to the Public Administration Committee Annual Conference, September.

Finlay, R. (2004), *Modern Scotland 1914–2000*, Profile Books.

Forrester, T. (1975), *The Labour Party and the Working Class*, Heinemann.

Foulkes, G. (1989), 'The Claim', in O. Dudley Edwards (ed.), *A Claim of Right for Scotland*, Polygon.

Fox, A. (1978), *Shop Floor Power Today*, Fabian Society.

Fraser, D. (2004), 'New Labour, New Parliament', in G. Hassan (ed.), *The Scottish Labour Party: History Institutions and Ideas*, Edinburgh University Press.

Fraser, D. (2008), *Nation Speaking Unto Nation: Does the Media Create Cultural Distance between England and Scotland?*, IPPR North.

Freeman, R. (2007), 'Social Democracy, Uncertainty and Health in Scotland', in M. Keating (ed.), *Scottish Social Democracy: Progressive Ideas for Public Policy*, Peter Lang.

Fry, M. (1987), *Patronage and Principle: A Political History of Modern Scotland*, Aberdeen University Press.

Gall, G. (2005), *The Political Economy of Scotland: Red Scotland? Radical Scotland?*, University of Wales Press.

Gall, G. (2012), *Tommy Sheridan: From Hero to Zero? A Political Biography*, Welsh Academic Press.

Gallagher, M. and Marsh, M. (eds) (1988), *Candidate Selection in Comparative Perspective*, Sage.

Galloway, G. (1982), 'Devolution Challenge', *New Socialist*, January–February.

Galloway, G. (1983), 'If Thatcher wins', *Radical Scotland*, April–May.

Gamble, A. (1974), *The Conservative Nation*, Routledge and Kegan Paul.

Gillies, D. (2008), 'The Politics of Scottish Education', in T. Bryce and W. Humes (eds), *Scottish Education*, Edinburgh University Press, 3rd edn.

Gleeson, D. and Knights, D. (2006), 'Challenging Dualism: Public Professionalism in "Troubled" Times', *Sociology* 40 (2).

Gordon, E. (1991), *Women and the Labour Movement in Scotland 1850–1914*, Clarendon Press.

Gould, P. (1998), *The Unfinished Revolution: How the Modernisers Saved the Labour Party*, Little, Brown and Co.

Gould, P. (2007), 'A heroic campaign', *New Statesman*, 14 May.

Gray, I. (1988), 'Committee of 100 Wanted', *Chartist*, April–May.

Gray, N. and French, L. (2010), 'The empire in miniature', *Scottish Left Review* No. 58, May–June.

Greenleaf, W. H. (1983a), *The British Political Tradition: Volume One: The Rise of Collectivism*, Routledge.

Greenleaf, W. H. (1983b), *The British Political Tradition: Volume Two: The Ideological Heritage*, Routledge.

Greener, I. and Powell, M. (2008), 'The changing governance of the NHS: Reform in a post-Keynesian Health Service', *Human Relations* 61 (5).

Greer, S. (2004), *Territorial Politics and Health Policy*, Manchester University Press.

Greer, S. (2006), 'The politics of health-policy divergence', in J. Adams and K. Schmueker, *Devolution in Practice 2006: public policy differences within the UK*, IPPR North.

Greer, S. (2007), 'The Fragile Divergence Machine: Citizenship, Policy Divergence, and Devolution', in A. Trench (ed.), *Devolution and Power in the UK*, Manchester University Press.

Greer, S. (2008), 'Options and the Lack of Options: Healthcare Politics and Policy', *Political Quarterly* 79 (S1).

Griffiths, N. (1989), 'Retrospect and Prospect', in O. Dudley Edwards (ed.), *A Claim of Right for Scotland*, Polygon.

Hain, P. (2011), 'Rebuilding Political Parties: Lessons from Labour', *Social Europe Journal*, 22 June.

Hall, S. (1979), 'The Great Moving Right Show', *Marxism Today*, January.

Harvie, C. (1983), 'Labour in Scotland during the Second World War', *The Historical Journal* 26 (4).

Harvie, C. (1989), 'The Recovery of Scottish Labour 1939–51', in I. Donnachie, C. Harvie and I. S. Wood (eds), *Forward!: Labour Politics in Scotland 1888–1988*, Polygon.

Hassan, G. (2002a), 'A Case Study of Scottish Labour: Devolution and the Politics of Multi-Level Governance', *Political Quarterly* 73 (2).

Hassan, G. (2002b), 'The Paradoxes of Scottish Labour: Devolution, Change and Conservatism', in G. Hassan and C. Warhurst (eds), *Tomorrow's Scotland*, Lawrence and Wishart.

Hassan, G. (ed.) (2004), *The Scottish Labour Party: History, Institutions and Ideas*, Edinburgh University Press.

Hassan, G. (ed.) (2009a), *The SNP: From Protest to Power*, Edinburgh University Press.

Hassan, G. (2009b), 'Don't Mess with the Missionary Man: Brown, Moral Compasses and the Road to Britishness', in A. Gamble and T. Wright (eds), *Britishness: Perspectives on the British Question*, Blackwell/Political Quarterly.

Hassan, G. (2011), 'Anatomy of a Scottish Revolution: The Potential of Post-nationalist Scotland and the Future of the United Kingdom', *Political Quarterly* 82 (3).

Hassan, G. and Barnett, A. (2009), *Breaking Out of Britain's Neo-Liberal State*, Compass.

Hassan, G. and Fraser, D. (2004), *The Political Guide to Modern Scotland*, Politico's.

Hassan, G. and Lynch, P. (1999), 'The Changing Politics of Scottish Labour: Culture and Values and Political Strategy and Devolution 1979–1999', Paper to Political Studies Association Annual Conference.

Hassan, G. and Lynch, P. (2001), *The Almanac of Scottish Politics*, Politico's Publishing.

Hassan, G. and Shaw, E. (2010), 'Doctrine and Ethos in the Scottish Labour Party', Paper to Political Studies Association Annual Conference.

Heald, D., Jones, C. A. and Lamont, D. W. (1981), 'Braking Mr Younger's Runaway Train: The conflict between the Scottish Office and Local Authorities over Local Government Expenditure', in H. M. Drucker and N. Drucker (eds), *The Scottish Government Yearbook 1982*, Unit for the Study of Government in Scotland.

Health and Community Care Committee (2000), *Inquiry into the Delivery of Community Care in Scotland*, Scottish Parliament.

Health and Community Care Research Findings No. 3 (2001), *Public attitudes to the provision of free personal care*, http://www.scotland.gov.uk/cru/resfinds/hcc3-00.asp.

Hepburn, I. (1983), 'The Foulkes Memorandum', *Radical Scotland*, August–September.

Hetherington, P. (1979), 'The 1979 General Election Campaign in Scotland', in N. Drucker and H. M. Drucker (eds), *The Scottish Government Yearbook 1980*, Paul Harris.

Hine, D. (1982), 'Factionalism in West European parties: A framework for analysis', *West European Politics* 5 (1).

Hirsch, D. (2006), *Paying for long-term care: Moving forward*, Joseph Rowntree Foundation.

Hood, C. (1995), 'The "New Public Management" in the 1980s: Variations on a Theme', *Accounting, Organizations and Society* 20 (2/3).

Hopkin, J. (2001), 'Bringing the Members Back in?: Democratising Candidate Selection in Britain and Spain', *Party Politics* 7 (3).

Hopkin, J. (2003), 'Political decentralization, electoral change and party organizational adaptation', *European Urban and Regional Studies* 10 (3).

Hopkin, J. (2009), 'Party Matters: Devolution and Party Politics in Britain and Spain', *Party Politics* 15 (2).

Hopkin, J. and Bradbury, J. (2006), 'British statewide parties and multilevel politics', *Publius: the journal of federalism* 36 (1).

Horton, T. and Gregory, J. (2010), 'Whose middle is it anyway?: Why universal welfare matters', *Public Policy Research* 16 (4).

Hume, D. (1742), 'Of Parties in General', in *Essays: Moral, Political and Literary*, Liberty Fund. http://www.econlib.org/library/LFBooks/Hume/hmMPL8.html.

Hutchison, D. (2008), 'The History of the Press', in N. Blain and D. Hutchison (eds), *The Media in Scotland*, Edinburgh University Press.

Hutchison, I. G. C. (1986), *A Political History of Scotland 1832–1924: Parties, Elections and Issues*, John Donald.

Hutchison, I. G. C. (2001), *Scottish Politics in the Twentieth Century*, Palgrave.

Inglehart, R. (1977), *The Silent Revolution*, Princeton University Press.

Issakyan, I., Lawn, M., Ozga, J. and Shaik, F. (2008), *The social and cognitive mapping of policy: The education sector in Scotland Centre for Educational Sociology The University of Edinburgh Final Report WP6*. http://www.know andpol.eu/fileadmin/KaP/content/Scientific_reports/Orientation1/O1_Final_ Report_Scotland_educ.pdf.

Janda, J. (1980), *Political Parties: A Cross-National Survey*, Free Press.

Jeffery, C. and Hough, D. (2009), 'Understanding Post-Devolution Elections in Scotland and Wales in Comparative Perspective', *Party Politics* 15 (2).

Jervis, P. (2008), *Devolution and Health*, Nuffield Trust.

Johns, R., Denver, D., Mitchell, J. and Pattie, C. (2010), *Voting for a Scottish Government: The Scottish Parliament Election of 2007*, Manchester University Press.

Johnston, T. (1952), *Memories*, Collins.

Jones, P. (2000), 'The First Laws of the New Parliament', in G. Hassan and C. Warhurst (eds), *The New Scottish Politics: The First Year of the Scottish Parliament and Beyond*, Stationery Office.

Jones, P. (2005), 'The Modernising Radical', in W. Alexander (ed.), *Donald Dewar: Scotland's first First Minister*, Mainstream.

Katz, R. (2001), 'The Problem of Candidate selection and Models of Party Democracy', *Party Politics* 7 (3).

Katz, R. S. and Mair, P. (2002), 'The Ascendancy of the Party in Public Office: Party Organizational Change in Twentieth-Century Democracies', in R. Gunther, J. R. Montero and J. J. Linz (eds), *Political Parties: Old Concepts and New Challenges*, Oxford University Press.

Kavanagh, D. and Cowley, P. (2010), *The British General Election of 2010*, Palgrave Macmillan.

Keating, M. (1975), 'The Role of the Scottish MP in the Scottish Political System, in the United Kingdom Political System and the Relationship Between the Two', Glasgow College of Technology Ph.D. thesis.

Keating, M. (1988), Glasgow: the City That Refused to Die, Aberdeen University Press.

Keating, M. (1989), 'The Labour Party in Scotland 1951–64', in I. Donnachie, C. Harvie and I. S. Wood (eds) (1989), Forward!: Labour Politics in Scotland 1888–1988, Polygon.

Keating, M. (2001), 'Devolution and Public Policy in the United Kingdom: Divergence or Convergence?', IPPR Seminar on Devolution in Practice.

Keating, M. (2003), 'Social Inclusion, Devolution and Policy Divergence', Political Quarterly 74 (4).

Keating, M. (2005), 'Policy Convergence and Divergence in Scotland under Devolution', Regional Studies 39 (4).

Keating, M. (2007), 'Public Services: Renewal and Reform', in M. Keating (ed.), Scottish Social Democracy: Progressive Ideas for Public Policy, Peter Lang.

Keating, M. (2010), The Government of Scotland, Edinburgh University Press, 2nd edn.

Keating, M. and Bleiman, D. (1979), Labour and Scottish Nationalism, Macmillan.

Keating, M. and Cairney, P. (2006), 'New Elite? Politicians and Civil Servants in Scotland after Devolution', Parliamentary Affairs 59 (1).

Kemp. A. (1993), The Hollow Drum: Scotland since the War, Mainstream.

Kerr, D. (2005), Building a Health Service Fit for the Future, Scottish Executive.

Kerr, D. and Feeley, D. (2007), 'Collectivism and Collaboration in Scotland', in S. L. Greer and D. Rowland (eds), Devolving Policy, Diverging Values: The Values of the UK's NHS, Nuffield Trust.

King, A. (2007), The British Constitution, Oxford University Press.

Knox W. W, (1999), Industrial Nation: Work, Culture and Society in Scotland 1800–Present, Edinburgh University Press.

Knox, W. and Mackinlay, A. (1995), 'The Re-Making of Scottish Labour in the 1930s', Twentieth Century British History 6 (2).

Kogan, D. and Kogan, M. (1981), The Battle for the Labour Party, Fontana.

Köllner, K. and Basedau, M. (2005), Factionalism in Political Parties: An Analytical Framework for Comparative Studies, Working Papers Global and Area Studies GOI-WP-12/2005 German Overseas Institute.

Kynaston, D. (2007), Austerity Britain 1945–51, Bloomsbury.

Labour Party (1982), Labour's Programme 1982, Labour Party.

Labour Party NEC (1996), Inquiry into Monklands District Council, Labour Party.

Labour Party NEC (1997a), Partnership in Power, Labour Party.

Labour Party NEC (1997b), City of Glasgow Labour Group: Further Report of the NEC Inquiry, DO:6/10/97, Labour Party.

Laclau, E. and Mouffe, C. (1985), Hegemony and Socialist Strategy, Verso.

Laffin, M. and Shaw, E. (2007), 'British Devolution and the Labour Party:

How a National Party Adapts to Devolution', *British Journal of Politics and International Relations* 9 (1).

Laffin, M., Shaw, E. and Taylor, G. (2007), 'The New Subnational Politics of the British Labour Party', *Party Politics* 13 (1).

Lally, P. (2000), *Lazarus Only Done It Once: The Story of My Lives*, HarperCollins.

Law, A. (2005), 'Welfare Nationalism: Social Justice and/or Entrepreneurial Scotland', in G. Mooney and G. Scott (eds), *Exploring Social Policy in the 'New' Scotland*, Policy Press.

Law, A. and Mooney, G. (2006), '"We've never had it so good": The "problem" of the working class in devolved Scotland', *Critical Social Policy* 26 (3).

Lebas, E. (2007), 'Sadness and Gladness: The Films of Glasgow Corporation 1922–1978', The Lighthouse: Scotland's Centre for Architecture and Design, Exhibition, 5 March–7 May.

LCC (Scotland) (1980), *Building Real Unity: Making Councils Accountable*, LCC (Scotland).

LCC (Scotland) (1987), *Discussion Paper*, LCC (Scotland).

Le Grand, J. (2003), *Motivation, Agency and Public Policy*, Oxford University Press.

Le Grand, J. (2007), *The Other Invisible Hand*, Princeton University Press.

Leopold, J. (1989), 'Trade Unions in Scotland: Forward to the 1990s', in A. Brown and D. McCrone (eds), *The Scottish Government Yearbook 1989*, Unit for the Study of Government in Scotland.

Lewis, H. (1988), 'Scottish Labour: Flag-bearer or enabler', *Chartist*, September-October.

Lingard, B. (2008), 'Scottish Education: reflections from an International Perspective', in T. Bryce and W. Humes (eds), *Scottish Education*, Edinburgh University Press, 3rd edn.

Lipset, S. M. and Rokkan, S. (eds) (1967), *Party Systems and Voter Alignments: Cross-National Perspectives*, Collier-Macmillan.

Lynch, P. (1995), 'The Scottish Constitutional Convention 1992–95', *Scottish Affairs* 15.

Lynch, P. (1996a), 'New Labour in Scotland: Hegemony, Autonomy, Ideology', Paper to the Conference of the Elections, Public Opinion and Parties Specialist Group, Political Studies Association.

Lynch, P. (1996b), 'Labour and Scottish Devolution: Securing Consensus and Managing Opposition', *Regional Studies* 30 (6).

Lynch, P. and Birrell, S. (2004), 'The Autonomy and Organisation of Scottish Labour', in G. Hassan (ed.), *The Scottish Labour Party: History, Institutions and Ideas*, Edinburgh University Press.

Macdonald, C. M. M. (2009), *Whaur Extremes Meet: Scotland's Twentieth Century*, Birlinn.

Mackay, F. (2004), 'Women and the Labour Party in Scotland', in G. Hassan (ed.), *The Scottish Labour Party: History, Institutions and Ideas*, Edinburgh University Press.

Macwhirter, I. (1990), 'After Doomsday . . . The Convention and Scotland's Constitutional Crisis', in A. Brown and R. Parry (eds), *The Scottish Government Yearbook 1990*, Unit for the Study of Government in Scotland.

Macwhirter, I. (1992), 'The Disaster That Never Was: The Failure of Scottish Opposition after the 1992 Election', *Scottish Affairs 1*.

Major, J. (1999), *John Major: The Autobiography*, HarperCollins.

Mann, J. (1962), *Woman in Parliament*, Odhams Press.

Marquand, D. (1991), *The Progressive Dilemma*, Heinemann, 2nd edn.

Marquand, D. (2008), *Britain since 1918: The Strange Career of British Democracy*, Weidenfeld and Nicolson.

Marriott, J. (1991), *The Culture of Labourism*, Edinburgh University Press.

Martin, D. (1989), 'The Democratic Deficit', in O. Dudley Edwards (ed.), *A Claim of Right for Scotland*, Polygon.

Marwick, W. H. (1967), *A Short History of Labour in Scotland*, W. & R. Chambers.

Maver, I. (2000), *Glasgow*, Edinburgh University Press.

McAlpine, J. (2011), 'When did the media lose its Scottish accent of mind?' in G. Hassan and R. Ilett (ed.), *Radical Scotland: Arguments for Self-Determination*, Luath Press.

McConnell, A. (2004), *Scottish Local Government*, Edinburgh University Press.

McConnell, J. (1999), 'Modernising the Modernisers', in G. Hassan and C. Warhurst (eds), *A Different Future: A Moderniser's Guide to Scotland*, Centre for Scottish Public Policy/The Big Issue in Scotland.

McConnell, J. (2004), 'New Scots Attracting Fresh Talent to meet the Challenge of Growth' speech, *Scottish Executive*, 25 February, http://www.scotland.gov. uk/Publications/2004/02/18984/33667.

McCormick, J. and Alexander, W. (1996), 'Firm Foundations: Securing the Scottish Parliament', in S. Tindale (ed.), *The State and the Nations: The Politics of Devolution*, IPPR.

McCrae, R. (1991), 'Women in the Labour Party', in Woman's Claim of Right Group (ed.), *A Woman's Claim of Right in Scotland: Woman, Representation and Politics*, Polygon.

McCrone, D. (1992), *Understanding Scotland: The Sociology of a Stateless Nation*, Routledge.

McCrone, D. (2001), *Understanding Scotland: The Sociology of a Nation*, Routledge, 2nd edn.

McGarvey, N. and Cairney, P. (2008), 'Narratives of Scottish Politics: Time for a New Debate?', Paper to the Territorial Politics Conference, Edinburgh.

McKenzie, R. T. (1964), *British Political Parties*, Heinemann Educational Books 2nd edn.

McLean, I. (1975), *Keir Hardie*, Allen Lane.

McLean, I. (2004), 'Scottish Labour and British Politics', in G. Hassan (ed.), *The Scottish Labour Party: History, Institutions and Ideas*, Edinburgh University Press.

McLean, R. (1990a), *Labour and Scottish Home Rule: Part One: Mid-Lanark to Majority Government 1888–1945*, Scottish Labour Action.

McLean, R. (1990b), *Labour and Scottish Home Rule: Part Two: Unionist Complacency to Crisis Management 1945–1988*, Scottish Labour Action.

McLean, R. (1990c), 'Labour Conference Review', *Radical Scotland*, February–March.

McLean, R. (2005), *Getting It Together: The History of the Campaign for a Scottish Assembly/Parliament 1980–1999*, Luath Press.

McLeish, H. (1999), 'The Negotiation Diaries', *Scottish Affairs* 28.

McLeish, H. (2004), *Scotland First: Truth and Consequences*, Mainstream.

McSmith, A. (1994), *John Smith: A Life 1938–1994*, Mandarin, 2nd edn.

Melucci, A. (1989), *Nomads of the Present: Social Movements and Individual Needs in Contemporary Society*, Hutchinson Radius.

Menter, I., Elliot, D., Hall, S., Hulme, M., Lowden, K., McQueen, I., Payne, F., Coutts, N., Robson, D., Spratt, J. and Christie, D. (2010), *Research to Support Schools of Ambition: Final Report*, Scottish Government.

Michels, R. (1962), *Political Parties: A Sociological Study of the Oligarchical Tendencies of Modern Democracy*, Collier-Macmillan.

Middleton, B. (2001), *Whatever happened to Labour?*, Gopher Publishing.

Milburn, A. (2007), *A 2020 Vision for Public Services*, London School of Economics.

Millan, B. (1983), 'Scotland', in G. Kaufman (ed.), *Renewal: Labour's Britain in the 1980s*, Penguin.

Miller, J. (2007), *The Dam Builders: Power from the Glens*, Birlinn.

Miller, W. L. (1980), 'The Scottish Dimension', in D. Butler and D. Kavanagh (eds), *The British General Election of 1979*, Macmillan.

Miller W. L. (1981), *The End of British Politics?*, Oxford University Press.

Minkin, L. (1980), *The Labour Party Conference*, Manchester University Press, 2nd edn.

Minkin, L. (1991), *The Contentious Alliance: Trade Unions and the Labour Party*, Edinburgh University Press.

Mitchell, J. (1990), *The Myth of Dependency*, Scottish Centre for Economic and Social Research.

Mitchell, J. (1996), *Strategies for Self-Government: The Campaigns for a Scottish Parliament*, Polygon.

Mitchell, J. (2004), 'Scotland: Expectations, policy types and devolution', in A. Trench (ed.), *Has Devolution Made a Difference?*, Imprint Academic.

Mitchell, J. (2005), 'The Election in Scotland', in A. Geddes and J. Tonge (eds), *Britain Decides: The UK General Election 2005*, Palgrave Macmillan.

Mitchell, J. (2006), 'Evolution and Devolution: Citizenship, Institutions and Public Policy', *Publius: The Journal of Federalism* 36 (1).

Mitchell, J. (2009), *Devolution in the UK*, Manchester University Press.

Mitchell, J. and Bradbury, J. (2002), 'Scotland and Wales: The First Post-Devolution General Election', in A. P. Geddes and J. Tongue (eds), *Labour's Second Landslide: The British General Election 2001*, Manchester University Press.

Mitchell, J. and Bradbury, J. (2004), 'Devolution: Comparative development and policy roles', *Parliamentary Affairs* 57 (2).

Mitchell, J. and Seyd, B. (1999), 'Fragmentation in the Party and Political System', in R. Hazell (ed.), *Constitutional Futures*, Oxford University Press.

Mitchell, J. and van der Zwet, A. (2010), 'A Catenaccio Game: The 2010 Election in Scotland', in A. Geddes and J. Tongue (eds), *Britain Votes 2010*, Oxford University Press.

Mooney, G. and Poole, L. (2004), 'A Land of Milk and Honey'? Social Policy in Scotland after Devolution', *Critical Social Policy* 24 (4),

Mooney, G. and Scott, G. (2005), 'Introduction', in G. Mooney and G. Scott (eds), *Exploring Social Policy in the 'New' Scotland*, Policy Press.

Mooney, G. and Williams, C. (2006), 'Forging new "ways of life"? Social policy and nation building in devolved Scotland and Wales', *Critical Social Policy* 26 (3).

Morgan, K. O. (1997), *Callaghan: A Life*, Oxford University Press.

Morley, D. (2007), *Gorgeous George: The Life and Adventures of George Galloway*, Politico's Publishing.

Moschonas, G. (2002), *In the Name of Social Democracy*, Verso.

Mullin, C. (2009), *A View from the Foothills: The Diaries of Chris Mullin*, Profile Books.

Murray, G. T. (1973), *Scotland: The New Future*, STV/Blackie.

Naughtie, J. (1989), 'Labour 1979–1988', in I. Donnachie, C. Harvie and I. S. Wood (eds), *Forward!: Labour Politics in Scotland 1888–1988*, Polygon.

Norris, P. and Lovenduski, J. (1995), *Political Recruitment: Gender, Race, and Class in the British Parliament*, Cambridge University Press.

Orriols, L. and Richards, A. (2005), 'Nationalism and the Labour Party: Differential Voting in Scotland and Wales since 1997', Estudio Working Paper 2005/213.

Osterle, A. (1999), *Equity and Long-term Care Policies: A Framework for Comparative Analysis*, European University Institute.

Panebianco, A. (1988), *Political Parties: Organization and Power*, Cambridge University Press.

Park, A. (2002), 'Scotland's Morals', in J. Curtice, D. McCrone, A. Park and L. Paterson (eds), *New Scotland, New Society?*, Polygon.

Paterson, L. (1994), *The Autonomy of Modern Scotland*, Edinburgh University Press.

Paterson, L. (2002), 'Scottish Social Democracy and Blairism', in G. Hassan and C. Warhurst (eds), *Tomorrow's Scotland*, Lawrence and Wishart.

Paterson, L. (2003), 'The Three Educational Ideologies of the British Labour Party, 1997–2001', *Oxford Review of Education* 29 (2).

Paterson, L., Bechhofer, F. and McCrone, D. (2004), *Living in Scotland: Social and Economic Change since 1980*, Edinburgh University Press.

Paterson, L., Brown, A., Curtice, J., Hinds, K., McCrone, D., Park, A., Sproston, K. and Surridge, P. (2001), *New Scotland, New Politics?*, Polygon.

Pattie, C., Whiteley, P., Johnston, R. and Seyd, P. (1994), 'Measuring Local Campaign Effects: Labour Party Constituency Campaigning at the 1987 General Election', *Political Studies* 42 (3).

Pearce, N. (2011), 'Scoping Scotland's Future', *IPPR*, 11 February, http://www.ippr.org/?p=54&option=com_wordpress&Itemid=17.

Peter, B. G, Pierre, J. and King, D. (2005), 'The Politics of Path Dependency: Political Conflict in Historical Institutionalism', *Journal of Politics* 67 (4).

Phillips, J. (2008), *The Industrial Politics of Devolution: Scotland in the 1960s and 1970s*, Manchester University Press.

Pierson, P. (2004), *Politics in Time: History, Institutions, and Social Analysis*, Princeton University Press.

Poole, L. and Mooney, G. (2006), 'Privatising Education in Scotland? New Labour, Modernisation and "public" service', *Critical Social Policy* 26 (3).

Pollock, A. (2001), 'Social Policy and Devolution', *British Medical Journal* 10, February.

Ponsonby, B. (1990), 'Searching for a Place in History', *Radical Scotland*, October–November.

Putnam, R. (1971), 'Studying Elite Political Culture: The Case of "Ideology"', *American Political Science Review* 65 (3).

Quinn, L. (1999), 'The structural implications of devolution for the Scottish Labour Party', Labour Party papers, GS5/11/99.

Radical Scotland (1983), 'In the Red Corner', *Radical Scotland*, August–September.

Radical Scotland (1985), 'The Guinea Pig Nation: A Question of Dignity', *Radical Scotland*, June–July.

Radical Scotland (1987), 'Grasping the Thistle', *Radical Scotland*, October–November.

Radice, G. (1992), *Southern Discomfort*, Fabian Society.

Radice, G. and Pollard, S. (1993), *More Southern Discomfort*, Fabian Society.

Raffe, D. (2004), 'How Distinctive is Scottish Education?: Five Perspectives on Distinctiveness', *Scottish Affairs* 49.

Raffe, D. (2005), *Devolution and Divergence in Education Policy*, IPPR.

Ranney, A. (1965), *Pathways to Parliament*, Macmillan.

Ranson, S. (2003), 'Public accountability in the age of neo-liberal governance', *Journal of Education Policy* 18 (5).

Ranson, S. (2008), 'The Changing Governance of Education', *Educational Management Administration and Leadership* 36 (2).

Rawnsley, A. (2000), *Servants of the People: The Inside Story of New Labour*, Hamish Hamilton.

Rawnsley, A. (2010), *The End of the Party: The Rise and Fall of New Labour*, Penguin.

Regional Trends (1996), Central Statistical Office.

Richards, S. (2010), *Whatever It Takes: The Real Story of Gordon Brown and New Labour*, Fourth Estate.

Robertson, D. (2011), 'The State of Scotland's Housing and How We Change It', in G. Hassan and R. Ilett (ed.), *Radical Scotland: Arguments for Self-Determination*, Luath Press.

Robson, K. (2007), *The NHS in Scotland*, Scottish Parliament Information Centre (SPICe).

Rokkan, S. and Urwin, D. (eds) (1982), *The Politics of Territorial Identity: Studies in European Regionalism*, Sage.

Rose, R. (1973), *The Problem of Party Government*, Penguin.

Ross, E. (1983), 'Devolution', in J. Lansman and A. Meale (eds), *Beyond Thatcher: The Real Alternative*, Junction Books.

Ross, J. (1988), 'A Fond Farewell to Devolution', *Radical Scotland*, December–January.

Routledge, P. (1998), *Gordon Brown: The Biography*, Simon and Schuster.

Royal Commission on Long Term Care (The Sutherland Report) (1999), *With Respect to Old Age*, The Stationery Office.

Rush, M. (1969), *The Selection of Parliamentary Candidates*, Nelson.

Russell, M. (2005), *Building New Labour: The Politics of Party Organisation*, Palgrave Macmillan.

Saren, J. and McCormick, J. (2004), 'The Politics of Labour's Scottish Heartlands', in G. Hassan (ed.), *The Scottish Labour Party: History, Institutions and Ideas*, Edinburgh University Press.

Saville, J. (1973), 'The Ideology of Labourism', in R. Benewick, R. N. Berki and B. Parekh (eds), *Knowledge and Belief in Politics: The Problem of Ideology*, Allen and Unwin.

Scandrett, E. (2011), 'Environmental Self-Determination and Lifelong Education', in G. Hassan and R. Ilett (ed.), *Radical Scotland: Arguments for Self-Determination*, Luath Press.

Scarrow, S. (1996), *Parties and their Members Organising for Victory in Britain and Germany*, Oxford University Press.

Scarrow, S., Webb, P. and Farrell, D. (2000), 'From social integration to electoral contestation', in R. Dalton and M. Wattenberg (eds), *Parties Without Partisans*, Oxford University Press.

Scharpf, F. (1997), *Games Real Actors Play: Actor-Centred Institutionalism in Policy Research*, Westview Press.

Schlesinger, P., Miller, D. and Dinan, W. (2001), *Open Scotland? Journalists, Spin Doctors and Lobbyists*, Polygon.

Schon, D. and Rein, M. (1994), *Frame Reflection*, Basic Books.

Scott, J. D. (1954), *The End of an Old Song: A Romance*, Eyre and Spottiswoode.

Scottish Constitutional Convention (1990), *Towards a Scottish Parliament*, Scottish Constitutional Convention.

Scottish Constitutional Convention (1995), *Scotland's Parliament, Scotland's Right*, Scotland's Constitutional Convention.

Scottish Executive (2003), *Educating for Excellence: Choice and Opportunity: The Executive's Response to the National Debate*, Scottish Executive.

349

Scottish Executive (2004), *Ambitious, Excellent Schools: Our Agenda for Action*, Scottish Executive.

Scottish Executive (2006), *Transforming Public Services: The Next Phase of Reform*, Scottish Executive.

Scottish Executive and the STUC (2002), *Memorandum of Understanding*, http://www.scotland.gov.uk/Resource/Doc/46905/0025821.pdf.

Scottish Executive Health Department (SEHD) (2003), *Partnership for Care: Scotland's Health White Paper*, Scottish Executive.

Scottish Executive Health Department (SEHD) (2005), *Delivering for Health*, Scottish Executive.

Scottish Office and Department of Health (1997), *Designed to Care: Renewing the National Health Service in Scotland*, The Stationery Office.

Scottish Labour Action (1988a), *Founding Statement*, Scottish Labour Action.

Scottish Labour Action (1988b), *Gubbed in Govan*, Scottish Labour Action.

Scottish Labour Action (1989), *Proposals for Scottish Democracy*, Scottish Labour Action.

Scottish Labour Party (1983), *Executive Statement*, Scottish Labour Party.

Scottish Labour Party (1984), *Green Paper on Devolution*, Scottish Labour Party.

Scottish Labour Party (1986), *Executive Statement*, Scottish Labour Party.

Scottish Labour Party (1987), *Executive Statement*, Scottish Labour Party.

Scottish Labour Party (2003a), *The Road to the Manifesto*, Scottish Labour Party.

Scottish Labour Party (2003b), *On Your Side: Scottish Labour Manifesto*, Scottish Labour Party.

Scottish Labour Party (2007), *Building Scotland: Scottish Labour Manifesto*, Scottish Labour Party.

Scottish Labour Party (2010), *Report of the Scottish Policy Forum*, Scottish Labour Party, http://www.scottishlabour.org.uk/.../905cf288-8d97-3754-ad0a-56424633.

Scottish Labour Party (2011a), *Fighting for What Really Matters: The Scottish Labour Party Manifesto 2011*, Scottish Labour Party.

Scottish Labour Party (2011b), *Review of the Labour Party in Scotland*, Scottish Labour Party, http://www.scottishlabour.org.uk/review.

Scottish Unionist Association (1951), *The Year Book for Scotland 1951*, Scottish Unionist Association.

Scottish Unionist Association (1955), *The Year Book for Scotland 1955*, Scottish Unionist Association.

Scottish Unionist Association (1959), *The Year Book for Scotland 1959*, Scottish Unionist Association.

Scottish Unionist Association (1964), *The Year Book for Scotland 1964*, Scottish Unionist Association.

Seawright, D. (1999), *An Important Matter of Principle: The Decline of the Scottish Conservative and Unionist Party*, Ashgate.

Seldon, A. (1997), *Major: A Political Life*, Weidenfeld and Nicolson.

Seyd, P. and Whiteley, P. (2004), 'British Party Members: An Overview', *Party Politics* 10 (4).

Sharpe, L. J., 'The Labour Party and the Geography of Inequality', in D. Kavanagh (ed.), *The Politics of the Labour Party*, Allen and Unwin.

Shaw, E. (1988), *Discipline and Discord in the Labour Party*, Manchester University Press.

Shaw, E. (1994), *The Labour Party since 1979: Crisis and Transformation*, Routledge.

Shaw, E. (1996), *The Labour Party since 1945*, Blackwell.

Shaw, E. (2001), 'New Labour: New Pathways to Parliament', *Parliamentary Affairs* 54 (1).

Shaw, E. (2002), 'New Labour: New Democratic Centralism?', *West European Politics* 25 (3).

Shaw, E. (2003), 'The Control Freaks?: New Labour and the Party', in S. Ludlam and M. Smith (eds), *Governing as New Labour*, Palgrave.

Shaw, E. (2007), *Losing Labour's Soul?: New Labour and the Blair Government 1997–2007*, Routledge.

Sheppard, T. (1997), *A New Scottish Labour Party*, Scottish Labour Action.

Sheridan, T. and McAlpine, J. (1994), *A Time to Rage*, Polygon.

Sillars, J. (1986), *Scotland: The Case for Optimism*, Polygon.

Smart, I. (1988), 'Dual Mandate', *Radical Scotland*, December–January.

Smart, I, (2011), 'Ten Reasons Labour Lost', unpublished paper.

Smith, J. (1983), 'John Smith, MP, talks to "Radical Scotland"', *Radical Scotland*, February–March.

Smith, T. and Babbington, E. (2006), 'Devolution: a map of divergence in the NHS', *Health Policy and Economic Research Unit Health Policy Review* 2.

Smout, T. C. (1986), *A Century of the Scottish People 1830–1950*, Collins.

Smyth, J. J. (2000), *Labour in Glasgow 1896–1936*, Tuckwell Press.

Stewart, J. (2004), *Taking Stock: Scottish Welfare Policy after Devolution*, Policy Press.

Steed, M. (1975), 'The Results Analysed', in D. Butler and D. Kavanagh (eds), *The British General Election of October 1974*, Macmillan.

Stewart, D. (2009), *The Path to Devolution and Change: A Political History of Scotland under Margaret Thatcher*, Tauris.

Strategy Unit (2006), Prime Minister's Strategy Unit, *The UK Government's Approach to Public Service Reform*, The Stationery Office.

Stuart, M. (2005), *John Smith: A Life*, Politico's Publishing.

STUC (2011), 'About the STUC', STUC, http://www.stuc.org.uk/about/welcome.

Surridge, P. (2004), 'The Scottish Electorate and Labour', in G. Hassan (ed.), *The Scottish Labour Party: History, Institutions and Ideas*, Edinburgh University Press.

System Three (1996), *The Views of Scottish Floating Voters*, unpublished paper.

Tannahill, C. (2005), 'Health and Health Policy', in G. Mooney and G. Scott (eds), *Exploring Social Policy in the 'New' Scotland*, Policy Press.

Taylor, B. (1999), *The Scottish Parliament*, Polygon.

Taylor, B. (2002), *Scotland's Parliament: Triumph and Disaster*, Polygon.

Taylor, M. (1999), 'They have to toe the Labour line', *The Guardian*, 11 May.

Taylor R. (2001), 'Employment Relations Policy', in A. Seldon (ed.), *The Blair Effect: The Blair Government 1997–2001*, Little, Brown & Co.

Taylor, C., Fitz, J. and Gorard, S. (2005), 'Diversity, Specialisation and Equity in Education', *Oxford Review of Education* 33 (1).

Tetteh, E. (2010), *Councillors and Council Control 1979–2010*, House of Commons Library.

Thatcher, M. (1993), *The Downing Street Years*, HarperCollins.

Thorlakson, L. (2009), 'Patterns of Party Integration, Influence and Autonomy in Seven Federations', *Party Politics* 15 (2).

Thorlakson, L. (2010), 'Party organizational strategy in multi-level systems', Paper to the Canadian Political Science Association Annual Conference, Montreal.

Torrance, D. (2009), *'We in Scotland': Thatcherism in a Cold Climate*, Birlinn.

Torrance, D. (2010), *Salmond: Against the Odds*, Birlinn.

Torrance, D. (2011), *Salmond: Against the Odds*, Birlinn, 2nd edn.

van Biezen, I. and Hopkin, J. (2006), 'Party organization in multi-level contexts', in D. Hough and C. Jeffery (eds), *Devolution and Electoral Politics*, Manchester University Press.

van Houten, P. (2009), 'Multi-level Relations in Political Parties: A Delegation Approach', *Party Politics* 15 (2).

Vidler, E. and Clarke, J. (2005), 'Creating Citizen-Consumers: New Labour and the Remaking of Public Services', *Public Policy and Administration* 20 (2).

Wainright, H. (1987), *Labour: A Tale of Two Parties*, Hogarth Press.

Watson, M. (2001), *Year Zero: An Inside View of the Scottish Parliament*, Polygon.

Webster, C. (1998), *The National Health Service: A Political History*, Oxford University Press.

Whiteley, P. (2009), 'Where Have All the Members Gone?: The Dynamics of Party Membership in Britain', *Parliamentary Affairs* 62 (2).

Whiteley, P. and Seyd, P. (1992), *Labour's Grassroots*, Clarendon Press.

Whiteley, P. and Seyd, P. (2003), 'How to win a landslide by really trying: the effects of local campaigning on voting in the 1997 British general election', *Electoral Studies* 22.

Wilson, J. Q. (1995), *Political Organizations*, Princeton University Press.

Winchester, N. and Storey, J. (2008), *Devolved Governance Systems*, NHS/SDO Working Paper No. 2.

Wolfe, B. (1973), *Scotland Lives: The Quest for Independence*, Reprographia.

Wood, F. (1989), 'Scottish Labour in Government and Opposition, 1964–1979', in I. Donnachie, C. Harvie and I. S. Wood (eds), *Forward!: Labour Politics in Scotland 1888–1988*, Polygon.

Wood, I. S. (1989), 'Hope Deferred: Labour and Scotland in the 1920s', in I. Donnachie, C. Harvie and I. S. Wood (eds), *Forward!: Labour Politics in Scotland 1888–1988*, Polygon.

Woods, K. (2002), 'Health Policy and the NHS in the UK 1997–2002', in J. Adams and P. Robinson (eds), *Devolution in Practice*, IPPR.

Wright, C. (2011), 'Labour's Scottish election campaign is a disaster', *Labour Uncut*, 29 April, http://labour-uncut.co.uk/2011/04/29/labours-scottish-election-campaign-is-a-disaster/.

Wright, E. (1960), 'Kelvingrove', in D. E. Butler and R. Rose (eds), *The British General Election of 1959*, Macmillan.

Wright, K. (1997), *The People Say Yes: The Making of Scotland's Parliament*, Argyll Publishing.

Yule, E. (2010), 'Scots Miserablism', *Glasgow Centre for Population Health*, 16 February, www.gcph.co.uk/assets/0000/0635/eleanor_yule_summary_final.pdf/.

Zahariadis, N. (1999), 'Ambiguity, Time, and Multiple Streams', in P. A. Sabatier (ed.), *Theories of the Policy Process*, Westview Press.

Index